Korea and the World

Korea and the World
Beyond the Cold War

edited by
Young Whan Kihl
IOWA STATE UNIVERSITY

Westview Press

BOULDER · SAN FRANCISCO · OXFORD

Published in 1994 in the United States of America by Westview Press, Inc., 5500 Central Avenue, Boulder, Colorado 80301-2877, and in the United Kingdom by Westview Press, 36 Lonsdale Road, Summertown, Oxford OX2 7EW

Library of Congress Cataloging-in-Publication Data
Korea and the world : beyond the Cold War / edited by Young Whan Kihl.
    p.   cm.
   Includes bibliographical references and index.
   ISBN 0-8133-1928-5. — ISBN 0-8133-1929-3 (pbk.)
   1. Korean reunification question (1945–   ) 2. Korea (South)—
Foreign relations.   3. World politics—1989–   I. Kihl, Young W.,
1932–   .
DS917.444.K66   1994
951.904'3—dc20   93-39865
                                                                                      CIP

Printed and bound in the United States of America

The paper used in this publication meets the requirements
of the American National Standard for Permanence of Paper
for Printed Library Materials Z39.48-1984.

10   9   8   7   6   5   4   3   2

Contents

Preface

The rapidly changing environment surrounding the Korean peninsula in the dawn of this new post–Cold War era has necessitated a thorough review and reassessment of Korea's position and status in the changing world order. Whereas Korea in the past has been passive and even victimized by external changes, the Korean people today seem more active and determined to take charge of their own destiny. As we move into the twenty-first century, the unprecedented dynamic transformation currently under way around the globe provides new challenges to the Korean people for their creative action and meaningful participation in the changing world.

This awareness and concern led to the creation of *Korea and the World: Beyond the Cold War*. It is hoped that the book will reach a broad audience of college students, Korea scholars, and policymakers. Progress in human endeavor is possible only through confronting challenges with timely and creative responses. As we focus on the Korean question in the present book, the Chinese character for "crisis" expresses these challenges appropriately, symbolizing as it does both the "danger" and the "opportunity" for problem solving. In the process of seeking new solutions to old problems, such as the age-old "Korean question" that forms part of the legacy of Cold War politics, we will need to explore alternative paradigms and new ideas. The issue of Korean reunification is a fundamental part of the Korean question; its answer will demand creative and energetic responses by the new generation.

The Research Council on Korean Reunification, which sponsored *Korea and the World: Beyond the Cold War*, was founded in 1984 as a nonprofit academic organization to promote research and scholarship on the subject of Korea's future and coming reunification. The council has sponsored numerous academic forums and symposiums for both members and their friends on a regular basis. These meetings include the council-sponsored Roundtable on Korean Reunification, regularly scheduled on a courtesy listing basis during the annual convention of the Association for Asian Studies. The council has been an unofficial subgroup of this association.

This book is the result of the workshop conducted by the council on April 5, 1992, during the annual convention of the Association for Asian Studies in

Washington, D.C. Although the council sponsored this project, the responsibility for the book chapters rests solely with the contributing authors rather than with the council, which does not take any political or partisan stand on issues. With Young C. Kim and Chae-Jin Lee, I was part of a three-member committee appointed by the council president, Han Kyo Kim of the University of Cincinnati, to oversee the task of putting the material into a publishable format. The book project was undertaken by the three editors, but in the course of contacting the publisher and editing the manuscripts, Young C. Kim and Chae-Jin Lee entrusted their responsibility to me as the primary editor.

On behalf of the editorial committee, I would like to express appreciation to each of the contributing authors of this volume, who gave their invaluable support and cooperation to make this book possible. I also wish to thank several individuals who have assisted in the completion of the project: Leila Hertzberg, Deborah J. Lynes, Ida May B. Norton, and Westview senior editor Susan McEachern. Two anonymous reviewers also made their contributions to enhance the quality of the book.

For readers familiar with the Korean *Hangŭl* pronunciation, a word of caution and clarification is needed. All Korean words are given in the text according to the McCune-Reischauer system of romanization or transliteration, with some stylistic modifications. Exceptions include individual names that are widely recognized and accepted in their idiosyncratic renderings, such as Syngman Rhee, Park Chung Hee, Kim Il Sung, Roh Tae Woo, Kim Young Sam, and Kim Jong Il. Other exceptions are certain place names, such as Seoul, and official terms like *Juche*. Otherwise, family names precede given names, and the given names are hyphenated (Kim Dae-Jung, Chung Wonsik). As for the ordering of authors' names in the reference material, I have tried to follow individual preferences (e.g., Sung Chul Yang, B. C. Koh) or style (Han-Kyo Kim, Dae-Sook Suh) if they are known to me. These Westernized names, including those of contributors to this book, have their surnames listed last.

Throughout the book, references are made to Korean and Japanese newspapers and periodicals such as *Han'guk Ilbo, Rodong Sinmun,* and *Asahi Shimbun.* No attempt is made to translate these titles into English because they are known worldwide by these proper names. For instance, *ilbo* and *sinmun* (*shimbun* in Japanese) mean "daily newspaper"; and *Han'guk* (Korea), *Rodong* (Workers'), and *Asahi* (Rising Sun) are proper names and not translated in the text.

Rapid changes characterized the volatile situation surrounding the Korean peninsula during the preparation of this book for publication. These changes pertained to the political drama of North Korea's "suspected" nuclear weapons program and South Korea's democratic reform politics. In order to capture some of the dynamics of these developments, the authors of Chapter 13 added a Postscript on North Korea's nuclear program, and I added an Epilogue to the book to place North Korea's nuclear program controversy in broader regional and global contexts, including peaceful alternatives and solutions to the problem as well as the South Korean response.

Finally, I wish to acknowledge a grant of Faculty Improvement Leave from Iowa State University during the spring 1992 semester. This enabled me to spend time at Harvard University's John King Fairbank Center for East Asian Research and Korea Institute and also at the Rand Corporation, Santa Monica, California, as a visiting fellow in May 1992. Several graduate students in my political science class, Asia in World Politics, assisted me in completing the project by providing a forum for lecture and discussion on some topics covered in this volume. The students include Sang-joon Cho, Bum-suk Kim, Dong-jin Lee, Heung-sik Park, and Hyung-lae Park. Particular thanks also must go to Edward Baker, Roger Benjamin, James Cotton, Carter Eckert, Hajime Izumi, Richard Mansbach, James McCormick, Chung-In Moon, Tony Namkung, Joseph Nye, Jonathan Pollack, Robert Scalapino, David Steinberg, and Edward Wagner.

This book is dedicated to the memory of C. I. Eugene Kim, who served as the founding member and the first president of the council from 1984 to 1986.

Young Whan Kihl
Ames, Iowa

About the Contributors

Ralph C. Hassig is lecturer in the School of Business and Economics, California State University, Los Angeles.

In Kwan Hwang is professor of political science and director of the Institute of International Studies, Bradley University, Peoria, Illinois. He has authored several books on Korea, including, most recently, *The United States and Neutral Reunified Korea* (1990) and *One Korea via Permanent Neutrality: Peaceful Management of Korean Unification* (1987).

Young Whan Kihl is professor of political science at Iowa State University, Ames. He has authored or edited twelve books on Korean politics and Asian affairs, including, most recently, *Rethinking the Korean Peninsula* (coeditor, 1993) and *Security, Strategy, and Policy Responses in the Pacific Rim* (coeditor, 1989).

Han-Kyo Kim is professor of political science at the University of Cincinnati, Cincinnati, Ohio. He has published widely on Korean politics and history. One of his most recent publications is *Sourcebook of Korean Civilization* (editor on modern period, 1992).

Hong Nack Kim is professor of political science at West Virginia University, Morgantown. He has published widely on Japanese and Korean politics. One of his most recent publications is *Korea and the Major Powers After the Seoul Olympics* (coeditor, 1989).

Ilpyong J. Kim is professor of political science at the University of Connecticut, Storrs. He has authored or edited twelve books on the politics of China and Korea. One of his most recent publications is *The Korean Challenge and American Policy* (editor, 1991).

Samuel S. Kim is senior research scholar at the East Asian Institute of Columbia University, New York. He is the author or editor of fifteen books, including, most recently, *China and the World: Chinese Foreign Relations in the Post–Cold War Era* (editor, forthcoming).

Young C. Kim is professor of political science and director of the Gaston Sigur Center of East Asian Studies, George Washington University, Washington, D.C. He has published widely on Japanese and Korean politics. His most recent publications include *Asia and the Decline of Communism* (coeditor, 1992) and *Economic Cooperation in the Asia-Pacific Region* (coeditor, 1990).

B. C. Koh is professor of political science at the University of Illinois, Chicago. He has published widely on Korean and Japanese politics. His most recent publications include *Japan's Administrative Elite* (1989) and *The Foreign Relations of North Korea* (coeditor, 1987).

Tae Hwan Kwak is professor of international relations at Eastern Kentucky University, Richmond. He has authored and edited several books on Korean politics. His most recent publications include *The Korean-American Community: Present and Future* (coeditor, 1991) and *Forty Years of U.S.-Korean Relations* (coeditor, 1990).

Chae-Jin Lee is professor of government and director of the Keck Center for International and Strategic Studies, Claremont McKenna College, Claremont, California. His most recent publications include *The Korean War* (editor, 1991) and *The Prospects for Korean Reunification* (coeditor, 1993).

Hong Yung Lee is professor of political science and chairman of the Center for Korean Studies, University of California, Berkeley. He is a specialist on Chinese and Korean politics. One of his recent publications on Korea is *Korean Options in a Changing International Order* (coeditor, 1993).

Hy Sang Lee is professor of economics at the University of Wisconsin, Oshkosh. He is a frequent contributor on the North Korean economy; his recent articles include "The Economic Reforms of North Korea: The Strategy of Hidden and Assimilable Reforms," *Korea Observer*, Vol. 23, No. 1 (Spring 1992), pp. 45–78. His 1989 publication "North Korea's Economic Opening: Programs and Prospects," in *Search for Inter-Korean Interaction and Cooperation* (Seoul), was credited with influencing the Seoul government to establish an Inter-Korean Economic Cooperation Fund.

Manwoo Lee is professor of political science at Millersville State University, Millersville, Pennsylvania, and director of the Institute for Far Eastern Studies, Kyungnam University, Seoul, Korea. His most recent publications include *The Odyssey of Korean Democracy* (1990) and *The Changing Order in Northeast Asia and the Korean Peninsula* (coeditor, 1993).

Kongdan Oh is policy analyst in the International Policy Department of the RAND Corporation, Santa Monica, California. Her most recent publications include *North Korea in the 1990s* (1992) and *Background and Options for Nuclear Arms Control on the Korean Peninsula* (1992).

Han Shik Park is professor of political science at the University of Georgia, Athens. He visited North Korea in November 1992. One of his most recent publications is *The Politics of North Korea* (editor, forthcoming).

Tong Whan Park is associate professor of political science at Northwestern University, Evanston, Illinois, and adjunct research fellow at the Korea Institute for Defense Analysis, Seoul. He is the author of *U.S. Forces in Korea and Their Strategic Missions* (1990).

Sung Chul Yang is professor of political science and academic dean, the Graduate Institute of Peace Studies, Kyung Hee University, Seoul, Korea. His most recent publications include *The Changing World Order: Prospects for Korea in the Asia-Pacific Era* (coeditor, 1992) and *The North and South Korean Political Systems: A Comparative Political Analysis* (forthcoming).

1

Korea After the Cold War: An Introduction

Young Whan Kihl

A new era dawned with the passing of the Cold War, the dominant dynamic in world politics in the years after World War II. During the Cold War era, the Korean security agenda was defined largely by considerations of the U.S. global strategy of ideological competition with the Soviet Union. U.S. strategy, as reflected in the Truman Doctrine, was to stem the tide of communist expansionism and contain Soviet power within its existing border. This containment policy was put to the test in Korea when war resulted from the communist North Korean invasion of South Korea on June 25, 1950. The dominant analytical paradigm of this era regarding the Korean peninsula was geopolitical thinking; Korea played a sensitive role as the buffer and fulcrum in the balance of power among the major powers surrounding the Korean peninsula.

Now that the Cold War is over, a new perspective is needed on the Korean peninsula's strategic role in global and regional politics. The authors of this book address some of the new questions that have arisen in regard to Korea's changing role in the new world order. What are the implications of the dramatic end of the Cold War in global politics for East Asia and the Korean peninsula? Will peace and prosperity return to the region, followed by the reunification of divided Korea? Alternatively, will history repeat itself in East Asia in the form of the violence-prone conflict and rivalry of the late nineteenth and early twentieth centuries? Answers to these and related questions will depend largely on an assessment of the emerging trends in the strategic environment of East Asia and Korea's place in it.

An end to the Cold War does not mean that security is no longer important in the international politics of East Asia. Rather, it means that a new concept of security is needed because the foreign policy issues are more complex and tend to be intertwined with economic issues and domestic politics. Korea's security role in the post–Cold War era will be determined by the ways in which the emerging trends in Korea's external environment are evaluated, Korea's new foreign policy goals are formulated, and Korea's relationships with its allies and neighbors are managed. As Han Sung-joo, who subsequently became South Korea's foreign minister in 1993, has argued, South Korea in its diplomacy may need to change its policy goals and methods of policy implementation by (1) diversifying partnership and policy issues, (2) overcoming competition with North Korea, (3) injecting a new moral and ethical dimension in diplomacy, and (4) institutionalizing the policymaking and implementation processes.[1]

An End of the Cold War and the New Security Environment

A new environment for Korean reunification has arisen in the post–Cold War era.[2] The new world order emerging in the 1990s will be shaped and influenced by the interplay of various forces and factors manifest in the years 1989–1993. These include such dramatic events as the collapse of the Berlin Wall in November 1989 and the subsequent reunification by absorption of East Germany by West Germany; the Persian Gulf war of 1990–1991, prompted by the Iraqi invasion of Kuwait; the abortive coup in the Soviet Union and the subsequent demise of the Soviet empire in 1991; and the ethnic conflict and Balkanization of Eastern Europe in 1992.[3] These historic events, when added together, will result in changes and shifts in the existing balance of power and relations among the major powers.

These dramatic events in Europe and the Persian Gulf added up to the greatest transformation of the international system in the post–World War II era. More history was made—and unmade—in these several years since 1989 than during the previous two generations since 1945. In the post–Cold War security environment, new policy agendas and new regional powers are bound to arise to dominate the pattern of international relations.

For instance, if economic issues and powers can be assumed to dominate the future, the role of world leadership may pass from the United States to Japan and to Germany in the shaping of an emerging new world order. The demise of the Soviet empire and East European communism will mean, as James Kurth has argued, "the resurrection and return of Mitteleuropa" (Middle Europe) in which a reunified Germany is bound to play a more decisive role.[4] Likewise, in East Asia the rising Japan and China will come to play a greater regional role in the future. Although Japan has provided much less of a historical and cultural model for East Asia than Germany has for Mitteleuropa and than China has for East Asia, the Japanese economic success has inspired several neighboring countries, including South Korea, to emulate Japan's model of "mercantilistic" capitalism and also a new concept of "comprehensive" security.[5]

The environment for Korea's shifting balance of power, however, has been unique to the Korean context. For instance, through the ages Korea has had "a strategic importance far out of proportion to its size."[6] This importance was derived from geography and history: the geopolitical location of the Korean peninsula in Northeast Asia and Korea's past history in the context of rivalry between the continental forces in Asia and maritime powers offshore. Throughout history China was such a continental power, often in violent competition with Japan as a maritime power. In the past century, for instance, three major wars were fought over control of Korea: the Sino-Japanese war of 1894–1895; the Russo-Japanese clash of 1904–1905; and the Korean conflict of 1950–1953, an "internationalized" civil war involving primarily the United States and China as belligerents.[7]

During the Cold War years, the strategic value of Korea stemmed from its geopolitical position between the United States and the Soviet Union in their ideological and military confrontation. Two separate states, a capitalist South and a socialist North, waged their proxy wars, both hot and verbal, on behalf of their respective patron states. Whereas the former Soviet Union and China were the continental forces, the United States and Japan were the maritime powers in the Cold War era.

The Korean peninsula, a heavily armed camp, became a security flashpoint in the Asia-Pacific region. The theater of the Korean conflict served two useful purposes strategically: as the focal point of competition between two ideologies (capitalism and socialism) and as a strategic fulcrum among the four major powers maintaining active interests in Korea and Northeast Asia. The intersection of these two contending forces worked to transform the Korean peninsula into one of the most sensitive security barometers in global and regional Cold War politics.[8]

U.S. Hegemony and Diffused World Order

The defeat of communism and the disappearance of a bipolar system have brought change in the security role of Korea, and this will mean change in the strategic value of the Korean peninsula in U.S. policy. As the post–Cold War era dawns, the strategic environment surrounding the Korean peninsula is certainly favorable to the United States and its security ally, the Republic of Korea (ROK, or South Korea), but it is adversarial to the interests of the surviving Leninist states of the Democratic People's Republic of Korea (DPRK, or North Korea) and the People's Republic of China (PRC).

This change in strategic environment has enhanced the prospect of greater peace and stability on the Korean peninsula provided that a post–Cold War new world order is led by the United States as the dominant hegemonic world power. Under these circumstances, South Korea as a U.S. security ally will be favored by a U.S.-led regional order. Although the security environment continues to remain unsettled and volatile, the threat of communist revolution and expansionism in Asia is practically nonexistent for the time being; so is the danger of aggressive moves by the surviving Leninist states in Asia beyond their existing borders.[9] The PRC under Deng Xiaoping, for instance, is preoccupied with the domestic agenda of economic development and modernization of the country. The DPRK under the dualistic rule of President Kim

Il Sung and his son, Kim Jong Il, appears to be focusing on the task of putting its domestic house in order, including consolidation of political succession and reinvigoration of its stagnant socialist economy.

Paul Kennedy's *The Rise and Fall of the Great Powers* was a timely and appropriate book to appear on the eve of the collapse of the Soviet empire.[10] This book triggered a debate as to whether the United States was overextending itself militarily and financially with an escalating economic burden to maintain its military presence worldwide. To counter the deterministic implication of the Kennedy thesis, Joseph Nye led a debate on the nature of U.S. power as being "soft" rather than "hard." According to Nye, the United States as a hegemonic power was able to withstand pressure and sustain itself militarily because of its leadership capability in alliance and coalition with friendly countries. This leadership capability, the power of persuasion rather than coercion, is the "soft" rather than "hard" side of U.S. power.[11]

However, because of the dynamics of economic competition in the capitalist world system, the power of the United States has undergone a relative erosion vis-à-vis the strong economic performance of its allies, Japan and West Germany, and the newly industrializing countries (NICs). Given this relative decline of the United States as an economic power and the concomitant rise of Japan as an economic superpower, the United States regards its relationship with Japan as "the critical linchpin" of its Asian security strategy.[12] To the extent that Japan can compensate for declining U.S. capabilities in the region, the United States and Japan will need to share leadership in managing security and economic tasks and to develop a "new special relationship."[13] Future U.S. policy toward Korea will be influenced by such strategic thinking in Washington about Tokyo.

Regional Trends and Patterns

The post–Cold War strategic environment remains basically unsettling and undefined. Some analysts project the rise of a multipolar world structure; others envision a more unipolar structure led by the United States. According to Nye, theoretically there are five alternative forms of the new distribution of power possible in the post–Cold War environment. These alternatives are return to bipolarity, multipolarity, three economic blocs (the European Community, Japan, and the United States), unipolar hegemony led by the United States, and multilevel interdependence.[14] The diffused world order is far from a U.S.-led unipolar hegemony, or Pax Americana as it is popularly known, but is closer to a multilevel or layered-cake image of international interdependence in which the United States is involved inextricably.

As for the future security environment in the Asia-Pacific region in the 1990s and beyond, the following contours and patterns seem visible.

- Threat of global and regionwide war diminishing
- China and Japan security alliance unlikely
- Northern triangular ties of Pyongyang, Moscow, and Beijing eroding due to Seoul's successful opening of diplomatic ties with Moscow and Beijing

- Greater prospect for a unified Korea
- Intraregional conflict and cooperation in Southeast Asia increasing in intensity

The following broad trends are also visible in the Asia-Pacific region of the post–Cold War world that will influence the pattern and style of foreign policy of the United States and regional actors.

- Domestic political concerns and constituency support overriding foreign and security policy agenda
- Economic interests emerging as greater than political and security interests while economic and trade disputes likely to escalate
- Multilateral diplomacy and institutions gaining prominence as a regional forum for policy coordination and adjustment

Both stable and dynamic forces are clearly evident in the post–Cold War global and regional environment. Resolution of international conflict issues in East Asia, including the Korean question, will be influenced largely by the interplay of these ongoing patterns and processes that are manifest in the new environment globally and regionally. Three emerging forces are particularly noticeable in the regional environment of Northeast Asia: a U.S.-led and U.S.-dominant system, the primacy of economics over security, and sustained economic growth of the Pacific Rim.

First, the new post–Cold War security order in the region is no longer a bipolar system. Instead, it is a U.S.-dominant system and a unipolar security order globally with the rising regional-bloc systems. As the threat of global war is gone, so is the threat of regionwide wars diminished. The U.S. strategic plan in the post–Cold War era, according to a Pentagon document, is intended to "thwart emergence of a rival superpower" to challenge U.S. supremacy.[15] The plan as submitted to the White House in 1992 was subsequently modified slightly to give greater responsibility for the "collaboration" and "collective security" activities of the United Nations and other international organizations.[16] Nevertheless, the hegemony and primacy of the United States as "balancer, stabilizer, and guarantor" will not disappear in the Asia-Pacific strategic framework in the 1990s.

Second, the relative decline of the United States as an economic power and the concomitant rise of Japan and Germany as economic superpowers have led to a greater role of economics in strategic thinking and foreign policy considerations by the world powers.

In place of traditional concern for security, there is a new accent on economics (trade, investment, exchange rates, and so on) being given in the diplomatic corridor of world politics in the post–Cold War era. The trend toward regionalization of economic blocs, such as the Japan-led yen-bloc formation in the Asia-Pacific region and the North American Free Trade Agreement (NAFTA) in the North American region, has risen as an emerging and new concern of diplomacy.

Third, the Asia-Pacific countries registered sustained growth in their economies in the 1980s, far above the world average of economic growth in other regions. This trend was pioneered by Japan in the 1960s and 1970s through its export-led strategy of industrialization. The four little tigers of East Asian NICs—South Korea, Taiwan, Hong Kong, and Singapore—achieved their "economic miracles" in the 1970s and 1980s. The East Asian NICs' success story is now being emulated and repeated by other semi- and near-NICs in the region, such as Thailand, Malaysia, Indonesia, and others. China has also emerged to become a rapidly growing economy through its open door policy and economic linkage with the outside world via Hong Kong and Taiwanese trade and investments.

Under the circumstances of the aforementioned regional trends and patterns, the threat of Asian communist revolution and expansion in the region has diminished in the post–Cold War era. The rise of a global superpower and regional hegemons in an attempt to fill a vacuum in the new environment is not likely to happen in the foreseeable future so long as the United States remains as a dominant power in the Pacific. This does not mean, however, that sources of instability in the region are absent.

First, the danger of a mini–arms race is real in the region, and so is the prospect of nuclear proliferation as the regional actors increase defense spending. Second, the uncertainty of political transition and leadership succession in several East Asian countries, depending on the outcome, may also lead to domestic turmoil and civil disturbances. Third, civil war conflict in some countries may spill over the borders and lead to interstate disputes. Finally, although a regionwide war is less likely, crisis may also erupt over the control of resources and movement and migration of refugees. The East Asian conflict zones include disputes over territory and resources in the South China Sea, the Sea of Japan, the northern territories of Japan, and Cambodia in Indochina.[17]

Greater Regional Order and Stability in a New Era?

Given these regional trends and patterns, what is the prospect of peace and security in the new Asia-Pacific age? Is Asia in the post–Cold War world more or less prone to conflict?

Whether the end of the Cold War will enhance stability and peace in East Asia is neither clear nor obvious. More likely is that the passing of the Cold War will usher in a new form of regional conflict and tension in East Asia. This is particularly so because, unlike in Europe, the Asian communist states have survived the test and crisis of legitimacy generated by communism's demise in the former Soviet Union and Eastern Europe. More likely, the post–Cold War regional security environment in Northeast Asia will have its own dynamics in terms of the structure and pattern of relationship.

John Mearsheimer, in a controversial article in 1990 entitled "Back to the Future," warned of the dangers accompanying the end of bipolarity in post–Cold War Europe.[18] "The next decades in Europe without the superpowers would probably not be as violent as the first 45 years of this century, but would probably be substantially more prone to violence than the past 45 years."[19] Although the same argument can be made about the future security environment in Asia, it is more likely that the Northeast Asian security process will have its own dynamics and unique ways of balancing it out in the end.

Ultimately, peace and stability in the region will depend on domestic political movements and tendencies in several key Asian countries, such as Japan and China. This aspect may take the form of Japan's domestic political reform and greater political and security participation in regional affairs. The latter was evidenced by the 1992 passage of the UN peacekeeping operations (PKO) bill in the Japanese Diet, rammed through by the Miyazawa Liberal Democratic Party (LDP) government, to facilitate Japanese involvement in the Cambodian peace process. Japan's enhanced future activities, including the nuclear option, are strenuously opposed by neighboring countries. Regional conflict may take the form of intensified economic and trade disputes between Japan and its Asian neighbors. Unless managed, these economic conflicts may spill over and escalate into acute international crisis.

Another concern is China's rising power and status in the region. Given the rapid economic growth of the Chinese economy—an average annual growth rate of 10–12 percent in the decade 1982–1992—it is a matter of time before China will emerge to become Asia's largest economy in the twenty-first century. The end of the Cold War has reduced China's leverage in world politics. China is no longer the valuable partner it was in the Cold War–era strategic triangle. More important, China harbors ancient fears and suspicion about outsiders. The sale of advanced weapons to Taiwan, for instance, is taken as a Western conspiracy against China, and it continues to enhance its own security posture by purchasing advanced weapons and technology from Russia and exporting advanced weapons of its own to third countries.[20] China's stepped-up naval presence in the South China Sea and its rumored construction of aircraft-carrier capability are factors injecting a new element of fear and insecurity among the neighboring countries in the region.

Whatever shape regional dynamics may take in the post–Cold War environment, the Korean peninsula will continue to occupy center stage in the regional balance-of-power system. As in the past, the peninsula will provide strategic options and opportunities to the major powers in the region into the twenty-first century.

From a broader historical perspective, East Asian conflict zones may be taken as dormant volcanoes. One cannot rule out the possibility of the clash of ethnic and cultural nationalist movements in Asia that may very well take the form, for instance, of an irredentist claim by certain Asian countries over contiguous territory in neighboring countries. These explosive volcanoes will flare up with slight provocation by the interested parties. From this perspective, the Korean demilitarized zone (DMZ) that separates the two sets of heavily armed troops in North Korea and South Korea is one such crisis region and the fault line forged during the Cold War era. Efforts are obviously needed to defuse the potential for explosion and to restore the groundwork for stability. Changing the Korean conflict zone into an active peace zone is an urgent policy agenda for the countries involved in the region.

Peace and New Détente in the Korean Peninsula

As noted in the preceding discussion, the maintenance of peace and stability on the Korean peninsula has been the function of a delicate balance of power among the major powers having active interest in the region, such as Japan, China, Russia, and the United States. During the Cold War era, this status was also determined by the nature of the relationship between the two rival states and regimes of North Korea and South Korea. This pattern will continue in the post–Cold War era as long as Korea remains a divided nation-state.[21] More important, however, future Korean peace and stability will depend on the internal peace and cohesion in each of the two Koreas (see Chapter 8).

The changes in external environment, such as the removal of the Berlin Wall in November 1989 and the collapse of East European and Soviet communist states soon thereafter, were both debilitating and traumatic to the North Korean regime. Nevertheless, both Korean states responded to the external shocks positively and creatively, albeit in varying degrees and intensity, with the inauguration of a new détente in their mutual relations. As a result, the ideological glacier has begun to thaw, and prospects for normalizing inter-Korean relations have improved considerably in the early 1990s.

The signing of the agreement on reconciliation, nonaggression, and exchanges and cooperation between the South and the North on December 13, 1991, and the adoption of a joint declaration on the denuclearization of the Korean peninsula on December 31, 1991, marked a historical landmark in inter-Korean relations. (For the texts, see Appendixes B and C.) Both agreements were put into effect with the exchange of ratified documents during the sixth high-level talks held in Pyongyang February 19, 1992, and by a series of measures undertaken subsequently to implement the terms of the agreements, such as establishing the North-South joint nuclear control commission, the North-South liaison offices in Panmunjom, and other functional commissions and committees.[22]

North Korean accession to the International Atomic Energy Agency (IAEA) safeguards accord on January 31, 1992, and to several on-site inspections subsequently of its nuclear facilities has also improved the prospect for institutionalizing the peace process on the Korean peninsula. However, a year later North Korea reneged on its promise to allow inspection of its facilities on grounds that the IAEA demand to inspect a newly designated site exceeded its authority and thus infringed upon North Korea's sovereignty. The North also used the pretext of the announced Team Spirit 1993 U.S.-ROK joint military exercises, which Pyongyang finds objectionable.

For the new détente on Korea to work, needed is a series of tension-reduction measures, such as a breakthrough in arms-control negotiations and agreements that will enhance transparency and confidence-building measures between North and South Korea (see Chapter 12). The abortive mutual exchange of visits by dispersed families and artist troupes between North and South Korea (on the occasion of commemorating the forty-eighth anniversary of Korea's liberation from Japanese rule on August 15, 1945) clearly dampened the prospect for normalizing relations and achieving the nationalist aspiration of reunification. The announced withdrawal of North Korea from the nuclear NPT (nonproliferation treaty) regime on March 12, 1993—the withdrawal was subsequently suspended on June 11, one day before it was to take effect—also set the clock backward on the timetable of restoring peace and stability on the Korean peninsula and keeping Korea denuclearized.

Nevertheless, a new era of reconciliation and cooperation in inter-Korean relations has thus begun, at least in principle, with a heightened anticipation that Korean reunification might somehow be attained at the end of this difficult and uncertain journey toward greater harmony and anticipated exchanges between the two Koreas.

Korea's Future and Reunification

The question of whether, when, and how to achieve Korean reunification will be determined primarily by the Koreans themselves and secondarily by the concerted efforts of other major powers. Three principles of reunification, as agreed on in the July 4, 1972, North-South joint communiqué, provide the political guidepost. These entail the principles of "independence without reliance on external forces," "peaceful reunification," and "great national unity transcending ideologies, ideas, and systems" (see Appendix A).

What path Korean reunification will take—if and when it comes—remains to be seen. At least three scenarios are possible, according to Young C. Kim: reunification by war, reunification by mutual consent, and reunification by default (see Chapter 14). However, both Korean states seem to have ruled out the path of reunification by conquest (as in Vietnam) or by absorption (as in Germany) (see Chapter 15). Instead, both Koreas are committed to the path of reunification by agreement (as in Yemen) that incorporates either confederal or commonwealth plans (see Chapters 9 and 16). More likely, the end result of inter-Korean relations via interaction will be reunification by association if the terms of the 1991 agreement are faithfully carried out in the direction toward peaceful coexistence as an intermediary stage (see Chapter 8).

ROK President Kim Young Sam, soon after his inauguration on February 25, 1993, proclaimed "a new diplomacy" for South Korea that would incorporate "a future-oriented policy" on the unification issue. His government, as he put it, "will move from the initial step of reconciliation and cooperation to the next step of a Korean Commonwealth, and to a final stage of an united nation of one people and one state." He also accentuated the theme of "open and global diplomacy" and upholding universal values of "democracy, liberty, welfare and human rights" as components of his "new diplomacy."[23]

DPRK President Kim Il Sung unveiled a new "Ten-Point Program of Great Unity of Korean Nation and Reunification," which was subsequently adopted by North Korea's legislative body on April 7, 1993, as an official policy of the government. This latest proclamation reaffirmed the founding of "a unified state" based on the principles of "independent, peaceful and neutral" government and "patriotism." It also recognized the principle of "enhancing unity" and promoting "coexistence" and "coprosperity" as well as building trust "through contacts, travels, and dialogues" between the North and the South.[24]

The character of a reunified Korean state will be a legitimate concern of the major powers surrounding the Korean peninsula (see Chapters 4 through 7). For instance, as John Blodgett has argued, U.S. interest dictates (1) that North Korea be nullified as a destabilizing political-military factor in the region; (2) that ultimate arrangements on the peninsula produce a Korea that is as secure as any nation can be in a potentially unstable region; and (3) that the new Korea work with—or at least not work against—the United States in constructing a regional security framework that will protect vital U.S. political and economic interests in the western Pacific.[25]

From the Korean perspective, a reunified Korea will have the option of pursuing a nonaligned diplomacy or retaining an alliance with the United States. Whereas the former is the preferred policy of North Korea's confederation scheme, the latter is that of South Korea's commonwealth plan of unification. If the latter option is chosen, a reunified Korea is more likely to remain as a nonnuclear country, with the U.S. security umbrella and nuclear-protection commitment remaining intact. This arrangement may be more rational and cost beneficial (see Chapters 8 and 9).

For more than four decades, socialist North Korea and capitalist South Korea were the frontline states in the Cold War era, engaging in cutthroat competition and remaining estranged. As a by-product of the Cold War system, the two Koreas epitomized the value premise of Cold War global politics and acted as partners in rivalry and enmity.

With the end of the Cold War, globally and locally, continued estrangement and hostility between the two Koreas seem anachronistic and counterproductive. Because the old habit of rivalry and mistrust will not and cannot be eliminated overnight, however, each regime is expected to continue its politics of competitive legitimacy in the name of achieving Korean reunification according to its own proposed scheme—that is, a hegemonic reunification.

The challenge in the post–Cold War era is to transform the nature and stake of inter-Korean relations from one of confrontation to coexistence in an orderly and peaceful manner. This task of institutionalizing the peace process on the Korean peninsula will take time. The latest controversy over nuclear issues shows how difficult it is to overcome the suspicion and enmity between the old foes (see Chapters 12 and 13).

However, by opening the channel of communication at the prime-ministerial level, the two Koreas initiated the process of relying on peaceful means of diplomacy and dialogue rather than making overt strategic moves of coercion and threats of war. If war is politics carried out by other means, to borrow the dictum of Karl von Clausewitz, diplomacy is politics carried out by peaceful means rather than by violence and war. To the extent that the two Koreas have decided to play the game of diplomacy and negotiation rather than war and conflict, the prospect of institutionalizing the peace process on the Korean peninsula has improved immeasurably.

Outline of the Book

The chapters presented here are organized in four parts according to key themes: (1) historical context, (2) policies of major powers toward the Korean peninsula, (3) inter-Korean relations, and (4) prospects of Korean reunification in the post–Cold War era. The introductory overview of Korea in the new world order given in this chapter is followed by expanded discussion of the context: In Chapter 2 by Han-Kyo Kim and Chapter 3 by Samuel S. Kim, the context of both history and world order is provided. These contributors place today's Korean unification issue in historical perspective and in the broader context of world-order issues and emerging global and regional trends in the changing world.

The four chapters in Part 2 deal with the major powers' relationship with and policies toward Korea in the changing post–Cold War environment of global and regional politics. In Chapter 4, Chae-Jin Lee describes the dynamics of changing relations between the United States and South Korea leading up to the inauguration in those countries of new presidents, Bill Clinton and Kim Young Sam respectively. Chapter 5 by Ilpyong J. Kim details the dynamics of "new thinking" that Mikhail Gorbachev's *glasnost* and *perestroika* instituted, as manifested in the changed policy of Moscow toward Seoul and Pyongyang and the normalization of relations between Seoul and Moscow. In Chapter 6, Hong Yung Lee analyzes the emerging triangular relationship between Beijing and its traditional ally, communist North Korea, and its new diplomatic and trade partner, the noncommunist and capitalist South Korea. Hong Nack Kim in Chapter 7 provides a detailed picture of the unfolding drama of the normalization talks initiated in September 1990 between Pyongyang and Tokyo and explains the stalemate in the relationship.

The six chapters in Part 3 examine the various aspects and dimensions of the politics of inter-Korean relations in the post–Cold War environment. In Chapter 8, Young Whan Kihl discusses the ongoing process of inter-Korean dialogue and negotiation and prospects for the two Koreas' coexistence or reunification. In Chapter 9, B. C. Koh compares the official unification plans put forth by Pyongyang and Seoul—North Korea's confederation plan and South Korea's commonwealth plan—and notes how they are similar yet different. Chapter 10 by Manwoo Lee examines the dynamics of South Korea's unification politics during the country's political transition beyond the administration of President Roh Tae Woo. In Chapter 11, Hy Sang Lee examines the economic dimension of inter-Korean relations with particular emphasis on North Korea's economic difficulties and the reasons for its failed economic reform measure. In Chapter 12, Tong Whan Park focuses on the controversy and stalemate in inter-Korean dialogue on military and security relations, including the proposed CBMs (confidence-building measures) and related tension-reduction measures. In Chapter 13, Kongdan Oh and Ralph C. Hassig review the controversy surrounding North Korea's suspected nuclear weapons program, including its announced withdrawal from the nuclear nonproliferation treaty regime, a decision subsequently reversed June 11, 1993.

The six chapters in Part 4 examine the various facets of Korea's future and reunification. In Chapter 14, Young C. Kim provides an overview of scenarios for Korean reunification and assesses how and why these will or will not materialize. Sung Chul Yang gives a realistic and cautious picture in Chapter 15 of why Korean reunification will take a form different from German reunification and what lessons Korea might learn from that experience: a costly and hastily drawn process that led to West Germany's costly and hasty absorption of East Germany. In Chapter 16, In Kwan Hwang draws a useful contrast of Korea with the successful cases of reunification of Yemen, Austria, and other previously divided countries. Tae Hwan Kwak in Chapter 17 surveys the ways the United Nations became involved in the Korean reunification issue, including the admission of both Korean states to UN membership in September 1991. In Chapter 18, Han Shik Park explores future shapes and possibilities of value congruence between the divided halves of Korea and the implication these have for reunification. Chapter 19, an epilogue, surveys the most recent developments regarding North Korean nuclear weapons capabilities.

Of all the family of divided nations after World War II, only such unlucky ones as Korea and China still remain separated. A few lucky ones, including Vietnam, Germany, and Yemen, have subsequently been reunified. Hence, in the chapters where contrast is drawn between Korea and countries that exemplify successful reunification, the time reference is often given in the present rather than the past tense. For instance, in Chapter 15, South Korea and North Korea are compared with the former West Germany and East Germany as if the latter still existed as separate countries.

Notes

1. Han Sung-joo, "Chonhankiŭi Han'guk oekyoŭi kwajewa sŏnt'aek" (Transitional-era Korean diplomacy mission and options), *Kegan Sasang* (Quarterly ideology), Vol. 14, No. 1 (Summer 1992), pp. 235–263, as cited in Kim Kyung-won et al., "Roundtable on Korean Diplomacy," *Han'guk Ilbo,* July 17, 1992.

2. Young Whan Kihl, "New Environment and Context for Korean Reunification," *Korea and World Affairs,* Vol. 16, No. 4 (Winter 1992), pp. 621–637. Also see Young Whan Kihl, "Rethinking Korean and Asia-Pacific Security and United States–Korea Relations," in Bum-Joon Lee and Sung-Chul Yang, eds., *The Changing World Order: Prospects for Korea in the Asia-Pacific Era* (Seoul: Korean Association of International Studies, 1992), pp. 167–174, 184–186.

3. Young Whan Kihl, "A New World Order and the Korean Peninsula," *Pacific Focus,* Vol. 8, No. 1 (Spring/Summer 1993), pp. 27–42.

4. James Kurth, "Things to Come: The Shape of the New World Order," *The National Interest,* No. 24 (Summer 1991), pp. 3–12.

5. For an exposition of the "comprehensive" security concept, see Umemoto Tetsuya, "Comprehensive Security and the Evolution of the Japanese Security Posture," in Robert A. Scalapino et al., eds., *Asian Security Issues: Regional and Global* (Berkeley: University of California Institute of East Asian Studies, 1988), pp. 28–49. "Comprehensive security" (*sogo anzen hoshyo*), according to Umemoto, "is a term coined in Japan

that purports to capture the multifaceted character of the quest for national security" (p. 28).

6. Norman D. Levin and Richard L. Sneider, *Korea in Postwar U.S. Security Policy* (Santa Monica, CA: RAND Corporation, 1982). Also see Young Whan Kihl, "The Korean Peninsula and the Balance of Power: The Limits of Realism," *Korea and World Affairs*, Vol. 13, No. 4 (Winter 1989), pp. 689–707.

7. For an analysis of the Sino-Japanese and Russo-Japanese rivalries, respectively, and the collapse of Korea's old kingdom, see C. I. Eugene Kim and Han-Kyo Kim, *Korea and the Politics of Imperialism 1876–1910* (Berkeley: University of California Press, 1967), especially pp. 61–120. On the origin and background of the Korean War, see Peter Lowe, *The Origins of the Korean War* (London: Longman, 1986), and the two-volume study by Bruce Cumings, *The Origins of the Korean War* (Princeton, NJ: Princeton University Press, 1981 and 1990). Also see Carter J. Eckert et al., *Korea Old and New: A History* (Seoul: Ilchokak, 1990), especially chapters 14 and 18.

8. Young Whan Kihl, "The Korean Peninsula Conflict: Equilibrium or Deescalation?" in Lawrence Grinter and Young Whan Kihl, eds., *East Asian Conflict Zones* (New York: St. Martin's Press, 1987), pp. 97–122.

9. Robert A. Scalapino, *The Last Leninists: The Uncertain Future of Asia's Communist States* (Washington, DC: Center for Strategic and International Studies, 1992).

10. Paul Kennedy, *The Rise and Fall of the Great Powers: Economic Change and Military Conflict from 1500 to 2000* (New York: Random House, 1987).

11. Joseph S. Nye, *Bound to Lead: The Changing Nature of American Power* (New York: Basic Books, 1990).

12. Byung-joon Ahn, "Strategic Trends in East Asia," *Pacific Review*, Vol. 4, No. 2 (1991), pp. 6, 109–115.

13. Takashi Inoguchi, "Shaping and Sharing Pacific Dynamism," *Annals of the American Academy of Political and Social Sciences*, No. 505 (September 1989), pp. 46–55.

14. Joseph S. Nye, "What New World Order?" *Foreign Affairs*, Vol. 71, No. 2 (Spring 1992), pp. 86–89. Also see Joseph S. Nye, *Understanding International Conflicts: An Introduction to Theory and History* (New York: Harper Collins, 1993), pp. 190–192.

15. *New York Times*, March 8, 1992.

16. Ibid., May 24, 1992.

17. Grinter and Kihl, *East Asian Conflict Zones*.

18. John Mearsheimer, "Back to the Future: Instability in Europe After the Cold War," *International Security*, Vol. 15, No. 2 (Summer 1990), pp. 5–56; "Why We Will Soon Miss the Cold War," *The Atlantic*, Vol. 269, No. 8 (August 1990), pp. 35–50.

19. Mersheimer, "Back to the Future," p. 6.

20. *Far Eastern Economic Review*, December 3, 1992, pp. 8–9.

21. My overall perspective on divided Korea appears in Young Whan Kihl, *Politics and Policies in Divided Korea: Regimes in Contest* (Boulder, CO: Westview Press, 1984).

22. For the text of these protocol agreements, see *Intra-Korean Agreements* (Seoul: ROK National Unification Board, 1991).

23. This address was delivered to the Seoul meeting of the Pacific Basin Economic Council (PBEC) May 24, 1993, which convened on a theme of "Open Regionalism: A New Basis for Globalism?" *Korea Newsreview* (Seoul), May 29, 1993, p. 5.

24. *Korean Report* (Tokyo), No. 273 (April 1993), pp. 1–6. For the text of this proclamation, see Chapter 8.

25. John Q. Blodgett, "Korea: Exploring Paths to Peace and Reunification," *Washington Quarterly*, Vol. 15, No. 3 (Summer 1992), p. 180.

PART ONE

The Context

2

Korean Unification in Historical Perspective

Han-Kyo Kim

As the division of Korea approaches its half-century mark amid some guarded hopes for reunification, it may be useful to view the peninsula's contemporary problems in broad historical perspective. History may not repeat itself, but with the help of hindsight, we can distinguish events of lasting significance from those that are ephemeral and understand the main themes of human and social evolution over time. In particular, the occurrence of similar events at different times invites inquiry into their underlying causes. Such an exercise may help us not only to formulate a theoretical and comparative framework for problems we face today but also to transcend the passion of the moment and arrive at a more balanced judgment.

Historical Overview of the Korean Nation

Historians trace the origin of the Korean nation to the prehistoric peoples who inhabited not only the Korean peninsula but also a wide region north of the Yalu and Tumen rivers. Known by such names as Puyŏ, Old Chosŏn, Ye, Maek, Okcho, Chin, and others, they evolved over a period of centuries into the three kingdoms of Koguryo (conventionally dated 37 B.C.–A.D. 668), Paekche (18 B.C.–A.D. 660), and Silla 57 B.C.–A.D. 935). Koguryo, astride today's northwestern Korea and southern Manchuria, was a powerful military power in its heyday and had close contacts—including frequent military conflicts—with the expanding empires in China proper. Paekche occupied the southwestern part of the peninsula although its rulers originated from the Puyŏ region. Silla, isolated from China in the southeastern corner of the peninsula, was the last to benefit from the advanced Chinese civilization.

Unified Silla

For many years, the three kingdoms were in a state of constant warfare against one another until Silla, probably the least likely prospect at the outset, managed to defeat first Paekche and then Koguryo. The victor, "Unified Silla," ruled for nearly 300 years all of the former Paekche land and a southern portion of Koguryo, or roughly two-thirds of the Korean peninsula. Most historians, with the notable exception of those in North Korea, hold the view that Silla's success laid the foundation for the formation of a Korean nation.[1] For that reason, our examination of historical analogies to today's Korean question must start at that point.

The final phase of the military rivalry on the peninsula pitted a north-south alliance of the Turks (T'u-chueh), Koguryo, Paekche, and Japan against an east-west counteralliance of Silla and Sui (later T'ang). The Turks in north-central Asia found Koguryo a natural ally against China, while Paekche called on Japan to counter the growing menace from the Silla-China alliance. Similar considerations drew Silla and China closer against their immediate neighbor-rivals.[2] The combined sea-land assault on Paekche by the east-west alliance forced the former to surrender, but almost immediately, Silla had to resort to force to prevent its Chinese ally from creating a T'ang colony in the former Paekche territory. A few years later, the Silla-T'ang forces launched a pincer-like offensive against the capital of Koguryo, which had been seriously weakened by internal dissension. No sooner had Koguryo surrendered than the winning coalition disintegrated again, and it was eight years before Silla could drive the T'ang forces from the region south of Pyongyang. Beyond Unified Silla's northern boundary, a new kingdom of Parhae (Chinese: P'o-hai) was created by a former Koguryo general who ruled over a mixed nation of Koguryo and the seminomadic Malgal peoples.

Geography can explain much of Korea's history. The topography of the Korean peninsula, with mountain ranges running east-west in the north and north-south in the south, may have been one of the primary reasons for the territorial boundaries of the three kingdoms. Koguryo's location astride the land route from the continent to Korea accounted for its wars with China, which pressured Koguryo to shift its political center southward to Pyongyang (A.D. 427). Paekche's tie to Japan to the south was logical given the presence of threats to its security coming from the other three directions. Silla's strenuous—and successful—efforts to forge a military alliance with China was crucial for its survival and eventual triumph over its neighbors. The inability of Koguryo and Paekche to form a strong united front against the Silla-T'ang coalition gave the latter the opportunity to defeat one opponent at a time. Little evidence suggests that there were great disparities among the three rival kingdoms in such factors of political-military power as level of technology, economic life, quality of leadership, and so on. Thus, geopolitical factors and the alliance strategy may well have been crucial in determining the outcome of the tripartite struggle.

Once united, Silla introduced throughout its greatly expanded domain a uniform centrally controlled government system that accommodated the newly subjugated peoples in its administrative and military organizations.[3] At the same time, the power of the throne was deliberately strengthened. By the end of the seventh century, the foundation for a unified nation under a powerful monarchy was laid. In other words, the history of the Korean nation starts with the inauguration of Unified Silla in A.D. 668. Despite internal dissension and foreign encroachment, the national framework and identity have survived for over 1,300 years to this day.

The preceding narrative emphasized foreign intervention. A related and intriguing question is whether the three neighboring kingdoms, at this early stage of Korean nationhood, were cognizant of the common Korean tie among them. In all probability they were not. It is difficult to argue that any one of the three Korean states had a Korean identity separate from its Silla, Paekche, or Koguryo identity because it had shared no common Korean experience or symbol. By the same token, the non-Korean identity of their foreign allies, be it China or Japan, probably was not clearly registered in the minds of the Silla or Paekche leaders. To Silla, for example, T'ang China was another foreign—that is, non-Silla—state, as was Paekche or Koguryo. Machiavellian maneuvers drew Silla and T'ang together against common foes, but the alliance broke up once the enemy had been defeated.[4] As stated earlier, Korean nationhood evolved out of common life experiences as one political community after Silla's unification.

Koryo

When the central authority of Unified Silla began to decline in the late ninth century, rebellious local leaders resurrected the memories of the Three Kingdoms period: The Later Koguryo kingdom came to be located near the northern border; Later Paekche rose in the southwestern region of the rapidly weakening Silla. A three-sided contest ensued, and intermittent battles, mostly between the forces of Later Koguryo and Later Paekche, lasted for about forty years. In the end, Later Koguryo, now renamed Koryo (A.D. 918–1392) under a new leader, Wang Gŏn, reunited the nation by accepting the surrender of the last Silla king (A.D. 935) and defeating the Later Paekche forces for the last time (A.D. 936).

About the same time as Silla's demise, its northern neighbor Parhae also succumbed to the rising power of the Khitan people who, by controlling a vast land in southern Manchuria reaching into northern China, posed a new threat to the fledgling Koryo Korea. There were three major Khitan invasions during the early years of Koryo. Through diplomatic as well as military actions, Koryo survived; more than that, it managed to establish solid control over much of north Korea with the important exception of the northwest region, where the Khitans and the Jurchens, another seminomadic people, became entrenched. Another noteworthy development connected with the fall of Parhae was the influx into Korea of a large number of Parhae refugees who were descendants of former Koguryo people. By the late tenth century, all Koreans lived in the Korean peninsula, and Koryo was the only state of Korea.

Unlike in the case of Silla, the process of unification by Koryo did not entail any direct foreign intervention, largely because of disunity and internal warfare within China, the most serious potential intervener. None of the Later Three Kingdoms had any serious political-military ties to forces outside the peninsula. After reunification, the Koryo rulers attempted gradual consolidation of a centralized bureaucratic structure at the expense of powerful local aristocratic families but encountered much difficulty. Nevertheless, in theory at least, a Confucian-based bureaucracy was established on the basis of recruitment through a civil service examination system modeled after the Chinese prototype (A.D. 958). The Koryo dynasty lasted 475 years through several palace coups and damaging foreign—in particular, Mongol—invasions. For an extended time (over a century and a half in the case of the Mongols), Koreans suffered enormously at the hands of these intruders. Their presence undoubtedly stimulated the growth of national sentiment or awareness among the Koreans. Their efforts to fight off the invading Khitans included invocation of divine protection by laboriously carving Buddhist canons on thousands of woodblocks (an operation repeated during the first Mongol invasion); the process produced the so-called Koryo Tripitaka (the canons) carving that is preserved to this day at Hein-sa temple in southeastern Korea. Also significant as a monument to the growth of national awareness was the preparation of the first written histories of Korea: *Samguk sagi* (History of the three kingdoms) and *Samguk yusa* (Memorabilia of the three kingdoms) in the twelfth and thirteenth centuries respectively.

Chosŏn

In the late fourteenth century, the Koryo dynasty faced not only the ever-present military threat from the north but also incessant incursions by bands of Japanese pirates from the south. A general, Yi Sŏng-gye, who won fame fighting invaders from both directions, waged a successful coup against the debilitated Koryo court using the issue of foreign policy toward China as a pretext. As the dynastic change from Yuan to Ming proceeded in stages within China, Koryo was forced to choose one over the other. General Yi sided with Ming and forcibly purged those who had advocated a continued tie with Yuan; ousted was the last Koryo monarch. Yi then declared a new state of Chosŏn with a new capital city of Seoul.

During the founding of Chosŏn or the Yi dynasty (1392–1910), Korea experienced neither territorial division nor direct military intervention by a foreign power in its internal political strife. But the question of national security was foremost in the minds of its new leaders, who sought a suzerain-tributary relationship with Ming and political settlement of the Japanese raids. At the same time, Korea steadily incorporated the territories to its north and northwest up to the Yalu and Tumen rivers, eventually establishing a firm hold on the entire region of the peninsula. To hold and develop the newly acquired territory was a constant challenge—and a heavy burden—for Chosŏn.

The government of Chosŏn was a quintessential Confucian bureaucratic system that prided itself on being culturally "Little China."[5] Sinophilism was not, however, negation of Korea's sense of national identity. On the contrary, throughout most of the 500 years of Chosŏn, a policy of tightly limited foreign contacts was pursued that fostered an inward-looking and isolationist orientation within Korean society. The painful episodes of Japanese and Manchu invasions, in the 1590s and 1630s respectively, reinforced antiforeignism, often the other and extreme side of nationalistic sentiment. The development of *Hangŭl*, the Korean script, is further evidence of Korean efforts to nurture its own national linguistic and cultural traditions.

The founders of Chosŏn adopted the seclusion policy as a shield to protect its security and independence. Their worst fear materialized in the second half of the nineteenth century in the wake of Korea's opening to the outside world. After establishing ties with Japan in 1876, Korea entered into political and economic relations with Western countries based on Western concepts of international law. China too signed formal trade agreements with Korea, but its objective was to preserve, not to abdicate, its traditional suzerain status in Korea. When the newly Westernizing Japan chose to challenge China, a Sino-Japanese war resulted entailing many battles fought on Korean soil in 1894 and 1895. China's defeat whetted Japan's appetite for Korea and points beyond on the Asian continent; ten years later, the island empire took on Russia and was again victorious. Unrestrained by any more competition, Japan completed its conquest of Korea by forcing the last Chosŏn monarch to sign a treaty of annexation in 1910.

The Sino-Japanese conflict over Korea represented the clash between the old China-centered international order of East Asia and the new Western rules of power politics; the former lost and disintegrated altogether because Japan, encouraged by the Western powers, permitted no compromise. The Russo-Japanese war, in contrast, was a contest between two expansionist powers unable to reach a lasting compromise that, among other matters, would have entailed partitioning Korea into two zones of influence, the north under Russian and the south under Japanese domination. For such a purpose, both the thirty-eighth and the thirty-ninth parallel lines were considered, the former by the Japanese in 1896 and the latter by the Russians in 1903.[6] Korea escaped partition at this time only to face total extinction as an independent nation a short time later (in 1910)—the first time the entire nation had to submit to foreign colonial domination.

The Twentieth Century

For thirty-six years, Japan imposed harsh militarist rule that totally disfranchised and exploited the Koreans. Once again, mistreatment by foreign conquerors induced Koreans to cherish their national identity even more. Fertilized by the Western concept of nationalism and nurtured by the overall process of socioeconomic modernization, a new, more urgent, and more widespread sense of nationhood was created.[7] The colonizers' attempts to assimilate the subjugated people were mostly counterproductive, especially when they were eclipsed by a ubiquitous pattern of discrimination. In short, nationalism and its goal of independence easily became the primary concern among a wide circle of politically conscious Korean individuals and groups. Whether exiled in foreign lands or living in their enslaved homeland, these Koreans carried on anti-Japanese activities in one form or another to keep alive their dream for Korea's independence.[8]

The partition of Korea in 1945 by the victorious Allies split a nation with a long-standing sense and historical experience of unity and homogeneity. Partition was one of those hasty and callous decisions the powerful nations imposed upon powerless peoples in the name of military and other expediencies. Unprepared, uninformed, and unconsulted, Koreans were preoccupied at first with the prospect of immediate independence; the thirty-eighth parallel appeared more like a temporary nuisance than a lasting barrier. Only when the issue of a separate election under UN supervision was raised did the specter of a permanently divided nation assume a fearsome proportion.

To the superpowers, especially on the U.S. list of priorities, Korea was a desirable but dispensable political and military asset. With the advent of the Cold War, however, Korea was turned into a bargaining chip or a test case in the global strategy of confrontation. Korea itself was not as important as were the impact and the perception of a nation's Korea policy in a wider regional and world context. When the U.S.-British-USSR decision in Moscow in 1945 to impose a trusteeship on Korea fizzled out, the only chance for great-power cooperation in Korea was lost. Each side became determined to try out its own solution and paid little attention to the problem of Korea's reunification. In rapid succession, two rival regimes were established in 1948, each under the protective wing of one or the other Cold War protagonist. The stage was set for fratricidal conflict.[9]

Both the initial North Korean offensive in mid-1950 and the UN forces' counteroffensive a few months later encountered unanticipated responses, frustrating expectations for quick reunification. A modified version of the historical pattern of East-West versus North-South alignment pitted North Korea, China, and the Soviet Union against South Korea, the United States, and, indirectly, Japan. The 1953 truce silenced the guns but failed to resolve the political issues arising from the division; four decades later, the nation remains split.

In the intervening years, circumstances within and outside the peninsula have greatly changed. As described in greater detail elsewhere in this book, the inter-Korean balance of power has shifted in favor of the South largely because of its rapid economic development since the late 1960s. In the world beyond Korea, the Cold War has ended with the implosion of the communist bloc in the early 1990s. The interplay between these internal and external factors has produced a peaceful but torturously slow dialogue between the two Koreas that has begun to produce some tangible if uncertain results. History still awaits the conclusion of this unfinished story.

Generalizations from History

What can we generalize and learn from this history of the Korean nation? We shall start with six straightforward and simple observations.

1. *Korea's nationhood has a long historical root dating back to the Unified Silla period that began in the seventh century.* For over 1,300 years, the national framework for Korea's political and social life has survived to induce a sense of national identity in the Korean psyche. The geographical boundaries of Korean states have fluctuated slightly, but the peninsula has remained the homeland. Repeated foreign invasions and the recent experience of alien rule have had the effect of stimulating, not eradicating, the Korean identity. In any comparison of the Korean case with similar examples of divided nations, the deep-rooted nature of Korean nationalism must be borne in mind.

2. *Historically, division is an anomaly or aberration for the Korean nation.* Prior to 1945, it experienced only once the disintegrative process from unity to division: the breakdown of political order in the waning years of Unified Silla. The Later Three Kingdoms period that followed lasted less than half a century and left no lasting legacies injurious to the unity of the nation. Difficult as the historical path has been for over thirteen centuries, Korea has been and is a homogeneous nation ethnically, culturally, linguistically, and psychologically.

3. *External and geopolitical factors have been ever-present and important parts of Korea's external environment.* Time and again, Korea faced invasion from neighboring states, mostly from the north but, intermittently, from the south as well. The agrarian Korean society, ruled most of the time by civilians, tended to be defensive or passive in its external behavior. Either Korea's weakness or one of its neighbor's aggressiveness, or the combination of the two, resulted in such an invasion. On occasion, Korea itself was not the ultimate prize for the invaders; it was instead a passage and an intermediate objective en route to a final target—for example, during the invasions by the Mongols (in the thirteenth century) and the Japanese (in the sixteenth century as well as in more recent times). Korea's vulnerability to these external factors becomes even more striking when we consider that in pre-modern Japan or China, major political changes resulted primarily from internal or domestic factors.

4. *Chronologically, the rise and fall of the Korean states parallel the experience of the Chinese state.* To show it in tabular form:

In Korea	In China
The rise of Unified Silla (668)	The rise of T'ang (618)
The rise of Koryo (936)*	The rise of Liao (947), Sung (960)
The rise of Chosŏn (1392)	The rise of Ming (1368)
The rise of ROK and DPRK (1948)	The rise of PRC (1949)
The fall of Unified Silla (935)*	The fall of T'ang (907)
The fall of Koryo (1392)	The fall of Yuan (1368)
The fall of Chosŏn (1910)	The fall of Ch'ing (1912)
The fall of Japanese rule (1945)	The fall of ROC (1948)

With the possible exception of the events in the midtenth century (marked by asterisks in the table), one can readily find a causal linkage between Korean and Chinese developments. Silla's unification efforts were aided by the emerging T'ang after the latter had overthrown Sui, which had exhausted itself and its adversary, Koguryo, in a series of massive battles. Koryo's fall coincided with the decline of the Mongol Yuan that had overshadowed—and undermined—the Korean dynasty. Japan's conquest of Korea in the twentieth century was preceded by Ch'ing China's forced exit from Korea, one of the last straws that brought down the Chinese dynasty. In the aftermath of the collapse of the Japanese empire, Korea was liberated, and the Nationalist Chinese government entered the last phase of its rule on the mainland. U.S. and Soviet decisions endorsing the creation of their client regimes in a divided Korea were undoubtedly influenced by the two superpowers' assessment of the Chinese civil war. To borrow a Chinese expression, the relationship between Korea and China has been that of "lips and teeth"—of interdependence.

5. *The Sino-Korean interrelationship, however, has not been one of equals; China has seized the initiative and projected its influence on Korea.* From the days of Wiman (a semilegendary Chinese refugee who founded a dynasty called Wiman Chosŏn in A.D. 194) and the Han dynasty (206 B.C.–A.D. 220), Korea was at times an extension of Chinese politics. On innumerable occasions during the early vigorous years of such Chinese and quasi-Chinese dynasties (non-Chinese nomadic peoples who established their rule in northern China) as Han, T'ang, Liao (Khitan), Chin (Jurchen), Yuan (Mongol), and Ch'ing (Manchu), military expeditions were sent to Korea, often even before completion of their occupation of China proper.

6. *Military conquest has been the only means of achieving unification in Korea.* Silla defeated Paekche and Koguryo on the battlefield; the last act in Koryo's reunification drama was its military victory over Later Paekche. This is not at all surprising because everywhere in the premodern period, military means was the ultima ratio in statecraft. It should be noted, however, that the unifiers quickly moved to accommodate and incorporate the people and even the sociopolitical systems of the defeated foes. Unified Silla admitted the people in the newly acquired regions into its nobility and its military organizations. Koryo likewise was generous in its treatment of the former Silla ruling class and waited a judiciously long time before revamping the governmental system.[10]

The Lessons of History

What lessons can be drawn from these historical cases? The following suggestions and caveats are deduced from or related to the preceding generalizations.

1. The long historical root of Korea's nationhood supports the expectation that Korea will be reunited sooner or later. This is an issue that touches the hearts of Koreans due to their sense of national identity. Although there are sharp political cleavages between the two Korean halves that are not easily bridged, in historical perspective, an eventual return to normality seems assured. A review of the last two decades and especially the years 1991–1992

shows how much inter-Korean relations have changed toward mutual accommodation.

2. The period of division and confrontation does not end without leaving some damaging aftereffects on homogeneity among the people. In the seventh and tenth centuries, the Unified Silla and the Koryo rulers strove to accommodate and assimilate the peoples in newly won regions—with some success. Wounds from intranational conflicts, as opposed to international wars, are often more difficult to heal. The fratricidal conflict in the 1950s left bitter memories. Efforts to mend the psychic wound and minimize its hurtful impact on their sense of homogeneity deserve the full attention of the Korean people.

Koreans should feel gratified that they still share today a common cultural heritage after almost fifty years of political division. The current generation of Koreans would surely be amiss if they failed to preserve this common heritage and caused irreparable damage to the shared sense of national identity. After all, their ancestors were able to safeguard their national culture and identity through centuries of foreign wars and domestic turmoil.

A potentially serious problem affecting homogeneity involves localism or provincialism that uses place (province) of origin as a point of reference in ordering one's interpersonal relations. The invidious distinction between the people from the southwest (Cholla province) and those from the southeast (Kyongsang province) has recently attracted attention in South Korean politics. In a future united Korea, a similar chasm may develop between the people of the north (*ipuk*) and the south (*inam*). To become aware of and ready to contain such a cleavage is a matter of crucial importance for the leaders of Korea even as the process of unification gets under way.

3. The role of external and geopolitical factors in Korea's political fortune is as undeniable today as it was in the past. Obviously, some of these factors, such as geographical location and topography, are relatively immutable. Nevertheless, technology can alter the nature and intensity of impacts of geopolitical factors, as evidenced in the case of transportation technology that has shrunk the world in terms of travel time. The United States is a neighbor of Korea in all but a narrow technical sense. As we update our perception of these factors, Korean issues must be considered not only in inter-Korean and bilateral terms but also in regional, multilateral, and global contexts.

A related suggestion concerns the question of neutrality of a united Korea.[11] Nonalignment is an attractive and seemingly logical formula inasmuch as it removes Korea from an international political arena of competition, alliance, and counteralliance.

4. The causal linkage between the dynastic cycles in Korea and those in China in the past underscores Korea's need today and in the future to be aware of China's role in and concerns about Korea's political future. Not only does China possess huge economic and military potentials, but it also has displayed time and again a high degree of sensitivity about its security interests in the Korean peninsula and particularly along the Sino-Korean border. Mao Zedong's decision to intervene in the Korean War is only a recent example. Indeed, throughout Korean history until the late nineteenth century, China was

the most important source of outside influence in both quantitative and qualitative terms. That China played practically no role in Korea during the first half of the twentieth century was due to Japan's domination over Korea and China's own internal difficulties—conditions that were transitory and unique. In the coming decades, as China undergoes economic and perhaps political reforms, it is likely to carry much greater weight in regional affairs; Korea, divided or united, will need to take the China factor even more seriously than it has in the recent past.

5. As for the other neighbors of Korea, the interests of the United States and Japan in Korea during the past century have been largely compatible except, of course, during World War II. Once Japan opened Korea in 1876—only five years after a U.S. expeditionary force had failed in its forcible attempt to do so—the United States became the first Western nation to conclude a treaty with Korea (1882). Despairing of Korea's ability to reform on its own, the U.S. government chose to accept at face value Japan's professed interest in Korea's modernization—even at the cost of Korean independence. Only when Japan threatened U.S. interests in East Asia, more specifically in China, did the United States go to war. Liberation of Korea was a by-product of the dismemberment of the Japanese empire.

In the postwar period, Japan was a willing and useful collaborator for U.S. policies in Korea and profited handsomely in the process. The United States and Japan are today the principal backers of South Korea, but their roles within the trilateral coalition—and indeed, in what used to be the two opposing alliances surrounding Korea—are undergoing basic changes. In the long run, Japan is likely to be a more important factor in Korea than it has been since 1945, whereas the U.S. role will slowly decrease.

For the last of the four neighbors of Korea, Russia, history offers little clue except that it has been largely unsuccessful in its dealings with Korea. Czarist Russia made a half-hearted attempt to establish a foothold in nineteenth-century Korea, but Japan rebuffed the move. The Bolshevik revolution (1917) and its aftermath temporarily removed Russia as a factor in Korean life except for its mesmerizing ideology. As one of the architects of the postwar plans for Korea, the Soviet Union was initially successful in blocking U.S. and UN policies and setting up a client state. For the last three decades or more, however, the Russian presence has gradually receded. Physically joined to Korea by a short land border, Russia, with all its military and economic potential, remains a significant actor in the Korean play. But its shadow over Korea will remain relatively small for some time to come.

Most important of all, perhaps, is the growing weight of Korea's own role in resolving its problems. The two Koreas, especially the South, have made remarkable gains in developing their power capabilities. They have ceased being mere objects of big-power manipulations. Their international behavior has reflected a growing sense of independence. The complexity and fluidity of the emerging political configuration surrounding the two Koreas require vigilance, flexibility, and wisdom on the part of Koreans in both halves of the peninsula.

6. The division of Korea in 1945 was imposed externally, not from within as were the precedents in the seventh and ninth centuries. In the first of these early cases, the three kingdoms were the results of a confederal union of smaller clans and tribes, while the Later Three Kingdoms arose out of spontaneous local uprisings within the decaying Unified Silla kingdom. Application of force and absorption of the defeated rival produced unity in these instances. A similar military formula was tried in 1950 and failed. For decades thereafter to this very day, the protagonists have been continually engaged in massive preparations for another conflict. History is no guide in predicting if and how these forces will be used to bring about reunification.

However, everyone in responsible positions in and outside Korea has publicly favored a peaceful process. A survey of the contemporary world scene presents a conflicting picture—the end of the Cold War but a large number of small local conflicts. The recent progress in North-South dialogue, especially the agreements signed in 1991 and put into effect in 1992 (see Appendixes B and C), encourages the hopeful expectation that reconciliation is more than propaganda or an empty promise.

What should be clearly stated here is that the process of reintegration of the two societies after some form of political union is achieved must be fair and equitable to all in order for the new union to survive. The leaders of Unified Silla and Koryo showed foresight as well as practical wisdom in accommodating and assimilating former adversaries. The longevity of these unifier regimes, 267 and 475 years respectively, resulted in no small measure from the lenient and conciliatory policies they adopted toward erstwhile foes. The time is not too soon to start planning similar policies for reunited Korea.

Notes

1. Silla's role as the first unifier of the Korean nation is recognized in Yi Ki-baek, *Han'guksa sillon* (A new history of Korea) (Seoul: Ilchokak, 1967), p. 90; and Han U-gǔn, *Hangil t'ongsa* (The history of Korea) (Seoul: Ullyu Munhwa Sa, 1969), p. 90. Historical writings in North Korea, however, mention "merger" (*t'onghap*) of the southern region by Silla and reserve "unification" (*t'ongil*) to describe Koryo's exploits in the tenth century. See, for example, Sin Hyon-sik, "T'ongil Silla e taehan *Chosǒn chǒnsa* ǔi sǒsul kwa kǔ pip'an" (Description and critique of *Chosǒn chǒnsa* account of Unified Silla), in Kim Chong-bae, ed., *Pukhan i ponǔn uri yǒksa* (Our history as viewed in North Korea) (Seoul: Ullyu Munhwa Sa, 1989), pp. 93–94.

2. Carter J. Eckert, Ki-baik Lee, Young Ick Lew, Michael Robinson, and Edward W. Wagner, *Korea Old and New: A History* (Seoul: Ilchokak Publishers, 1990), p. 31.

3. The postunification "national" army of Silla—nine "oathbannermen" divisions and ten garrison units—was recruited "not only from the native Silla population but also from the former inhabitants of Koguryo and Paekche, and from Malgal tribesmen as well." At the same time, aristocratic families from the conquered states were accorded Silla's own nobility ("bone-rank") statuses and resettled in "secondary capitals." See ibid., p. 48.

4. It makes little sense, therefore, to accuse Silla of having collaborated with a foreign (T'ang) power against another "Korean" state. Current North Korean historiography charges Silla with "flunkeyism" (*sadae chuǔi*); see Historical Research Institute, Acad-

emy of Social Sciences, *Chosŏn t'ongsa* (Survey history of Korea), Vol. 1, No. 1 of North Korean Academic Works Series (Seoul: Owŏl, 1988), pp. 136–.

5. Chu Hsi's teaching, often referred to as neo-Confucianism, flourished in Korea as official orthodoxy; one of its most ardent disciples, Song Si-yŏl (1607–1689), was known for his open admiration of Chinese culture. At the time of the fall of Ming China, he considered Korea to be the only bastion of Confucianism, a "Little China." See Kajimura Hideki, *Chosenshi no wakugumi to shiso* (The framework and thought in Korean history) (Tokyo: Kenbun Shuppan, 1982), pp. 24–28, 32.

6. Yi Sŏn-gŭn, *Han'guksa: Hyŏndae P'yon* (The history of Korea: Modern period) (Seoul: Ullyu Munhwasa, 1963), pp. 761–777. Also see William L. Langer, *The Diplomacy of Imperialism, 1890–1902*, Vol. 1 (New York: Alfred A. Knopf, 1935), p. 406; C. I. Eugene Kim and Han-Kyo Kim, *Korea and the Politics of Imperialism, 1876–1910* (Berkeley: University of California Press, 1968), pp. 101–102.

7. An extended discourse on "cultural nationalism" appears in Michael Edson Robinson, *Cultural Nationalism in Colonial Korea, 1920–1925* (Seattle: University of Washington Press, 1988).

8. Chong-Sik Lee, *The Politics of Korean Nationalism* (Berkeley: University of California Press, 1963). Although dated, this remains the most comprehensive one-volume survey available in English that deals with the complex array of events, personalities, and organizations.

9. For three informative monographs dealing with such controversial topics as the decision for partition, U.S. policy in Korea, and the events leading to the outbreak of the Korean War, see Bruce Cumings, *The Origins of the Korean War*, 2 vols. (Princeton, NJ: Princeton University Press, 1981 and 1990); James Irving Matray, *The Reluctant Crusade: American Foreign Policy in Korea, 1941–1950* (Honolulu: University of Hawaii Press, 1985); Michael C. Sandusky, *America's Parallel* (Alexandria, VA: Old Dominion Press, 1983).

10. The founder of Koryo "took to wife a woman from the Silla royal house, and … treated the Silla nobility with extreme generosity. Because of this, many individuals of Silla lineage entered into the Koryo bureaucracy, thus initiating the tradition of elite continuity that would characterize Korean political culture down into the twentieth century." See Eckert et al., *Korea Old and New*, p. 63. It was Koryo's fourth king, Kwangjong (949–975), who began serious restructuring of the government and bureaucracy; ibid., p. 64.

11. For a forceful exposition of the neutrality issue, see In K. Hwang, *One Korea via Permanent Neutrality: Peaceful Management of Korean Unification* (Cambridge, MA: Schenkman Books, 1987).

3

The Two Koreas and World Order

Samuel S. Kim

The Korean Problematique

In 1991 and 1992, Korea was back in the news and on the agenda of a "new world order." This is hardly surprising because the torments of divided polity have been closely keyed to the situational and structural changes in global high politics overlaid by Cold War bipolarity over the years. History and geography have condemned Korea to be a stepchild of great-power conflict. The opening of Korea during the heyday of international social Darwinism and imperialistic power play in the late nineteenth century instantly transformed the "hermit kingdom" into a vortex of great-power rivalries. Five external powers—China, Japan, Russia, Great Britain, and the United States—all pushed their way into this Confucian tributary state long protected by the Sinocentric world order. A century later, the Korean peninsula is still considered the strategic intersection where four of the world's five centers of power—the United States, Russia, China, and Japan—uneasily meet and interact. Korea is said to be "the fuse on the nuclear powderkeg in the Pacific."[1]

Although the thirty-eighth parallel was initially imposed as part of a U.S. ad hoc zonal plan—agreed to by the Soviet Union—for dividing up Japanese troop surrender arrangements in August 1945, its hardening was a direct consequence of intensified superpower conflict in the Cold War. Would not the end of the Cold War and superpower conflict enable both Koreas to liberate themselves from the shackles of the two competing Cold War systems for national reunion? Yet the Korean situation is far more complicated than this conventional wisdom would suggest. The life cycle of divided Korea is now almost a half century old, exceeding the entire tenure of the thirty-five-year Japanese colonial rule by more than a decade. In the process, one nation has

29

been dissolved into two states with two systems, spawning two incomplete nation-states. Such divided polities are prone to an extreme and often violent version of the politics of national identity to maximize their exclusive security and legitimacy. The dynamics of state formation and conflict formation developed in tandem over the Cold War years. Four decades after the Korean War ended, the so-called demilitarized zone (DMZ) is perhaps the most militarized conflict zone in the post–Cold War world; more than 1.8 million military personnel confront each other there, armed to the teeth with the latest weapons systems.

And yet the momentous but unexpected peaceful changes in the international system in the late 1980s and early 1990s—events unprecedented in the history of international relations—have overturned much of mainstream international relations theories.[2] In addition, the perceived wisdom about the traditional Korean security predicament—of Korea being so weak in the region of the strong, as captured in the old Korean saying "A shrimp gets crushed to death in the fight between whales"—is not as reliable a guide as of yore in explaining some epochal inter-Korean developments that occurred in the early 1990s (e.g., the entry of the two Koreas into the United Nations; the historic North-South agreement on reconciliation, nonaggression, and exchanges and cooperation [see Appendix B]; the joint declaration for a nuclear-free Korean peninsula [Appendix C]; the cancellation of the 1992 Team Spirit U.S.–South Korea military exercise; and North Korea's signing of the nuclear safeguards accord with the International Atomic Energy Agency [IAEA]). Apparently, there are several ironies and role reversals emanating from the intensified vertical and horizontal interaction of forces at the societal, state, regional, and global levels.

Although the destructive pattern of superpower bipolarity and rivalry has passed away with the collapse of communism in Eastern Europe and the Soviet Union and the demise of the socialist superpower, the shape and content of an emerging world order remain indeterminate. The post–Cold War world seems increasingly like a turbulent multicentric one faltering at a crossroads where contradictory forces—globalism, regionalism, bilateralism, and unilateralism—are vying for supremacy. The rapidly changing global situation lends itself to diverse prognostications about the shape of international life to come. At a time of such acceleration of world history, not "the end of history" as Francis Fukuyama would have us believe,[3] it is easy to succumb to the fallacy of premature optimism or pessimism on the changing relationship between the future of the two Koreas and the future of the world order.

The Korean situation in the post–Cold War context can be assessed from two levels of generalization. At the situational level, not only has the Cold War come to an end in global high politics, but both Koreas seem to be undergoing an important dynamic of societal and economic change prodding their respective governments to be more receptive to peacemaking and peacekeeping approaches in the ongoing inter-Korean dialogue. As well, wider regional developments in East Asia seem far less constraining than at any time in the long Cold War period of seeking more space and pathways of securing peace and stability in the Korean peninsula. With the end of the Cold War and the emergence of a more cooperative East-West relationship, new possibilities and opportunities have arisen in the local, regional, and global political space. At a deeper level, however, the structures of militarization remain securely embedded in the topography of East Asian international politics.

The purpose of this chapter is both analytic and prescriptive: to develop a broader understanding of the Korean question by exploring the complexities of its relationship with a changing world order and the range of situational and structural factors at the global, regional, and local levels that relate to the prospects for securing a long peace in the Korean peninsula; and to suggest alternative ways of enhancing common security for the Korean people. For this line of empirical and normative inquiry, the approach applied is drawn from the model of a "just world order." This particular approach, which developed analytical techniques and normative orientations over the twenty-five years of transnational collaborative research under the rubric of the World Order Models Project (WOMP), suggests a basis for nonviolent system transformation that encompasses the world-order values of peace, economic equity and well-being, social justice and human rights, ecological integrity, and humane governance and participatory democracy.[4] As a transnational and transdisciplinary enterprise, this world-order approach offers an alternative road map, a broad focus, and a comparative frame of analysis for rethinking the Korean problem. Given the contending images of preferred futures and the uneven realization of world-order values throughout the world, however, the challenge here presupposes the absence of a single, universally valid master key to the resolution of the Korean conflict. In the spirit of "thinking globally but acting locally," this world-order approach envisions a series of adaptable strategies keyed to existing local circumstances and opportunities to be treated as building blocks for the synergistic linkage process among global, regional, and national circumstances as they pertain to complex Korean realities.

The importance of the two Koreas as a world-order challenge is that both states have distinctive as well as general characteristics that will further extend the comparative basis for understanding how diverse societies cope with the common problems of nation building and development processes in an ever more complex and interdependent world.

The Two Koreas in a Changing World Order

The invocation of "a new world order" by President George Bush in 1990 and 1991 at a time of rapid global change seemed to catalyze a global debate on the subject. For all its conceptual and normative elusiveness and diverse responses from many places, the call for a new world order, already a household term in the United States, was perhaps the most official acknowledgment that the structural simplicity and rigidity of superpower bipolarity had given way to a new sense of global system transition. Indeed, it may be accepted as the coming of the Grotian moment to enact a new global politics. With the end of the Cold War in 1989 and 1990, the United Nations had, for the first time in a half century, the historical opportunity to initiate a truly multilateral approach to the creation of a new, just, and peaceful world order. In short, the United Nations suddenly became an arena and an actor in world-order transition politics. The Security Council found itself expanding and deepening its conflict-coping roles and resources in relation to a series of sanguinary state-making conflicts in trouble spots around the world from Central America to the Balkans through Africa and the Middle East to Southeast Asia. In the process, the nature and scope of UN peacekeeping expanded considerably to encompass a variety of new roles and functions—such as the disarmament of insurgents (Nicaragua and Cambodia), the provision of humanitarian and welfare assistance (Cyprus, southern Lebanon, and the Kurdish region of Iraq), and even the monitoring and supervision of elections (Namibia, Haiti, Cambodia, and Western Sahara)—even as the organization at the same time was experiencing the widening "Lippman Gap" between commitments and capabilities (cash). At any rate, the United Nations as the world organization provides a testing ground in the 1990s for exploring the nexus between the politics of the two Koreas and the new politics of world order in the normative domain of global politics.

Against this backdrop, North Korea and South Korea finally entered the United Nations as two separate but equal member states on September 17, 1991.[5] In fact, the remarkable event took place in the Security Council a month earlier. Indeed, the 3,001st meeting of the Security Council on August 8, 1991, may well be remembered as one of the most remarkable nonevents in the annals of UN politics. Since 1947, the Korean question, in various contentious manifestations, has proved to be one of the most divisive, enduring, and intractable problems constantly intruding upon wider East-West geopolitical and ideological rivalries in and out of the world organization. Yet the Security Council that August day spent only five minutes in finally crossing the Rubicon on the Korean membership issue. Without any debate, the council unanimously adopted the report of the Committee on the Admission of New Members concerning the application of the Democratic People's Republic of Korea (DPRK) and the application of the Republic of Korea (ROK) for admission to membership in the United Nations.

Equally revealing is the manner in which the Security Council took action. The two separate membership applications were merged into a single draft resolution, and the council decision (and recommendation to the General Assembly) was adopted without a vote as Resolution 702 (1991).[6] Likewise, the General Assembly decided without a vote to admit the DPRK and the ROK as the 160th and 161st member states in the form of a single resolution (General Assembly Resolution 46/1).

Clearly, there was far more than met the public eye in the Security Council action. This historical event was a direct consequence of the sweeping changes beginning in the late 1980s in the global political situation. The brevity of the action merely underscored the behind-the-scenes negotiations and understanding among the five permanent members (Perm Five) of the council to accept the two separate membership applications as a package deal—and without a vote—so as to minimize the intrusion of zero-sum inter-Korean politics in the council. The tactic seemed deliberately designed to soothe Pyongyang's bruised national ego by projecting the council action as the triumph of the principle of universality and, as such, as the triumph of both Koreas in their global quest for international legitimation. That an understanding on such a delicate collective diplomatic surgery of separating the Korean Siamese twins was possible in 1991 was another testimonial to the expanding virtuous circle of cooperation the United States and the former Soviet Union were creating in the United Nations. This cooperation on the Korean UN membership question took place before Russia slipped into the Security Council and replaced the USSR's permanent seat on December 24, 1991, with tacit encouragement from the United States and other members of the Perm Five.

Of course, UN membership is only part of the larger inter-Korean conflict. To really put an end to the Cold War legacy in the Korean peninsula requires more than the symbolism of the two Koreas' presence in the world organization. Still, the parallel membership suggests that the two Koreas have become moving targets on slippery trajectories subject to multiple pressures, both domestic and external. Over the years, Seoul and Pyongyang have taken turns playing Dr. Jekyll and Mr. Hyde in the now-on and now-off competitive international game, constantly changing the rules of entry and play. Since 1947, the Korean quest for legitimation has been closely keyed to the jagged development of the UN politics of collective legitimation and delegitimation. After all, the real "power" of the United Nations lies not in military and economic resources (which the world body is congenitally ill-endowed to mobilize anyway except as an expression of superpower hegemony) but in "legitimacy power." Legitimacy facilitates the exercise of UN authority; it is the oil that lubricates global normative politics—this is what the so-called UN politics of collective legitimation and delegitimation is all about. As well, legitimacy is the outer limit that nonstate actors outside the UN can aspire to reach.

In tracing the long tortuous journey to Korean UN membership, one is struck by some paradoxical twists and turns—and remarkable role reversals. In the 1950s and 1960s, it was Seoul, not Pyongyang, that was advancing claims for absolute legitimation. Pyongyang made no claim in 1949, 1952, and 1957 when it applied for UN membership that the DPRK was the only legitimate government representing the whole Korean peninsula. Pyongyang's primary focus was largely on shoring up the domestic base of legitimation, whereas Seoul pursued absolute legitimation via its repeated attempts to gain UN membership. The situation began to change dramatically in the first half of the 1970s with a role reversal: It was Pyongyang's turn to launch a global diplomatic offensive in search of absolute legitimation; Seoul retreated into a more realistic claim for relative legitimation (i.e., separate but equal UN membership).

The perennial debate on the Korean question came to a strange and inconclusive closure in 1975 when the General Assembly adopted two contradictory resolutions on the same day, one pro-ROK (Resolution 3390A) and the other pro-DPRK (Resolution 3390B). Ignoring the pro-ROK resolution, the DPRK pronounced the other one "an epochal event" and "a great turning point" in the history of UN politics. In retrospect, however, the 1975 UN debate and pro-DPRK resolution proved to be a Pyrrhic victory in Pyongyang's search for absolute legitimation. The 1975 UN debate merely forced the world organization to dramatize and legitimize the reality of the two separate states in the Korean peninsula. It is hardly surprising, then, that Pyongyang rather abruptly dropped its UN card in the wake of this "epochal event" and brought no more pressure to bear on its allies to open the issue.

By September 1988 when the DPRK and the ROK both turned forty, the symbolic and diplomatic contrast between the two was rather striking. While Kim Il Sung in the North was seeking international legitimation of hereditary socialism with the succession crisis still unresolved, Roh Tae Woo in the South seemed busy polishing up his image as the first freely elected president in almost twenty years. In the race for diplomatic recognition, Seoul surged ahead from an almost dead-even position in the mid-1970s, enjoying an advantage of 128 countries having official diplomatic relations with the ROK over 99 countries with the DPRK as of August 1988 (and an advantage of 153 over 112 as of the end of 1991).[7] At the same time, the number of countries recognizing both Seoul and Pyongyang increased from 49 in mid-1976 to 66 in mid-1988 to 90 in mid-1991. In the international organization membership race—both international intergovernmental organizations (IGOs) and international nongovernmental organizations (INGOs)—Seoul had a 2:1 advantage in IGO membership (41 for the ROK as against 20 for the DPRK) and an almost 6:1 advantage in INGO membership (820 for the ROK and 141 for the DPRK) as of the end of 1989.[8]

Greatly buoyed by a series of triumphs in its Nordpolitik, Seoul in November 1989 submitted documents to UN member states explaining its post-1973 position on the Korean UN membership question: that both Koreas should be allowed to enter the world organization as two separate but equal member states. Thus, the issue of Korean membership that had remained dormant for almost three decades was reopened in a low-key way only to provoke Pyongyang's vehement opposition.

The rapid Moscow-Seoul rapprochement in the wake of the Seoul Olympic Games led to full diplomatic relations in September 1990 and was a major diplomatic breakthrough in Seoul's bid for UN membership. Like post-Mao China, Gorbachev's Soviet Union—a state that in the late 1970s had arrived at strategic parity and seemed on the verge of claiming primacy in the superpower rivalry then pervading the globe—had become newly aware of the economic burden of its "imperial overstretch" as well as of technological backwardness and economic stagnation and suddenly retreated from an aid-donor to a supplicant role. The Soviet Union made it clear at the third Gorbachev-Roh summit meeting on Cheju Island in April 1991 that it would no longer help Pyongyang's quest for absolute legitimation by vetoing Seoul's application for UN membership. (Indeed, in the Gorbachev years, the veto completely vanished from Soviet voting behavior in the Security Council.)

In late 1990, Seoul was further encouraged by the mounting support expressed by many speakers in the 1990 General Assembly session. Of the 162 heads of state and other delegation leaders who spoke, for instance, a record

71 (up from 49 in 1989) backed Seoul's basic line—simultaneous but separate membership for both Koreas. In the end, however, Seoul decided to let the December 18 deadline pass without submitting its formal membership application, partly because of the preoccupation of the Security Council with the Gulf crisis and partly to give a little more time for its behind-the-scenes diplomacy to overcome or neutralize a possible Chinese veto. On March 8, 1991, South Korea finally made a decisive shift from secret to open diplomacy when Foreign Minister Lee Sang-Ock publicly announced that Seoul would apply for UN membership in 1991, irrespective of North Korea's opposition. This was followed by the announcement that Seoul would send its current and former prime and foreign ministers to join top diplomats abroad on a tour of thirty-six nations to drum up support for simultaneous entry of the two Koreas into the UN if possible and Seoul's unilateral entry if necessary.

After failing to obtain Beijing's explicit support, Seoul decided in March 1991 to go for broke, banking on the notion that China would not dare risk its international reputation and economic interests by casting a solo veto. This diplomatic gamble paid off. Rather, the issue became moot with Pyongyang's dramatic reversal of its long-standing party line announced May 27, 1991, and its jump start on a separate UN membership application. Still, the China factor was certainly one of the major determinants in the reversal of Pyongyang's principled opposition to simultaneous entry. As late as November 1989 the Chinese Foreign Ministry publicly reaffirmed its support of the Pyongyang line by opposing simultaneous entry. In 1990 Beijing followed an indeterminate line—that the international community should encourage both Koreas to settle this issue properly through consultation.

Prime Minister Li Peng's state visit to Pyongyang May 3–6, 1991, confirmed what had been widely suspected in diplomatic circles: that China would not permit Pyongyang to dictate its voting behavior in the Security Council. There are several reasons China would find it difficult to cast a veto, especially a solo veto, in the service of Pyongyang's stand. First, despite its "principled opposition" to a wide range of issues in the Security Council, China has consistently expressed its opposition in the form of "nonparticipation in the vote." In almost two decades of participation in the Security Council (1971–1991), China cast only two vetoes—one on the Bangladesh membership issue and one on the Middle East question in 1972. Given its long-standing assault on the veto as an expression of hegemonic behavior, China would refuse to be cornered into a situation of having no choice but to cast its veto. Second, despite its ritualistic lip service to Korean reunification, the central challenge of post-Mao foreign policy has been how to make the external environment safe and peaceful for China's modernization drive. Like the United States, Japan, and Russia, China is more interested in maintaining peace and stability in the Korean peninsula than in bringing about Korean reunification.

Third and perhaps most important, Beijing cannot help but notice that there have been only two ways of reunifying divided nations in the postwar era: by war (the Vietnam model) and by peaceful evolution and absorption (the German model). Each of the two reunifying models is unattractive, even threatening, to post-Tiananmen China with its own acute identity-legitimacy crisis. In the wake of German unification on October 3, 1990 (which in fact as well as in law was the *accession* of East Germany to the Federal Republic of Germany), the Chinese leadership began to wake up to the worst possible scenario for Korean reunification: South Korea swallowing up North Korea. After numerous secret contacts, visits, and talks, Beijing reportedly finally persuaded Kim Il Sung to shift to a "two countries, two systems" strategy and join the United Nations by piggybacking on Seoul's membership application. Faced with the collapse of socialism in Europe and the danger of collapse of socialism in East Asia, Beijing quietly adopted in 1991 a new strategy of establishing a Beijing-Pyongyang-Hanoi socialist united front so as to extinguish the spark of the Western "peaceful evolution" co-optation strategy. The stepping up of Sino–North Korean military cooperation is said to be the price Beijing had to pay for Pyongyang's shift from its absolute legitimation-via-reunification strategy to this Stalinist "socialism in one country" strategy.[9] Such was Beijing's definition of the international situation throughout 1991 when the question of Korean UN membership was injected into the UN politics of collective legitimation and delegitimation. (And yet, with the virtual demise of Western sanctions and the collapse of the Soviet Union by the end of 1991, Chinese foreign policy seemed to be turning its back on Pyongyang, as the official state visits in the latter half of 1992 by the South Korean president, the Japanese emperor, and the Russian president were widely publicized as crowning achievements of post-Tiananmen diplomacy.)

By mid-May 1991 Pyongyang was so trapped in the ever-tightening encirclement imposed by Seoul's Nordpolitik that there were only two escape options: to have a showdown and face certain defeat, possibly missing the last chance to join the world organization, or to jump the gun on Korean UN membership. The May 27, 1991, statement of the DPRK Foreign Ministry, submitted to the Security Council in a bitter tone, acknowledged Pyongyang's entrapment.

> Taking advantage of the rapid changes in the international situation, the south Korean authorities are committing the never-to-be condoned treason to divide Korea into two parts ... by trying to force their way into the United Nations. ... As the south Korean authorities insist on their unilateral United Nations membership, if we leave this alone, important issues related to the interests of the entire Korean nation would be dealt with in a biased manner on the United Nations rostrum and this would entail grave consequences. We can never let it go that way. The Government of the Democratic People's Republic of Korea has *no alternative but to enter the United Nations at the present stage as a step to tide over such temporary difficulties created by the south Korean authorities.*[10]

Pyongyang's principled stand was self-defeating as far as UN membership was concerned. Faced with a clear and continuing challenge from the South, the best Pyongyang could do in late 1990 was to reformulate Kim Il Sung's 1980 formula for "a Democratic Confederal Republic of Koryo" as a transitional step to reunification: to wit, the two parts of Korea should apply for joint UN membership with each side taking turns sharing one revolving seat on a yearly basis. "If the north and the south are sincere in their negotiation, with good will for reunification, the legal substance of joint UN membership could easily be arranged and the Security Council and the General Assembly of the United Nations will support whatever both the north and the south agree, as shown in the settlement of the Cambodian seat."[11]

Yet Pyongyang's proposal for joint UN membership of the two Koreas as a confederation of states was a legal oxymoron. Despite the "We the *Peoples* of the United *Nations*" opening line in the preamble of the charter, the United Nations, in law and in practice, has remained a state-centric organization giving little space for the representation of nations and peoples. Otherwise, there would be some 800 member *nations* rather than the present 183 member *states* (as of May 28, 1993). UN membership, as stipulated in article 4 of the charter, is open to states, not nations. As a primary juridical person and subject in international law, a state, by evincing several characteristics it shares in common with other states, such as territory, population, government, and independence of action (as stipulated in article 1 of the 1933 Montevideo Convention on the Rights and Duties of States), fulfills the basic requirements for entrance into the international community. A confederation of states, as implied in the DPRK proposal for joint UN membership, is a rather loose association of independent sovereign states based on an international treaty and has nothing to do with the question of state making (state succession) or state membership in international organization. It is little wonder, then, that there are no precedents for admitting a confederation of states as one single member state into any IGO, including the United Nations.

The significance of this historic event for the future of the world organization as well as for the future of the two Koreas cannot be denied. In the UN setting, at least, the end of superpower conflict disposed of the Korean question as a last festering Cold War problem. At long last the four major membership problems relating to the divided polities of China (1971), Germany (1973, 1990), Vietnam (1977), and Korea (1991) that plagued the world organization over the Cold War years were cleared off the deck. As a result, the United Nations became better poised to shift its institutional identity from being an arena of Cold War politics to being an actor of world-order politics. The UN Security Council summit declaration on "New Risks for Stability and Security" issued January 31, 1992, despite all the hidden structural problems that the declaration conveniently papers over, was a first major normative step in the redefinition of the organization's role as an agent of the new world order: "The ending of the cold war has raised hopes for a safer, more equitable and more humane world. ... The non-military sources of instability in the economic, social, humanitarian and ecological fields have become threats to peace and security. The United Nations membership as a whole needs to give the highest priority to the solution of these matters."[12]

Although it is still premature to adumbrate the future shape of Korea's international life, several possible consequences can be suggested. First, developments indicate that perhaps in the short run peaceful coexistence of the two Korean states has prevailed over national union. The means was a Grand Bargain of a two-plus-four—or perhaps more accurately, a two-plus-two (the former Soviet Union and China)—game on the UN's diplomatic chessboard. The irony is that Pyongyang emerged as the greatest beneficiary of the Grand Bargain because UN membership provided a face-saving exit from the entrapment of absolute legitimation. It became Pyongyang's turn of misfortune to feel threatened by the Second Image Reversed effect of its own magnificent obsession with national unity. In the 1990s, it is in Pyongyang's survival interests to accept the UN legitimation of the two Koreas as the only diplomatic way to prevent the German reunification model from being actualized in the Korean peninsula. The German model—as well as the Chinese reunification drive—resembles a Taoist paradox and lesson: Talking less and less is really achieving more and more. To hold together different parts of a whole, one must let them go their separate ways.

The combined weight of UN membership and the German model seemed to give rise to a new realism in Pyongyang. "If the stark realities existing in north and south are disregarded and reunification through unification of the systems is advocated," Prime Minister Yon Hyong-muk of the DPRK said in Pyongyang's first "state of the world" address on October 9, 1991, "it will inevitably increase mistrust and confrontation, not reunification, and will lead, furthermore, to the recurrence of the national scourge of conflict and fratricidal war."[13] Kim Il Sung's growing apprehension about the German model—unification by absorption—was made even more explicit in Yon's keynote speech at the fourth North-South high-level talks.[14] North Korea's de facto acceptance in 1991 of the two Korean states under the formula of "one nation, one state, two systems, two governments" was a significant departure from its past unification-first stand.[15] Almost overnight, Pyongyang was compelled to shift its national identity and role from a revisionist to a status-quo power. By accepting and legitimizing the two Koreas as two separate but equal member states, the world organization expanded the possibilities that the North and South could accommodate each other in and out of the world organization. The North-South agreement on reconciliation, nonaggression, and exchanges and cooperation (Appendix B) stood out as an unprecedented compromise package deal combining Seoul's peacemaking approach (exchanges and cooperation) and Pyongyang's peacekeeping approach (nonaggression). Such a breakthrough would not have been possible without a prior mutual acceptance of legitimacy of the two Korean states that UN membership captured and institutionalized. For the moment, Korean peace won over national union. Despite the primordial passions for national union, as made evident in so many state-making internal wars under way today, there is nothing intrinsically empowering about it when so many others seem to prosper without it. National union per se does not automatically bring about power, prosperity, and democracy.

Second, the UN provides a convenient and legitimate venue for cross-bloc diplomatic contacts and negotiations in gradually reducing lingering Cold War contradictions on the Korean peninsula. It was at UN headquarters in New York that Soviet Foreign Minister Eduard Shevardnadze and South Korean Foreign Minister Choi Ho-Joong on September 30, 1990, issued a joint communiqué for the establishment of full diplomatic relations. The UN again was the site when China's Foreign Minister Qian Qichen and South Korea's Foreign Minister Lee Sang-Ock met officially for the first time in late 1991 with the former praising the latter's efforts in resolving the China membership issue in the Asia-Pacific Economic Cooperation (APEC) and the latter commending the former's efforts on the Korean UN membership issue. Thanks to Pyongyang's entry into the world organization, the United States and the DPRK held their high-level talks in New York in late 1991 for the first time since the end of the Korean War. Between June 2 and June 11, 1993, the United States and the DPRK held a series of high-level negotiations in New York on the Korean nuclear crisis catalyzed by Pyongyang's announcement that it would withdraw from the nuclear nonproliferation treaty (NPT). As a result, the clock was stopped as the unusual joint U.S.-DPRK joint statement said that Pyongyang would "suspend as long as it considers necessary" its March 12, 1993, decision to withdraw from the NPT. On December 23, 1991, the DPRK and Cyprus signed an agreement in New York to establish diplomatic relations. Moscow had already taken the first major normative leap in erasing its part of the ideological fault-lines on the Korean peninsula. With full normalization of diplomatic relations between China and the ROK as of August 24, 1992, there no longer remains any compelling reason for Washington and Tokyo not to cross the Cold War Rubicon in establishing full diplomatic relations with the DPRK.

Third, not just the UN proper but the entire UN system with all of its subsidiary organs and specialized agencies can enmesh both Pyongyang and Seoul, especially the former, into the global networks of functional cooperation. In late 1991 Seoul became a member of the International Labor Organization, thus completing its full membership in all the specialized agencies, and at the same time signaled its support of Pyongyang's entry into the World Bank. In 1989 the Pyongyang government permitted an unprecedented release of demographic data to the UN Population Fund as a way of seeking technical assistance for the preparation of a national census (scheduled for January 1992), apparently the first census since the 1940s.[16] The UNDP-initiated Tumen River Area Development Program (TRADP)—a $30 billion project over fifteen to twenty years involving North Korea, China, Russia, Mongolia, South Korea, and Japan—is another example of how the world organization can serve as a legitimizing conduit for meshing inter-Korean development with a larger regional multilateral setting. It is, in theory at least, a multilateral functional solution to a subregional political problem.[17]

Fourth, the world organization can help reshape the politics of the two Koreas by creating global transparency in the behavior and expectations of its member states, thus making any norm-defying behavior more detectable and costly. Both Koreas have already started the politics of competitive legitimation of another kind, with each making its own brief before the world audience on the nuclear issue—who is threatening whom in what way and over what period of time.[18] The entire UN system is now poised to exert its normative influence through its own world-order agendas on the shaping of a more peaceful order in the Korean peninsula. Both Koreas are now confronted, in varying degrees and for different reasons, with the challenge of restructuring their attitudes, beliefs, policies, and laws to the reality of UN legitimation of North Korea and South Korea with all the rights and responsibilities the UN charter specifies for member states.

Finally, the world organization can produce Second Image Reversed effects for critical social movements in local and national settings. To cite one example, the ratification of two human rights covenants by the communist Czech government in pre–Havel years provided Charter 77, the Czech human rights group, with a legitimating instrument in its human rights and democratizing struggle at home. The entry of the two Koreas into the UN in the post–Cold War setting has already empowered the critical social/peace movements in South Korea calling for major cuts in military spending. These peace activists believe Seoul's annual military spending of about $10.6 billion—twice Pyongyang's military expenditure—should be drastically reduced to make room for more spending in such neglected areas as social welfare, housing, and the environment.[19]

The Two Koreas in a Changing Regional Order

This is obviously an opportune time to reconsider the Korean question not only against the background of accelerated improvement in great-power politics in the UN but also in the post–Cold War context of a rapidly evolving East Asian regional geopolitical and geoeconomic landscape. Viewed from a regional perspective, the termination of the Cold War does not mean the beginning of global peace, let alone the fading of trouble spots in the Third World. We are witnessing distinctively crosscutting pressures and tendencies.

Even in Europe where the Cold War began and ended in a most dramatic manner, both centripetal and centrifugal forces are developing in tandem. While social and economic density and interdependence are leading Western Europe, by fits and starts, toward greater economic and political integration with a new supranational identity, Eastern Europe and the constituent national republics of the former Soviet Union are unraveling at dizzying speed with ominous implications for the new regional order. With the sweeping repudiation of Marxism that formerly functioned as a legitimating transnational lingua franca for Pax Sovietica, the Second (socialist) World seems to have simply vanished beyond recall. If the old East-West military and ideological divide has been erased, a new North-South economic divide has already emerged. At the same time, both the European Community and the North Atlantic Treaty Organization (NATO) seem unable or unwilling to deal with the state-making internal war in ex-Yugoslavia, exporting the trouble to the Security Council in New York to handle.

The situation of the Asia-Pacific region is vastly more complex and volatile, dominated by the twin pressures of globalism and nationalism with little of pan-Asian regionalism. This is the only region in the world where so many combinations and permutations of two-, three-, four-—and even two-plus-four or three-plus-three—power games can be played on the regional chessboard with all their complexities and variations. The difficulty of accurately assessing the changing pattern and distribution of power in the region is greatly conflated by the fact that in international politics the perception of power matters as much as the reality of power and that the perception of what constitutes "power" has changed dramatically in the wake of the demise of the socialist superpower. As a result, the geopolitical realities of the region are now more amenable than ever before to diverse interpretations, especially in view of China's shifting and unpredictable strategic behavior: In one sense, the region is more bipolar today than ever before given the overlay cast by two global/regional powers—the world's lone superpower (the United States) and the world's largest credit power (Japan). In another sense, the region is more multipolar than elsewhere, a status that developed especially after the emergence of China as a new and independent nuclear power in 1964 and U.S. decline after the Vietnam War. In still another sense, the region is more unipolar than elsewhere because of the largely unchallenged U.S. hegemony in East Asian international politics.[20]

Even the notion of a strategic triangle has numerous regional and subregional variations. The most well-known and widely debated triangle has been (until the Soviet breakup) the Sino-Soviet-U.S. grouping with at least four possible configurations.[21] Since 1965 the U.S.–Japan-South Korean North Pacific triangle, as Kent Calder argues, has emerged as another key feature of the highly dynamic but unbalanced economic and security relationships of the region.[22] According to Peter Hayes, Northeast Asia is overlaid by twin informal strategic triangles: The United States "has linked China and Japan in an informal security triangle, and is the common hypotenuse between this great-power triangle on the one hand, and the informal security triangle among South Korea, United States, and Japan on the other."[23] The collapse of the Soviet Union has already given rise to a debate on the possibilities of a new strategic triangle involving the United States, Japan, and Russia.[24]

Like great tectonic plates of the earth's crust, any collision or collusion between and among the Big Four would impact upon the patterns of international amity and enmity as well as of international power distribution not only regionally but also globally. In other words, the demarcation between regional and global politics is substantially blurred. Given the presence of four of the world's five centers of power in the region, including three of the five nuclear powers, it is hardly surprising that there is only endless debate on the shifting international alliances and alignments. The absence of any multilateral regional arms-control and disarmament negotiations, let alone multilateral security regimes, stands out as a defining feature of the region.

The most dominant dialectics of a new regional order can be seen in the sharpening contradictions and tensions between the omnipresent economic dominance of Japan and the omnipresent military dominance of the United States, as China waits on the sidelines ready to respond to any anti-China condominial regional order. The new topography of post–Cold War East Asian international politics suggests a shift in the center of gravity from geopolitical to geoeconomic axis with intensifying conflict to gain access to market opportunities, direct foreign investment, technology, and control of resources. The game nations now play, according to the current Chinese definition of the international situation, is said to be an all-out Darwinian struggle for the enhancement of "comprehensive national strength" (*zonghe guoli*) in a multipolar world.[25]

Obviously, Japan looms large in world politics. However, the difficulty of assessing Japan's role as a global/regional hegemon is vastly compounded by the long shadows of the imperial past. Despite some regional differences, especially between Northeast Asia and Southeast Asia, there pervades deep Asian ambivalence toward U.S. hegemony, Japanese hegemony, or even "Nichibei bigemony" (U.S.-Japanese). It would be no exaggeration to say that most Asians prefer U.S. hegemony to any other type, for although it is regarded, to paraphrase Winston Churchill, as the worst form of international leadership, there is nothing better to replace it. Still, the changing global situation has altered strategic calculus in practically every capital city in Asia, setting in motion the politics of post–Cold War adjustment. Like it or not, Asian countries have to accept the primal reality that the United States no longer has the necessary domestic consensus or resources to assume the costs and responsibilities of global/regional leadership.

As a result, more and more Asian countries, especially members of the Association of Southeast Asian Nations (ASEAN), are looking to Tokyo for another kind of Japanese miracle—a benign international leadership. Asia eyes Japan with a mixture of amity and enmity, wanting more and more of Japanese aid, know-how, technology, market, and even developmental model and less and less of Japanese preconditions believed to be infringing upon their state sovereignty or national dignity. This view represents an East Asian equivalent of the continuing U.S. pressure upon Japan for greater burden sharing without power sharing.

Japan's Asian identity is no less ambivalent and problematic. As one of a few true nation-states—a state's jurisdiction coincides perfectly with its own nation (homogeneous people)—Japan should have escaped the wrenching identity problems that have afflicted so many old and new multinational states. Yet by a more comprehensive and synthetic definition of national identity,[26] the state defines and differentiates itself not only behaviorally but essentially by what it "is" as well as what it "does." National identity is thus embedded in the national symbol system that the Japanese refer to as *kokutai* (national essence). Asia and the West—and after the end of World War II the United States—constituted two opposite poles, the former standing for civilization and modernity (power and plenty) and the latter for barbarism and backwardness in the making of modern Japanese national identity. Even today, in Japanese eyes, the United States represents peace, democracy, and prosperity, whereas Asia is a temptation to trigger Japan's predatory chauvinism and attitudinal conceit—all of which bespeaks a curious mixture of inferiority complex toward the West and superiority complex toward Asia. Across the ideological spectrum, as Masaru Tamamoto has written, there still exists abiding self-doubt about Japan's ability to control itself in assuming East Asian leadership.[27] Furthermore, the widely shared perception in East Asia that Japan is *in* Asia but not *of* Asia and thus unfit to be a new successor leader or hegemon has much to do with pendulum swings in Japan's Asian identity, which rotate between escaping and conquering Asia. Of course,

China and the two Koreas will never accept Japanese leadership of any kind in East Asian international politics.

Distance seems to make Japan's heart grow fonder. Japan and South Korea are so close geographically, ideologically, and developmentally and yet so far apart in myriad other ways. Nationalism is not the sole culprit because it is never inherently pathological. Its manifestation is time-specific, issue-specific, and situation-specific. What is surprising was a steady rise in the 1980s of respondents in public opinion polls expressing strong anti-Japanese and anti-Korean sentiments—in the range of 60-70 percent, including among young people. It seems that anti-Japanese demonstrations have become a favorite sport in South Korean society, and the Japanese government, as if to rub more Japanese salt in the Korean nationalistic wound, seems chronically unable or unwilling to put an end to old historical enmities. There is no need to describe in detail a seemingly endless series of historical controversies plaguing Japanese-Korean relations—Prime Minister Nakasone's August 1985 official visit to the Yasukuni Shrine, which made him the first postwar head of government to worship the Japanese war dead (including top war criminals); the Ministry of Education's intervention to sanitize the history textbooks about Japan's aggression in the 1930s; and the so-called comfort girls who were abducted and sent to Japanese military "comfort stations" (brothels) in occupied China and Southeast Asia during World War II.

Despite such national-identity clashes, South Korea, more than any other East Asian NIC (newly industrialized country), has followed the Japanese model of development. Korea Inc. is a poor imitation of Japan Inc., just as Korean *chaebŏl* (business conglomerates) are both the linguistic and institutional imitation of Japanese *zaibatsu*. Japan has already become South Korea's chief source of imports (technology and components) and, after the United States, its largest export market; South Korea has become Japan's second-largest export market and its second-largest import source.[28] Faced with searing labor-management conflicts and declining global competitiveness, the Roh government and his ruling party made a great leap of faith in 1990: In an apparent attempt to emulate the Japanese political system as the master key to the Japanese-style economic miracle, they established a one-party developmental state. Herein lies the logic of merging the ruling party and the two opposition parties into the Democratic Liberal Party (mimicking Japan's ruling Liberal Democratic Party) in the attempted—and by 1992 largely aborted—system transition from a strongman developmental state to a one-party developmental state. Not only did South Korea's economic woes grow unabated, but more tellingly, South Korean voters administered a crushing blow to the ruling DLP by denying it a majority in the March 24, 1992, parliamentary elections.

Clearly, East Asia emerged in the 1980s as the most dynamic region of the global economy with seemingly ever-expanding concentric waves of regional economic integration. Japan led the way with its first big developmental wave (with a large dosage of state interventionism and generous help from the Korean War); the East Asian NICs (South Korea, Taiwan, Hong Kong, and Singapore) initiated a second; and Thailand, Malaysia, Indonesia, and coastal China produced a third—a repetitive cycle with a curious mixture of state interventionism and liberal international economic norms. Most Anglo-U.S. neoliberal developmental economists—and the World Bank—got it all wrong in touting East Asian economic success as the triumph of capitalism and in prescribing this model as the wave of the future for Third World development. "Command capitalism," "state capitalism," "dirigist capitalism," or "capitalism with socialist characteristics"—these are better labels for describing East Asian developmental neoauthoritarian states and city-states. Post-Mao China emulates this model with its slogan "socialism with Chinese (read capitalist) characteristics."

As the most important investor, trader, technology transmitter, and aid donor, Japan is beyond comparison in shaping the political economy of the region. According to the so-called V-formation "flying-geese" model—an influential but still self-serving interpretation of Japan-led East Asian economic integration explicated by former Japanese Foreign Minister Okita Saburo— the dynamic of East Asian regional development is seen as a natural "process of consecutive takeoffs with a built-in catch up process. ... And because the geese that take off later are able to benefit from the forerunners' experience to shorten the time required to catch up," Okita argues, "they gradually transform the formation from a V-formation to eventual horizontal integration."[29] This process is easier pronounced than performed. Although the real test of this theory may not come until the twenty-first century, it seems more plausible to argue that this regional economic integration is locked into a pyramidlike hierarchical integration and interdependence of an unequal kind with Tokyo as the main destination of profits—something akin to what Maoist China meant in likening the trilateralists' concept of "interdependence" to the relationship between "a horseman and his mount."[30]

At the deep structural level are the U.S. military presence and an impressive overlay of a series of bilateral security ties the United States has with most countries of the region. Despite Mikhail Gorbachev's overtures for a comprehensive security system for the entire Asia-Pacific region—from Vladivostok (July 1986) to Krasnoyarsk (September 1988) to New York (December 1988) to Beijing (May 1989)—the United States remained more concerned with maintaining the integrity of its Cold War alliance systems and its naval supremacy in the region.[31] In this spirit, the United States quashed not only Gorbachev's Pacific overtures but also all other similar Australian, Canadian, and Japanese proposals for a multilateral Asia-Pacific security conference—a sort of Conference on Security and Cooperation in Asia (CSCA).

As true for the United States but for different obvious reasons, bilateralism is at the core of Chinese regional policy. As Li Luye, director-general of the China Center for International Studies, put it: "Any attempt to copy Europe's model of collective security or to duplicate the pattern of integration of the two Germanies in Northeast Asia is not realistic and could by no means bring peace and stability to this area. It would be desirable to start establishing a security mechanism in the Asia-Pacific region, including Northeast Asia, on a bilateral basis."[32] At the second international conference on "Joint Efforts for Development: Prevention of Conflicts," held in Bandung, Indonesia, in August 1991, Chinese officials strongly opposed both the establishment of a multilateral regime for handling territorial disputes and the intrusion of outside powers (i.e., Japan, the United States, and the Soviet Union), maintaining instead that disputes should be resolved by the countries directly involved on a bilateral basis.[33] China's general silence and passivity on regional arms-control and disarmament issues, in contrast to its activism in the UN, speak directly to Beijing's acute concern that the establishment of an Asian-Pacific security framework would impinge on its expansive regional security zone as well as on its bargaining leverage in a bilateral setting.[34]

Indeed, the Gorbachev challenge represented a sharp break from the zero-sum style of thinking and behavior and expanded the limits of the possible for a new regional order. And yet the United States failed to respond to the Gorbachev challenge for a comprehensive security system in the region. Part of the problem lies in the tenacious assumption that a hegemonic power is ipso facto a naval power, that naval power is readily fungible, and that any arms-control and disarmament negotiations can only compromise U.S. naval supremacy in the Asia-Pacific region. The Pacific Force, the Cold War alliance structure of the United States for the Asia-Pacific region, emerged largely unrevised in 1990 in a much-awaited Department of Defense blueprint for U.S. military strategy for the decade.[35] In subsequent vigorous attempts to invent a menu of seven alarming war scenarios outlining a $1.2 trillion strategy to keep the world safe for Pax Americana II—to draw up the bottom line for the U.S. military budget—the Pentagon shifted from "a single monolithic global scenario" (read the Soviet threat) to a "regionally focused national military strategy." The notion of a unipolar world order resonated in the initial draft of the Pentagon's document for defense planning guidance for fiscal years 1994–1999: "We must account sufficiently for the interests of the large industrial nations to discourage them from challenging our leadership or seeking to overturn the established political or economic order," and "we must maintain the mechanisms for deterring potential competitors from even aspiring to a larger regional or global role."[36] Paradoxically, multilateral approaches to regional and global problems in a multipolar post–Cold War world were rejected by the Bush administration. Of course, this requires new regional enemies. Not surprisingly, Kim Il Sung has been placed on the hit list as "most-favored-enemy." As Adm. Charles Larson, commander in chief of the Pacific Command, put it: "North Korea poses the greatest immediate threat to regional stability."[37]

U.S. foreign policy in general and U.S. policy in this important region in particular have been shaped and guided by one central organizing creed of anticommunism and its former corollary, "the Soviet threat." In the process, a strategic culture emerged that was critically dependent on a Manichaean vision of stark bipolarity and the Cold War system. It was this creed that formed the postwar national symbol system, which in turn provided the ark and anchor of the postwar U.S. national identity. It was also this creed that imposed a measure of unity and coherence upon the Asia-Pacific region, which lacked any sense of shared cultures and ideologies, via a series of geopolitical and geoeconomic ties stretching from Japan and South Korea to ASEAN states to Australia and New Zealand. Ironically, President Reagan's strategy of hegemonic restoration only accelerated the hegemonic decline that first became visible in the course of U.S. involvement in Vietnam. Reagan's instigation of the largest military expansion in U.S. peacetime history simply worked to undercut the economic and technological bases of hegemony as well as U.S. global competitiveness. By 1985, the United States had become a net debtor (and five years later the world's largest debtor nation) for the first time since 1914 and Japan the world's largest credit power. In sum, this creed transformed the hegemon's dividends into the hegemon's debts, and compound interest placed the United States on a trajectory of decline.[38]

Paradoxically, the ending of the Cold War in 1989 and 1990 seems to be having mixed effects. "In Asia it has brought perhaps the deepest peace that Asians have known this century," as *The Economist* put it, "together with the world's fastest growth in arsenals and the arms trade."[39] Throughout the Asia-Pacific region, the deep structure of militarization and the competing war systems remain largely intact in the post–Cold War setting. The military still remains as the most powerful and cohesive social system in most East Asian countries. Most countries resist pressure to reduce their military spending on various grounds: They have to spend more to catch up with their neighbors; they have to spend more to replace outdated weapons systems; they have to spend more to back up their territorial claims; and so forth. North Korea (21.5 percent), Pakistan, Burma, Brunei, Sri Lanka, Taiwan, and Singapore all exceed the global average of 4.5 percent of GDP spent on defense, and South Korea just barely escaped with a 4.4 percent of GDP (dropped to 3.8 percent in 1992).[40] The military spending curve has suddenly begun to rise sharply (about 13–15 percent per year) in post-Tiananmen China. The U.S. high-tech military victory in the 1991 Gulf war has set in motion another catch-up race to make smart bombers even more brilliant. Even the "pacifist" Japan now has the third-largest navy in the world, and its defense budget ($32.89 billion in 1991), though still only slightly over 1 percent of its GNP, is the world's third largest in absolute terms and is more than four times China's official defense budget ($7.56 billion).[41] Finally, Japan is constantly pressured by the United States for greater "burden sharing," which means burden sharing without power sharing—indeed, it means Japanese subsidization of U.S. hegemony in the region and beyond (for example, the Persian Gulf). This unique and ultimately unsustainable situation of the rising power underwriting the costs of the declining power is what the burden-sharing controversy is all about.

Still, the cumulative weight of events—the fading of the Cold War, the collapse of the Soviet Union, and the decline of U.S. hegemony—has reflected and effected the end of old certainties and the beginning of more complex, shifting, and diffuse patterns of power and influence in the region. Almost every country in the area, including Japan, is now coping with wrenching problems of redefining national identity and role conceptions in a rapidly changing world. The more polycentric and less ideological system that is emerging in the region gives more room to maneuver for small powers. Indeed, small powers in the area have become increasingly more assertive and less amenable to hegemonic control. Much to Washington's dismay, Malaysian Prime

Minister Mahathir Mohammed served the first shock, without much success, by proposing the establishment of an East Asia Economic Group (EAEG) in December 1990 that would exclude the United States, Australia, and New Zealand. On September 16, 1991, the Philippine Senate delivered the second blow—and with success owing in part to the force majeure of the Mt. Pinatubo eruption that affected Clark Air Base—when it rejected a controversial draft treaty that would have permitted the U.S. Navy to remain at its Subic Bay base for another ten years. Even South Korea got caught up in this politics of readjustment, delivering the third blow to Washington by moving too fast—and too softly—in its dialogue and détente with Pyongyang, especially on the nuclear issue. Each of these three cases suggests that globalism breeds nationalism—a kind of Second Image Reversed process in which external economic interdependence returns home to fuel greater state autonomy. Robert Gilpin has called this phenomenon the "new mercantilism" that pervades practically all the trading nations; it is a new threat to international security.[42]

The Gulf war has also greatly increased tensions between East Asian states and their traditional allies outside the region. Only two East Asian countries—Japan and South Korea—acquired the dubious honor of making the "hit list of six" (Germany, Saudi Arabia, the United Arab Emirates, and the exiled government of Kuwait were the other four) of Secretary of Treasury Nicholas Brady's globe-trotting mission for "burden sharing" to defray the costs of the U.S.-led military buildup and the Desert Storm operation in the Gulf crisis of 1990–1991. Tokyo and Seoul were pressured to contribute some $13 billion and $500 million respectively in cash and other material and paramilitary supplies; the pressure added more fuel to the already inflamed alliance relationships. Despite the habitual pro forma assurances from national security managers in Seoul and Washington ("If it ain't broke, don't fix it"), U.S-ROK relations are now plagued with a host of disputes that in essence involve the difficult transition from Cold War military collaboration to a new post–Cold War normal relationship.

The key to the integrity and stability of U.S. bilateral alliance systems in the region, especially to the "Nichibei bigemony"—euphemistically called the "US-Japan global partnership"—has been the shared perception of the former Soviet threat. Korea per se was never all that important to U.S. strategic planners. From beginning to end of the long Cold War era, Japan remained the linchpin of U.S. East Asian strategy. In other words, Korea was important to the United States only as a strategic tripwire for its Japan-centered extended deterrence in the region. At most, then, Korea was symbolic of America's Cold War resolve to draw the containment line in East Asia.

Because of built-in mutual assured dependency and damage, the U.S.-Japan relationship is more capable of surviving (or at least muddling through) the post–Cold War strains. The same cannot be said about the U.S.-ROK relationship, partly because of the distinctive dynamic of divided polity and irresistible primordial passions for national reunion that undergird Korean politics and partly because of the marginality of Korea in U.S. domestic politics. In the post–Cold War context, then, the strategic importance of Korea as a frontline domino to be protected at any cost becomes increasingly problematic. At long last, there is now a clear and continuing possibility for the two Koreas to recapture security sovereignty that they had forfeited in their entangling alliances with outside powers.

Interestingly, the Korean peninsula is also regarded by Chinese military thinkers as a vital strategic shield. Necessarily, China's Korea policy in an uncertain and complex multipolar regional and global order is a balancing act reflecting and affecting its basic principles and interests as well as its consecutive and simultaneous participation in multiple games on the bilateral, regional, and global chessboards with all their complexities and variations. By fits and starts, this policy has evolved through several phases, shifting from a policy of one Korea to a policy of one Korea de jure and two Koreas de facto to a policy of two Koreas de facto and de jure. China's Korea policy has been guided by the realist maxi-mini strategy of enhancing its own drive for modernization and status. In the pursuit of such interest-driven policy toward the Korean peninsula, Beijing has adopted a multitasking approach of emphasizing different but mutually complementary priorities in different issue areas. Despite the inauguration of formal diplomatic relations with Seoul in August 1992, Beijing still takes a dual-track approach of strengthening its traditional geostrategic ties with North Korea even as it actively promotes new geoeconomic ties with South Korea.

The reactions of the two Koreas to major changes in great-power relations in East Asia are instructive. President Richard Nixon in 1971 administered the first shock—popularly known in Japan as "the Nixon Shokku"—to Tokyo, Seoul, and Pyongyang. The ensuing Sino-U.S. rapprochement of 1971–1972 sufficiently traumatized the "reactive state"[43] (Japan) to normalize its relations with China and forced the two recalcitrant Koreas into the first round of inter-Korean dialogue. The shared sense of fear and suspicion that great powers were once again slicing the Korean melon catalyzed both Koreas to come together for the first time since division and sign the "Three Principles for Unification of the Fatherland," issued in the form of the North-South joint communiqué of July 4, 1972 (see Appendix A). The entire process of détente II in the early 1970s involving the United States, the Soviet Union, China—indeed, there was a ménage à trois possibility in the strategic triangle at the time—Japan, North Korea, and South Korea soon collapsed as far as Soviet-U.S. and inter-Korean relations were concerned.

Undoubtedly, the Gorbachev challenge for a new Asia-Pacific regional order had the greatest impact in siring another phase of superpower cooperation—détente III—as well as in terminating the Cold War. Even during the pre-Gorbachev years, the Soviet threat was more smoke than fire, more like a thermostat that could be calibrated in the service of mobilizing bipartisan foreign policy consensus in the United States and intrabloc alliance cohesion in the region. At the core of the Soviet "new thinking" in the Gorbachev years was a revolutionary concept of security that transcended both the Marxist class struggle and the Western realist notion of struggle for power among nations. Indeed, the proposition, advanced by Foreign Minister E. A. Shevardnadze at the 1988 UN General Assembly, that a voluntary transfer of certain sovereign rights to the world community as the surest and cheapest way of enhancing national security *and* global security was "revolutionary" in Soviet foreign policy.[44] The Soviet proposal for a comprehensive security system (first expounded in Gorbachev's unusual newspaper article "Realities and Guarantees for a Secure World" in the September 17, 1987, issue of *Pravda* and *Izvestia* and subsequently refined and elaborated in various official documents and scholarly literature 1987–1990)[45] was significant both in terms of its normative content and the new opening it offered to the creation of a new global and regional order. "The idea of a comprehensive system of security," as Gorbachev put it, "is the first project of a possible new organization of life in our common planetary home. In other words, it is a pass into a future where the security of all is a token of the security of each."[46]

As a result, Sino-Soviet relations were renormalized and the region no longer faced imminent danger of being drawn into a Sino-Soviet armed conflict. Yet the greatest impact of the Gorbachev Pacific challenge can be seen in the Korean peninsula. The 1988 Seoul Olympiad was a watershed in accelerating cross-bloc functional cooperation between Seoul and Moscow as well as between Seoul and Beijing. Soviet interest in Korea shifted from a passive desire to avoid an unwanted confrontation with the United States to a more active solicitation of South Korean support in Soviet Far Eastern development and greater integration of the Soviet economy with that of the North Pacific triangle. The unexpectedly rapid Moscow-Seoul rapprochement from 1989 to 1991 suggests an interesting case for testing the functionalist "peace by pieces" approach to world order. In any case, this cozying-up process certainly melted at least one of the major pillars propping up the Cold War alliance systems in the Korean peninsula. In the short space of ten months (June 1990–April 1991), no fewer than three Gorbachev-Roh summit meetings took place in San Francisco, Moscow, and Cheju Island; Soviet–South Korean relations were fully normalized; and Moscow played the most crucial role in paving the way for the Korean UN membership. Seoul-Moscow trade soared to $1.5 billion in 1991, up from $889 million in 1990, and there were projections it could reach $10 billion by the mid-1990s.[47] Despite the uncertainties bedeviling Russia in the wake of the failed coup and the demise of the Soviet Union, there is as yet no danger of Moscow returning to the Korean peninsula as part of the problem.

Such rapid progress in Moscow-Seoul relations, coupled with an equally rapid decompression of Moscow-Pyongyang relations, has taken the sting out of the long-festering ideological and geopolitical rivalry China and the former Soviet Union engaged in over North Korea. The ending of Cold War bipolarity has meant the demise of not only the vaunted China card in the collapsed strategic triangle but also the Pyongyang card in the old Soviet-Sino rivalry. Another important consequence of the changing nature of the former Soviet (now Russian) factor in Beijing's overall cost-benefit calculation is that Moscow sets the pace for Beijing's diplomatic marathon. "In recent years," as two PRC scholars have put it, "it has been China's practice to let Moscow take the lead in approaching Seoul while it avoided lagging too far behind."[48] What Moscow can do in a more decisive—and sweeping—fashion, Beijing can do as well or even better in a more measured and calculating fashion.

Whereas Gorbachev's Soviet Union shifted from being part of the problem to being part of the solution as it pertains to the Korean question, the Bush administration remained part of the problem. The underlying reasons for Soviet change and U.S. continuity are both normative and practical. The Soviet Union during the Gorbachev years moved decisively toward a new conception of comprehensive security as a way of creating a more peaceful and stable external environment for domestic reform, but the Bush administration or at least the Pentagon and realist "national security managers" seemed unable or unwilling to resist the unipolar temptation to reclaim U.S. hegemony. "In effect, U.S.-orchestrated military integration substitutes for political integration," Peter Hayes has argued, "avoiding the political-ideological headaches of collective security organizations."[49]

It became evident during the 1991 Gulf war that a "new world order" is another name for Pax Americana II in the post–Cold War era. The most striking and inescapable feature of the post–Cold War world, according to neoconservative journalist Charles Krauthammer, is its unipolarity. The United States is the center of world power, the unchallenged and unchallengeable superpower—indeed, the lone global supercop, "the only country with the military, diplomatic, political and economic assets to be a decisive player in any conflict in whatever part of the world it chooses to involve itself."[50] The best and brightest prescription for a future world order lies in "American strength and will—the strength and will to lead a unipolar world, unashamedly laying down the rules of world order and being prepared to enforce them."[51] Although President Bush himself maintained calculated ambiguity, the Pentagon's post–Cold War blueprint for the 1990s embraced such a unipolar/hegemonic conception of a new world order. Perhaps there was more a touch of showmanship than the necessary normative and material power needed to put into effect such a unipolar conception of the new world order. Spurred by a rapidly spreading arms race in Asia, especially North Korea going nuclear, alarmed by China's growing military power ("China-threat theory") that would in turn force Japan to drift toward rearmament, and encouraged by the blessing and participation of the Clinton administration, Japan and ASEAN states for the first time have just recently (as of this writing) begun to talk about the establishment of a new multilateral security forum for the Asia-Pacific region.[52]

The Dynamics of Inter-Korean Dialogue

To appreciate the historical significance of the recent inter-Korean dialogue, we need to go back to the beginning of liberated/divided polity. Ironically, the politics of divided Korea started with the end of Japanese colonial rule in 1945. As a true nation-state after A.D. 668 with only rare and temporary exceptions, Korea was liberated from one vanquished power only to be split by the victorious superpowers into two separate captive and dependent states. This divided liberation marked the beginning of an identity/legitimacy crisis in Korea. The politics of competitive legitimation started in 1945 from an identical cultural and historical baseline: The two Koreas took separate paths in the nation-building, identity-forming, and legitimacy-seeking processes under the sponsorship of the two competing superpowers. Even before the outbreak of the Korean War, both Koreas had already locked themselves into the competing Cold War alliance systems in charting out the separate state-making paths that culminated forty-six years later in UN legitimation as two independent states.

Since the division, the legitimation/identity crisis has become the most essential challenge of Korean politics, domestic and external.[53] Inter-Korean détente has become all the more intractable because of the zero-sum nature of competition, in which legitimation of one side has come to be viewed as largely dependent on the delegitimation of the other side. Each Korea committed itself to an intense version of the politics of fragmentation by overdifferentiating its half from the other half. One commonality in the inter-Korean relationship over the years has been use of the term "puppet" in defining—and delegitimizing—the government of the other Korea. Indeed, the sources of this legitimation/identity crisis have remained more or less the same in both Koreas: (1) leadership and succession crisis from within; (2) continuing challenge and/or threat from the other Korea; and (3) twin allied security dilemmas of entrapment and abandonment.

In short, the central challenge of both Koreas as insecure and incomplete nation-states has remained clear: how to make the world at large and the great-power allies in particular safe and congenial for the identity-defining and legitimacy-seeking processes. What has changed over the years in response to the logic of the changing domestic and international situation is the means with which to realize the end.

Because of its head start in diplomatic recognition in the 1950s and 1960s, thanks to its special relationship with the United States, Seoul, not Pyongyang, was seeking absolute legitimation. A role reversal occurred in the early 1970s: Pyongyang shifted gears toward absolute legitimation, and Seoul retreated into more realistic claims for relative legitimation. Indeed, the 1970s may well be remembered as *la belle époque* of Pyongyang's engagement in the global politics of collective legitimation. A number of major changes in the international environment joined to intensify President Park's sense of insecurity and siege mentality and to enhance President Kim's sense of confidence that the DPRK could join this international game and even beat the South by its own rules. The image South Korea projected in the 1970s was one of a crazy and dependent national insecurity state in search of allied support at any cost. The kidnapping of Kim Dae Jung and the Koreagate scandal merely represented the desperate reactions of a garrison state in a serious legitimation/identity crisis. By contrast, the 1970s witnessed Pyongyang's grand entry into global politics, where it had many more hits than misses in its identity-asserting and legitimacy-seeking global diplomacy. Seoul's seemingly insurmountable head start in diplomatic recognition all but vanished in the 1970s as Pyongyang pursued a more flexible, diversified, and omnidirectional policy. By mid-1976, the number of countries recognizing Seoul and Pyongyang stood respectively at 96 and 93. This turn of diplomatic fortune was not entirely of Pyongyang's own making. It had a lot to do with the fact that the

Third World as a collective global actor was promoted to the unusual, albeit fleeting, role of dominance in the normative domain of global politics in the 1970s with its clarion call for the establishment of a new international economic order (NIEO).

From the late 1970s, however, Pyongyang began to encounter staggering economic woes at home and serious diplomatic setbacks abroad. Until the mid-1970s, *Juche* (self-reliant) ideology commanded considerable credibility because North Korea seemed headed toward becoming an exceptional model island of autocentric, socialist economy in the sea of the capitalist world system. By the 1980s, it became increasingly obvious that *Juche* could no longer perform its multiple functions: to legitimize Kim Il Sung's (and his son Kim Jong Il's) consolidation of power at home; to delegitimize South Korea as a U.S. imperial outpost in Northeast Asia; to minimize allied control and interference without losing allied support; and to establish global solidarity with the Third World in the relentless pursuit of absolute legitimation.

To a certain extent, the new Seoul factor reflected and affected Pyongyang's growing legitimation/identity crisis. Because they lacked historical and constitutional claims to legitimacy, both Park Chung Hee and Chun Doo Hwan took a performance-based approach to legitimation, following three closely interconnected strategies: (1) a state-guided export-oriented strategy of economic development for exploiting the country's geostrategic U.S. connection to the fullest to maximize payoffs and minimize penalties; (2) a "development first, reunification later" strategy; and (3) a strategy of "bleeding North Korea dry" in the qualitative arms race by rejecting any discussion on mutual reductions of military forces on both sides of the DMZ. To win the international competitive bidding in 1981 to host the 1988 Summer Olympics in Seoul—and to win in the wake of the 1980 Kwangju massacre—must surely have helped boost Chun's lagging support. In January 1982, Chun launched a massive diplomatic offensive designed to shore up the external base of legitimation. The multifaceted and multidirectional approach entailed a new foreign policy, so-called Nordpolitik, coupled with "economic diplomacy," a combination designed to diversify and globalize Seoul's foreign policy—and thus to rectify its international reputation as an indebted and dependent client regime. As well, it constituted Seoul's opening to the socialist world.

The 1988 Seoul Olympiad spotlighted the contrast between the South and the North—two Koreas so near yet so far apart. As if to add insult to injury, Roh was now claiming dual legitimation (e.g., cross recognition and separate but equal UN membership) only to accentuate Kim's national identity angst and to intensify his search for absolute legitimation. Smarting under the crushing ideological and economic impact of the collapse of communism in Eastern Europe and the rapid demise of international socialist support, the monolith of Leninist North Korea was beginning to show cracks and strains. From the latter half of 1990, Pyongyang's "searching" behavior became more flexible and forthcoming, as evidenced by its endorsement of confidence-building measures (CBMs) coupled with a serious arms-control proposal (gradually thinning down to 100,000 on each side of the DMZ) as an integral part of the inter-Korean dialogue. Pyongyang also opened its door wider to

Japan for diplomatic relations and economic aid and to various UN agencies for technical assistance.

A role reversal in the Korean politics of competitive legitimation in the 1988–1991 period is rather revealing. In return for Moscow's full diplomatic recognition of the ROK—and with it also the implied support for Seoul's bid for UN membership—the South Korean government pledged $3 billion in foreign aid. In addition to this major diplomatic blow, Moscow also served notice that Pyongyang would have to start servicing its debt to Moscow (estimated at about $4.6 billion) and trading in hard currency (as of January 1, 1991). The change in Soviet policy could not have come at a worse time, as North Korea's GNP for 1989 stood at its 1984 level. The Soviet Union as the DPRK's largest trade partner (about 57 percent of total trade as late as 1990) vanished in 1991—two-way trade for the first six months of 1991 dropped to 1.2 percent of the same period in 1990. The drastic reduction of Soviet supply of cheap oil (e.g., from 800,000 tons in 1987 to 500,000 tons in 1990, 42,000 tons in 1991, and 25,000 tons in January–September 1992), coupled with the 1991 drought that dried up the reservoirs on which the country depends for hydroelectric power, caused a critical energy crisis. The consequences of such a conflation of economic and diplomatic misfortunes were made manifest everywhere: Factories running at about 40–50 percent of capacity; military airplanes grounded; few vehicles seen on the roads; cities remaining unlighted at night; and a "let's eat two meals a day" campaign under full swing.

In the field of economic relations with North Korea, too, as in the ROK recognition question, China's actual policy has been to let Moscow take the initiative without lagging too many steps behind. For instance, China had in the not distant past supplied about 1.2 million tons of crude oil to North Korea a year—650,000 tons in the form of barter trade and the remaining 550,000 tons on credit. At the beginning of 1993. China stopped supplying crude oil to North Korea in barter trade following the breakup of trade talks between the countries in November 1992 and the subsequent Chinese decision to follow the Moscow lead in demanding cash payment for trade. Apparently, China imposed this shift from the barter trade system to the hard currency trade system in the course of bilateral talks between Li Lanqing (China's foreign trade minister) and Kang Jong-mo (vice chairman of North Korea's External Economy and Trade Commission) even as both sides tried to put the best possible face on the shift. Pyongyang announced that the talks were held in "a warm and friendly atmosphere" without giving any details; the Chinese press reported that under all the "new circumstances," China and North Korea had to seek new ways of developing a bilateral economic and trade relationship. Although the change of system from barter to cash payment may present North Korea "certain difficulties for a while," the shift has been explained as being of eventual benefit for both countries.[54]

One of the hidden factors driving inter-Korean détente in 1990 and 1991 was a new partnership in economic misery. The "miracle" economy of South Korea is a testimonial to the fact that the time required for economic catch-up through late industrialization has shrunk steadily over the centuries. It took fifty-eight years for the United Kingdom to double its per capita output

(1780–1838), forty-seven years for the United States (1839–1886), thirty-four years for Japan (1885–1919), eighteen years for Brazil (1961–1979), eleven years for South Korea (1966–1977), and only ten years for China (1977–1987).[55] After experiencing double-digit growth for nearly three decades without paying much attention to social, political, and environmental problems, South Korea rather suddenly entered another critical transition period to encounter a confluence of such situational and structural problems as high wages, labor shortage, cash deficiency, technological bottlenecks, high inflation, high consumption, erosion of infrastructure and social discipline, high crime rates, declining global competitiveness, environmental degradation, and so on. Most economists in Seoul now concede that the national economy is seriously plagued by the "four highs" and "four shortages"—high wages, high interest rates, high consumption, and the high value of the Korean won, coupled with shortages of labor, cash, transportation facilities, and high technology. A summary list of the new economic woes would include the following:[56]

- The four golden years of trade surplus (1986–1989) seemed like a flash in the pan, weakening the incentive to make a necessary structural change from labor-intensive to knowledge-intensive products.
- The sudden transition from authoritarianism to democratization in 1987 gave rise to soaring labor-management conflict with over 7,000 industrial strikes and skyrocketing wage increases (e.g., 34.5 percent in 1988, 36.2 percent in 1989, and 17.4 percent in 1992). The gap widened between labor-cost increase and productivity increase (e.g., averages in South Korea rose by more than 18 percent a year in the period 1987–1992, whereas productivity rose by only 10 percent a year), forcing more than 300 labor-intensive footwear companies to shut down in 1991 and 1992 as Nike, Reebok, and other big buyers took their business elsewhere.
- Declining competitiveness and growing protectionism in South Korea's most important market, the United States, coupled with rising consumption and imports, placed its export-oriented development strategy back on the track of rising trade deficits ($4.83 billion in 1990, $9.65 billion in 1991, and $4.3 billion in 1992) and growing external debts.
- About 91 percent ($8.8 billion) of the $9.65 billion trade deficit in 1991 was incurred with Japan. In order to increase exports to reduce trade deficits, however, South Korea has to increase imports of Japanese plant, machinery, and industrial materials, further raising trade deficits with Japan. Such a structural problem with Japan had been papered over during the heyday of South Korean authoritarianism and the open U.S. market but no longer can be.
- Skyrocketing land prices have drastically increased production costs, reduced South Korea's global competitiveness, and engendered rampant speculation. The total value of land in South Korea is now reported to be equivalent to 70 percent of the entire U.S. land value. Under such conditions, it is rational for South Korean investors and businesspeople

to channel their money into whatever speculative opportunity offers fast and high returns rather than into the manufacturing sector and re-search and development.

- Just as President Roh's decision to fulfill his electoral promise of building 2 million units of affordable apartments in Seoul's sprouting satellite cities diverted much capital and labor away from the manufacturing sector and ignited inflation (around 10 percent per year), the 1992 electoral campaigns consumed a huge amount of money. Some 5 trillion won (the government's annual budget is about 33 trillion won) reportedly was spent for the March 19 parliamentary elections alone, which undermined official antiinflation policy. The chronic labor shortage in the manufacturing industry was greatly exacerbated in February 1992 as the illegal early election activities of numerous politicians sapped a fair amount of the country's manpower, pushing up the labor shortage rates for some industries above the 40 percent level.[57]

In short, South Korea is mired down in the product-cycling march to the promised land. Seoul has already lost its global competitiveness in labor-intensive products to Southeast Asian countries and China (where average labor cost is about one-tenth that in South Korea but labor productivity is only 10–30 percent below South Korean levels) without being able to make a breakthrough in moving up to knowledge-intensive high-value products with the exception of dynamic random access memory (D-RAM) chips.

There is another ironical twist in Korean development. It was not until the 1980s that South Korea's phenomenal late industrialization finally became a subject of great interest for both theoreticians and policymakers. It seemed as if a basket case had become a model for Third World development. Articles and books addressing the Korean political economy—"Is [South] Korea the next Japan?"—became legion.[58] Understandably, South Korean development excited such theoretical and policy interest because, unlike most Third World states and like Japan, South Korea could offer virtually no resources other than human resources. The onset of problems in the early 1990s has underscored the social and structural problems of the so-called miracle economy.

At the same time, this new reality of South Korea's economy adds another potent but unpredictable element in the cost-benefit computations of inter-Korean economic exchange and cooperation. What greatly complicates our understanding of the shape of things to come is the changing balance of primordial, ideological, military (nuclear), political, legal, and social factors involved in greater economic integration of the two Koreas. The German case suggests the inordinate economic costs of full-scale inter-Korean economic integration—on the order of $90 billion a year. The cost of absorbing North Korea's stagnant or collapsing economy is estimated at about $200–500 billion over five to ten years, although such figures are little more than shots in the dark given the uncertainties of domestic and external factors involved in the total calculus of Korean reunification.[59] Although there is a high degree of complementarity (e.g., Seoul's capital, experience, and entrepreneurship and Pyongyang's cheap, disciplined labor, raw materials, and shortage of hard currency), the actual trade pattern has been determined more by political and military than by purely economic considerations. The inter-Korean trade ratio in 1991, when Seoul suddenly emerged as Pyongyang's major trading partner, ran at about 10:1 in favor of the North. In effect, inter-Korean trade has become foreign aid in disguise. North-South economic cooperation, though suddenly on the rise following the inter-Korean dialogue of 1990–1991 that culminated in a series of historic accords in December 1991, shrank in 1992 and 1993 largely due to the North's shortage of hard currency and growing tensions on the Korean peninsula caused by North Korea's suspected nuclear weapons program. In March 1993, for instance, the South's exports to the North amounted to only $130,000 on an approval basis, a hefty drop of 90.8 percent from a year earlier, and its merchandise imports from the North fell to $17.4 million, off 27.5 percent during the same period.[60] The South Korean government has adopted a flexible carrot-and-stick approach as a cost-effective way of responding to the suspected nuclear weapons program in the North; President Kim Young Sam ordered on March 17, 1993, that all South Korean moves to invest in the North's crippled economy should be held in abeyance until Pyongyang reversed its March 12, 1993, decision to withdraw from the NPT. The nuclear issue looms large as a sword of Damocles over the ongoing inter-Korean cooperation. In short, the two Koreas have made a great leap, but a long and tortuous road still lies ahead in the stop-go Long March toward the promised land of national union.

Toward a Common Security System

Despite all of the positive changes at the situational level, Korean security remains elusive. A list of normative and structural obstacles standing in the way of establishing an alternative common security system would include at least the following: (1) the general resistance of national security managers to consider new ideas that challenge traditional zero-sum security thinking; (2) the secretive nature of the national decisionmaking process exempting security issues from any public debate or scrutiny; (3) the overlay of the Korean peninsula by external military ties, though in a highly asymmetrical way; (4) the presence of military-industrial complexes in the two halves of divided Korea; (5) deformed authoritarian culture in which resort to violence is widely accepted and practiced as the arbiter of social and political conflicts; (6) the absence of any comprehensive regional security framework or institution comparable to the Conference on Security and Cooperation in Europe (CSCE); and (7) the general tendency of most domestic and transnational nonstate actors and movements to concentrate on human rights and environmental issues. Moreover, the conflation of divided polity and the war systems constitutes a continuing source of insecurity to both Koreas as well as to others in the region and beyond.

In light of these seemingly insurmountable obstacles, it is tempting to settle for a modest "realistic" change within the existing framework. Yet there are several reasons that argue against the logic of such "realism." To begin with, the extraordinary changes and surprising developments accompanying the end of the Cold War have already changed our definition of what is real and what is possible in a rapidly changing world. Historically, all great transformations have been preceded by the progressive decay of the dominant social paradigm and propelled by the introduction of a totally new conception of social reality—by an alternative worldview that shifted the flow of history. Such a new conception of social reality helps us to see more clearly where we are today and where we want to be tomorrow and how we need to build new bridges to make the world-order transition. The only question is whether this system change will come about by a series of local and regional upheavals or whether we can intervene to shift it into a nonviolent direction guided by new security thinking and policy objectives.

The most urgent task is redefining security in the post–Cold War setting. "Security" has remained the prime motive of state behavior in international relations since the inception of the modern-states system at Westphalia. Yet the perennial quest for security, especially since the dawn of the nuclear age, seems to bring only perennial insecurity. How can we explain such a paradox? Is security a utopian goal or a Sisyphean pursuit?

Ironically, the concept of security began to acquire a predominantly military character in the postwar era. The notion that a state must be prepared militarily at all times to defend itself against external military threats became popular just as new sources of nonmilitary threat (oil depletion, soil erosion, shrinking forests, climatic change, political oppression, population explosion, and debt crisis) began to proliferate. The assumption that the state can and must have both guns and butter has been a major factor in militarizing the world economy. All the security principles of historical and contemporary international systems are based on the notion that security is an outcome of managing or balancing military power between contending actors in the international system.[61] This reductionist conception of security, though theoretically parsimonious and politically expedient, conveys a distorted and dangerous image in an increasingly interconnected and interdependent world. Such militarized conception condemns humanity to a multiplicity of mutually insecure states—a global system of collective insecurity. Moreover, in an age of scarcity, it entails high opportunity costs in both developed and developing worlds. The world-order perspective adopted in this chapter argues that planet Earth is now constituted biologically, materially, and ecologically in such a way as to make the collective survival of the human species the starting point for our journey from "here to there." Security in the nuclear-ecological age can only mean common security.[62]

It is increasingly obvious that the traditional concept of national security makes no sense even for the great powers in a nuclear-ecological age. In the case of divided and incomplete nation-states whose security structures are overlaid by great powers, national security breeds destabilizing fear, insecurity, searching alliance behavior, and arms race. National security cannot escape from the reactive—and self-fulfilling—consequences a state's security behavior brings for the security behavior of its adversary. Over the years, both Koreas have conceptualized and pursued security in such an exclusive zero-sum manner. Herein lies the Korean security problematique. Clearly, there is a need for an alternative security—common security—in the sense that the security of one enhances the security of all.

Common security is a comprehensive security in terms of locating an array of threats situated in and flowing from a set of interlocking processes and relationships between and among seemingly discrete social problems and conflicts. Its comprehensive nature is to be found in at least four principal defining characteristics:

1. It proceeds from the premise that any fair and effective security framework must address the legitimate concerns and interests of all its members. As such, it is an advance on the concept of collective security premised on the problematic and ultimately partial division between the aggressive and peace-loving states. In the Korean context, then, to enhance the security of the weaker, less privileged half (the DPRK) is the safest and cheapest way of enhancing the security of the stronger half (the ROK). A cornered North Korea can launch a preemptive strike, igniting a major armed conflagration in the Korean peninsula and beyond.

2. It is defined multidimensionally and horizontally as the safeguarding of human beings against those conditions endangering or negating their most essential values as humans. Insecurity extends to all major threats to human life, health, and freedom. The minimization of violence, in both a direct/physical and indirect/structural sense, is what human security is all about. If we see this planet as a web of interconnected ecosystems—and follow Plato's analogy of politics to medicine as the art of healing the soul and of helping the body polity—violence can be seen as a pathological agent that destroys, degrades, or diminishes life-sustaining, life-enhancing, and life-expanding processes. Such an approach opens up new paths to explore both military and nonmilitary threats to security and to examine interrelationships among military, economic, demographic, ecological, and human rights dimensions of security. The world-order values of peace, economic well-being and equity, human rights, and ecological balance are organically linked with the enhancement of four prerequisite conditions for security: human survival, human needs, human rights, and human habitat.[63] In other words, common security is not likely to be realized if it is defined narrowly to refer only to one's military security.

3. It is defined vertically as encompassing all system levels of human organization. The problem with the dominant realist statecentric approach is that the state has become more often than not a primary source of threat to *global* security as well as to its own *people's* security, all in the name of *national* security. Threats to security manifest themselves in varying forms and degrees in different locations and at different levels of human life. The common security approach stresses the importance of thinking about security at the level of human beings, local communities, states, and regions as well as at the global level. Given the enormous scale, complexity, and diversity of the security problematique, different

requirements of security must be keyed to different situations and levels. A single global solution (e.g., a world government) or a single national solution (e.g., an arms buildup) fails to integrate the many levels of security requirements.

4. It is defined normatively as a value-realizing, threat-minimizing cooperative process rather than as an outcome of a state or a group of states maintaining a dominant position over other nations (e.g., hegemonic stability). Security is not conceptualized as a state's end goal, the pursuit of which necessarily requires a tremendous sacrifice in human freedom, but rather as an ongoing process of minimizing obstacles and threats to the protection and promotion of human life and potential—it is conceived as a relative, not absolute, concept. True humanism recognizes that there has never been and never can be absolute security in human life. Any approach that assumes that conflict or threat can be completely eliminated is practically irrelevant as a basis for scholarship or policy. The pursuit of absolute national security through absolute weapons systems has exacted enormous, avoidable opportunity costs that detract from the enhancement of human security.

What is required for the enhancement of common security is a new form of politics empowered by a new conception of power. The realist conception of power as control and dominance is rejected. The resort to force as an expression of power is really an expression of powerlessness, an expression of peacemaking and peacekeeping incompetence. Instead, we embrace a softer, feminist conception of power as a positive, sharing, problem-solving "competence" for the establishment of a common security system.[64] Power is thus "defined more by the ability to do than by the possibility of forbidding."[65] Common security calls for a redefinition of social power as a way of guiding the new politics. At the same time, such redefinition of power as collective problem-solving competence opens up a more empowering way of "thinking globally but acting locally."

If Korean security is to be endowed with this wider meaning, it would seem appropriate to think about a strategy of multiple connections and linkages. If a more stable and peaceful order is to emerge in the Korean peninsula and East Asia, cooperative connections and linkages sensitive to the requirements of common security will have to be established in different but interrelated issue areas and at different system levels. What is required is *a synergistic intersystemic approach linking up all the progressive forces working in, around, and among three systems of intersecting politics in the world today*—the first system of territorial states and their supporting infrastructure of corporations, banks, and media; the second system of international organizations, including the United Nations and regional international organizations; and the third system of "the peoples of the world" acting individually and collectively through various critical social movements and NGOs.[66] Security should no longer be conceived as the exclusive preserve of the politician, the general, or even the international diplomat—let alone as the exclusive responsibility of the state. Common security by definition assumes extensive public participation of actors both within and across state boundaries. Such a multisystem approach could provide the desired popular pressure to keep the inter-Korean détente process alive and at the same time provide alternative backup systems to prevent the process from degenerating into an armed confrontation. Despite uncertain prospects, the TRADP underlines one way of establishing intersystemic functional cooperation involving social actors from all three systems. The synergistic intersystemic approach is premised upon the creative interplay of new understandings and new opportunities opening up in the first, second, and third systems in the post–Cold War setting. An appropriate common security response at one system level should facilitate positive reciprocal response at another. However, the greatest burden for normative initiatives for a common security system is to be found among critical social actors and movements in the third system both within and outside the Korean peninsula. Unlike for opposition parties and revolutionary movements of the twentieth century, the overriding objective of critical social movements today is not aimed at seizing state power but at transforming and reconstituting civil society.

The green peace movement represents a rare example of horizontal and vertical linkages with substantial impact on the first system. It not only rejects nuclear weapons but also offers an alternative conception of security that draws attention to the intricate interconnections among local, national, and international factors and that widens the meaning of security to include environmental as well as military threats. New Zealand's policy against nuclear ships is another potent reminder of what third-system actors can accomplish in changing the established policy of their government. In the wake of the two Koreas' entry into the world organization, the Citizens Coalition for Economic Justice in Seoul has been advancing claims that the defense budget should not only be drastically cut but also subject to thorough public scrutiny in the media.

The impact of most social movements on the second system varies from issue to issue. They have greatest influence in the UN's norm-making and standard-setting activities in the human rights and environmental fields and virtually no influence in the economic field. Still, the modest achievements of the United Nations in the field of arms control and disarmament came about largely through the normative initiative and pressure of nonstate peace activists. The proliferation of nuclear-free zones is suggestive of the manner in which diverse social actors are carrying out the local responsibility of global problems. "The entire nuclear-free-zone concept," as Elise Boulding has written, "which was embodied in successive treaties including the 1959 Antarctica Treaty, the 1967 Outer Space Treaty, the 1967 Treaty of Tlatlolco, and the 1971 Seabed Treaty was developed and lobbied through the international system by INGOs."[67]

To flesh out these possibilities in the post–Cold War Korean context, the critical social movements can accept common security as a point of departure for directly meeting the challenges of dealignment, demilitarization, development, and democratization. The lessons of the divided/allied polities of Germany, China, Vietnam, and Korea seem clear enough. International alliances promote the politics of fragmentation as well as conflict escalation. Despite the frenzied searching behavior to escape from the twin alliance dilemmas of abandonment and entrapment over the long Cold War years, both Koreas have forfeited in varying degrees and at different times substantial portions of their sovereignty in the security sphere for the sake of allied support. By rejecting the two-plus-four formula and by signing several historic accords in late 1991, both Koreas have taken a first dealigning step. A reunified allied procommunist Korea—or for that matter a reunified pro-Japan Korea—can be dismissed as being beyond the realm of possibility. A reunified allied pro-U.S. Korea, however, would be unacceptable to China and possibly to Russia. The most viable and acceptable option for Korean reunification is a dealigned, demilitarized, denuclearized, and democratizing Korea that refuses to be drawn into some new geopolitical alliance or maelstrom in the region.

The synergistic intersystemic approach is premised on the belief that no single perspective or monocausal paradigm can be more than partial.[68] All the antecedent conditions, processes, and mechanisms of peaceful system change suggested in the preceding discussion may not be very significant or sufficient separately; it is rather their dynamic interplay and confluence that expand the outer possibilities of enhancing common security in the Korean peninsula. For the first time since Korean liberation/division, it is now possible to speak of the correlative possibility of a new emerging world order becoming part of the Korean solution and of the new inter-Korean détente becoming part of the world-order solution. Herein lies the central challenge of linkage between Korea and the new world order. Of course, there is no assurance any of these conditions and processes can be realized. When all the conditions are fulfilled, however, the problem of a common security system might become moot. It is only in the spirit of a Manhattan (or rather Hiroshima) project for a working peace system that the synergistic intersystemic approach is suggested for an alternative way of securing a long peace in the Korean peninsula.

Notes

1. For a detailed if somewhat overly dramatized analysis of this point, see Peter Hayes, *Pacific Powderkeg: American Nuclear Dilemmas in Korea* (Lexington, MA: Lexington Books, 1991); quotation at p. xiv.

2. See Daniel Deudney and G. John Ikenberry, "Soviet Reform and the End of the Cold War: Explaining Large-Scale Historical Change," *Review of International Studies* 17 (Summer 1991); and James N. Rosenau, *Turbulence in World Politics: A Theory of Change and Continuity* (Princeton, NJ: Princeton University Press, 1990).

3. See Francis Fukuyama, "The End of History?" *National Interest*, No. 16 (Summer 1989), and *The End of History and the Last Man* (New York: Free Press, 1992).

4. Richard Falk and Samuel Kim, *An Approach to World Order Studies and the World System* (New York: Institute for World Order, 1982).

5. This section draws from my more detailed analysis of the subject. See Samuel S. Kim, "The Long Road to the Two Koreas' UN Membership," *Hogaku Semina* (Jurisprudential seminar) (Tokyo) 36:11, special issue on "The New Era of the United Nations: The First Step of Reform" (November 1991): 65–71.

6. UN Doc. S/PV. 3001 (August 8, 1991).

7. *North Korea News*, No. 610 (December 23, 1991), p. 5; No. 612 (January 6, 1992), p. 6.

8. *Yearbook of International Organization* 1989/90, Vol. 2, 7th ed. (Munich, New York, London, and Paris: K. G. Saur, 1989), Table 3.

9. Lo Ping and Lai Chi-king, "Secret Talks Between Chinese, Vietnamese Communist Parties and Between Chinese, Korean Communist Parties," *Cheng Ming* (Hong Kong), August 1, 1991, pp. 12–13, in *Foreign Broadcast Information Service: Daily Report, China* (hereafter cited as *FBIS-China*), August 1, 1991, pp. 1–2.

10. UN Doc. S/22642 (June 3, 1991), emphasis added.

11. UN Doc. S/21836 (October 2, 1990).

12. For the text of the declaration, see *New York Times,* February 1, 1992, p. 4.

13. For the text of Yon's speech, see UN Doc. A/46/PV 18 (October 9, 1991), pp. 61–78, quote at pp. 69–70.

14. Yon said: "Pursuing ideological and institutional confrontation … is a manifestation of an idea of encroachment to impose one's ideology and institutions upon the other. … [If] you attempt to 'prevail over communism' and 'absorb and annex the North,' … you will be condemned by our fellow countrymen." *Pyongyang Times,* October 26, 1991, p. 4.

15. Rhee Sang-Woo, "North Korea in 1991: Struggle to Save Chuch'e Amid Signs of Change," *Asian Survey* 32, 1 (January 1992): 57.

16. Nicholas Eberstadt and Judith Banister, "Military Buildup in the DPRK: Some New Indications from North Korean Data," *Asian Survey* 31, 11 (November 1991): 1099.

17. Japan's interest in the TRADP is passive and minimal, and South Korea's interest has greatly diminished in the wake of the August 1992 Seoul-Beijing normalization and the rise of the North Korean mischief on the nuclear issue. The original grandiose multilateral project is now being sliced into smaller bilateral and trilateral pieces. On March 19, 1993, China and North Korea signed a treaty on bilateral cooperation in developing the Tumen River basin that would allow China to use all the facilities at the Rajin port on the northeastern coast of North Korea. It is also reported that North Korea has been making desperate efforts to assure a measure of economic cooperation with China as the last remaining ally and patron. On May 9, 1993, China, Russia, and North Korea agreed to give long-term land leases to foreigners to attract investment for a proposed economic development zone on their borders. The next day, five of the original six—China, DPRK, ROK, Mongolia, and Russia—also reached agreement to establish a coordinating committee to harmonize activities of the riparian countries in the Tumen River delta and an international cooperative to attract investors from the public and private sectors.

18. In his maiden speech before the world audience immediately after North Korea's entry into the UN, Prime Minister Yon pronounced: "The most pressing issue involved in ensuring a durable peace in the world is to effect arms reduction and abolish nuclear weapons and other weapons of mass destruction. As a nation exposed to continual nuclear threat, the Korean people have put forward the abolition of nuclear weapons as an urgent demand related to our national destiny. The Government of the Democratic People's Republic of Korea regards the achievement of a comprehensive ban on nuclear testing within a short period of time as one of the most pressing tasks in the field of disarmament today. It will actively join the international community in its endeavors to prevent the testing and production of nuclear weapons, to reduce nuclear weapons and, eventually, to abolish all nuclear weapons." UN Doc. A/46/PV.18 (October 9, 1991), p. 66.

19. *Far Eastern Economic Review* (hereafter cited as *FEER*) September 26, 1991, p. 27.

20. I owe this multiple though somewhat modified reading of the East Asian geopolitical landscape to Richard Falk.

21. For a penetrating analysis of the four configurations of this strategic triangle, see Lowell Dittmer, *Sino-Soviet Normalization and Its International Implications, 1945–1990* (Seattle: University of Washington Press, 1991), chaps. 9–16, pp. 156–255; and "Mainland China's Position in the Pacific Strategic Balance: Looking Toward the Year 2000," *Issues and Studies* 28, 1 (January 1992): 1–17.

22. Kent Calder, "The North Pacific Triangle: Sources of Economic and Political Transformation," *Journal of Northeast Asian Studies* 8, 2 (Summer 1989): 3–17.

23. Hayes, *Pacific Powderkeg*, p. 181.

24. A two-day international conference on this theme held at Princeton University May 5–6, 1992, attracted important foreign policy players from Russia, Japan, and the United States.

25. For more on this point, see Samuel S. Kim, *China In and Out of the Changing World Order* (Princeton, NJ: Center of International Studies, Princeton University, 1991).

26. For the reconceptualization of national identity along this line, see Lowell Dittmer and Samuel S. Kim, "In Search of a Theory of National Identity," in Lowell Dittmer and Samuel S. Kim, eds., *China's Quest for National Identity* (Ithaca, NY: Cornell University Press, 1993), chap. 1, pp. 1–31.

27. For an excellent analysis of Japan's national identity along this line, see Masaru Tamamoto, "Japan's Uncertain Role," *World Policy Journal* 8, 4 (Fall 1991): 579–597.

28. Shim Jae Hoon and Mark Clifford, "South Korea," in *Japan in Asia* (Hong Kong: Review Publishing Co., 1991), p. 28.

29. Saburo Okita, "Asian-Pacific Prospects and Problems for the Further Development of the Asian-Pacific Cooperative Framework," paper presented at the symposium In Search of a New Order in Asia, Santa Barbara, CA, February 1–3, 1990, p. 2.

30. See Dick Nanto, *Pacific Rim Economic Cooperation* (Washington, DC: Congressional Research Service, April 3, 1989); and Walden Bello and Eric Blantz, "Perils and Possibilities: Carving Out an Alternative Order in the Pacific," *Alternatives* 17, 1 (Winter 1992): 1–22.

31. See Samuel S. Kim, "Superpower Cooperation in Northeast Asia," in Roger E. Kanet and Edward A. Kolodziej, eds., *The Cold War as Cooperation: Regional Patterns and Prospects* (London: Macmillan, 1991), pp. 367–401; "The United States Policy Toward Northeast Asia: The Gorbachev Challenge," *Korean Journal of International Relations* 30, 2 (1990): 371–400; and Selig S. Harrison, "A Chance for Détente in Korea," *World Policy Journal* 8, 4 (Fall 1991): 599–631.

32. Li Luye, "The Current Situation in Northeast Asia: A Chinese View," *Journal of Northeast Asian Studies* 10, 1 (Spring 1991): 78–81, quote at p. 80.

33. See Xinhua (New China News Agency), in *FBIS-China*, August 6, 1991, pp. 8–9.

34. See Alastair I. Johnston, "China and Arms Control in the Asia-Pacific Region," in Frank C. Langdon and Douglas A. Ross, eds., *Superpower Maritime Strategy in the Pacific* (London and New York: Routledge, 1990).

35. U.S. Department of Defense, *A Strategic Framework for the Asian Pacific Rim: Looking Toward the 21st Century* (Washington, DC: U.S. Government Printing Office, April 1990).

36. "Excerpts from Pentagon's Plan: 'Prevent the Re-emergence of a New Rival,'" *New York Times*, March 8, 1992, p. A14.

37. Admiral Larson's congressional testimony, quoted in Bello and Blantz, "Perils and Possibilities," p. 5.

38. See Robert Gilpin, *The Political Economy of International Relations* (Princeton, NJ: Princeton University Press, 1987), pp. 328–340; "The United States as a Debtor," in *The*

United States and Japan (Princeton, NJ: Center of International Studies, March 1988), pp. 1–15; and Masaru Tamamoto, "Japan's Search for a World Role," *World Policy Journal 7*, 3 (Summer 1990): 513.

39. "Asia's Arms Race," *The Economist*, February 20, 1993, pp. 19–22; quote at p. 19; and Michael T. Klare, "The Next Great Arms Race," *Foreign Affairs 72*, 3 (Summer 1993): 136–152.

40. See Tai Ming Cheung and Jonathan Friedland, "Asian Governments Resist Pressure to Cut Arms Budgets," *FEER*, November 7, 1991, pp. 52–53; *Asia 1992 Yearbook* (Hong Kong: Review Publishing Co., 1992), pp. 6–9.

41. International Institute for Strategic Studies, *The Military Balance 1991–1992* (London: Brassey's, 1991), pp. 150, 165.

42. Robert Gilpin, "The Economic Dimension of International Security," in Henry Bienen, ed., *Power, Economics, and Security* (Boulder, CO: Westview Press, 1992), pp. 51–68.

43. For a persuasive interpretation of Japan as a "reactive state," see Kent Calder, "Japanese Foreign Economic Policy Formation: Explaining the Reactive State," *World Politics 40*, 4 (July 1988): 517–541.

44. For the text of Shevardnadze's UN speech of September 28, 1988, see *FBIS–Soviet Union*, September 28, 1988, pp. 2–9.

45. See Richard A. Falk, Samuel S. Kim, and Saul H. Mendlovitz, eds., *The United Nations and a Just World Order* (Boulder, CO: Westview Press, 1991), pp. 166–177, 188–197, 542–545.

46. Mikhail Gorbachev, *Realities and Guarantees for a Secure World* (Moscow: Novosti Press Agency Publishing House, 1987), p. 16.

47. Young-shik Bae, "Soviet-South Korea Economic Cooperation Following Rapprochement," *Journal of Northeast Asian Studies 10*, 1 (Spring 1991): 26; and *Asia 1992 Yearbook*, p. 191.

48. Jia Hao and Zhuang Qubing, "China's Policy Toward the Korean Peninsula," *Asian Survey 32*, 12 (December 1992): 1140.

49. Hayes, *Pacific Powderkeg*, p. 180.

50. Charles Krauthammer, "The Unipolar Moment," *Foreign Affairs 70*, 1 (1991): 24.

51. Ibid., p. 33.

52. David E. Sanger, "Asian Countries, in Shift, Weigh Defense Forum," *New York Times*, May 23, 1993, p. 16.

53. Legitimation crisis, according to Habermas, "is directly an identity crisis." Jurgen Habermas, *Legitimation Crisis*, trans. Thomas McCarthy (Boston, MA: Beacon Press, 1973), p. 46. For my analysis of Korean politics applying the notion of "legitimation/identity crisis" in the Habermasian sense, see Samuel S. Kim, "Research on Korean Communism: Promise Versus Performance," *World Politics 32*, 2 (January 1980): 281–310, and "North Korea and the Non-Communist World: The Quest for National Identity," in Chong-Sik Lee and Se-He Yoo, eds., *North Korea in Transition* (Berkeley, CA: Institute of East Asian Studies, University of California, 1991), pp. 17–42.

54. *North Korea News*, No. 665 (January 11, 1993), p. 3, and Beijing Radio International in Korea, December 30, 1992, in *FBIS-China*, December 31, 1992, pp. 4–5.

55. World Bank, *World Development Report 1991: The Challenge of Development* (New York: Oxford University Press, 1991), pp. 12–13.

56. See *The Economist*, March 27, 1993, p. 35; Hong Yung Lee, "South Korea in 1991: Unprecedented Opportunity, Increasing Challenge," *Asian Survey 32*, 1 (January 1992): 64–73, and "South Korea in 1992: A Turning Point in Democratization," *Asian Survey 33*, 1 (January 1993): 32–42; *Korea Newsreview*, February 29, 1992, p. 12; and Andrew Pol-

lack, "After Stall, Koreans See Need for Economic Reform, Too," *New York Times,* December 15, 1992, pp. A1, A18.

57. *Korea Newsreview,* February 29, 1992, p. 12.

58. Alice Amsden, *Asia's Next Giant: South Korea and Late Industrialization* (New York: Oxford University Press, 1989); Walden Bello and Stephanie Rosenfeld, *Dragons in Distress: Asia's Miracle Economies in Crisis* (San Francisco, CA: A Food First Book, 1990); Frederic C. Deyo, ed., *The Political Economy of the New Asian Industrialism* (Ithaca, NY: Cornell University Press, 1987); Stephan Haggard, *Pathways from the Periphery: The Politics of Growth in the Newly Industrializing Countries* (Ithaca, NY: Cornell University Press, 1990); T. W. Kang, *Is Korea the Next Japan?* (New York: Free Press, 1989); Robert Wade, *Governing the Market: Economic Theory and the Role of Government in East Asian Industrialization* (Princeton, NJ: Princeton University Press, 1990) and "East Asia's Economic Success: Conflicting Perspectives, Partial Insights, Shaky Evidence," *World Politics* 44, 2 (January 1992): 270–320; and Jung-En Woo, *Race to the Swift: State and Finance in Korean Industrialization* (New York: Columbia University Press, 1991).

59. For a cover story on the subject, see *FEER,* March 26, 1992, pp. 54–61.

60. *Vantage Point* 16, 4 (April 1993): 19–21.

61. For the classical treatment of this line of analysis, see Inis L. Claude, Jr., *Power and International Relations* (New York: Random House, 1962).

62. For full discussion on the notion of common security, see Independent Commission on Disarmament and Security Issues, *Common Security: A Blueprint for Survival* (New York: Simon and Schuster, 1982); Burns H. Weston, ed., *Alternative Security* (Boulder, CO: Westview Press, 1990); and Michael T. Klare and Daniel C. Thomas, eds., *World Security: Trends and Challenges at Century's End* (New York: St. Martin's Press, 1991).

63. For elaboration of this point, see Samuel S. Kim, "Global Violence and a Just World Order," *Journal of Peace Research* 21, 2 (1984): 181–192.

64. For further discussion on such an alternative conception of power, see Berenice A. Carroll, "Peace Research: The Cult of Power," *Journal of Conflict Resolution* 16, 4 (December 1972): 585–616; and Samuel S. Kim, "In Search of Global Constitutionalism," in Richard Falk, Robert Johansen, and Samuel Kim, eds., *The Constitutional Foundations of World Peace* (Albany: State University of New York Press, 1993), chap. 4, pp. 57–83.

65. Carla Pasquinelli, "Power Without the State," *Telos,* No. 68 (Summer 1986): 82.

66. For the elaboration of such a three-system approach, see Richard Falk, Samuel S. Kim, and Saul H. Mendlovitz, eds., Vol. 1, *Toward a Just World Order* (Boulder, CO: Westview Press, 1982), pp. 1–10.

67. Elise Boulding, "Peace Learning," in Raimo Vayrynen, ed., *The Quest for Peace* (Beverly Hills, CA: Sage Publications, 1987), p. 327.

68. For illustrative purposes, an analogy of cancer to the war system may be helpful. Medical researchers have discovered more than 1,000 pathological agents (carcinogens) as definite or suspected causes of cancer not only in nuclear dump sites and cigarettes we smoke but also in the air we breathe, the water we drink, the food we eat, the clothes we wear, the drugs we take, and so on.

PART TWO

Major Powers and Korea

4

The United States and Korea: Dynamics of Changing Relations

Chae-Jin Lee

Ever since the end of World War II the United States has played a direct and important role in the management of Korean affairs. In 1945 the United States joined the Soviet Union in dividing the Korean peninsula along the thirty-eighth parallel and set up a military government in South Korea. After the failure of its prolonged reunification negotiations with the Soviet Union, the United States brought about the establishment of the Republic of Korea (South Korea) in 1948 as a rival to the Soviet-sponsored Democratic People's Republic of Korea (North Korea). Hence the two opposing Korean regimes developed a hostile relationship under the auspices of the two global superpowers.

During the Korean War, which broke out in 1950, the United States led the UN-mandated efforts to rescue South Korea from North Korea's armed conquest and thereby engaged China in a bloody and costly military confrontation. After the armistice agreements in 1953 left Korea again divided across the demilitarized zone (DMZ), the United States promptly embraced South Korea as a client state and continued to play a vital role in guaranteeing peace and stability in the Korean peninsula. As South Korea recovered from its war-torn and poverty-stricken situation, achieved rapid economic growth, and assumed an assertive diplomatic posture, the United States undertook a gradual process of structural change in its close relationship with South Korea. A transition from a hierarchical and unequal alliance to a new pattern of mature and complex interdependent partnership took place. This change has not been without difficulty, especially with respect to U.S. acceptance of South Korea's autonomous policy, but the United States now appears to recognize South Korea's increasing importance in determining the issue of Korea's reunification as well as the future of the Asian and Pacific region.

Meanwhile, in recent years the United States has taken a series of cautious steps to reduce its enmity toward North Korea and to pursue diplomatic and cultural contacts. Even though the United States has made no significant breakthrough in its estranged relations with North Korea, in the post–Cold War era it is prepared to explore the possibility of improving those ties.

Since the two Korean governments signed the agreement on reconciliation, nonaggression, and exchanges and cooperation (Appendix B) and the joint declaration for a nonnuclear peninsula (Appendix C) in the early 1990s, the United States has been challenged to reassess its policies toward South Korea and North Korea and to chart a new course of action in support of the peaceful reunification of Korea. In fact, the abrupt reunification of Germany suggests that the United States should be ready for a similar development in Korea. In view of the actual and potential transformation of U.S. policy toward Korea, it is useful to examine U.S. relations with both Koreas in diplomatic, economic, and military areas and to consider a range of policy options the United States is likely to face in the rest of the 1990s.

Diplomatic Relations

The United States has consistently supported and enhanced South Korea in its rivalry with North Korea in the international community. At the United Nations, the United States cosponsored a number of resolutions in favor of South Korea, maneuvered to reject the anti-Seoul campaign, and protected the United Nations Command and other UN operations involved in South Korea. Most important, the United States was instrumental in realizing the simultaneous admissions of South Korea and North Korea to the United Nations in 1991. Hence U.S. cooperation with South Korea in the United Nations and other international organizations was cemented.

Under the leadership of Presidents Ronald Reagan and George Bush, the United States effectively transcended a few thorny diplomatic problems, such as the Koreagate scandals and the violations of human rights that strained Washington-Seoul relations, and restored a generally cooperative and mutually beneficial diplomatic linkage between the two allies. In particular, Presidents Bush and Roh Tae Woo cultivated a warm rapport by holding several summit meetings and frequently consulted each other on a wide range of important issues. In February 1989 Bush assured Roh and other South Korean leaders in Seoul that the United States was "a faithful friend and a dependable ally" for South Korea and that "we work together in all things."[1] He also told the South Korean National Assembly that he was committed to support the mutual defense treaty and to maintain U.S. forces in South Korea. In order to clarify the U.S. position on Korea's reunification, Bush declared at the South Korean National Assembly in January 1992: "For 40 years, the people of Korea have prayed for an end to this unnatural division. For 40 years, you have kept alive the dream of one Korea. The winds of change are with us now. My friends, the day will come when this last wound of the Cold War struggle will heal. Korea will be whole again. For our part, I will repeat what I said here 3 years ago: The American people share your goal of peaceful reunification on terms acceptable to the Korean people. This is clear. This is simple. This is American policy."[2] His statement "Korea will be whole again" was reminiscent of the position taken by the United States in regard to the process of German unification: It was intended to dispel any suspicion in South Korea that the United States presented a major obstacle to the prospect of Korea's reunification.

The United States also endorsed South Korea's ambitious northern diplomacy (Nordpolitik) that was primarily designed to normalize its relations with the Soviet Union, China, and Eastern Europe but was also intended to ease its frozen confrontation with North Korea. President Roh explained in 1990 that because the road between Seoul and Pyongyang was totally blocked, "we have to choose an alternative route to the North Korean capital by way of Moscow and Beijing."[3] As the South Koreans made rapid progress in normalizing or expanding their diplomatic and economic relations with many socialist regimes, the United States had some trepidation about the speed and implications of their northern diplomacy, particularly about the prospect for South Korea's massive investments in and technology transfer to the Soviet Union. The United States probably was concerned that in contrast to the success of its northern diplomacy, South Korea might deemphasize the importance of its U.S. alliance. When the United States decided to support the sweeping reform measures taken first by Mikhail Gorbachev and then by Boris Yeltsin, however, it enthusiastically applauded the growing ties between Seoul and Moscow. In July 1991 President Bush clearly told President Roh that both countries shared an interest in seeing economic and political reform in the Soviet Union move forward.[4] More explicitly, Secretary of State James Baker stated: "Diplomatically, by effectively pursuing *nordpolitik*, the Republic of Korea is beginning to melt the last glacier of the Cold War. The establishment of full diplomatic relations with the Soviet Union, the exchange of trade offices with China, and ascension to the United Nations ... all clear the path for reducing tensions on the Korean Peninsula and ultimately for reunification—a goal that our two peoples shared for over 4 decades."[5]

In an attempt to buttress South Korea's northern diplomacy, the United States initiated a conciliatory posture toward North Korea. On October 31, 1988, the U.S. government authorized its diplomats to "hold substantive discussions with officials of the Democratic People's Republic of Korea in neutral settings" and to encourage "unofficial, non-governmental visits" from North Korea in academics, sports, culture, and other areas.[6] The United States expected that its initiative would increase mutual understanding between the two countries and would encourage those in North Korea who might advocate more open policies. This announcement was soon followed by formal talks between U.S. and North Korean political counselors at the International Club in Beijing. Those talks signified a change in the U.S. policy of diplomatic isolation against North Korea and provided an easily accessible diplomatic channel for the two governments to discuss all matters of mutual interest.

The Beijing talks were held more than twenty times in four years, and in that time the United States found the forum useful to explain its policy to North Korea, to reduce North Korea's misperceptions and miscalculations, and to present its requests and grievances to North Korea. Among other things, the U.S. side requested in Beijing that North Korea adopt tangible steps for improving its relations with South Korea, submit its nuclear facilities to full-scope inspections by the International Atomic Energy Agency (IAEA), account for about 8,200 U.S. soldiers listed as missing in action during the Korean War, and stop pursuing or supporting international terrorism. The United States also asked North Korea not to export ballistic missiles to the Middle East and to cease violations of its citizens' human rights. In the State Department's 1991 human rights report, North Korea was accused of denying its citizens the most fundamental human rights, persecuting religious activities, conducting a pervasive indoctrination program, and detaining about 150,000 political prisoners and their family members in maximum-security camps. The U.S. side indicated that if North Korea satisfied any aspects of the requests made in Beijing, the United States would take a positive step to improve bilateral relations. In order to deliver an "authoritative message" about U.S. positions that would reach North Korea's top leadership in "unfiltered form," Arnold Kanter (then undersecretary of state for political affairs) held a high-level meeting with Kim Yong-sun (secretary for international affairs of the Korean Workers' Party) in New York in January 1992. Kanter stated: "The U.S. is prepared to reciprocate positive DPRK behavior. We do see preliminary signs that North Korea has begun to make some of the decisions necessary to become a responsible international actor. We believe such behavior is in the best long-term interest of the DPRK and hope that Pyongyang takes timely action to prove us right."[7]

Indeed, the North Koreans considerably softened their anti-U.S. campaign and appreciated the Beijing talks and the Kanter-Kim meeting. They sought U.S. agreement to upgrade the Beijing talks to a regularized high-level diplomatic forum and to exchange liaison offices between the two countries. After the collapse of socialist regimes in Eastern Europe and the disintegration of the Soviet Union, Kim Il Sung evidently came to believe that as the only strategic superpower, the United States holds a key to the resolution of the Korean problems and is a potentially attractive partner for North Korea's economic and technological development. This is in sharp contrast with his continuing rhetoric that U.S. capitalism and imperialism are doomed. As a person who learned and practiced the balancing act between Moscow and Beijing, Kim has attempted to drive a wedge between the United States and South Korea and to create a sense of competition and balance between the United States and Japan. His southern diplomacy is intended to counter the success of South Korea's northern diplomacy. In his interview with *Washington Times* reporters in April 1992, he said he was ready to "bury the hatchet" and to welcome a U.S. embassy in Pyongyang "as quickly as possible." He stated: "If the statesmen who are responsible for the destiny of the United States amend their Korea policy farsightedly and in accordance with the trend of the present times toward independence, a smooth solution will be found to the question of improving Korea-U.S. relations. We hope that the United States will amend its Korea policy without hesitation, make a due contribution to the peaceful reunification of Korea and further join actively in the historic trend toward independence for the world."[8] The U.S. government, however, was not yet prepared to accommodate Kim's diplomatic overtures.

In the absence of bilateral diplomatic relations, North Korea has used the tactics of "people's diplomacy" in the United States. The North Koreans have sent a number of individuals to attend scholarly, artistic, and religious meetings in the United States and have invited to Pyongyang a variety of influential U.S. citizens ranging from Rep. Stephen Solarz (D–New York), Adm. Ronald Hays (former commander of U.S. forces in the Pacific), and Gen. Richard G. Stilwell (former commander of U.S. forces in South Korea) to Gaston Sigur (former assistant secretary of state for East Asian and Pacific affairs), Arthur Hummel (former ambassador to China), and the Rev. Billy Graham. In his luncheon meeting with Kim Il Sung in April 1992, Graham conveyed President Bush's "verbal message" to the host and discussed U.S.–North Korea relations.[9] The main objectives of North Korea's people's diplomacy are to demonstrate desire for reasonable, peaceful, and constructive relationships and to build up a popular support base for normalized relations between the two countries.

Economic Issues

Notwithstanding its new flexibility, apparent in preliminary diplomatic contacts and cultural exchanges, the United States has offered no basic change in its strict policy of economic sanctions against North Korea. The U.S. government continues to invoke the Foreign Assets Control Regulations (the Trading with the Enemy Act) and the Export Administration Act to prohibit almost all commercial and financial transactions with North Korea by individuals or firms subject to U.S. jurisdiction. U.S. citizens may not invest or use credit cards in North Korea but may spend money there for travel-related expenses. They may bring back to the United States no more than $100 worth of North Korean merchandise for personal use. Even though the U.S. government is not eager to enforce these legal provisions against individual travelers to North Korea, it prosecuted a company that had indirectly exported helicopters to North Korea. The United States allows exports or donations of humanitarian goods (medicine, clothing, foodstuffs) to North Korea, but a specific license from the Treasury Department is required. The Office of Foreign Assets is in charge of issuing licenses to U.S. travel agencies to arrange group tours to North Korea. A large number of Korean-Americans have traveled to North Korea to visit their separated family members.

The United States does not welcome North Korea's admission to international financial institutions such as the World Bank and the Asia Development Bank. Nor does the United States encourage North Korea's membership application to the General Agreement on Tariffs and Trade (GATT) or the Asia-Pacific Economic Cooperation (APEC). It is skeptical about the immediate prospect of North Korea's genuine economic reforms or multilateral development endeavors such as the Tumen River Development Project. In this sense the United States is much more cautious and conservative than South Korea, which is prepared to expand its fledgling economic contacts with

North Korea. The agreement on reconciliation, nonaggression, and exchanges and cooperation (Appendix B) stipulates that "both parties shall conduct economic exchanges and cooperation, including the joint development of resources, trade in goods as a kind of domestic commerce and joint investment in industrial projects." South Koreans tend to regard economic transactions with their northern counterparts as an important functional step toward Korea's peaceful reunification. The United States, however, refuses to recognize inter-Korean trade as "domestic commerce" entailing no tariffs and argues that the inter-Korean agreement violates the GATT provisions.

This disagreement between the United States and South Korea reflects a structural change in their bilateral economic relations. In the aftermath of the Korean War, massive U.S. economic assistance programs were indispensable to South Korea's survival and recovery. U.S. aid and advisers also played a role in supporting South Korea's ambitious economic development plans during the 1960s and 1970s. As a result, South Korea has successfully graduated as a major recipient of U.S. assistance and has compiled a remarkable record in economic development and foreign trade. South Korean gross national product (GNP) has grown at an average annual rate of 10 percent since the early 1960s. Per capita GNP increased from $88 in 1962 to $6,200 in 1990; its exports expanded from $50 million to $65 billion during the same period. The United States absorbs about 30 percent of South Korea's total exports. South Korea is the seventh-largest trading partner for the United States and the second-largest market for U.S. agricultural products. The United States no longer regards South Korea as an economic dependency but as an interdependent and competitive economic counterpart.

As their economic relations have become complex and competitive, the United States and South Korea have encountered a diverse array of disputes and conflicts. In the 1970s, the United States attempted to protect its domestic industries against inexpensive imports from South Korea. This protectionist policy stemmed from the collapse of U.S. hegemony in the world economy and the declining competitiveness of its industries in such important areas as textiles, steel, electrical appliances, automobiles, and electronics. The United States forced South Korea to accept the orderly marketing agreements (OMA) and the voluntary export restraints (VER) for limiting its penetration into U.S. markets.

When the United States accumulated an increasing deficit in its trade with South Korea in the 1980s ($9.6 billion in 1987 and $8.7 billion in 1988), it focused on the issues of fair trade and market access to South Korea. Equipped with a set of retaliatory legal devices such as Super Section 301 of the Omnibus Trade and Competitiveness Act (1988), the United States demanded that South Korea open its domestic markets to U.S. agricultural products (such as beef and tobacco) and service industries (such as banking, insurance, advertising, communications, and stock brokerage) and honor foreign intellectual property rights (copyright, patents, computer software, and the like). An increasing number of members of Congress threatened to impose a stiff protectionist legislative mandate against South Korea, Japan, Taiwan, and other major trading partners of the United States.

In his speech before the South Korean National Assembly in February 1989, President Bush profusely praised South Korea's economic progress as "an inspiration for developing countries throughout the world" and stated that "Korea has become an industrial power, a major trading power, and a first-class competitor." Yet he gently but unmistakably stated: "Korea's economy has benefited greatly from the free flow of trade. And yet today, in many countries, there is a call for greater protectionism. And I'm asking you to join the United States in rejecting these short-sighted pleas. Protectionism is fool's gold. Protectionism may seem to be the easy way out, but it is really the quickest way down. And nothing will stop the engine of Korea's economic growth faster than new barriers to international trade."[10] The Bush administration vigorously fought against the rising protectionist maneuvers in the U.S. Congress but was unhappy about the slow pace of market-opening and other liberalization measures taken by South Korea. Richard H. Solomon bluntly issued a thinly veiled warning in January 1991: "Americans are frustrated by what is seen as an anti-import campaign directed against foreign goods and services. Incidents of intimidation against U.S. exporters and their Korean partners can only further stimulate a protectionist mood in the United States. Economic issues between our countries urgently need a positive and constructive response; protectionism in Korea can only lead to pressure in the United States to restrict the access of Korean goods to the American market."[11] Solomon hoped that the robust economic ties between the United States and South Korea would continue to be a "fundamental pillar" of their relationship and would endure long after the confrontation between North Korea and South Korea is resolved.

In response to mounting U.S. pressure, the South Koreans have argued that their economy is still fragile with many "infant industries" and with high defense expenditures and heavily depends upon the imports of raw materials and crude oil. They point out that they have incurred large foreign debts and have suffered from a chronic trade deficit with Japan. They also suggest that in terms of growing anti-U.S. sentiment in South Korea, they cannot give the appearance of submitting to high-profiled U.S. pressure tactics. In his address before the U.S. Congress in October 1989, President Roh promised that South Korea would move toward "a more open, liberalized and self-regulating economy" and would achieve the same degree of market openness in the ensuing four or five years as found in the advanced industrialized countries.[12] In the case of agricultural imports from the United States, he asked for more time to avert political and social consequences among South Korean farmers. Roh subsequently took a series of steps to lower tariff and nontariff barriers against imports from the United States and to gradually accept U.S. service industries in South Korea. In her discussions with South Korean leaders in January 1992, Carla Hills (U.S. trade representative) expressed general satisfaction with the overall implementation of South Korea's trade liberalization, except in the area of agricultural products. The U.S. trade deficit with South Korea has drastically declined in the early 1990s.

The United States recognizes the importance of its bilateral partnership with South Korea in regard to multilateral economic issues. "As an emerging economic power," Bush said in early 1992, "Korea must now shoulder with other trading nations the burden of leadership on behalf of the multilateral trading regime."[13] More specifically, he elicited South Korea's active role in moving the Uruguay Round to a successful conclusion. Moreover, the United States greatly values South Korea as a strong pro-U.S. Asian country that promotes the APEC framework, which includes the United States, Canada, Australia, and New Zealand, and opposes a Malaysian proposal to exclude these four countries in an Asian trading bloc. Even if their bilateral trade disputes cannot be resolved easily to their mutual satisfaction, the United States shares a view with South Korea that their economic ties are bound to expand in the years ahead and that they need each other in managing the challenges of regional and global economic dynamics. The two countries also agree that the continuation of South Korea's economic prosperity is essential to promoting the interests of peace and cooperation in the Korean peninsula.

Military Containment

There is no doubt that South Korea's phenomenal economic achievements have been made in part because of the strong and effective security blanket provided by the United States. At the end of the Korean War, the United States signed a mutual defense treaty with South Korea as part of its worldwide military containment system against international communist threats. The treaty stipulated that the United States define an armed attack against South Korea as "dangerous to its own peace and safety" and act to meet the "common danger" in accordance with its constitutional processes. The United States also acquired the right to deploy its land, air, and sea forces on and around the territory of South Korea. The commander of U.S. forces in Korea, in his capacity as UN commander, was to continue his operational command authority over South Korean armed forces as agreed by President Syngman Rhee during the war.

After the war, the United States rapidly reduced the number of its troops deployed in South Korea from 302,000 in July 1953 to 60,000 in December 1955. In addition to its deterrent effect on North Korea, the continuing U.S. military presence in South Korea served a number of other purposes—to bolster U.S. political influence in South Korea, to protect South Korea's economic and diplomatic activities, to offer a training place for U.S. forces, and to demonstrate U.S. resolve in dealing with Cold War confrontations. Most important, the United States regarded its military position in the Korean peninsula as a pivotal buffer to protect Japan's security interests and to counterbalance the strategic ascendancy of the Soviet Union and China.

However, guided by the Nixon Doctrine, which was intended to remove the direct commitment of U.S. ground forces in Asia, Presidents Richard M. Nixon and Jimmy Carter decided to reduce U.S. military and financial burdens in South Korea and to gain a flexible strategic posture in the Asian and Pacific region. Although Nixon withdrew the Seventh Infantry Division from South Korea by March 1971, Carter found it difficult to withdraw all U.S. ground troops from South Korea over a period of four or five years primarily because he failed to convince his external allies (South Korea and Japan) and his domestic constituents that U.S. military disengagement from South Korea was acceptable at the time of the Cold War.

Unlike his predecessors, President Ronald Reagan, as a staunch Cold War warrior, decided not to reduce U.S. military forces in South Korea at all.[14] His eight-year presidency ushered in a stable and harmonious military relationship between the two allies. Upon his inauguration, President George Bush inherited his mentor's Korea policy and declared his position before the South Korean National Assembly in February 1989: "I am committed to maintaining American forces in Korea, and I am committed to support our mutual defense treaty. There are no plans to reduce U.S. forces in Korea. ... They will remain in the Republic of Korea as long as they are needed and as long as we believe it is in the interest of peace to keep them there."[15]

In spite of his categorical statement, however, Bush was compelled to modify his military policy toward Korea because of three major developments: the end of the Cold War, a significant change in inter-Korean relations, and the political and economic situation in the United States. In particular, a growing number of U.S. senators and representatives, irrespective of their party affiliations, exerted pressure upon Bush to scale down U.S. forces in South Korea. They argued that there be a "peace dividend" for the United States as a result of the passing of the Cold War and that taxpayers' money be saved by reducing U.S. military commitments abroad. They also contended that South Korea's successful Nordpolitik weakened the political basis of North Korea's military alliance with the Soviet Union and China and that South Korea could afford to defend itself because of its enormous economic and technological advantages over North Korea.

In response to mounting congressional pressure, the Bush administration issued an important report in April 1990 outlining the U.S. intention to retain its forward deployed forces, overseas bases, nuclear umbrella, and bilateral security arrangements in the Asian and Pacific region for the foreseeable future but to reduce incrementally the overall U.S. military presence in South Korea, Japan, and the Philippines.[16] More specifically, the report stated that "the Korean Peninsula will remain one of the world's potential military flashpoints." The United States defined its security objectives in South Korea as (1) deterring North Korean aggression or defeating it should deterrence fail, (2) reducing political and military tensions on the peninsula by encouraging North-South talks and the institution of a regime built on confidence-building measures (CBMs), and (3) transforming U.S. forces on the peninsula from a leading to a supporting role, including some force reductions. In the initial phase (from one to three years), the United States envisioned a modest force reduction of about 7,000 personnel (2,000 Air Force personnel and 5,000 ground force personnel) and promised to support "steady improvements" in South Korea's defense capabilities. For the second phase (from three to five years), the United States planned to adjust further its combat capability by assessing the North Korean threat, the state of inter-Korean relations, and the improvement of South Korea's military capabilities, and perhaps the United States would also restructure the Second Infantry Division. In the final phase (from five to ten years), fewer U.S. forces were projected to remain in South Korea because the South Koreans should be ready to take the lead role in their own defense by the year 2000.

After the United States successfully executed its military campaign in the Persian Gulf, President Bush told President Roh in July 1991 that "the United States remains today fully committed to protecting the peace and security of Korea—even as Korea assumes a leading role in its own defense."[17] The two leaders also agreed to make a concerted effort to prevent North Korea from developing nuclear weapons. In an attempt to dramatize U.S. concern about North Korea's nuclear weapons program, Secretary of Defense Dick Cheney announced in November 1991 that the United States would suspend the second phase of its military reduction plan in South Korea until North Korea submitted its nuclear facilities to full-scope safeguards inspections by the IAEA. In a speech to the South Korean National Assembly in January 1992, President Bush called on North Korea to demonstrate its sincerity to meet the obligations it undertook when it signed the nuclear nonproliferation treaty six years earlier.[18]

Although recognizing South Korea's leading role in its own defense, the United States does not wish to restructure drastically its basic containment policy toward North Korea because it assumes that despite his conciliatory southern diplomacy, Kim Il Sung has both the intention and the capability to initiate another Korean War. It also believes that he is irrational, unpredictable, and dangerous. This deep-seated belief is corroborated by a series of incidents North Korea has inflicted upon the United States, such as the seizure of the U.S.S. *Pueblo* and the downing of the naval reconnaissance plane EC-121. The United States rejects North Korea's proposals to change the armistice agreement to a bilateral peace treaty, to abrogate the U.S.–South Korean mutual defense treaty, and to completely withdraw U.S. forces from South Korea. As far as the settlement of inter-Korean military problems is concerned, the United States prefers to let South Korea assume a major responsibility but in close mutual consultation.

The United States agrees with South Korea that North Korea enjoys superiority over South Korea in a number of critical military categories such as ground troops, jet fighters, bombers, tanks, artillery, armored personnel carriers, attack submarines, amphibious craft, and commando forces. The two allies also conclude that North Korea poses a serious threat to South Korea by deploying its forces offensively near the DMZ and by developing nonconventional weapons of mass destruction and Scud-type missiles. In an attempt to counter the growing sentiment in the U.S. Congress that the United States should reduce its military presence in South Korea after the Cold War, Gen. Robert W. Riscassi (commander of U.S. forces in South Korea) argued before the Senate Armed Services Committee in March 1992: "As we emerge from the Cold War, it is critical that we not underestimate persisting regional tensions. Northeast Asia remains a divided region, full of emotional scars and distrust. Our military presence in Korea remains an irreplaceable investment, both for resolving the potentially volatile struggle within a divided Korea, and for sustaining peace and stability in one of the world's most dynamic and powerful regions."[19] Riscassi explained that North Korea has made an impressive increase in the speed, pace, and lethality of its offensive ground forces and that "the forward presence of the United States ground and air forces remains vital to counterbalancing North Korean strength."

In the long run, the United States hopes to see that the two Korean sides faithfully carry out all the commitments made in the joint declaration for a nonnuclear Korean peninsula as well as the agreement on reconciliation, nonaggression, and exchanges and cooperation. The United States contends that the Korean peninsula is the one place in East Asia where European-style confidence-building measures and arms-control agreements can be applied because heavily armed ground forces confront each other across a clearly demarcated land border.[20]

If North Korea can decisively address U.S. anxiety about its nuclear weapons program and ballistic missile exports to the Middle East, the United States is likely to reward North Korea by elevating the Beijing talks to a higher-level format, lifting economic sanctions against North Korea, or exchanging liaison offices between the two countries. The United States may also cancel the Team Spirit exercises and resume its plan for reducing U.S. forces in South Korea according to the 1990 report.[21] No matter what North Korea may do, however, the United States is not expected to overcome easily its deep-seated mistrust of Kim Il Sung's military intentions.

Conclusion

The preceding discussion suggests that since the Cold War system began to disintegrate, the United States has cautiously explored the possibilities of restructuring its overall policy toward Korea but has not yet articulated a clear long-term strategy toward the prospects of Korea's reunification. In spite of the inter-Korean agreements signed in December 1991, the United States appears to harbor a persistent doubt about Kim Il Sung's peaceful overtures and to take a relatively conservative attitude toward the future of relations between North Korea and South Korea. In light of the drastic changes taking place in the post–Cold War era, however, the United States faces the difficult task of seriously considering a range of possible policy options or scenarios in regard to Korean reunification: (1) the status quo, (2) the Vietnam model, (3) the German model, and (4) the model for gradual reunification.

The status-quo scenario envisions that despite the end of the Cold War in world politics, the United States continues to keep its strong pro-Seoul position intact and to pursue a policy of military containment, diplomatic nonrecognition, and economic sanctions toward Pyongyang. It assumes that the two Korean governments fail to implement the two bilateral agreements and that they sustain the old pattern of mutual mistrust and extreme tension in the Korean peninsula. Even if the United States offers some adjustments in its Korea policy, it may not assume a direct or active role in promoting Korea's peaceful reunification in the near future.

The United States is firmly determined to prevent North Korea from applying the Vietnam-type model of military action in South Korea. The Pentagon's "regionally focused national military strategy" spells out a precise and massive U.S. response to such a contingency in Korea even if North Korea has five to ten nuclear weapons deliverable by aircraft or missiles.[22] The United States has made it clear to all parties concerned that it will continue to uphold its treaty obligations for South Korea's defense. During his visit to Seoul in July 1993, President Bill Clinton stated that "The Korean peninsula remains a vital American interest. ... Our troops will stay here as long as the Korean people want and need us here."[23] He also warned that if North Korea makes nuclear weapons and uses them against South Korea, the United States would quickly and overwhelmingly retaliate so that North Korea would cease to exist. The United States may choose to take multilateral military action against North Korea's attack, as it did during the Korean and Gulf wars, but it is also conceivable that the United States will be ready to take a unilateral military approach in Korea, if necessary, so that it can demonstrate its preeminent strategic status in the post–Cold War international order. The Vietnam-type scenario is highly unlikely in Korea because both China and Russia are opposed to it and because South Korea has a formidable defensive capability.

It is more likely that the German-type scenario would take place and that South Korea would quickly absorb North Korea in a peaceful fashion. Just as President George Bush had done in January 1992, President Bill Clinton assured the South Korean National Assembly in July 1993 that the United States fully supports the goal of South Korea's peaceful reunification "on terms acceptable to the Korean people."[24] He added that "when the reunification comes, we will stand beside you in making the transition on the terms that you have outlined." There is an essential continuity in U.S. policy toward Korea's unification irrespective of a change in the U.S. presidency. However, some U.S. officials privately express concern that the German-type solution in Korea might impose too much of an economic burden upon the southern part of a unified Korea, create an element of instability in the Asian and Pacific region, or present a degree of uncertainty and risk to U.S. policy. Whereas the hard-liners in U.S. bureaucracies seem to favor the German model of quick absorption in Korea, the moderates tend to take a cautious approach. There is an influential view that the reunification process in Korea will prove far more tumultuous within the region than has German reunification in Europe.[25] If, however, the two Korean sides agree upon a process for a prompt, but peaceful reunification, the United States is not expected to veto the process.

If the two Korean governments can faithfully carry out both the letter and the spirit of the two bilateral agreements, especially the provision for an effective nuclear safeguards regime, and can solidify a system of mutual trust and peaceful cooperation, the United States is likely to resume its military withdrawal from South Korea in accordance with the 1990 plan, to modify the sharp edges of its containment policy toward North Korea, and to push for military confidence-building measures and arms control in the Korean peninsula. This scenario envisions that the United States will adopt a de jure two-Korea policy until the two Korean sides can work out a gradual process for peaceful reunification. Even though the South Korean government wishes to assume a primary role in dealing with the specific processes for Korea's reunification, the United States will promote a two-plus-four formula, in which the United States, China, Russia, and Japan may agree to endorse and guarantee the negotiated reintegration between North and South.[26]

It remains uncertain whether the United States is willing and able to pursue a role of assertive leadership or active mediation in transcending the stagnant status-quo scenario and in promoting the scenario for gradual and peaceful reunification in Korea. How the United States will determine and implement its option toward Korea will depend primarily upon the unfolding of inter-Korean relations and secondarily upon the direction of a new international order after the Cold War, especially the dynamic interactions among the United States, China, Russia, and Japan. Moreover, domestic political and economic factors in the United States are expected to play a more important role in shaping its policy toward Korea. Whatever options or scenarios the United States may ultimately choose or accommodate, it is likely to exercise more influence than any other foreign country in the management of Korean affairs throughout the 1990s.

Notes

1. George Bush, "Continuity and Change in U.S.-Korean Relations," *Current Policy* No. 1155 (1989).

2. George Bush, "The U.S. and Korea: Entering a New Age," *U.S. Department of State Dispatch*, January 13, 1992, pp. 23–25.

3. For the text, see Roh Tae Woo, *Korea: A Nation Transformed* (Elmsford, NY: Pergamon Press, 1990), pp. 47–49.

4. See "U.S.–South Korean Relations," *U.S. Department of State Dispatch*, July 8, 1991, pp. 484–485

5. For the text of Baker's speech, see ibid., pp. 485–486.

6. See the text of U.S. policy announcement in *Department of State Bulletin*, January 1989, p. 17.

7. Arnold Kanter, "North Korea, Nuclear Proliferation, and U.S. Policy: Collective Engagement in a New Era," testimony at the Subcommittee on East Asian and Pacific Affairs, Senate Foreign Relations Committee, February 6, 1992.

8. *Washington Times*, April 15, 1992.

9. *Rodong Sinmun*, April 3, 1992.

10. Bush, "Continuity and Change."

11. Richard H. Solomon, "The Last Glacier: The Korean Peninsula and the Post–Cold War Era," *U.S. Department of State Dispatch*, February 11, 1991, pp. 105–108.

12. Roh Tae Woo, *Korea*, pp. 11–17.

13. Bush, "The U.S. and Korea."

14. See the text of the Ronald Reagan–Chun Doo Hwan joint communiqué in *Department of State Bulletin*, March 1981, pp. 14–15.

15. Bush, "Continuity and Change."

16. See "A Strategic Framework for the Asian Pacific Rim: Looking Toward the Twenty-First Century," in U.S. Senate Armed Services Committee, *The President's Report on the U.S. Military Presence in East Asia* (Washington, DC: U.S. Government Printing Office, 1990).

17. "U.S.–South Korean Relations."

18. Bush, "The U.S. and Korea."

19. See "Briefing Remarks by Gen. Robert W. Riscassi" before the Senate Armed Services Committee, March 4, 1992.

20. Solomon, "The Last Glacier."

21. "A Strategic Framework."

22. See *New York Times*, February 17, 1992.

23. For President Clinton's statements and activities in Seoul, see *Los Angeles Times*, July 11, 1993, and *Korea Herald*, July 11, 1993.

24. See the text of his speech in *Los Angeles Times*, July 11, 1993, and *Korea Herald*, July 11, 1993.

25. See James A. Winnefeld, Jonathan D. Pollack, Kevin N. Lewis, Lynn D. Pullen, John Y. Schrader, and Michael D. Swaine, *A New Strategy and Fewer Forces: The Pacific Dimension—Executive Summary* (Santa Monica, CA: RAND, 1992), p. 13.

26. For the advocacy of a two-plus-four formula, see James Baker III, "America in Asia: Emerging Architecture for a Pacific Community," *Foreign Affairs* (Winter 1991-92), pp. 1–18.

5

The Soviet Union/Russia and Korea: Dynamics of "New Thinking"

Ilpyong J. Kim

The world has changed dramatically since the beginning of the Gorbachev era in the Soviet Union in March 1985. The Cold War ended after more than four decades of conflict between the United States and the Soviet Union, and the collapse of the Berlin Wall ushered in the reunification of the two Germanys. The East European nations achieved independence, abandoning the ideology of communism and severing the alliance relationship governed by the Warsaw Pact. The USSR disintegrated after seventy-three years of existence, and the Communist Party of the Soviet Union (CPSU) was disbanded after more than seven decades of control over the Soviet peoples and society. The fifteen republics of the USSR declared themselves independent, and the resulting Commonwealth of Independent States (CIS) has not achieved its original goal of bringing the republics together. However, the Russian Federation, under Boris Yeltsin, has emerged the great power of the CIS, with a population of 150 million people, a tremendous industrial base, vast natural resources, and a large share of Soviet military power.

Scholars of the Soviet Union and other communist systems will continue to analyze and evaluate the causes and consequences of the collapse of communism as an ideology and an economic system for many years to come. This chapter surveys only the development of Soviet–South Korean (ROK) relations under Gorbachev in the late 1980s, in the context of changing Soviet perceptions of and policy toward the Korean peninsula, and evaluates the foreign policy of the Russian Federation toward the reunification of the two Koreas in the 1990s.

Some of the issues dealt with here include the reasons that the Soviet Union reached the decision to establish diplomatic relations with the ROK in September 1990, despite North Korea's opposition, and the role of the Russian Federation in maintaining diplomatic and economic relations with both Koreas. For example, will it be possible for the Russian Federation, as one of the four major powers involved in Korean affairs, to make a significant contribution toward bringing about reunification? Did the Soviet Union normalize relations with South Korea because of economic reasons, as Kim Hak-joon asserted in his article,[1] or did the decision have something to do with the fundamental changes in Soviet foreign policy after adoption of the policy of "new thinking"?

From the Declaration of June 23, 1973, to Normalization

For the past half century, the northern problem, or unification, has been the primary issue of each ROK administration. From President Syngman Rhee of the First Republic in 1948 to President Roh Tae Woo of the Sixth Republic in the l980s, successive presidents have undertaken to approach the North in an effort to come to terms with unification peacefully. South Koreans yearn for the sense of security that such a resolution would bring. Their uneasiness over the division is caused by the harsh experience of the Korean War, which the North started for the purpose of reunification.

From the inception of the ROK government in 1948 to President Park Chung Hee's declaration of June 23, 1973, foreign and defense policies of the ROK had been subordinated to the Cold War policy of the United States, which was based on anticommunism and hostility toward the Soviet Union and its allies. In 1973 President Park declared that the ROK government was willing to approach communist nations such as the Soviet Union, China, and those in Eastern Europe regarding the establishment of diplomatic relations.[2] The declaration was the prelude to the "northern policy," or Nordpolitik, that President Roh announced on July 7, 1988.

The development of Soviet–South Korean relations had three phases: (1) the period from June 23, 1973, to 1988, during which the ROK government made a series of attempts to open up diplomatic relations with the Soviet bloc countries; (2) the period from 1988, when the Soviet bloc countries—except Cuba and Albania–decided to participate in the Seoul Olympic games, to 1990, when the USSR and South Korea normalized diplomatic relations; and (3) the post-1990 period. The ROK has now established diplomatic relations with every former Soviet bloc country except Cuba.[3]

Notwithstanding Nordpolitik, not much happened during the first phase of Soviet–South Korean relations in the 1970s and early 1980s because of the persisting Cold War and the rigidity of Soviet policy toward the Korean peninsula. However, the Soviet-U.S. détente and the Sino-U.S. rapprochement in the early 1970s brought about the North-South dialogue and negotiations that yielded the communiqué of July 4, 1972, and the declaration of June 23, 1973.

The North-South détente lasted a little over a year; tension escalated in subsequent years.

Despite the June 23 declaration, by which South Korea attempted to approach the Soviet Union and other communist countries in the 1970s, Soviet–South Korean rapprochement did not come about until the change in Soviet leadership from Leonid Brezhnev to Mikhail Gorbachev. Ever since the October 1917 revolution, the Bolsheviks had subscribed to the ideology of Marxism and Leninism, but it is unclear how much of Soviet foreign policy can be ascribed to ideology and how much to cold calculations of how to advance the interests of the Soviet state. Until Gorbachev initiated the policy of "new thinking" in the late 1980s, Soviet leaders insisted that their foreign policy was scientifically determined and that it sprang directly from the writings of Karl Marx and Vladimir Lenin.

Gorbachev developed a new concept of security, and in *Perestroika: New Thinking for Our Country and the World,* he wrote that "security can no longer be secured through military means. ... The only way to security is through political decisions and disarmament."[4] During the Gorbachev era of *perestroika* and *glasnost,* ideological rhetoric disappeared not only in domestic reform but also in the reformulation of foreign policy because of his pragmatism and realism. Gorbachev's "new thinking" brought a fundamental reorientation toward international affairs: The USSR would become a cooperative member of the international community. In a historic address to the General Assembly of the United Nations on December 7, 1988, Gorbachev said that in deideologizing the Soviets' relations with other states, "we are not abandoning our conviction, our philosophy, or our traditions, but neither do we have any intention to be hemmed in by our values."[5]

Soviet policy toward Asia in general and toward South Korea in particular had already shifted when Gorbachev presented a pragmatic economic development strategy for Siberia in an address in Vladivostok in July 1986, a year after he had succeeded Konstantin Chernenko as general secretary of the CPSU.[6] Gorbachev spoke there of improving relations with China and Japan and of having other nations participate in Siberian development projects. He committed to the withdrawal of Soviet troops from Sino-Soviet border areas and agreed to settle the territorial disputes along the main channel of the Amur River. He also called for regional cooperation in the areas of security and human rights in Asia consistent with the Helsinki accords. The Soviet approach to the Asia-Pacific region was becoming more pragmatic and increasingly conscious of economic considerations.

In a speech at Krasnoyarsk on September 16, 1988, Gorbachev made a seven-point proposal to strengthen the security of the Asia-Pacific region.[7] In the interim between these two speeches, Gorbachev was caught up in the politics of the making of Soviet foreign policy, specifically concerning Soviet policy toward rapprochement with South Korea. The turning point came in 1988, when the Soviet government decided its athletes would take part in the twenty-fourth Olympiad, which was to take place in Seoul in September. It would take another chapter to analyze the bureaucratic politics of Soviet policymaking, but a brief summary of the circumstances surrounding the decision is necessary to understand Soviet policy toward Korea.

George F. Kunadze, director of Japanese research in the Soviet Academy of Sciences (who later became deputy foreign minister of the Russian Federation) presented a paper in Seoul in June 1991 in which he explained that Soviet policymakers were divided into two camps: the conservatives and the reformers.[8] The traditional bureaucracy in the Foreign Ministry and the International Relations Department of the CPSU Central Committee were against participation in the Olympics because of the possible effects on Soviet relations with North Korea (DPRK). The important role North Korea played in the decisionmaking process of the Soviet bureaucracy was described by Kunadze:

> But as far as the conventional wisdom of the Soviet bureaucracy was concerned, both Soviet participation in the Seoul Olympics and a trade opening to the ROK were still subject to North Korean approval. Later thanks to the obstinate position of the DPRK, which absolutely refused to approve any Soviet contacts with Seoul whatsoever, this linkage was considerably softened. It happened simply out of necessity: the USSR was determined to take part in the Olympics, hence the Soviet government stopped its futile efforts to get North Korean approval, scaling them down to the search of some reasonable formula, to placate North Korea.[9]

A compromise solution to the stands of the conservatives and reformers on how to deal with North Korea had to be worked out because the conservatives supported the North Korean position, and the pragmatic reformers supported participating in the Olympics and the opening of trade relations with South Korea. "The final edition of this formula suggested that the DPRK was entitled to a certain compensation for not making an open scandal out of the Soviet athletes' voyage to Seoul," Kunadze recalled. "In this vein the Soviet government made a pledge not to establish official-level relations with the ROK."[10] "The most important thing is that at the moment of this pledge people in Moscow apparently meant to honor it," Kunadze stressed. "In other words, it was still considered sufficient enough to maintain just low-level private exchanges with the ROK. So once again the issues of the USSR-ROK relations appeared closed for a time being."[11] What were the reasons, then, that the Soviet policymakers decided to establish diplomatic relations with South Korea?

For several decades, Soviet policy toward Korea had been dominated by conservative Soviet experts on Korea who had been trained exclusively within the framework of the fraternal relations between the USSR and the DPRK. In their training many had learned to speak the Korean language, but they had also picked up prejudices against South Korea that retarded their grasp of the realities of South Korea. "Unfortunately, the general tendency in Soviet policy towards Korea as well as the Soviet Korean research was rather conservative, not to say negative." However, Soviet research on Korea began to take on a different character in the Gorbachev era, and the new thinking brought out "a few Soviet experts somehow miraculously successful in developing an adequate vision of the Korean problem."[12]

The Institute of International Economy and World Politics (IMEMO) emerged as the leading organization devoted to bringing about change in Soviet research on Korea and Soviet Korean policy. "As a government think tank responsible mainly for the study of industrially developed countries, the IMEMO had had almost nothing to do with Korea," Kunadze asserted. "That exempted us from the lunacy of the ideological stereotypes compiled by the other institutes, traditional contributors to the Soviet Korean policy." IMEMO was also "spared the brainwashing instructions from the department of the Central Committee of the CPSU which deals with the socialist countries." He concluded, "In short, a newcomer to Korean research, IMEMO ironically found itself adequately equipped for the job with common sense, a good portion of radical ideas, and last but not least a comparatively good understanding of the logic and dynamics of the South Korean state and society."[13]

IMEMO entered Korean policy research with a determination to make a significant contribution to the "traditionally stagnant field of Soviet diplomacy," Kunadze declared. However, its scholars had to hesitate before advocating prompt recognition of the ROK. "Instead we proposed a gradual opening to the ROK in the firm belief that Soviet interests would be better served by taking carefully measured steps forward, one at a time," Kunadze recalled. "We also developed a system of arguments to back this stance up." He explained why IMEMO proposed a gradual approach to the recognition of South Korea:

> Although we did not share an orthodox view of the DPRK as a fraternal communist country, we argued that by rushing things through we would be endangering a delicate balance of interests of too many actors, including China, the USA and North Korea. Frankly speaking, China was the first on the list of our priorities. Conventional logic suggested that by leaving North Korea no other choice but to retaliate, we would be inviting China to fill the vacuum left after the Soviet departure from Pyongyang. What is more, by doing so, we might have also expected a direct negative reaction on the part of China, with some unclear implications for Sino-Soviet relations.[14]

There were two more important arguments against recognition of the ROK advanced by the bureaucracy. The Soviet military presented a very simple geopolitical argument to the effect that "we should not abandon an alliance without adequate compensation," Kunadze said. "The size and form of the compensation in question was never determined, but nevertheless the argument was considered sound." The second argument was that the Soviet Union had limited tactical reserves. "Everybody agreed that by recognizing the ROK the USSR would not be gaining much in terms of diplomacy or strategy," Kunadze emphasized. "So the only argument in favor of this decision had to be economic benefits. Our choice appeared clear: diplomatic recognition in exchange for economic benefits."[15]

TABLE 5.1   Trade Between the Soviet Union and the ROK (US $1,000)

	1988	1989	1990	1991	Percent Increase 1991 over 1990
ROK exports to USSR	26,021	207,746	519,147	641,807	23.6
ROK imports from USSR	178,312	391,700	369,652	581,532	57.3

SOURCE: Pak Yong-bok, "A Study on the Details of South Korea's Trade with CIS," unpublished research report, Korean Trade Association (Seoul), n.d., p. 15.

The Economic Factor in USSR-Korean Relations

In 1988 Korean President Roh Tae Woo issued his July 7 "northern policy" (Nordpolitik) declaration in which he called for improvement in relations with the socialist countries in general and, more specifically, better relations with the Soviet Union and China, the two major powers of the communist bloc. That September, Gorbachev, in the Siberian city of Krasnoyarsk, acknowledged the possibility of expanded economic exchange with South Korea. Thus, economic relations between the Soviet Union and South Korea received significant boosts before the normalization of diplomatic relations in September 1990.

According to Kim Hak-Joon, the most astute observer and policy analyst of President Roh's office, the reason the Soviet Union set out to establish diplomatic relations with South Korea had much to do with the altered Soviet perception of Korean economic development and Roh's Nordpolitik.[16] After analyzing the contents of the articles and research papers written by such Soviet experts on East Asia as Oleg Davydov, Mikhail Kapitsa, Dimitry Petrov, Alexander Fedorovsky, V. Martinov, and George Kunadze, Kim concluded that "the Soviet Korean specialists proposed to start the economic cooperation with South Korea in the fields of light industry, the food processing industry, the pharmaceutical industry, the tourist industry, and trade. Moreover, they proposed to expand the scholarly exchange with South Korea in order to learn from the model of South Korean economic development."[17] The economic overtures were successful: Bilateral trade between the Soviet Union and South Korea grew enormously each year after 1986 and was projected to reach $9 billion by 1995. Trade data for selected years are shown in Table 5.1.

Gorbachev addressed the Supreme Soviet of the USSR after the third Soviet–South Korean summit in April 1991 and reported that during the ten months since the first summit in San Francisco in June 1990, rapprochement had moved along rapidly. "It will enhance the unification of Korea that the Korean people have hoped for," Gorbachev asserted. "In the process of unifying the two Koreas, the two governments should function as sovereign units and we are trying our best to provide an environment in which unification can take place." Gorbachev also reported on current and future economic and trade relations between the Soviet Union and South Korea, which was the subject of the summit on Cheju Island. President Roh agreed to provide South Korean credit of $3 billion to the Soviet Union. The two presidents had agreed the ROK would begin supplying consumer goods in May 1991 in order to relieve the shortage of consumer goods in the Soviet Union.[18] Gorbachev continued: "It has been promised that the commercial exchange of $1.5 billion this year [1991] and $10 billion in 1995 will be achieved. This is possible since our trade volume has increased 100% each year during the past four years. We have also agreed that investment, especially investment in the petroleum industry, should be increased. ... We have also discussed the construction of 48 industrial projects, which included exploration of the natural gas in Siberia and Far Eastern Russia."[19]

South Korea's overseas investment and markets with the Soviet Union and all East European countries expanded widely as the result of the ROK government's Nordpolitik of approaching the socialist states. Trade volume with the northern states increased by an average of 30 percent after the declaration of July 7, 1988. The volume of trade with the former socialist countries, $8.1 billion, helped Korea avoid an overall trade deficit. Although Korean investment in the Soviet Union and Eastern Europe and imports of natural resources from the region remained meager, indirect investment amounted to 367 projects, and the volume of induced resources reached $500 million as of November 1992, according to ROK government sources.[20]

The northern countries, including the former Soviet republics and the countries of Eastern Europe, have an enormous market potential: They account for 24 percent of the global area and 31 percent of the world population. Hence, South Korea's Nordpolitik not only helped those countries in their political and economic ordeals but also brought the Soviet Union into the Asia-Pacific region so that it could contribute to the region's peace and stability. South Korea's annual trade volume with the northern countries is projected to reach $26 billion by 1996 and rise to more than 14 percent of total volume by the year 2000. Thus, the Soviet Union and South Korea had a commonality of economic interests in establishing diplomatic relations.

From the perspective of Soviet policymakers, economic benefit was the priority consideration because South Korea was willing to provide a $3 billion loan for economic cooperation. However, the political consideration was an important element, as George Kunadze stressed. "The biggest motivation to recognize the ROK grew out of Soviet domestic politics."[21] In his report to the Supreme Soviet of the USSR about his visit to South Korea, Gorbachev asserted:

> We have to pay special attention to the experience of South Korea, which has overcome underdevelopment and reached the stage of industrial develoment within a short period of time. We all know that South Korea was a dictatorial country not too long ago. If the Soviet Union and South Korea can combine the potential power of each country for beneficial and future-oriented economic development, we can certainly establish a creative and efficient model of economic cooperation. ... The South Korean leader is preparing to help the Soviet Union to participate in the integration process of the Asian-Pacific economic community. President Roh has invited the Soviet Union to participate in the international body of the Asian-Pacific economic cooperation and in EXPO-93 which will take place in South Korea.[22]

From the South Korean perspective, implementation of the Nordpolitik resulted in the state visit of President Roh to Moscow December 13–17, 1990, the first such visit by the ROK head of state. It was reciprocated by Gorbachev's state visit April 19–20, 1991. The exchange of visits and the summits not only consolidated Soviet–South Korean relations but also enhanced the environment of peace and stability in East Asia and in the Korean peninsula. The improvement in Soviet–South Korean relations also influenced North Korea to open a dialogue with the South and convene meetings of the two Korean prime ministers. After six such meetings in Seoul and Pyongyang alternately, the two sides on December 13, 1991, reached an agreement on reconciliation, nonaggression, and exchanges and cooperation (Appendix B) that became effective February 19, 1992.[23]

The impact of Soviet–South Korean normalization on East Asia's new international order helped bring about the demise of the Yalta system and the diminishment of the Cold War in the region. When Gorbachev emerged as the new leader of the Soviet Union in March 1985 and implemented his policy of *perestroika* and *glasnost* in the late 1980s, a new international order was shaping up in Western Europe that ultimately brought the end of the Cold War there and the unification of the two Germanys. Still, the Cold War lingered in Northeast Asia, embodied in the conflict and hostility between the two Koreas. It was hoped the South-North agreement would inevitably reduce the tensions and bring on an atmosphere conducive to reunification.

After the dissolution of the USSR in December 1991, the CIS was created. It comprises nine independent republics, of which the Russian Federation is the largest. For a short period in early 1992, the Russian–South Korean relationship retrogressed because of uncertainty about the future. However, economic relations resumed after the state visit of Russian President Boris Yeltsin in November 1992 during which he presented twenty-three economic projects that the Russian Federation and South Korea could jointly develop. The proposed projects cover such fields as natural resources exploration, cooperation in science and technology, the construction of infrastructure such as roads and ports, and tourism. Yeltsin also asked for more active Korean investment to help the troubled Russian economy. He pledged further efforts to expand bilateral relations under the terms of the September 1990 establishment of diplomatic ties. The Russian Federation has now become heir to the treaty obligations of the former Soviet Union. It is interesting that Yeltsin spoke of selling military technology and equipment to South Korea and that President Roh was interested in the proposal.[24]

In the November 1992 ROK-Russia treaty (Appendix D), Presidents Roh and Yeltsin affirmed "their conviction that the development of friendly relations and cooperation between the two countries will contribute not only to their mutual benefit but also to the peace, security and prosperity of the Asian and Pacific region and throughout the world." The leaders thus underscored their commitment to the purposes and principles of the charter of the United Nations. They also recognized that "the Moscow Declaration of 14 December 1990 shall continue to govern relations between the two countries." The declaration was incorporated into the treaty between the Russian Federation and the ROK.[25] The text of the treaty and its fifteen articles is similar to what Gorbachev and Roh signed when diplomatic relations were established in June 1990.

The North Korean Factor in Russian Policy

When Yeltsin met South Korean Foreign Minister Lee Sang-Ock in July 1992 to discuss his planned visit to Seoul four months later, he said, "Kim Il Sung will be awfully jealous when I visit Seoul."[26] The Russian also declared that the ideological bonds between Moscow and Pyongyang no longer existed. It is clear that North Korea does not figure importantly in the foreign policy calculations of the Russian Federation.

The Soviet Union was first among the nations that recognized the DPRK when it was founded in September 1948, and Joseph Stalin placed Kim Il Sung in a leadership position. The Soviets gave the DPRK economic and military assistance, and during the Korean War (1950–1953) Stalin supported North Korea's effort to unify the country by military means. In the post–Korean War period, 1954 to 1960, the Soviet Union provided grants and credits totaling 1.3 billion rubles. (North Korea still owes 2.2 billion rubles to the former Soviet Union.) The Soviets also dispatched 6,000 technicians and experts to help rebuild the North Korean economy, and more than 20,000 students from North Korea were trained in various institutions of higher education in the Soviet Union in the 1950s and 1960s. The former Soviet Union was the source of 60 percent of North Korea's electric power; 33 percent of its iron and steel; 60 percent of its petrochemical products; and 40 percent of its textile goods.

The Soviets continued to support Kim Il Sung in the 1960s and 1970s despite North Korea's standing apart from Sino-Soviet disputes regarding influence in the Pyongyang government. After the death of Stalin and the de-Stalinization initiated by Nikita Khrushchev in 1956, however, Kim Il Sung had to face up to factional struggle in North Korean politics. By using Stalin's tactics of setting one faction against another, he was able first to purge the pro-Soviet faction and then to eliminate the Chinese faction, thereby instituting his own *Juche* (self-identity) ideology. According to a former deputy minister of internal affairs in the North Korean government who was exiled to the Soviet Union, *Juche* ideology "has nothing to do with the ideology of Marxism or Leninism; it is Kim's own ideology based on Korean tradition and his own cult of personality."[27] Thus, the ideological bond between the Soviet Union and North Korea had disappeared long before the Russian leader Yeltsin declared it dead in 1992.

The policies of *perestroika* and *glasnost* of the former Soviet Union changed fundamentally the Soviet–North Korean relationship. Under Gorbachev's "new thinking," Soviet policy toward the Asia-Pacific region in general and more specifically toward the Korean peninsula took on a new coloration. The strategic interest of the Soviet Union during the Cold War years became economic interests during the Gorbachev era (1985–1991). North Korea was important to the Soviets when it served their strategic interests, but it is now South Korea that is important to the Russians because it serves their economic interests. In consequence, Soviet–North Korean relations were downgraded when diplomatic relations between the Soviet Union and South Korea were established in September 1990.

As early as 1988, when the Soviet Union decided to participate in the Seoul Olympic games, North Korea's response was somewhat ambivalent about the new Soviet approach. The Soviets promised not to open diplomatic relations with the South and to continue economic and military aid to the North. However, when Hungary established diplomatic relations with South Korea in 1989, the spokesman for North Korea's Foreign Ministry charged that the way Hungarian officials handled the matter constituted a betrayal and an unjustifiable act for which they should take full responsibility. The attack indicated North Korea's sense that Eastern Europe and the Soviet Union were double-crossing an erstwhile ally.

The Soviet media began to take a more realistic and pragmatic approach to the Korean problem, as signaled by the suggestion in September 1989 by *Izvestia*, the government newspaper, that Soviet–South Korean normalization of relations be initiated by recognizing the existence of two independent states in the Korean peninsula. On January 8, 1990, *Pravda*, an organ of the Central Committee of the CPSU, called for normalization. These recommendations were followed by the official statement of Foreign Minister Eduard Shevardnadze after the U.S.-Soviet foreign ministers conference on February 14, 1990, that "The Soviet Union supported the reduction of tensions in the Korean peninsula and the North-South Korea dialogue in which the Soviet Union is willing to serve as a mediator."[28] Thus, the Soviet role in the resolution of the Korean question was being perceived as that of mediator between the two sides rather than as ally of North Korea.

In the early months of 1990, the Soviet press and Moscow radio began to criticize the dictatorship and isolation of North Korea. It was reported that more than 8,800 students and technicians, including 500 students in China, were called back to North Korea for ideological reorientation. A weekly magazine of the reformist group, *Issues and Facts*, on April 1, 1990, speculated that if North Korea opposed reform and an opening to the outside world, it might face the fate of Romanian President Nicolae Ceauşescu and his wife: death by execution. The Soviet media were laying the groundwork for the Soviet–South Korean summit meeting, which took place in June 1990 in San Francisco and led to the Soviet–South Korean normalization of relations on September 30, 1990.

The North Korean responses to the Soviet–South Korean rapprochement were not as critical as they had been regarding the East European normalization with South Korea. The North Korean party newspaper, *Rodong Sinmun*, carried a commentary on April 4, 1990, stressing that "the Soviet–South Korean normalization of diplomatic relations cannot be tolerated because it perpetuates the division of Korea." The same newspaper emphasized on June 6, 1990, that the summit in San Francisco was nothing but "a plot to divide Korea into two halves by the splitists"—they would never be forgiven. In responding to the official announcement of normalization, *Rodong Sinmun* on

October 5, 1990, described "the establishment of Soviet–South Korean relations [as] an act of betrayal" that North Koreans found shocking.

When the Soviet Union established diplomatic relations with South Korea, it did not sever its relations with North Korea. The treaty of friendship and mutual assistance that had been concluded in July 1961 was automatically renewed in July 1991 for ten more years. Although relations with the DPRK declined for two or three years as a result of Soviet–South Korean normalization, the Russian Federation is planning to renegotiate the 1961 treaty. Yeltsin said in Seoul in November 1992 that Moscow would consider repealing an article in the treaty that provided for the automatic intervention of Russia in the event of a war involving either North Korea or Russia.[29] Thus, Russian policy in Korea is oriented toward peace and stability in East Asia rather than toward military conflict, the characteristic of Soviet policy in the Cold War era.

Conclusion

During the Cold War, Soviet foreign policy was preoccupied with Western Europe and the United States. The policy regarding East Asia in general and more specifically the Korean peninsula was subordinated to the strategic interest of the Soviet Union. However, "that was then and this is now." The Russian Federation, the preeminent republic of the successor CIS, is likely itself to become a major power if not a superpower. Its policy focus is shifting from Europe to the Asian Pacific because "it has become quite clear that the world community is entering a new Pacific era and the Asia-Pacific region is growing into a new center of world civilization," as one Russian expert on Asia declared. In addition, "relations with the Korean states carry a special meaning for Russia because of a century-old community living now in Russia and the strategic importance of the Korean peninsula."[30]

The convergence of Soviet interest in economic benefits and South Korean interest in normalization of relations with the Soviet Union under Nordpolitik resulted in the establishment of diplomatic relations between the two countries. Their 1961 treaty of friendship and mutual assistance is intact and has been renewed to the year 2001. The realities of the international scene are not reflected in the treaty, especially the military clause. Hence, the Russians expect to renegotiate it to correspond to the new realities of Russian–North Korean relations.

In bilateral relations with Pyongyang, the Russian interest would be best served if Russia can help the two Koreas to conduct discussions aimed at reducing tensions and fostering stability and peace in the peninsula. "It is in the Russian national interest," Gennady Chufrin, deputy director of the Russian Institute of Oriental Studies, asserted, "to promote the unification process even though the unification of Korea is first of all and above all an internal affair of the Korean people." Further, according to his perception, a unified Korea "may contribute positively to the state of international relations because Korea is to become a natural ally of Russia in opposing the revival of Japanese militarism."[31] Such a revival would not only unify the two Koreas but also contribute to the convergence of the strategic interests of the Russians, Koreans, and Chinese.

Russia would be best served if it continues to coordinate its policies with the two Korean governments and also cooperates with them in promoting regional security in Asia and the Pacific. One of the foreign policy issues on which Russians and North Koreans may see eye to eye is a special economic zone in Northeast Asia in which Russian natural resources, North Korean labor, and South Korean capital and technology could be brought together to make a significant contribution to the economy of the region. Such a development would include exploration of Russia's Far East and development of the Pacific Rim and the Tumen River basin, where the vital interests of Russia, China, Japan, and the two Koreas would converge. The development of the basin, which borders on Russia, China, and North Korea, under the auspices of the United Nations could serve as a model for future cooperation by the potential beneficiaries.

Notes

1. Kim Hak-Joon, "South Korean–Soviet Détente and South-North Korean Relations," in *The Korean Peninsula and International Politics in Transition* (Seoul: Publication Committee of Essays for the Commemoration of Kim Ilpyong's Sixtieth Birthday, 1991), pp. 3–19.

2. Ilpyong J. Kim, "Policies Toward China and the Soviet Union," in Youngnok Koo and Sung-joo Han, eds., *The Foreign Policy of the Republic of Korea* (New York: Columbia University Press, 1985), pp. 198–218.

3. Ilpyong J. Kim, "The Normalization of Chinese–South Korean Diplomatic Relations," *Korea and World Affairs* 16, 3 (Fall 1992): 483–492.

4. Mikhail S. Gorbachev, *Perestroika: New Thinking for Our Country and the World* (New York: Harper and Row, 1987), p. 69.

5. For Gorbachev's speech to the United Nations General Assembly on December 7, 1988, see *New York Times*, December 8, 1988.

6. Mikhail S. Gorbachev, "The Soviet Role in Asia" (speech in Vladivostok, July 29, 1986), *Current Digest of the Soviet Press* 38 (August 27, 1986).

7. For Gorbachev's speech in Krasnoyarsk, "Asian Policy," see *Current Digest of the Soviet Press* 40 (October 19, 1988).

8. George F. Kunadze, "USSR-ROK: Agenda for the Future," in *ROK-USSR Cooperation in a New International Environment* (Seoul: Institute of Foreign Affairs and National Security, 1991), pp. 81–94.

9. Ibid., p. 82.

10. Ibid.

11. Ibid., p. 83.

12. Ibid.

13. Ibid.

14. Ibid., p. 84.

15. Ibid. (emphasis added).

16. Kim Hak-Joon, "South Korean–Soviet Détente."

17. Ibid., p. 15.

18. For Gorbachev's statement, see *Pravda*, April 27, 1991.

19. Ibid.

20. *Korea Times*, November 25, 1992.

21. Kunadze, "USSR-ROK," p. 86.

22. For Gorbachev's speech, see *Pravda,* November 22, 1991.

23. For the text of the basic agreement, see *Intra-Korean Agreements* (Seoul: National Unification Board, 1992).

24. See "Yeltsin's Visit Enhances Seoul-Moscow Ties," *Korea Newsreview,* November 28, 1992.

25. For the text of the treaty on basic relations," see *Korea Times,* November 20, 1992.

26. *Korea Newsreview,* November 28, 1992.

27. For Kang Sang Ho's interviews with the Russian magazine *Ogoneok* (Children), No. 1 (1991), see "Ivan Ipanashivech Changes Occupation," in *Source Materials on Soviet Relations with the Korean Peninsula, 1986–1991* (Seoul: Sejong Institute, 1991), pp. 219–238.

28. Ibid., pp. 78–79.

29. *Korea Newsreview,* November 28, 1992.

30. Gennady Chufrin, "Russian Policy Towards the DPRK: Goals and Uncertainties," paper presented to the International Conference on Four Major Powers' Policies Towards the DPRK, September 30, 1992, Seoul.

31. Ibid.

6

China and the Two Koreas:
New Emerging Triangle

Hong Yung Lee

On August 24, 1992, the Republic of Korea and the People's Republic of China formally established diplomatic relations with a terse joint communiqué. This historic breakthrough in bilateral relations was followed by President Roh Tae Woo's visit to Beijing, where he was received with all protocols reserved for a foreign head of state. It has been almost a half century since the two newly established Korean states fought a bloody war (from 1950 to 1953). The 1992 normalization laid down an important cornerstone for regional peace, but its implications for Korean unification are uncertain. In the communiqué, the Republic of Korea acknowledged the People's Republic of China as the sole legitimate government of all China and promised to respect the PRC's position that there is only one China and that Taiwan is a part of China. Instead of mentioning the existence of two Korean states, the Chinese promised to respect the Korean people's desire for early unification of the Korean peninsula through peaceful means and to support the peaceful unification of Korea by Korean people.[1] In short, Korea pledged to "one China," whereas, by omission, the PRC implied a de facto two-Korea position. The rapprochement thus hinted a possible emergence of a triangular relationship, with the PRC in the best position to exert influence on both Koreas.

Korea has had a long and close relationship with China, even though this small country on the periphery of China has often been regarded by the latter over the past 2,000 years as an important tributary country. Frequently comparing the Korean peninsula to a "lip" protecting China's "teeth," the rulers of the great Asian continental power have tended to regard any foreign influence in the peninsula as a security threat, sometimes invading the region to enforce submission from Korean rulers and other times rendering military assistance to the Korean court to repel incursions from powers outside. In modern times, China's fate has been closely tied with that of Korea. For instance, China's defeat in the 1895 Sino-Japanese war paved the way for foreign powers to "slice the Chinese melon" and reduce China to a semicolony. After colonizing the Korean peninsula, Japan encroached upon Manchuria, from which it then initiated a full-scale invasion into China's heart that eventually led to World War II.

Chinese domestic political development also had profound implications on the Korean peninsula. For instance, the communist victory over the Nationalists in 1949 helped make it possible for the Kim Il Sung regime to survive as an independent political entity in the northern part of the peninsula. When UN forces approached the Yalu River during the Korean War, Mao decided to intervene despite enormous risks for his newly established regime.[2] China paid a high cost for its intervention on behalf of North Korea. Because of the frontal clash with the United States in the conflict, Beijing lost an opportunity to "liberate Taiwan" and acquired number-one status on the U.S. enemy list. Subjected to maximum pressure from the United States, China had to rely on the Soviet Union to strengthen its national security. When Khrushchev neglected to pay attention to China's interests—he knew China had no other nation to rely on except the Soviet Union—Mao challenged him in the Sino-Soviet dispute. Worried about the possible collaboration of Washington and Moscow against him, Mao made the historic decision to invite President Nixon to Beijing in 1972. Thus was created a strategic triangle among Washington, Beijing, and Moscow.

The end of Cold War bipolarity resulting from the collapse of the socialist regimes in Eastern Europe and the former Soviet Union has had profound implications for the way each nation conducts its international affairs. These fundamental changes in the international system have facilitated a shift of focus in international politics from military security to economic issues. These transformations have increased the opportunities for cooperation and reduced the danger of large-scale military conflicts. They have further blurred the boundary between internal and external politics, making it easier for such external factors as the world market to influence a nation's domestic politics or for domestic special interest groups to intervene more forcefully in the making of state foreign policy.

These new trends in international politics turn out to be a blessing for South Korea because its sustained efforts to develop its national economy enable it to exploit its economic resources in the interests of its foreign policy goals. In the case of China, these external changes took place after the post-Mao leadership had initiated sweeping reforms, redirecting the regime's primary goal from revolutionary change to economic development. The new goal required that China restructure its command economy and open itself to the outside world to acquire technology, capital, and trade. This trend in domestic policies made it easier for China to adjust its external policy after the end of the Cold War. Even the Democratic People's Republic of Korea, although unprepared for these drastic changes in contemporary world politics and having suffered economic decline as its trade partners in the communist camp collapsed, appears to be taking the first steps toward redefining its foreign policy objectives in light of the changed international environment.

North Korea and China

North Korea and China have been important allies to each other—they built a comradeship tested on the battlefield during the Cold War era—although their relationship has soured from time to time. For instance, Chinese criticism of Kim Il Sung as a revisionist strained Beijing-Pyongyang relations during the initial stage of the Cultural Revolution of 1966–1968. However, as Sino-Soviet relations deteriorated into open hostility, North Korea's strategic value to China increased proportionally. In turn, North Korea skillfully exploited the Sino-Soviet conflict to preserve its autonomy and to obtain maximum concessions from both the Soviet Union and China. Unable to compete with the Soviet Union in providing sophisticated weapons and economic aid to Pyongyang, China compensated for these weaknesses with stronger political support to the North Korean rulers and their official position on the Korean question, which can be summarized as a "one-Korea" policy. This does not mean that Beijing and Pyongyang did not diverge on some issues. For instance, North Korea undoubtedly did not appreciate it when China played the "U.S. card" against the Soviet Union in the late 1970s and the early 1980s. Nonetheless, after normalizing its diplomatic relations with Washington and Japan, Beijing tried subtly but unsuccessfully to help North Korea open a high-level dialogue with Washington and Tokyo.

Even after the end of the Cold War, the two countries continue to share many common interests on such matters as defense of a broadly defined socialism, safeguards of national security, and promotion of economic development. Despite the collapse of socialist regimes in other parts of the world, China and North Korea continue to claim to be socialist countries committed to socialist values, although the relevance of these values to internal politics, economic structure, and foreign policy behavior has been diminishing. North Korea publicly endorsed Beijing's suppression of the incipient democratic movement in spring 1989.[3] China and North Korea, however, no longer justify their socialist systems in terms of the universal validity of Marxism and Leninism. Instead, their justification tends to be defensive, apologetic, and muted, with the point stressed that the ideology is suitable to the two countries' presumably unique and specific conditions.[4]

The two countries also hold similar perceptions of the post–Cold War international situation. Both accept the end of the bipolarity that was based on the ideological division between capitalist and socialist camps, and these changes may be "beneficial to maintaining world peace and promoting economic and social development." However, they are not very optimistic because "the world is not stable, and economic competition is intensifying." The two nations share similar concerns about the U.S. policy of "beyond containment" aimed at "peaceful evolution" of their internal systems; in their view, the policy amounts to a continuation of the Cold War era.[5] The two also hope that rising nationalism and increasing economic power of other developing countries will act as a counterbalance to continuing U.S. military hegemony.

Despite their shared interests in the ideological and security arenas, Beijing and Pyongyang may nonetheless diverge on the issues of the unification of the Korean peninsula or the importance of the military threat to North Korea's national security. Even if Pyongyang were to deem that the use of military force to resolve the reunification issue a feasible option, that strategy is unacceptable to China because such a move would disrupt stability and peace in Northeast Asia and thus threaten the success of China's modernization programs. Therefore, China has tended to portray North Korea as a weaker party compelled to respond to South Korea's military buildup, and when it concedes that North Korea's military capability is superior to that of South Korea, it stresses that Pyongyang has neither offensive capability nor aggressive intention.[6]

There is no way of knowing whether North Korea has the technical capability and political will to manufacture nuclear weapons. On the one hand, it is possible that Kim Il Sung, concerned about the increasingly unfavorable military balance between the two Koreas, may attempt to produce nuclear weapons as deterrent against the South. But the potential cost for this option is high and contains a significant element of risk. On the other hand, Kim may see the nuclear issue as a bargaining chip and seek to exploit it to draw international attention to the Korean problem. Whatever North Korea's long-term calculations might be, it is unlikely that Kim Il Sung has made a final commitment to produce a nuclear bomb. However, it is possible that North Korea is committed to achieving a nuclear capability in terms of materials and technical know-how pending a final decision based upon later assessment of its security needs.

Whatever may be North Korea's real intention on nuclear weapons, a nuclear North Korea is no more acceptable to China than to South Korea and the United States. Yet so far Beijing has shown reluctance to bring public pressure on Pyongyang to renounce its nuclear program. Initially, Beijing insisted that it "was not clear about the scope of North Korea's nuclear development program." At the same time, the Chinese government has publicly stated that it does not want to see "any nuclear weapons on the Korean peninsula" and expressed hope that "all related parties will resolve that problem through negotiations for the goal of making the Korean peninsula a nuclear-free zone."[7] There also have been unconfirmed reports that Beijing refused North Korea's requests to aid its nuclear development program. In short, Beijing seems to be pursuing a cautious and skillful policy to defuse the North Korean nuclear issue. On the one hand, it pledges to guarantee North Korea's territorial integrity even as it underscores the North's military vulnerability and economic weakness and encourages other nations to adopt a moderate policy that will induce North Korea to open itself to the outside world. On the other hand, it publicly warns that North Korea should end its diplomatic isolation and reform its economic structure to achieve economic growth.

For Beijing, the Sino–North Korean economic relationship is evolving from one of mutual benefit to one of burden as China's international trade volume increases, its trade network diversifies, and North Korea's economy deteriorates.[8] Until recently, China and North Korea conducted trade by official agreement. Consequently, the trade volume stayed at a certain level a few years and then increased to the next level of volume for a few years.

After the Korean War cease-fire, the volume of Sino-North Korean trade expanded rapidly. North Korea proved to be an important trade partner when China was internationally isolated because of its radical internal politics. For instance, Sino-North Korean trade as a proportion of China's total trade volume reached its peak (5.19 percent) in 1963 when China's total trade fell because of the Great Leap Forward. During the Cultural Revolution period when Beijing was isolated from the rest of the world, North Korean trade constituted about 4 percent of China's trade. The balance of trade favored China except for the period 1982–1987 when China was on a buying spree. However, since China's economic reforms, the importance of North Korea as China's trade partner has been decreasing steadily (it accounted for about 0.5 percent of China's total trade by 1990), whereas North Korea's dependence on China has been steady or increasing. For instance, Sino–North Korean trade constituted 16–19 percent of North Korea's total trade in the 1980s. China exports largely agricultural products (soybean, maize, cotton, and edible oil) and petroleum (about 1.2 million metric tons annually since 1984). In return, North Korea's major export items include steel products and some minerals.

North Korea faces extremely severe economic difficulties caused partially by the collapse of the Soviet Union and new Russian demands to restructure its trade relationship on the basis of hard currency. Largely equipped with Soviet-made machinery and heavily dependent upon petroleum supplies from the former Soviet Union, North Korean industry suffers from a shortage of parts and energy, typically operating at less than 50 percent of capacity. Under such conditions, North Korea has no other nation to ask for economic assistance except China. In his thirty-eighth visit to Beijing in October 1991—which lasted an unprecedented twelve days—Kim Il Sung reportedly pleaded for "a loan of 35 billion yuan without any political conditions attached [and] three millions tons of oil per year." Deng Xiaoping is said to have promised a delivery of 1.7 million tons—about 500,000 tons more than China was then supplying to North Korea.[9] There is also an unconfirmed report that Kim made a secret trip to Beijing in 1992 in search of economic aid. But despite the continuing cordial relationship between Beijing and Pyongyang, China is taking a tough stance on North Korea's economic plight by demanding that trade between the countries be settled through hard currency.[10]

If Kim Il Sung failed to obtain what he wanted in economic aid and technological assistance for his nuclear program, Beijing apparently assured him that China would continue its political support to the North Korean regime even after the first-generation revolutionary leaders with whom Kim has close personal ties are replaced by a new generation of bureaucratic technocrats.[11] After several days together with Jiang Zemin, the highest-ranking bureaucratic technocrat, Kim declared that "I became further familiar with General Secretary Jiang. During this trip of mine, I became very familiar with the Chinese leaders of the third generation."[12] China's bureaucratic technocrats must have promised continuing political support to North Korea even after Kim's son, Kim Jong Il, succeeds him. "The main objective of Chairman Kim Il Sung's visit is to further strengthen the traditional friendship between the two parties, the two states, and the two peoples. ... Regardless of whatever change may take place in the international situation, the friendship between China and the Democratic People's Republic of Korea will not change, and will remain permanent."[13]

In brief, unlike Russia, which totally lost the trust of North Korea after it suddenly normalized diplomatic relations with Seoul, China has continued to foster its ties with North Korea while gradually improving its association with South Korea to the point of formal diplomatic relations. However, it is obvious that the strategic importance to China of North Korea as a buffer zone with respect to either the United States or Russia has been declining as China's relations with the two other major players in the region have improved. Thus, the Sino–North Korean relationship appears to be built largely upon traditional ties and common efforts to preserve the two countries' respective political systems. But as China changes its foreign policy priorities to economic development through a deepening of its economic reforms and a measured opening to the outside world, the distance between Beijing and Pyongyang will continue to widen.

Despite constant protest from Pyongyang, China has been steadily, although cautiously, improving its relations with Seoul, initially insisting on the principle of separating politics from economics and justifying the deepening of its economic ties with Seoul in terms of practical necessity. Shandong and Liaoning provincial authorities have been authorized to engage in direct trade with South Korea, and Beijing established semiofficial trade offices in Seoul before normalizing diplomatic relations. This careful, step-by-step approach is the main reason China has been successful in establishing diplomatic relations with the South without incurring too much disruption of its relations with the North. Although resentful of China's two-Korea policy, North Korea is not in a position to alienate China too much, because it is the only close ally that still demonstrates some interest in Pyongyang's survival.

While improving its ties with the South, China has continued to exert subtle pressure on North Korea to reform its autarkical economic system and to widen trade relations with the outside world. North Korea also knows it is imperative to resolve its mounting economic difficulties and to achieve rapid economic development in order to preserve its system. But North Korea's internal political conditions are quite different from those existing in China when it embarked on its reforms in the early 1980s. Whereas the reformer Deng Xiaoping, who suffered two purges during the Cultural Revolution, nevertheless gained control of China after the death of Mao largely on the strength of his commitment to economic change, Kim Il Sung handpicked his own son as his successor specifically in order to assure the continuity of the regime's political line. Because Kim Jong Il must rely exclusively upon the legitimizing authority of his charismatic father and be elevated to power by conservative forces, his policy options are necessarily much more constricted than those of Deng, whose alliance with the progressive currents in the Chinese Communist Party made possible his successful departure from the line associated with Mao. Mao was already partially discredited by the disastrous social consequences of his policies, but Kim Jong Il will not be able to demythologize his father and his *Juche* philosophy without undermining his own political legitimacy.

Moreover, when China initiated reforms, its economic condition was not as desperate as that of North Korea in 1993. In addition, North Korea has had to face challenges from the southern half of the peninsula, which is becoming stronger economically and militarily as time passes. There appears to be no other option for North Korea but to follow cautiously in the footsteps of China's reformers, albeit in a distinctly North Korean style. Also, it seems that China is actually succeeding in persuading Kim Il Sung to adopt "neoauthoritarianism" and carry out economic reforms while pledging China's guarantee of North Korean national security. Despite its possible misgivings about North Korea's economic viability, China remains supportive of North Korea's domestic political process.

South Korea and China

In contrast to the strategic security concerns and ideological affinity that constitute the basic bond in Sino–North Korean relations, China's policy toward South Korea has been dictated largely by economic considerations. As is well known, China sought rapprochement with the United States in the early 1970s to counterbalance the perceived threat from the Soviet Union, and the shared strategic interests between Washington and Beijing eventually led to diplomatic normalization in 1979. After improving its relations with Washington, China embarked upon an ambitious modernization program, which required economic reforms and an opening to Western powers in order to gain access to capital and technology. China thereafter began softening its position on South Korea, for China's economic development definitely requires a peaceful international environment, particularly in East Asia.

Throughout this period, Seoul sought to expand economic ties as a means to open a direct dialogue with Beijing. Since the years of the Park regime, all South Korean political leaders have expressed their eagerness to expand official ties with Beijing even at the cost of sacrificing relations with Taiwan. For instance, in 1983, the South Korean government returned a hijacked Chinese airplane after treating all Chinese passengers well and likewise returned a Chinese naval ship that mutinous soldiers brought to South Korea. The Seoul government even declined to officially condemn the Tiananmen Square massacre.

The success of South Korea's economic growth drew the attention not only of China's economists but also of a post-Mao leadership committed to economic development rather than social revolution. Elected by popular vote, President Roh could afford to discard the strong anticommunist stand that the previous military-backed regime frequently used to justify its authoritarian rule; he embarked on his program of Nordpolitik through which he sought to expand formal ties with other socialist countries in Eastern Europe and in

East Asia and yet ostensibly encourage the United States and other Western countries to adopt more flexible policies toward Pyongyang. The timing of the new South Korean diplomatic thrust turned out be fully coincident with the political and economic transformations taking place in the socialist world.

During the 1980s and early 1990s, the originally different policy objectives of the two states converged as China realized the impracticality of separating economic from political relations, finding it imperative to have some kind of official contacts. South Korea also found China, with its ever-increasing trade with the outside world after the death of Mao, to be a potentially important trade partner that could render material benefit to the export-oriented Korean economy. Consequently, the initial indirect trade through unofficial channels gradually changed to semiofficial and finally direct and official channels with the establishment of diplomatic missions in both Beijing and Seoul. As the trade volume increased, both sides recognized the numerous difficulties compounded by the absence of official ties, but Beijing moved cautiously to expand semiofficial contacts with Seoul, largely because of its concern about North Korea's reaction. In April 1991, Seoul and Beijing exchanged trade representatives. (The arrangement provides ample flexibility for each side to handle many diplomatic functions; the South Korean office in Beijing is staffed by personnel from the Ministry of Foreign Affairs and enjoys all diplomatic immunity.) This exchange was followed by a bilateral trade agreement on January 31, 1992. Although it took the form of a private accord between the China Chamber of International Commerce and the Korea Trade Promotion Corporation, the agreement ended discriminatory customs duties levied by China on goods imported from South Korea and provided mutual most-favored nation treatment. Finally, the two sides agreed to exchange official diplomatic missions in August 1992.

As the normalization indicates, Beijing has dropped its previous preconditions that its future relations with Seoul must be dependent on a further improvement between the two Koreas, conditions similar to what the South Korean government asks the United States and Japan to observe in their dealings with Pyongyang. The normalization also reflects the great changes in international politics in the post–Cold War era and augur well for further improvements in Asian international relations. The fact that the Chinese government decided to establish diplomatic relations, despite its political and ideological affinities with North Korea, indicates that economic considerations currently override political and strategic ones in China's foreign policy.

The trade data for the decade preceding normalization graphically illustrate the increasing economic ties between Seoul and Beijing.[14] A turning point in terms of trade volume between Seoul and Beijing took place in the two-year period 1980–1981 immediately after China set up four special economic zones for the purpose of drawing foreign capital and investment. During this period, China's trade with Seoul increased to $183 million (from 0.48 percent of China's total trade volume to 0.82 percent), whereas China's trade with North Korea decliend from $678 million (1.79 percent of China's total trade) to $544 million (1.39 percent).[15] In this early stage of burgeoning bilateral relations, China would probably have asked North Korea to understand that China needed trade relations with Seoul for economic and industrial reasons and that economic links would not affect China's overall policy toward the Korean problem. Moreover, Beijing would have underscored its willingness to offer South Korea access to its vast markets, in part to induce Taiwan and Japan to offer better terms in their economic negotiations.

Thereafter, Sino–South Korean trade steadily increased, whereas Sino–North Korean trade stagnated. In 1984 and 1985, China's trade with South Korea surpassed that with the North as a percentage of China's total volume; Sino–North Korean trade decreased from 1.01 percent to 0.79 percent, whereas Sino–South Korean trade increased from 0.89 percent to 1.07 percent. The total volume of Sino–South Korean trade made a quantum jump in the period 1986–1989. By 1989, China's trade with South Korea reached over $3 billion, almost ten times that with North Korea. South Korea's decision not to officially condemn the Tiananmen massacre probably helped promote the trade increase.

China's unofficial but direct contacts with South Korea rapidly expanded even after the Tiananmen tragedy. The total trade volume in 1991 was three times that of 1987, the year before the inauguration of Roh. In 1991, with the two-way trade volume reaching about $5.8 billion, China became South Korea's fourth-largest trade partner, after Japan, the United States, and Germany; South Korea is China's fifth-largest trade partner. Expectations are high that diplomatic normalization will stimulate further trade between the two countries, although Korea's high expectations for the China market are perhaps at times unrealistic. The trade volume between the two was projected to reach about $8 billion in 1992 and about $10 billion by 1995.[16]

South Korea's direct investment in China is on the rise too. By 1991, total investment reached about $125 million. In terms of regional distribution, nearly 80 percent of investment is concentrated in the three northeastern provinces and north China. Shandong province leads in investment, accounting for 23.3 percent of the total, followed by Liaoning (18.5 percent) and Heilongjiang (10.5 percent). If the coastal areas of Liaoning and Shandong provinces and Tianjin are added, the Bohai rim district accounts for close to a half of the total.[17]

Many new joint ventures are on the drawing board. The Korean Land Development Corporation has negotiated with the Chinese to establish a "Korean industrial zone" of 1.2 square kilometers within Tianjin's special economic zones where about 150 enterprises owned solely by Koreans will produce textiles, electronics, clothing, and building materials. Weihai, which signed almost 70 agreements of economic cooperation and investment with South Korean firms in 1991, also decided to designate certain areas for Korean enterprises to set up Korean industrial zones.[18] The Chinese side promised to expand the domestic market for Korean enterprises in China and asked Seoul to invest in specific industrial sectors such as electronics.[19]

Although South Korea's investment in China so far has come chiefly from small and medium-sized enterprises, South Korea's big-business community, despite such unresolved issues as double taxation, is actively planning for investment in China. There has been interest in building several facilities:

Hyundai large department stores in Beijing and Shanghai and a joint-venture petrochemical plant in Liaoning province; Samsung an electronic production base in the Shenzhen; Daewoo a tent and bag plant as well as a joint-venture automobile factory in Dalian; and Lucky Goldstar a container manufacturing factory. Chinese provinces are eager to attract South Korean investment. Heilongjiang seeks South Korean participation in developing the Sajiang Plain, and Hainan authorities in creating a large industrial park.

The two economies are complementary to each other as well as competitive. For instance, Chinese exports to Korea include basic raw materials (such as coal, petroleum, building materials) and agricultural and fishery products. Korea's major export items are electronics, textiles, and petrochemicals. China exports a large quantity of agricultural products—15 percent of South Korea's overall imports of such products. South Korea's economy also benefits from China's abundant cheap labor. The Northeast Asia Development Company in Yanji plans to dispatch 20,000 laborers to South Korea every year under the pretext of training, and about 20,000 ethnic Korean-Chinese are reported working in South Korea illegally.[20] The significance of the economic complementarity and potential mutual benefit of Sino–South Korean economic cooperation will become more obvious as economic regionalization intensifies. In China such concepts as "Asia-Pacific Economic Cooperation," "Northeast Asian Economic Sphere," "Southeast Asia Economic Zones," and "Yellow Sea Rim Economic Sphere" are drawing increasing attention from economists and government officials.

There still remain potential sources of friction. In 1991, Korea accumulated a $1 billion trade deficit with China—11 percent of Korea's total—and the deficit is expected to grow. Moreover, because of the low cost of Chinese materials, highly competitive freight charges, and shorter delivery time, Chinese goods in these categories will soon dominate Korea's import market. Particularly remarkable is the penetration of the Korean market by Chinese agricultural products, largely at U.S. expense.[21] In addition, South Korea finds itself in competition with China in third countries. Largely because of differential labor costs—Korea's average wage is 28 times that in China—Korea is losing some of its share of the U.S. market to China, particularly for such labor-intensive goods as simple house appliances. Korea's share declined from 3.5 percent to 3.1 percent in 1991; whereas China's share increased to 4.1 ($8.5 billion) from 3.9 percent in the same year.[22] Likewise, Korea is losing some of its share of the Japanese market to China. For instance, Korea's agricultural exports to Japan have been falling, whereas China's exports of all types have been rising.[23] This loss of Japanese markets has further contributed to Korea's trade deficit with Japan, which reached $9.6 billion in 1991.

More worrisome to South Korea is the close cooperation recently developed between China and Japan, which have complementary economies. The Chinese economy will not pose a challenge to the Japanese economy until it reaches the present level of South Korean industrialization. Understandably, therefore, Japan seeks to maintain a certain distance from South Korea, keeping it at a middle level in the vertical division of labor as envisioned in the "flying-geese model." Although South Korea may hope to act as a balancer between Japan and China in the political arena, its economy can nevertheless be squeezed by both in the economic arena.

South Korean Model of Economic Development for China and North Korea?

By establishing formal diplomatic ties with the Republic of Korea, China became at a stroke the power occupying the pivotal point from which it can exert influence over both Pyongyang and Seoul as its current may require. Thus, China has succeeded not only in preserving its traditional close strategic and political ties with North Korea but also in parlaying its gradually expanding economic relations with Seoul into full-fledged diplomatic relations. China's success in retaining North Korea's trust while improving its ties with South Korea is attributable to several factors: China's sensitivity in understanding North Korea's dilemma, its ability to offer a practical model for reform efforts based on its own experiences, and its diplomatic subtlety compared with that of the Western nations.

The new triangular relationship is in part the result of North Korea's realization that the balance of power is shifting in favor of the South. Encouraged by the favorable international environment and able to exploit its increasing economic capability, Seoul is quietly shifting its policy from "two Koreas" to "one Korea" under its hegemony. Thus, Pyongyang may be justified in fearing that the very survival of the North Korean system is at stake. North Korea, perhaps for this reason, has been cautiously redirecting its unification initiatives from "one Korea" to "two Koreas," as indicated by its decision to join the United Nations simultaneously and separately from South Korea.

Yet there is no doubt that China's decision to normalize diplomatic relations with Seoul must have been a great disappointment to Pyongyang. It is possible, although unlikely, that China consulted with Pyongyang on the normalization; in any case, North Korea may have had no leverage to dissuade Beijing. Extremely isolated in international politics, North Korea cannot afford to alienate Beijing by condemning its new ties with Seoul. Instead of publicly criticizing Beijing's decision, Pyongyang seems at the moment to have accepted (although grudgingly) China's de facto two-Korea policy and to be maintaining its close ties with its most important ally. At the same time, freed from its obligation to support China's policy of "one China," North Korea has recently developed a keen interest in expanding its economic relations with Taiwan.[24]

In fact, unwilling to offer the economic assistance once provided by the former Soviet Union and unable to control Pyongyang's internal politics, China has been attempting to persuade North Korea to "change course toward economic construction, stand on its own feet, and open the country to the outside world." By pursuing reforms and adopting a more flexible and open policy line, China argues, North Korea can overcome the current economic difficulties; cooperation between China and North Korea in this respect will be productive for both sides, both for the Korean peninusla and for Asia.[25] At the same time, China seems willing to guarantee the North's external security. For that purpose, Chinese are eager to prove to North Korea the benefit of economic reform by sharing their experiences.

It is ironic that China's overall strategy in dealing with the many conflicting pressures arising through reform of the socialist economic and political systems has come to approximate South Korea's successful experience of economic development. The need to adapt socialist economic structures to the market, combined with demands for political democratization from social forces liberated by economic reforms, will result in a structure characterized by the "hard" state—a state relatively autonomous from the influence of social forces and capable of implementing its own policies—and the "soft" economy. The South Korean model thus serves well China's conflicting needs: to open its economy to foreign capital and technology yet minimize undesirable external influence on its internal political and social processes, and to carry out economic reforms yet preserve the state sufficiently strong to guide the reform step-by-step through the gradual process. In fact, Chinese intellectuals have been debating the South Korean experience in academic journals since the mid-1980s.

In turn, China has been pressing North Korea to adopt the formula of the hard state and the soft economy, and North Korea seems to be heeding the advice. Apparently even Kim Il Sung realizes that priority should be directed to economic development lest South Korea absorb North Korea as West Germany did its eastern counterpart. But Kim's dilemma has been how to reconstruct the economy and open the country to outside influence without endangering a fragile political system in which large numbers of ruling elite have vested interests.[26] Following the Chinese strategy of reform might enable North Korea to resolve the two conflicting goals, even though opening up to the outside world will entail more political risk to North Korea than it did to China.

The argument presented in this chapter is that North Korea is gradually adopting the South Korean model of economic development transmitted through China, just as the North once copied the Chinese model of the Great Leap Forward in its ch'ŏllima (flying horse) movement or incorporated Mao's philosophy of self-reliance in its Juche ideology. There are additional reasons that North Korea will eventually follow in China's footsteps. As is the case in China, most of North Korea's new leaders who are replacing the old revolutionary generation of Kim Il Sung are bureaucratic technocrats. Moreover, the model of political authoritarianism is congruent with Korea's historically strong elitist tradition, reinforced by Leninist political practice in North Korea. Economic logic also argues for the authoritarian option. North Korea possesses an untapped supply of cheap labor but lacks capital and technology, both of which must come from abroad. Only some kind of neoauthoritarianism will enable North Korea to resolve the delicate task of importing technology and capital from abroad while trying to preserve the Leninist party's dominant position in the political process.

If it is correct to believe that China and North Korea will follow the model of political authoritarianism and economic and social pluralism by turning to a market economy, the ideological differences among the three nations in the triangle will further diminish. In turn, increasing economic interaction between China and South Korea will further influence each society's domestic politics and developmental strategy.

Although China at the moment occupies the pivotal point in the triangle, this formation is intrinsically unstable and cannot last long. Of course, China may try to preserve the triangle because it offers the most promising way of dealing with the Korean problem (barring the ideal but unlikely resolution of a unified Korea friendly or even subordinate to China, as has been the case during various historical periods). Nonetheless, the present axis of the two Koreas is extremely unstable. The only way to stabilize the triangle might be to have a politically stable and economically flourishing North Korea. If North Korea succeeds in economic development, the social and political consequences will be far-reaching—at the least, reduced social, economic, and political differences between the two Koreas, and this shift could pave the way toward an eventual peaceful unification. But at the moment, China has no capacity to help North Korea achieve economic development and yet ensure the survival of its present political system.

At the same time, China, a power with a long history, is well aware that unification of Korea is inevitable. At the moment, chances for economically weak North Korea to unify on its terms are extremely minimal. Furthermore, no unification of the peninsula will be possible without the cooperation of China, which has a higher stake in the Korean peninsula than does Japan, the United States, or Russia, particularly in light of the possibility that China will rapidly expand its economic and military power in the coming years. Thus, the issue is under what conditions and in what form China might be willing to accept unification of the peninsula. Will China help the Republic of South Korea to unify the peninsula? This remains the most critical question for the fate of the unification efforts that both South Koreans and North Koreans regard as an inevitable mission.

Notes

1. *Han'guk Ilbo,* August 25, 1992.

2. For Beijing's decision to enter the Korean conflict, see Yao Yu, "In Commemoration of Thirty Years Anniversary for Entering Korea War," in *Lishi Yanjiu.* For the Korean translation, see Hong Yung Lee, *Sino-Soviet Affairs,* Vol. 8, No. 4 (Winter 1985), pp. 213–235.

3. *Foreign Broadcast Information Service* (Daily Report on East Asia) [hereafter cited as *FBIS*], July 7, 1989.

4. *FBIS,* November 24, 1989, p. 1.

5. *FBIS,* November 17, 1989, pp. 1–2.

6. *Guoji Wenti Yaniu* (Research on International Problems), No. 4, 1987, pp. 15–20.

7. *FBIS,* November 14, 1991.

8. The trade figures are compiled from numerous issues of *Almanac of China's Foreign Economic Relations and Trade,* published in Beijing.

9. *FBIS,* October 31, 1991, p. 15.

10. *Han'guk Ilbo,* February 13, 1993.

11. For this point, see Hong Yung Lee, *From Revolutionary Cadres to Party Technocrats* (Berkeley: University of California Press, 1991).

12. *Renmin Ribao,* October 14, 1991.

13. *Renmin Ribao,* October 15, 1991.

14. *Almanac of China's Foreign Economic Relations and Trade.*

15. *South China Morning Post,* May 26, 1982.

16. *Chosŏn Ilbo,* December 28, 1991; and *Kyonghyang Sinmun,* December 21, 1991.

17. *JETRO: China Newsletter,* No. 97, pp. 13–18.

18. *Shijie Ribao,* March 4, 1992.

19. *Han'guk Ilbo,* September 4, 1992.

20. *Han'guk Ilbo,* April 24, 1992.

21. *FBIS,* July 2, 1991, pp. 17–18.

22. *Han'guk Ilbo,* August 15, 1992.

23. *FBIS,* May 27, 1992, p. 22.

24. *Shijie Ribao,* May 3, 1991.

25. *FBIS,* December 4, 1991, p. 8.

26. Selig Harrison, "Text of Statements by Four Witnesses at the Hearing on Korean Reunification Held by House Foreign Affairs Subcommittee on East Asia and Pacific Affairs, Washington, 24 May 1988," *Korea and World Affairs,* Vol. 12, No. 2 (Summer 1988), pp. 377–378.

7

Japan and North Korea: Normalization Talks Between Pyongyang and Tokyo

Hong Nack Kim

Japan and Korea are close geographically, yet far apart psychologically because of the bitter residue of Japanese colonial domination of Korea from 1910 to 1945. Despite their past relationship, since 1965 the ROK and Japan have normalized diplomatic relations and have remained close political allies and valued partners in economic and trade relations. It was only recently, however, that the North Korean regime's attitude toward Japan began to thaw, leading in 1990 to the beginning of normalization talks between Pyongyang and Tokyo, although little progress resulted. This chapter addresses that episode and chronicles the unfolding drama of improving relations between North Korea and Japan.

After nearly a half century of diplomatic estrangement, Japan and North Korea have embarked on a series of negotiations for the purpose of normalizing diplomatic relations between the two countries on the basis of the joint declaration signed by the representatives of Japan's ruling Liberal Democratic Party (LDP), the Japan Socialist Party (JSP), and the Korean Workers' Party (KWP) in Pyongyang on September 28, 1990. In addition to outlining eight basic principles to govern the process of normalizing relations between Japan and North Korea, the joint declaration stipulated that the three signatories "urge" their respective governments to initiate negotiations in November 1990 for the early establishment of diplomatic ties between Tokyo and Pyongyang.

Despite the initial euphoria and optimism expressed by the political leaders of both countries regarding the prospects for early normalization, Japanese–North Korean talks have not made satisfactory progress because of a number of problems, including the parties' disagreement on the scope and nature of Japan's compensation to North Korea (for the period of colonial rule) and Pyongyang's refusal to accept fully the international inspection of its nuclear facilities and to abandon its nuclear development program.

This chapter will focus especially on recent Japanese–North Korean relations, emphasizing the LDP government's handling of the problem of normalizing Japanese–North Korean diplomatic ties from September 1989 to July 1993.

Japan's Postwar Policy

The basic framework of Japan's Korea policy in the post–World War II period was laid down at the time of the Japanese–South Korean normalization treaty in 1965. In the treaty, Japan recognized the government of the Republic of Korea (South Korea) as the "sole legal" government of Korea as defined by UN General Assembly Resolution 195 (III) in 1948.[1] After normalizing relations with South Korea, Japan virtually ruled out diplomatic relations with North Korea and limited Japanese contacts with it to a bare minimum. Except for a modest amount of trade carried out by private Japanese firms, there were few contacts between the two countries. In a sense, Japan's Korea policy strongly reflected the influence of the United States, which has long guaranteed South Korea's security while not recognizing North Korea. In view of the U.S.-Japan alliance, it was natural for Japan to maintain basically pro-Seoul and anti-Pyongyang policy throughout the Cold War period.

In the early 1970s, the JSP spearheaded a movement to normalize Tokyo-Pyongyang relations, but there was no real progress.[2] Instead, the bilateral relationship began to deteriorate in the latter half of the 1970s. A number of factors help explain this situation:

First, North Korea resented the growing political and economic cooperation between Tokyo and Seoul after the establishment of diplomatic ties between Japan and South Korea in 1965. Recognizing the importance of South Korea's security to Japan, the LDP government provided political and economic support to South Korea.[3] Perceiving that the increasingly close ties between Seoul and Tokyo were detrimental to Pyongyang's grand design to reunify the two Koreas under its domination, North Korean leaders not only denounced the Tokyo-Seoul normalization treaty of 1965 but also demanded that Japan abrogate it. However, leaders of the LDP were unyielding to North Korea's pressure, as they conceived a strong linkage between the security of South Korea and that of Japan.

Second, from the mid-1970s, North Korea also accused Japan of conspiring with South Korea and the United States to perpetuate the division of Korea by implementing the scheme of "cross recognition" of the two Koreas by the four major powers (the United States, the Soviet Union, Japan, and China) and the simultaneous admission of the two Koreas to the United Nations. At the same time, Pyongyang ruled out the possibility of normalizing diplomatic relations with Japan on the grounds that such a move would serve the cause of cross recognition as "contrived" by Seoul, Tokyo, and Washington.[4]

Third, Japanese–North Korean relations were exacerbated further by Pyongyang's inability to pay its trade debt to Japan. It owed over $380 million by 1976, of which $120 million was in arrears. Although Japanese creditors agreed to reschedule Pyongyang's repayment of trade debt three times (1976, 1979, and 1983), North Korea unilaterally terminated the agreement after 1984. As a result, Pyongyang's trade debt to Japan totaled over 80 billion yen (or over $600 million). In 1986, the Japanese Ministry of International Trade and Industry (MITI), under the export insurance program, had to pay 30 billion yen to Japanese creditors for losses incurred because of the North Korean defaults.[5] At the same time, MITI suspended the export insurance program for North Korea. The net effect of MITI's decision was to restrict Japanese–North Korean trade by forcing North Korea to trade with Japan strictly on a cash basis. These developments in turn undermined the credibility as well as the creditworthiness of North Korea among the Japanese.

Fourth, during the 1980s, Japanese–North Korean relations were strained further by North Korean terrorist attacks against South Korea, which prompted Tokyo to impose sanctions against Pyongyang. For example, Japan imposed sanctions against North Korea in retaliation for the bombing by Pyongyang in Rangoon in October 1983, which killed seventeen prominent leaders including four cabinet members. Although sanctions were lifted in January 1985, Japan reimposed similar penalties when North Korean agents destroyed a Korean Air Lines' (KAL) passenger plane by planting a time bomb, killing 115.[6] These acts of violence perpetrated by North Korea not only tarnished its image in Japan but also soured Japanese–North Korean relations.

A fifth factor that worsened relations was Pyongyang's refusal to release two Japanese seamen seized in November 1983. The captain and chief engineer of the *18th Fujisanmaru* were arrested for allegedly having helped a North Korean stowaway, Min Hong-ku, sail to Japan on the ship in October 1983. Subsequently, they were tried as spies and were sentenced to fifteen years of imprisonment at hard labor. In order to seek their release, Japanese diplomats carried out without success a series of negotiations with North Korean officials. Pyongyang refused to release them unless Japan would repatriate Min to North Korea. Because Min clearly indicated his intention to seek political asylum in Japan, Tokyo rejected Pyongyang's demand.

Overtures by Japan

Japan's relations with North Korea began to improve following the issuance of South Korean President Roh Tae Woo's "special declaration of northern policy"—Nordpolitik—on July 7, 1988. Among other things, Roh indicated Seoul's willingness to help its friendly neighbors improve relations with North Korea. Seoul's new policy was encouraging to Japan, for hitherto South Korea's opposition to Japan's attempts to improve relations with Pyongyang had constituted a major constraint on Japan's North Korea policy.

Immediately after President Roh's declaration, Japan proposed opening a dialogue with North Korea on the condition that the two Japanese seamen detained in North Korea be released. However, North Korea's reactions to the Japanese overture were negative. In a statement issued January 11, 1989, the North Korean Ministry of Foreign Affairs not only denounced Japan's "hostile" policy toward the DPRK but also demanded that Tokyo remove major "obstacles" in Pyongyang-Tokyo relations.[7] Specifically, it insisted that Japan abandon its pro-Seoul and anti-Pyongyang policy, stop its participation in the "plot" to create two Koreas by advocating "cross recognition" and "cross contacts," and stop repressive measures against the Ch'ongryŏn (a pro-Pyongyang Korean residents association in Japan). It also criticized the Japan-ROK normalization treaty of 1965 in which Japan had recognized the ROK as the "sole legal" government on the Korean peninsula. Until the obstacles were removed, it contended, "nothing can be expected out of holding talks" with Japan. In addition, after criticizing Japan's failure to apologize for the suffering inflicted on Koreans during Japan's colonial rule, Pyongyang declared that Japan "is obligated to pay reparations to the DPRK."[8]

In a statement issued about a week later, the Japanese Ministry of Foreign Affairs refuted Pyongyang's allegations about Japan's "hostile" policy toward North Korea and expressed its willingness to negotiate with Pyongyang without any precondition for the settlement of outstanding issues between the two countries.[9] However, North Korea again responded negatively.

In an attempt to indicate Japan's willingness to improve relations with North Korea, on March 30, 1989, Prime Minister Takeshita Noboru expressed "deep remorse and regret" to Koreans both in the South and the North for Japan's past actions on the Korean peninsula and reiterated Japan's willingness to improve relations with the "Democratic People's Republic of Korea" (DPRK).[10] This was the first time a Japanese prime minister had called North Korea by its official title. The Takeshita statement was warmly received. Apparently, Kim Il Sung was pleased with it when he said that "some Japanese officials are making positive statements."[11] Kim also indicated his willingness to welcome the proposed visit to Pyongyang by an LDP delegation headed by Kanemaru Shin in September 1989. But the collapse of the Takeshita government in May 1989 as a result of the Recruit scandal (a bribery case involving discount sales of unlisted stocks by the Recruit Cosmos Company to prominent political leaders for political favors) sidetracked the diplomatic initiative. It was not until summer 1990 that Japan and North Korea began to show renewed interest in improving bilateral relations.

On July 24, 1990, North Korean Vice President Li Chong-ok informed Kubo Wataru, deputy chairman of the JSP, that North Korea would welcome a joint visit to Pyongyang by JSP and LDP leaders. This change in North Korea's Japan policy can be attributed to a number of factors.[12] First, Pyongyang came to accept the necessity of dealing with Japan's ruling LDP after the party rebounded from the political crisis triggered by the Recruit scandal by winning a comfortable majority (286 out of 512 seats) in the general election in February 1990. Initially, Pyongyang leaders anticipated the replacement of the LDP government by a JSP-led coalition government because the LDP had suffered a stunning defeat in the upper house election in July 1989.

Second, the Soviet–South Korean summit conference held in San Francisco on June 4, 1990, shocked North Korea, as the dramatic meeting between Roh and Gorbachev strongly signaled imminent establishment of diplomatic ties between Seoul and Moscow. In an apparent move to compensate for the diplomatic setback dealt by the Moscow-Seoul rapprochement, Pyongyang decided to seek rapprochement with Tokyo.

Third, no less important was North Korea's desperate economic need for foreign capital and technology to revitalize its economy, which was stagnating with less than a 2 percent annual growth rate. However, Pyongyang could not count on the economically troubled Soviet Union and East European countries for economic assistance, nor could it look to China, which had its own share of economic difficulties. Under the circumstances, tapping Japan's capital and technology was the best option available for Pyongyang.

Japan's reaction to Pyongyang's overture conveyed through Kubo was quite favorable, for there was a growing feeling among Japanese leaders that Japan should normalize its relations with North Korea. In a statement delivered in the Diet on June 15, 1990, Prime Minister Kaifu Toshiki declared that he would like to "contact with North Korea without any precondition attached."[13] He also expressed the hope that the proposed trip to North Korea by an LDP delegation headed by Kanemaru Shin would materialize as soon as possible.

The Kaifu government's positive posture toward Pyongyang can be attributed to a number of factors: First, the Soviet–South Korean summit meeting in June 1990 also shocked Japan, partly because it did not expect such a sudden breakthrough in Moscow-Seoul relations and partly because President Roh had not informed Prime Minister Kaifu of the scheduled Roh-Gorbachev meeting during his visit to Japan in late May. Although the Japanese government officially welcomed the summit, it was unhappy about Seoul's lack of diplomatic courtesy.[14]

Second, Japanese leaders began to feel upstaged by South Korea's initiative with the Soviet Union. Such a feeling was natural in view of the fact that Japan had not made much progress in negotiating a peace treaty with Moscow after 1956. Under the circumstances, they felt it necessary for Japan to seize the diplomatic initiative to enhance its international prestige and influence. In this respect, mending fences with North Korea was regarded as a necessary step, for such a move would resolve the last remaining issue arising from Japan's defeat in World War II: North Korea is the only country with which Japan has not maintained diplomatic relations in the postwar period in spite of geographical proximity and historical and cultural ties. In addition, the normalization of diplomatic ties between Tokyo and Pyongyang would provide the advantage of establishing ties with both North Korea and South Korea. Rapprochement with Pyongyang was regarded as essential for Japan because the Soviet Union was on the verge of acquiring such a position on the Korean peninsula.

Third, Japanese leaders tended to believe that increased contacts between Japan and North Korea would enable Pyongyang to acquire a more realistic picture of the outside world and to facilitate the process of cross recognition of the two Koreas by the four major powers.[15] They also believed in the merit of inducing North Korea to participate in the main arena of international politics as a more prudent way of reducing tension on the Korean peninsula than isolating the Pyongyang regime. Such a feeling became stronger as Japan perceived the Cold War era as coming to an end in the wake of drastic political and economic change in the Soviet bloc in 1989 and 1990.

Preliminary Negotiations

The LDP delegation headed by Kanemaru Shin and the JSP delegation led by Tanabe Makoto arrived in Pyongyang on September 24, 1990. At the first meeting, Kim Yong-sun, the ruling KWP secretary for international affairs, emphasized the importance of a Japanese apology and compensation for its past colonial rule over Korea and Japan's responsibility for the abnormal relations between the two countries in the postwar period. If these issues could be resolved, according to Kim, other issues could be settled expeditiously.

On the apology issue, Kanemaru made an apology at a welcoming banquet held on the day of arrival in Pyongyang for the "intolerable sufferings and hardships" the Korean people had experienced under Japan's colonial rule. Kanemaru also carried with him a letter of apology from Prime Minister Kaifu in his capacity as LDP president; it was addressed to Kim Il Sung and was handed to the North Korean leader the next day.[16]

On the compensation issue, Kanemaru declared that "Japan is responsible for solving the compensation issue whether or not the two nations have diplomatic relations."[17] Kanemaru also told Kim Yong-sun that Japan should provide some compensation to North Korea even before the establishment of formal diplomatic relations between the two countries.

On the question of establishing a bilateral mechanism for improving ties, Kanemaru's initial plan was to seek an exchange of liaison offices between Tokyo and Pyongyang, because North Korea had steadfastly ruled out since the mid-1970s the possibility of establishing diplomatic ties with Japan. Such ties, North Korea had argued, would lead to the cross recognition of the two Koreas by major powers. However, Kanemaru's plan was drastically revised as a result of an unexpected turnabout in Pyongyang's policy toward normalizing relations with Japan.

North Korea's new policy toward Japan was revealed by a senior North Korean official at a bilateral meeting held September 27. However, it was Kim Yong-sun who explained to the Japanese the reasons for the apparent change in North Korea's Japan policy. Kim told Kanemaru and Tanabe that the policy change was made partly because of rapid changes in the international situation and partly because of the reported refusal by Japan to consider reparations to North Korea unless official bilateral negotiations for the establishment of diplomatic relations took place between the two countries.[18] Thus, North Korea decided to change its position on the normalization question primarily to obtain economic compensation from Japan.

On the basis of talks held with North Korean leaders, including Kim Il Sung, Japanese party leaders worked out a joint declaration with North Korean leaders, which was issued September 28.[19] In the eight-point declaration, representatives of the LDP, the JSP, and the KWP urged that Japan fully apologize "for the unhappiness and suffering caused to the Korean people during the 36 years of colonial rule." They also agreed that Japan should compensate North Korea not only for the damage caused during the colonial period but also for the "losses suffered by the Korean people in the 45 years" since World War II. They also agreed to remove the provision in the Japanese passport stipulating that "it is not valid in North Korea." In addition, Japan and North Korea should set up satellite links and inaugurate direct air flights to improve bilateral ties. In the declaration, the three signatories also recognized that "there is only one Korea" and called for peaceful reunification of North and South. The declaration stipulated further that the three signatories "urge" their respective governments to initiate talks in November 1990 for the early establishment of diplomatic ties between the two nations.[20]

Although it was not incorporated in the joint declaration, North Korea agreed to release the two detained Japanese seamen early in October 1990. Subsequently, the seamen were allowed to return to Japan with Japanese political leaders who came to Pyongyang on October 10.

Although the LDP and the JSP hailed the joint declaration, some influential Japanese leaders and media were highly critical of Kanemaru for his handling of the compensation and other related issues. Even if they acknowledged his role in the breakthrough in Japanese–North Korean relations, they were unhappy about his "excessive" concessions to North Korean demands.[21]

Several Japanese leaders and the Japanese Ministry of Foreign Affairs were also critical of Kanemaru's acceptance of Pyongyang's compensation demand for the "45 years of abnormal relations" in the postwar period. They believed Japan was neither legally responsible for the "abnormal relations" in the postwar period nor morally obligated to offer compensation.[22] Many Japanese believed that the relationship had been created by international circumstances like the Cold War, which were beyond Japan's control. They also believed that North Korea should share more of the blame for the estrangement because much of the deterioration had been caused by Pyongyang's unfriendly and reckless behavior.

South Korea and the United States also voiced concern about the terms and conditions of the proposed normalization of relations between Tokyo and Pyongyang. South Koreans were apprehensive because of the risks normalization poses for their national security. If Japan provides massive compensation and economic assistance to North Korea, and if the money is used to upgrade North Korea's conventional military capability, the existing balance of power on the Korean peninsula could be adversely changed.[23] The United States shares this concern.

Seoul's position was spelled out on October 8, 1990, by President Roh at a meeting with Kanemaru Shin, who called on Roh at Chong Wa Dae to brief the president on his meeting with North Korean leaders. Roh reaffirmed Seoul's position that it did not basically oppose Japan's improvement of bilateral relations with North Korea, provided that such an improvement would not disrupt meaningful progress in inter-Korean relations. More specifically,

Roh asked Japan to take into consideration the following five principles in approaching North Korea:[24] (1) Japan should consult with South Korea in normalizing relations with North Korea; (2) Japan should urge North Korea to sign the nuclear safety agreement with the International Atomic Energy Agency (IAEA); (3) Japan should pay adequate attention to the state of North-South dialogue; (4) Japan should withhold compensation or economic assistance to North Korea until the establishment of formal diplomatic ties between the two countries so as to ensure that Japanese funds would not be used for upgrading North Korea's military capability; and (5) Japan should take steps to prompt Pyongyang to move toward openness and reforms.

Japan agreed to respect South Korea's request in dealing with Pyongyang in the full-dress normalization talks.

Obstacles to Normalization

After three rounds of preliminary talks in fall 1990, the first round of full-dress normalization talks between Japan and North Korea took place in Pyongyang January 30–31, 1991, and the second round in Tokyo March 10–11, 1991. However, little progress was made in narrowing the gaps between the two nations on three major issues:

First, North Korea insisted that Japan should compensate North Korea for Japan's colonial rule over Korea in the pre–World War II period. In demanding reparations for the colonial period (1910–1945), North Korea insisted that Korea was "at war" with Japan because Koreans fought Japanese troops after Japan annexed the country in 1910.[25] In addition, North Korea demanded Japanese compensation for the forty-five years following World War II, on the grounds that Japan had been responsible for the division of Korea and that "she played the role of the supply base, the repair base and the attack base of the U.S. forces"[26] during the Korean War. Furthermore, North Korea contended that "Japan cannot avoid responsibility for the enormous damages she had inflicted upon our country after the war, while pursuing a hostile policy toward [North] Korea." Stressing that "Japan has gone through the past 45 years without making apology or compensation to North Korea," Chon In-chol, chief North Korean negotiator, declared that "the political and economic losses imposed upon the North Korean people in the postwar period are quite enormous."[27]

Japan, however, rejected North Korea's contention. According to Nakahira Noboru, chief Japanese negotiator, "Pyongyang's interpretation has no basis under international law."[28] Further, Nakahira maintained that Korea had not been one of the Allied powers that fought against Japan during World War II. Although he indicated Japan's willingness to compensate for the damage done to Koreans during the colonial period, Nakahira reaffirmed Tokyo's position that there was no legal ground for Japan to compensate for the alleged losses arising from "abnormal" relations between Japan and North Korea in the postwar period.

A second major obstacle was the inability of both sides to work out a compromise on the question of the international inspection of North Korea's nuclear facilities. Japanese negotiators told North Korea that the existing bilateral talks should be aimed not only at normalizing diplomatic relations but also at promoting peace and stability in East Asia, including the Korean peninsula. In this regard, Japan urged North Korea to open its nuclear facilities for inspection by the IAEA in accordance with the provisions of the nuclear nonproliferation treaty North Korea had ratified in 1985. During the second round of talks in Tokyo in March 1991, Japan reiterated the demand that North Korea permit IAEA inspection.

North Korea rejected the Japanese demand on the grounds that the nuclear inspection issue was not a proper topic for normalization talks and that such a problem should be decided between North Korea and the United States, since similar inspection should be conducted concerning U.S. nuclear weapons deployed in South Korea. "If this nuclear threat is removed," said Chon In-chol, "we will immediately sign the nuclear safety accord with the IAEA." Furthermore, Chon declared that Pyongyang would sign the safety agreement if the United States "gives legal[ly] binding assurances of non-use of nuclear weapons" to Pyongyang.[29]

Third, by spring 1991, the boundary of North Korea's jurisdiction was also shaping up as a major issue in the Pyongyang-Tokyo talks. Apparently, Japan was unwilling to conclude a normalization treaty with North Korea unless North Korea specified the boundary of its territorial jurisdiction on the Korean peninsula. In rejecting Japan's request for clarification, North Korea declared that "There is no need to ask about the bounds of jurisdiction. What the DPRK and Japan should do is to recognize the sovereignty of each other and establish relations in accordance with the international usage." It maintained further that "If a problem of jurisdiction arises in our country, it is an internal affair of the nation to be settled between the north and south of Korea, and Japan is not requested to meddle in and 'judge' it."[30] Thus, it was clear that North Korea was unwilling to admit that its jurisdiction is limited to territory north of the armistice line on the Korean peninsula. By refusing to admit the existence of the two Koreas, it pretended to insist on the position stipulated in article 1 of the North Korean constitution that nominally its jurisdiction extends over the entire Korean peninsula in defiance of political reality.

At the third round of normalization talks, held in Beijing May 20–22, 1991, Japan and North Korea failed to iron out differences on most of these issues. However, on the North Korean boundary, Pyongyang indicated its willingness to concede the effectiveness of its legal jurisdiction in only the northern "half" of the Korean peninsula.[31] By making such a concession, North Korea apparently wanted to normalize diplomatic relations with Japan first and discuss other issues, including compensation and international inspection of North Korea's nuclear facilities, later.

Japan was unwilling to entertain North Korea's revised proposal. According to Ambassador Nakahira Noboru, Japan would not normalize diplomatic relations with North Korea unless Pyongyang satisfied Japan's demand for international inspection of its nuclear facilities. Furthermore, Japan expressed its desire for progress in the inter-Korean dialogue and the simultaneous entry of the two Koreas into the United Nations, since these developments would not only facilitate normalization of Japanese–North Korean relations but also contribute to the promotion of peace and security in the region. In a sense, Japan regarded progress in these three areas (nuclear inspection, simultaneous entry into the UN, and North-South dialogue) as preconditions for normalization.

However, it was Japan's request for information concerning a missing Japanese woman, "Li Un-hye," that caused the abrupt adjournment of the third round of talks without a date even being set for the next round. The identity of the woman was verified from photographs dispatched from the Japanese police by Kim Hyŏn-hi (a former North Korean agent who had planted a time bomb that destroyed a Korean Air Lines [KAL] plane in November 1987) as her Japanese language instructor in North Korea. Information provided by Kim concerning the Japanese woman's background matched completely with Taguchi Yayeyo, believed to have been kidnapped by North Korean agents in 1978 and detained there.[32]

Although North Korea took an uncompromising stance on a number of issues at the third round of talks, its posture became much more accommodating and conciliatory toward the three major conditions laid down by Japan in the summer of 1991. First, on May 28, North Korea announced its intention to seek a separate seat in the UN along with South Korea. For the first time since 1958, when Pyongyang had gone along with Moscow's proposal for dual membership of the two Koreas, it now accepted the simultaneous entry of the two Koreas into the UN.[33] Furthermore, on June 7, 1991, Pyongyang notified the IAEA of its willingness to sign the nuclear safeguards agreement.[34] It was to dispatch experts to hold meetings with the IAEA in mid-July. Once the IAEA Assembly approved the agreement in September, Pyongyang would sign it. It was not clear, however, whether Pyongyang was making the signing of the agreement conditional on U.S. withdrawal of nuclear weapons from Korea. Furthermore, in mid-July, Pyongyang also announced its intention to convene the fourth conference of North Korean and South Korean prime ministers in Pyongyang toward the end of August 1991.

These developments were quite encouraging to Japan, which regarded progress in these areas as essential for normalizing Tokyo-Pyongyang relations. Japanese officials expressed their hope that Pyongyang's more flexible posture would have positive effects on the stalemated talks. In order to work out a compromise on the Li Un-hye issue, Japan dispatched a negotiator to Pyongyang in July. According to a Japanese source, an understanding was reached on the Li issue between Tokyo and Pyongyang that Pyongyang would agree to accommodate Japan's request for investigating the matter if Tokyo made such a request at a preliminary meeting at the outset of the next round of normalization talks.[35] On the basis of such an understanding, the fourth round of talks was scheduled for Beijing August 30–September 1, 1991.

At the Beijing talks, little progress was made in resolving the outstanding issues between Tokyo and Pyongyang. In accordance with the agreement reached in July, Japan at the outset requested that North Korea provide information concerning Li Un-hye. However, North Korea refused to comply with the Japanese request. Disgusted by North Korea's reneging on its earlier promise, Japanese Foreign Ministry officials wanted to suspend the negotiations but were instructed by Prime Minister Kaifu to continue.[36] After a lengthy debate, a compromise was worked out on August 31, 1991, when North Korea agreed to discuss the matter separately from the main agenda in the future.

In regard to the boundary of North Korea's jurisdiction, Japan requested Pyongyang to affirm specifically that "its territorial jurisdiction is limited only to territory north of the armistice line in Korea."[37] However, North Korea's response was somewhat evasive—it merely agreed to "study" the Japanese request on the issue. When Japanese Ambassador Nakahira urged Pyongyang to place its nuclear facilities "unconditionally" under international inspection, Chon In-chol criticized Japan's attempt "to interfere in the internal affairs" of North Korea.[38] The fourth round of talks ended with the understanding that the fifth round should be held in Beijing in November 1991.

Japan was clearly disappointed by the lack of progress in the fourth round of normalization talks, for it had anticipated a real breakthrough in the stalemated negotiations in view of Pyongyang's more conciliatory foreign policy announcements from May to July 1991.

Meanwhile, there were clear indications that some influential Japanese political leaders, such as Kanemaru Shin and Tanabe Makoto, had become unhappy and impatient with the lack of progress in Japanese–North Korean normalization talks. Among other things, they were critical of the Kaifu government's handling of the Li Un-hye issue. At a press conference September 1, JSP chairman Tanabe said that "It is Japan that raised a question about an issue [Li Un-hye] which has no direct connection with the agenda of the normalization talks." He then added: "Anyone with common sense can understand whether or not such an approach is in line with international customs and conventions."[39] Two days later, Kanemaru made a similar criticism of the Kaifu government at a meeting of the LDP Takeshita faction, saying that for Japan "to raise a question on the KAL passenger destruction incident constitutes merely a spiteful act [against North Korea]."[40] He urged the Kaifu government to complete normalization talks with Pyongyang as soon as possible. Furthermore, Kanemaru, Tanabe, and other influential Japanese leaders favoring early normalization intensified their efforts to build up broader public support for rapprochement. In spring 1991, the LDP, the JSP, and the pro-Pyongyang Ch'ongryŏn association began to step up campaigns to promote adoption of resolutions supporting "the early normalization of Japanese–North Korean diplomatic relations" by local and provincial legislative assemblies. By September, over 1,021 local assemblies, including the Tokyo Metropolitan Assembly, had adopted such resolutions. Also, a large delegation of over 300 local assemblymen (most of them LDP members) visited Pyongyang in July at the invitation of the North Korean government.[41]

By the beginning of September, in an apparent move to drum up support for early normalization, forces led by Kanemaru and Tanabe decided to organize a Japan–North Korea Friendship Association in conjunction with the first anniversary of the issuance of the three parties' joint declaration of September

28, 1990. Over 300 Japanese leaders were invited to attend a gala party hosted by Kanemaru and Tanabe in Tokyo on September 19. An organization committee for the friendship association was inaugurated at the party with the plan to establish the association in November. Its membership would include not only political leaders from government and opposition parties (except the Japan Communist Party) but also economic, labor, cultural, and intellectual leaders of Japan.[42] The planned strategy of the association was to parallel that used by the Japan-China Friendship Association in connection with the normalization of Sino-Japanese relations in the early 1970s; the planned objective was to build popular demand and support for the normalization of Tokyo-Pyongyang relations.

Apparently under pressure from Kanemaru and Tanabe, the Japanese Ministry of Foreign Affairs began to study the possibility of extending recognition to North Korea as a sovereign state in conjunction with the admission of the two Koreas to the United Nations. On September 11, Japan's chief cabinet secretary, Sakada Isoji, acknowledged at a press conference that the ministry was studying such a possibility.[43] However, ministry officials indicated that recognition of North Korea as a state and the normalization of Japanese–North Korean relations were separate issues. Although the specific procedure or date for extending recognition to North Korea was not decided, it was speculated that Japan would make such a move either immediately after North Korea's entry into the UN or at the fifth round of normalization talks in November.[44] South Korea was clearly unhappy about the plan and urged Japan to withhold recognition of North Korea until after normalization of Japanese–North Korean relations. The Japan–South Korea Dietmen's League (headed by former Prime Minister Takeshita Noboru) also declared its opposition to prenormalization recognition of North Korea.[45] Shortly thereafter, the Kaifu government ruled out the possibility of recognizing North Korea after it announced on September 13 its intention not to sign the nuclear safeguards agreement with the IAEA. North Korea's abrupt turnabout on this issue not only surprised many Japanese but also dashed any hope for a major breakthrough in the normalization talks.

Another significant development in fall 1991 that inevitably affected negotiations was the inauguration of the new LDP government headed by Miyazawa Kiichi. The new leadership replacing the Kaifu government included Miyazawa, a skilled hand in foreign affairs (foreign minister in the Miki government from 1974 to 1976) and known for his friendly attitude toward the United States, and the newly appointed foreign minister, Watanabe Michio, also a powerful faction leader and more conservative than his predecessor. Thus, the Miyazawa government was expected to pay more attention to the wishes of friendly powers, such as the United States and South Korea, and to be less susceptible to the pressure of pro–North Korean forces in dealing with North Korea than the Kaifu government had been.

At the fifth round of talks, held in Beijing November 18–20, 1991, North Korea indicated a more flexible stance on such issues as Japan's compensation to North Korea (it no longer contended that Korea was at war with Japan in the pre-1945 period) and the boundary of North Korea's territorial jurisdiction, but it was uncompromising on the issue of international inspection of North Korea's nuclear facilities. Japan urged North Korea to accept inspection unconditionally, since Pyongyang's basic demand for the condition of signing the nuclear accord had been met as a result of President Bush's announcement of the U.S. intention of withdrawing tactical nuclear weapons from abroad, including South Korea (September 1991), and of South Korean President Roh Tae Woo's declaration on the denuclearization of the Korean peninsula in early November. However, North Korea reiterated its intention not to sign the accord unless the United States withdrew its nuclear weapons completely from the South and unless both North and South (including U.S. bases) were placed simultaneously under the same international inspection.[46] Furthermore, North Korea indicated its displeasure at Japan for pressuring it to sign the nuclear pact, declaring that Pyongyang would not sign any accord "under unreasonable international pressure."[47]

In regard to the Li Un-hye issue, North Korea flatly rejected the Japanese request for investigation, contending that "the [KAL plane] incident was concocted by South Korea" and that "Li Un-hye therefore is non-existent."[48] The only positive result of the meeting was information provided by North Korea concerning the status of twelve Japanese wives of repatriated North Koreans. The talks ended with an agreement to hold a sixth round of normalization talks in Beijing in January 1992.

Impasse in Negotiations

By spring 1992, there had been a major breakthrough in inter-Korean relations. At the fifth conference of South and North prime ministers, held in Seoul December 11–13, 1991, the two leaders signed the agreement on reconciliation, nonaggression, and exchanges and cooperation (Appendix B).[49] It was an "epochal event"—for the first time since the division of the Korean peninsula in 1948, Seoul and Pyongyang had signed an official agreement. In addition to accepting legitimacy of each other's political system, both sides agreed not to interfere in each other's internal affairs or "to slander or vilify" each other. Furthermore, the two regimes agreed to resolve differences and disputes arising between them through peaceful means, not force, and to promote economic exchanges and cooperation and reunions and visits between separated family members. On December 31, 1991, North Korea and South Korea agreed to sign the joint declaration for denuclearization of the Korean peninsula (Appendix C), which prohibits both sides from possessing or developing nuclear weapons as well as nuclear processing facilities and uranium-enrichment technology.[50] Furthermore, to police any violation of the accord, they agreed to set up a Joint Nuclear Control Commission to handle the inspection of sites mutually agreed upon. These agreements were ratified at the sixth conference of prime ministers at Pyongyang in February 1992. In addition, North Korea signed the nuclear safeguard agreement with the IAEA on January 30, 1992. Against the backdrop of improving inter-Korean relations, Japan and North Korea held two additional rounds of talks in Beijing in spring 1992: the sixth January 31–February 2 and the seventh May 13–15. Because of the breakthrough in inter-Korean relations and partly because of the signing of the nuclear safeguard agreement with the IAEA, Pyongyang expected real progress in the stalemated normalization talks. However, nothing significant materialized because the two sides could not iron out differences on the nuclear issue and the compensation issue.

First, although Japan welcomed North Korea's decisions to sign the safeguards agreement with the IAEA and the joint declaration on denuclearization with Seoul, it was wary about Pyongyang's intention on the nuclear development program. At the seventh round of talks, Japanese Ambassador Nakahira demanded that Pyongyang implement the nuclear accords, stressing that Japan could not normalize relations with Pyongyang until North Korea allowed international inspection of its nuclear facilities.[51] Japanese apprehension about North Korea's intention on the nuclear issue stemmed partly from Pyongyang's recalcitrant attitude toward inspection and partly from U.S. and South Korean intelligence reports indicating that Pyongyang was not only continuing its nuclear development program but also on the verge of manufacturing nuclear weapons. Even North Korea's newly appointed chief delegate, Li Sam-ro, confirmed in Beijing in May 1992 that Pyongyang was producing plutonium, the key material needed in manufacturing nuclear weapons.[52] North Korea contended, however, that it was conducting nuclear research strictly for peaceful uses, and that it should no longer be an issue because it had signed the two nuclear agreements.

Second, Japan and North Korea could not reach an accord on the compensation issue. North Korea reiterated its position that "normalization of diplomatic relations is out of the question unless Japan admits and apologizes her past criminal deeds in explicit terms and makes sufficient compensation for it."[53] Japan maintained, however, that because Japan was not in a state of war with North Korea before and during World War II, Pyongyang's demand should be dealt with as an issue of North Korea's claim for property damages in the pre-1945 period. (Japan applied such a principle in settling similar issues with South Korea in 1965.) For this purpose, the Japanese chief delegate requested that his North Korean counterpart present documentary proof of damage caused by Japan during the colonial days.[54] Rejecting the Japanese viewpoint, the North Korean chief delegate declared that Pyongyang would never accept the settlement formula used by Japan with South Korea, for it sidestepped the problem of compensating for human and property damage Japan inflicted on Korean people from 1910 to 1945. North Korea also demanded that Japan compensate for the so-called Korean comfort women who were forced into Japanese military brothels during World War II.[55]

Third, in addition to these major issues, there were others on which Tokyo and Pyongyang could not agree. For example, North Korea proposed to include an "antidomination" clause in the normalization treaty with Japan. However, Japan rejected North Korea's request on the ground that there was no need for such a clause because both nations were members of the United Nations, which prohibits forceful domination of one member by the other. In addition, there was little progress in settling the Li Un-hye issue and the home visits by Japanese wives of North Koreans.

As a result of the parties' inability to settle these thorny issues, the seventh round of talks ended in stalemate on May 15, 1992. They agreed nevertheless to hold the eighth round sometime in July 1992.

It was not until November 5, 1992, that the eighth round of talks was held in Beijing. At the meeting, North Korea reiterated its claim for compensation for the pre-1945 period. North Korean chief negotiator Li Sam-ro insisted that there was no legal basis for Japan's contention that North Korean demands for compensation should be handled within the framework of property damage claims. Furthermore, he contended that the Japanese-Korean annexation treaty of 1910 was "invalid" from the beginning because it was not properly signed or ratified by the Korean government. Li also flatly denied the allegation that North Korea might be developing nuclear weapons, saying such a story was a Japanese "fabrication."[56] At the same time, he charged Japan with stockpiling more plutonium than it needed in order to arm itself with nuclear weapons. In response, Nakahira Noboru, the chief Japanese negotiator, expressed Tokyo's skepticism about North Korea's denials on the nuclear issue, demanding that Pyongyang implement mutual inspection of nuclear facilities with South Korea in addition to accepting IAEA inspection. He stressed that it would be difficult for Japan to normalize relations with North Korea unless the suspicion on Pyongyang's nuclear program were dispelled. There was no progress in narrowing the gap between the two sides, and the meeting was suspended abruptly in the afternoon of November 5 when the North Korean delegation walked out of the conference room in protest against the Japanese delegation's request for information concerning Li Un-hye, denouncing such a demand as a serious "insult" to North Korea.[57] As of mid-June 1993, there was no indication as to when the next round of talks would be held.

Conclusion

From the foregoing analysis a few basic conclusions can be drawn: First, Japan's North Korea policy has shifted since the fall of 1990 from one of nonrecognition to one of normalizing relations with Pyongyang. The policy change has been necessary in light of the successful implementation by South Korea of its northern policy (Nordpolitik) that brought about normalization of diplomatic relations with the former Soviet Union and the East European countries. South Korea has also substantially expanded economic relations with China. In order to play a greater role in building a new international order in East Asia in the post–Cold War era, it is necessary for Japan to mend fences with North Korea. Such a move can also contribute to the promotion of peaceful coexistence between the two Koreas because it would facilitate cross recognition of them by the four major powers (the United States, Japan, China, and Russia).

Second, Pyongyang has adopted changes in its policy toward Japan in order to compensate for the diplomatic setbacks dealt by Seoul's successful implementation of Nordpolitik. Under the circumstances, it has become necessary for Pyongyang to normalize relations with Japan and possibly with the United States. Without such compensatory face-saving measures, it would be difficult for the Kim Il Sung regime to balance its dismal record in foreign relations.

Third, North Korea's new policy toward Japan is clearly related to its desire to secure from Japan massive economic assistance, which is indispensable for revitalizing North Korea's economy. In light of the bankruptcy of the socialist economic system, North Korea cannot expect any help from the republics of the former Soviet Union, once its erstwhile patron. In fact, the Soviet Union required North Korea to trade with the Soviets strictly on a cash basis starting in 1991. China insisted on a similar arrangement in 1992. In view of the widening economic gap between North and South Korea ($23.1 billion GNP versus $230 billion in 1990), North Korea is desperately in need of foreign capital and technology to upgrade its stagnant economy. In fact, the growing disparity between the economic power of the two Koreas has aroused much speculation that North Korea would eventually meet a fate similar to what befell East Germany: unification by absorption under the terms of the economically more powerful side. Under the circumstances, the only logical solution for North Korea is to tap Japanese capital and technology to shore up its sagging economy. Especially attractive to Pyongyang is the huge compensation Japan is expected to make to North Korea in conjunction with normalization of relations. This potential benefit explains Pyongyang's new approach to Japan and the reversal of its long-standing opposition to cross recognition of the two Koreas by major powers.

Fourth, because there is no real urgency for Japan to normalize relations with the DPRK, and because it does not want to undermine its existing friendly relations with South Korea, Tokyo is likely to persist in its demand that Pyongyang accept international inspection of nuclear facilities and progress in the dialogue between North Korea and South Korea. In the November 5, 1992, round of talks, the Miyazawa government made it clear that Japan would not normalize relations unless Pyongyang fulfilled its obligations under the nuclear safeguards agreement with the IAEA and the joint North-South declaration on denuclearization of the peninsula. There is little prospect for a breakthrough in the stalemated Pyongyang-Tokyo normalization talks until North Korea implements the provisions of these agreements.

Fifth, although North Korea is eager to normalize relations with Japan as soon as possible, the talks are likely to drag on because of a number of thorny issues. In addition to the nuclear issue, which has been the major stumbling block, there is a substantial gap between Tokyo and Pyongyang concerning the proper amount of compensation (or "reparations" as demanded by North Korea) to be made by Japan for its prewar colonial rule over Korea. The Japanese Ministry of Foreign Affairs reportedly is inclined to offer $500 million, the same amount Japan offered South Korea in 1965, whereas sources close to North Korea believe Pyongyang would demand more than $5 billion by taking into consideration the inflation rate and other factors (e.g., Japan's total economic assistance to South Korea since 1965). Some even expect North Korea to demand as much as $10 billion by adding compensation for forty-five years of alleged losses in the postwar period. To hammer out a mutually acceptable compromise solution on the compensation issue is likely to be difficult.

Finally, in seeking rapprochement with North Korea, Japan cannot ignore the legitimate interest and concerns of its neighbors, particularly South Korea. Because a Tokyo-Pyongyang rapprochement will affect not only the interests of the two countries involved but also other countries, South Korea will pay close attention to the process of Japanese–North Korean normalization talks. If its legitimate interests are compromised by the terms of the Tokyo-Pyongyang rapprochement, South Korea will take issue with Japan. The same can be expected from the United States. If properly handled, the establishment of diplomatic ties between Japan and North Korea can contribute to peace and stability on the Korean peninsula by facilitating cross recognition of the two Koreas by the major powers. However, Japan's failure to pay adequate attention to the security interest of South Korea in seeking rapprochement with North Korea will undermine not only the existing balance of power on the Korean peninsula but also Japan's friendly ties with South Korea. It is therefore essential for Japan to consult closely with South Korea and the United States in dealing with North Korea.

Notes

1. For a full text of the treaty, see *Koreana Quarterly*, Winter 1965–Spring 1966, pp. 119–120.

2. For a detailed analysis, see Hong Nack Kim, "Japan's Policy Toward North Korea Since 1965," *Korea and World Affairs*, Winter 1983, pp. 658–660.

3. Japan provided over $1.13 billion in government credits and over $2.423 billion in commercial loans, and the total Japanese equity investment in South Korea amounted to $610 million from 1965 to 1979. See Hong N. Kim, "Japanese-Korean Relations in the 1980s," *Asian Survey*, May 1987, p. 498. In addition, on January 11, 1983, Japan decided to offer a $4 billion public loan, including $1.85 billion in ODA (official development assistance) funds and $2.15 billion in Export-Import Bank credits. See Hong N. Kim, "Politics of Japan's Economic Aid to South Korea," *Asia Pacific Community*, Spring 1983, pp. 95–96.

4. Yamamoto Tsuyoshi, "Hakusho: Nitcho Fuseijo Kankei" (White paper: Japan–North Korea abnormal relations), *Sekai*, May 1988, pp. 139–140.

5. Ibid., p. 158.

6. Asahi Shimbunsha, *Asahi Nenkan 1988* (Asahi yearbook 1988) (Tokyo: Asahi Shimbunsha, 1988), p. 20.

7. For a Japanese text of the North Korean Foreign Ministry's statement, see *Gendai Korea* (Contemporary Korea) (Tokyo), April 1989, p. 68.

8. Ibid.

9. *Asahi Shimbun*, January 21, 1989.

10. *Asahi Shimbun*, March 30, 1989 (evening edition).

11. *Asahi Shimbun*, April 4, 1989 (evening edition).

12. *Asahi Shimbun*, July 25, 1990.

13. *Asahi Shimbun*, June 16, 1990.

14. Hen Shinichi, "Kaifu vs Roh Tae-Woo no 'Kokusai Seijiryoku' o tou" (Inquiry on Kaifu versus Roh Tae Woo's international political ability), *Hoseki*, September 1990, pp. 112–113.

15. Kim, "Japanese-Korean Relations in the 1980s," pp. 510–511.

16. *Yomiuri Shimbun,* September 27, 1990.

17. *Japan Times,* September 26, 1990.

18. *Asahi Shimbun,* September 28, 1990.

19. For the text of the joint declaration, see *Asahi Shimbun,* September 29, 1990.

20. Ibid.

21. For a detailed analysis, see Hong Nack Kim, "The Normalization of North Korean–Japanese Diplomatic Relations: Problems and Prospects," *Korea and World Affairs,* Winter 1990, pp. 662–664.

22. *Yomiuri Shimbun,* September 29 and 30 and October 1, 1990 (evening edition).

23. For a detailed analysis, see Kim, "Normalization of North Korean–Japanese Diplomatic Relations," pp. 664–667.

24. *Japan Times,* October 9, 1990.

25. *Pyongyang Times,* February 2, 1991, and March 30, 1991. See also *People's Korea,* February 2–9, 1991, and March 30–April 6, 1991.

26. *Pyongyang Times,* February 2, 1991.

27. Ibid.

28. *Yomiuri Shimbun,* March 12, 1991.

29. *Pyongyang Times,* February 2 and March 20, 1991.

30. *People's Korea,* March 30–April 6, 1991.

31. *Yomiuri Shimbun,* May 22 and 23, 1991. See also *Pyongyang Times,* May 25, 1991.

32. *Han'guk Ilbo,* May 17, 1991. See also *Asahi Shimbun,* May 16, 1991.

33. For a detailed analysis, see Hong Nack Kim, "The Two Koreas' Joint Entry into the U.N. and the Implications for Inter-Korean Relations," *Korea and World Affairs,* Autumn 1991, pp. 397–414.

34. *Yomiuri Shimbun,* June 14, 1991.

35. *Yomiuri Shimbun,* August 31, 1991. See also Katsumi Sato, "Nitcho Mugensoku kosho no Enshutsusha" (Staging unprincipled negotiations between Japan and North Korea), *Shokun,* November 1991, p. 165.

36. Ibid.

37. *Yomiuri Shimbun,* September 1, 1991.

38. Ibid.

39. *Yomiuri Shimbun,* September 2, 1991.

40. *Sankei Shimbun,* September 3, 1991.

41. Sato, "Nitcho Mugensoku," pp. 166–167.

42. *Yomiuri Shimbun,* September 1 and 20, 1991. See also *Han'guk Ilbo,* September 12, 1991.

43. For a detailed analysis, see *Yomiuri Shimbun,* September 14, 1991; *Choong Ang Ilbo,* September 13, 1991; and *Han'guk Ilbo,* September 12, 1991. See also Sato, "Nitcho Mugensoku."

44. *Yomiuri Shimbun,* September 14, 1991.

45. *Yomiuri Shimbun,* September 12, 1991.

46. *Yomiuri Shimbun,* November 20 and 21, 1991. See also *Pyongyang Times,* November 23, 1991.

47. *Pyongyang Times,* November 23, 1991.

48. *Yomiuri Shimbun,* November 19, 1991.

49. For the text of the agreement, see *Korea and World Affairs,* Spring 1992, pp. 145–148.

50. For the text of the joint declaration, see ibid., p. 149.

51. *Yomiuri Shimbun,* May 14, 1992.

52. *Yomiuri Shimbun,* May 15, 1992.

53. *People's Korea,* February 8, 1992, p. 1.
54. *Yomiuri Shimbun,* May 15, 1992.
55. Ibid.
56. *Yomiuri Shimbun,* November 6 and 7, 1992. See also *Han'guk Ilbo,* November 6, 1992.
57. *Yomiuri Shimbun,* November 6, 1992.

PART THREE

Inter-Korean Relations

8

The Politics of
Inter-Korean Relations:
Coexistence or Reunification

Young Whan Kihl

For more than four decades, North Korea and South Korea were on the front line of the Cold War, where their cutthroat competition contributed to their continuing estrangement. The founding of two separate Korean states in 1948—the Republic of Korea (ROK, South Korea) and the Democratic People's Republic of Korea (DPRK, North Korea)—epitomized the values of the Cold War politics. As by-products of the Cold War system, they acted as partners in rivalry and enmity.

The dramatic end of the Cold War era, however, has changed both the atmosphere in world politics and the character of inter-Korean relations. With the dawning of the new post–Cold War era after the collapse of East European and Soviet communism in 1989–1991, the continuous rivalry and confrontation between the two Korean states seemed anachronistic, out of tune with the changing world. Therefore, in an effort to catch up with the changing times, the governments of South Korea and North Korea agreed—through a meeting between their prime ministers in December 1991—to initiate a "new détente" and to build a cooperative relationship.

However, the old habit of rivalry and mistrust would not and could not be eliminated overnight, and the two Korean regimes continued to engage in the politics of competing legitimacy in the name of achieving hegemonic reunification of Korea. Thus, the challenge for inter-Korean relations in the post–Cold War world is how to transform the nature of their relationship from one of confrontation into one of peaceful coexistence in an orderly and peaceful manner. This task of institutionalizing the peace process on the Korean peninsula has not been easy, as evidenced by the controversy in the early 1990s over the political and security issues, including North Korea's suspected nuclear weapons program.

In accounting for the historical breakthrough in inter-Korean relations in 1991 and 1992, one may look into both external and internal sources of influence. When the external shock waves created by the removal of the Berlin Wall in November 1989, the collapse of East German state, and the subsequent German reunification reached the shore of the Korean peninsula, they generated electrifying concern and interest. The respective Korean regimes reacted to external shocks with initial disbelief but responded to challenges more positively and aggressively, albeit in varying degrees and intensity. While the ROK continued to reap the benefits of a successful northern policy (Nordpolitik),[1] the DPRK reversed its stance of self-imposed isolation by joining the United Nations and by initiating the new "diplomacy of promotive adaptation."[2]

Although stimulated by these external changes, the key variables in the Korean context responsible for moving the issue of peace and reunification forward as the 1990s unfold seem to be the stakes associated with domestic politics within each Korea and the political relations between the two sides. This chapter addresses the internal political dynamics within each Korea pushing the issue of Korean reunification forward. Discussed first, however, is the context of Korea's "new détente" and the framework for peaceful coexistence, including the nuclear controversy. This is followed by an analysis of domestic political dynamics in each Korea and the problems and prospects for a negotiated settlement for Korea's future and reunification.

The Context of Korea's "New Détente"

Divided Korea was the symbol and legacy of the Cold War era. In its origin the Korean War (1950–1953) was a cause and consequence of the ideological rivalry between the two superpowers, the United States and the Soviet Union, in the post–World War II period.[3]

With the collapse of the Soviet communism, continued confrontation and rivalry between the two halves of divided Korea made little sense in the changed environment and context of world politics. Naturally, the people's desire to liquidate the legacy of the Cold War years was manifest in the nationalist aspiration for reunification of North and South Korea.

Inter-Korean relations have gone through several stages of ups and downs. Prior to 1972, the two Koreas were in violent contact during the Korean War; there followed a period of estrangement and internal consolidation punctured by an occasional border clashes, including North Korean commando raids across the demilitarized zone (DMZ). The major-power détente in the early 1970s with the Sino-U.S. rapprochement in 1972 shifted inter-Korean relations from the incommunicado phase to one of dialogue and negotiation. This phase did not last beyond 1974, however. The next phase of resumed inter-Korean dialogue was also brief—1984–1985; the discussion led to an exchange of visits by few dispersed family members and artist troupes from both sides in 1985. Thus, the inter-Korean dialogue in the 1970s and 1980s, with the familiar on-off pattern of relationship, was short-lived and failed to bear fruit.

The new relationship between North and South in the 1990s, however, represents a breakthrough in inter-Korean relations; it reflects the determination of the two Korean regimes to stay in touch with the changing environments of world politics. This new relationship thus seems to be in line with the search for a new world order and the two Koreas' determination to remain relevant in world affairs.

The new détente of 1991–1992 is the recognition by both Koreas that coexistence is the necessary condition for maintaining peace and stability in the post–Cold War era. It recognizes the self-evident truth that reunification of Korea is not likely, unless force and violence are used, without first establishing the framework for peaceful coexistence and also promoting cooperation and exchanges between the two sides.

These efforts to overcome hostility in inter-Korean relations resulted in the December 1991 signing of two historical documents by the two sides: an agreement on reconciliation, nonaggression, and exchanges and cooperation (Appendix B) and a joint declaration for denuclearization of the peninsula (Appendix C). As a result of these agreements, the possibilities and prospect for peace and reunification of Korea have improved measurably, although North Korea's suspected nuclear weapons program—now placed under an IAEA (International Atomic Agency) safeguards inspection—has raised a threshold of renewed danger and insecurity on the Korean peninsula.[4]

The Framework for Peaceful Coexistence?

Talks and Agreements Between Prime Ministers

A major breakthrough in inter-Korean relations occurred in 1990 with the holding of high-level talks between North and South at the prime ministerial level. The first meeting held in Seoul in September was historic in the sense that each side came to accept the other, for the first time, as a "legitimate" partner in negotiation.[5] The two subsequent meetings held in 1990, however, produced no substantive agreements.

The fourth meeting, scheduled for spring 1991, was unilaterally canceled by Pyongyang in protest over the U.S.-ROK joint military exercises called Team Spirit 1991. The rescheduled meeting, set for late August 1991, was postponed once again by Pyongyang because of the prevailing uncertain situation following the abortive coup in the Soviet Union. The meeting finally took place in Pyongyang in October, and an agreement was reached on October 22 that both sides would negotiate for a single text on the North-South agreement on reconciliation and cooperation to be worked out at a subsequent meeting.

It was during the fifth high-level talks in Seoul that the two sides successfully negotiated the agreement on reconciliation, nonaggression, and exchanges and cooperation (hereafter referred to as the basic agreement or the agreement) on December 13, 1991 (see Appendix B). This historic agreement was followed by the adoption of the joint declaration on denuclearization of the Korean peninsula (hereafter referred to as the joint declaration) on December 31, 1991 (Appendix C), which was later signed by the respective prime ministers on January 20, 1992. The final ratified documents of the basic agreement and the joint declaration were exchanged during the sixth high-level talks in Pyongyang on February 19, 1992.

The basic agreement was clearly a compromise between the two divergent approaches and positions held by the respective sides on inter-Korean negotiation. Whereas the North insisted that the major steps be taken first on political and military matters so as to achieve reunification, the South advocated confidence-building measures on economic and cultural matters as first priority so as to foster a climate of mutual trust. The text of the basic agreement is a comprehensive document that incorporates the varying positions of both sides. Although the interpretation of the text might differ between the two sides, thereby providing a new source of contention, the 1991 agreement constitutes a landmark in the forty-six-year history of inter-Korean rivalry and competition.

The Substance of the Basic Agreement

The agreement consists of twenty-five separate articles, apart from a preamble, that are grouped into four chapters. The first chapter with eight articles contains pledges on reconciliation: mutual recognition and respect for each other's system (article 1); noninterference in the other's internal affairs (article 2); cessation of hostile propaganda (article 3); forbearance from attempts to overthrow the other side (article 4); conversion of the armistice into a durable peace (article 5); measures to build cooperation and promote "national" interests abroad (article 6); establishment of a North-South liaison office at Panmunjom within three months of the exchange of ratified documents (article 7); and creation of a North-South political committee within one month thereafter to implement and enforce these measures (article 8).

The second chapter with six articles deals with pledges on nonaggression. It promises the nonuse of force and nonaggression against each other (article 9); establishes the peaceful settlement of disputes through dialogue and negotiation (article 10); maintains the existing military demarcation line established by the July 27, 1953, armistice to define a zone of nonaggression (article 11); establishes a North-South joint military commission within three months to advance various confidence-building measures and promote disarmament (article 12); provides for installing direct telephone links between the military authorities to prevent accidental conflict (article 13); and forms a North-South military subcommittee within one month to implement these provisions (article 14).

The third chapter with nine articles deals with pledges on exchanges and cooperation. The terms include the joint development of resources and economic exchange of goods and cooperation as a kind of "domestic commerce with joint ventures" (article 15); exchanges and cooperation in varied areas, including science and technology, education, arts, health, sports, environment, and publishing and journalism (e.g., newspaper, radio, television broadcasts) (article 16); free travel and contacts between the two Koreas (article 17); free correspondence, meetings, and visits between members of divided families (article 18); the reconnecting of railway lines and the opening of sea and air routes (article 19); postal and telecommunications contacts and efforts to guarantee their privacy (article 20); cooperation internationally to promote economic, cultural, and related activities abroad (article 21); the establishment of a joint economic exchanges and cooperation commission in three months (article 22); and the creation of an exchange and cooperation subcommittee within one month thereafter to carry out these agreements (article 23).

The final section of the agreement is composed of two articles, one regarding an amendment procedure based on mutual concurrence (article 24), the other providing for the agreement to take effect on the date the two sides exchange its text (article 25).

The agreement finally came into force February 19, 1992, the date of the exchange of ratified documents. The subsequent high-level talks in 1992 also made some progress toward institutionalizing the peace process by setting up the machinery to carry out the basic agreement. During the eighth high-level talks in Pyongyang on September 17, 1992, for instance, the two prime ministers signed and put into effect three separate protocols to implement the basic agreement. They included protocols on (1) nonaggression, (2) reconciliation, and (3) exchanges and cooperation. They also agreed to establish a joint commission on reconciliation; they had previously reached an accord to create a liaison office in Panmunjom during the seventh high-level talks, held in Seoul in May 1992. Despite this progress, the protocols failed to resolve several other key and controversial issues, such as the recognition of each other's government in the political arena, prohibition of arms buildup along the DMZ, and the on-site nuclear inspection guidelines, which were left for future discussion at related joint commissions and other forums.[6]

The significance of the basic agreement is that North Korea and South Korea finally came to accept its underlying premise regarding peace and reunification. Clearly, peaceful coexistence must precede any change in the status quo that reunification of North and South will entail. The agreement is also a reflection of political realism. Reunification, which both sides pursue as a policy, is obviously a condition in the Korean peninsula that is feasible at best only in the distant future.

The Nuclear Dimension and Stalemate

The inter-Korean agreement on peaceful coexistence does not amount to very much substantively unless the nuclear threat and nuclear blackmail are also eliminated from the strategic thinking and calculus in Korea. The danger of nuclear proliferation is real, and a nuclear arms race between North and South is also possible if North Korea continues to pursue its ambitious nuclear development program and South Korea is enticed to match the challenge. The nuclear dilemma was addressed by several important developments in the closing months of 1991.

First, U.S. President George Bush announced on September 28, 1991, a drastic reduction—and removal in some cases—of U.S. land-based tactical nuclear weapons deployed abroad; included, by implication, were U.S. forces stationed in South Korea. Second, President Roh Tae Woo of South Korea declared on November 8, 1991, that it would not manufacture, store, deploy, or use nuclear weapons and called upon North Korea to join him in making the Korean peninsula a nuclear-free zone. This statement by Roh was interpreted as his confirmation that U.S. nuclear weapons were no longer deployed in South Korea or were in the process of being removed. Third, before Roh's proposal, North Korea had already put forward its proposal for making the Korean peninsula a nuclear-free zone.

In order to forestall the danger of nuclear war, North Korea and South Korea agreed on the joint declaration on the denuclearization of the Korean peninsula on December 31, 1991; it was subsequently signed by their respective prime ministers January 20, 1992 and put into effect February 19, 1992 at the sixth high-level talks held in Pyongyang. The joint declaration outlines the two sides' desire "to eliminate the danger of nuclear war through denuclearization of the Korean Peninsula" and thereby "to create an environment and conditions favorable for peace and peaceful unification" of Korea and also to "contribute to peace and security in Asia and the world."[7]

The joint declaration consists of six points: The South and the North "shall not test, manufacture, produce, receive, possess, store, deploy or use nuclear weapons" (article 1); "shall use nuclear energy solely for peaceful purposes" (article 2); "shall not possess nuclear reprocessing and uranium enrichment facilities" (article 3); "shall conduct inspection of the objects selected by the other side and agreed upon between the two sides, in accordance with procedures and methods to be determined by the South-North Joint Nuclear Control Commission" (article 4); "shall establish and operate a South-North Joint Nuclear Control Commission within one month of the effectuation of this joint declaration" (article 5); and shall put the declaration into force "as of the day the two sides exchange appropriate instruments following the completion of their respective procedures for bringing it into effect" (article 6).

Between February 19 and March 14, seven rounds of contacts were held between South and North to discuss the formation and operation of the joint nuclear control commission. After serious discussion on the contents and wording, the two sides finally adopted a governing document on March 14, 1992. However, at the first commission meeting in Panmunjom on March 19, the two sides failed to make progress in how to interpret and implement the terms of the agreement. The fourth point in the document, for instance, was about the formation and operation of the commission, but they could not agree on how to proceed on the verification procedure and inspection methods.[8]

The two sides began substantive discussion on the proposed rules for mutual nuclear inspections at the ninth meeting on August 31. It soon became obvious in subsequent meetings that they could not agree on the basic principle of inspection: the "principle of reciprocity" (the South) versus the "principle of simultaneous dissolution of suspicion" (the North). According to the North, because the degree of concern and suspicion regarding nuclear development is different in the South and the North, the South could inspect one place in the North (the Yongbyon site), and the North should be allowed to inspect all the U.S. military installations in the South.[9] The South insisted, in the name of reciprocity, that other suspected sites besides Yongbyon, including Pyongsan, Pakch'on, Sunch'on and Taech'on, should also be made available for inspection.

Other differences over the rules of mutual nuclear inspections pertained to the targets and method of inspection. Whereas the North, in the name of "asymmetric inspection" rule, sought to inspect all military installations of the South, it insisted that the South should inspect only the Yongbyon facility (designated as civilian) and refrain from inspecting other suspected sites, including military bases. The South emphasized that special inspections, along with routine inspections, were needed to completely dispel nuclear suspicions.

The special inspection, also called "challenge inspection," would permit either side to designate a suspect area of the other side at any time and inspect it with twenty-four-hour advance notice to the other side. The North was against special inspection on the ground that this idea ran counter to article 4 of the joint denuclearization declaration, which calls for "inspections of objects which one side chooses and both sides agree on." The South, in turn, claimed that special inspection was permitted under the provision of article 4 that defined a positive concept: In order to effectively embody the purpose and spirit of the joint declaration, the other side should agree when one side selected a target for inspection.[10]

In the end, the North-South talks on the nuclear issues failed to materialize beyond the thirteenth meeting on December 17. The 1993 Team Spirit military exercises gave the North an excuse for unilaterally suspending all talks, including those by the joint nuclear control commission. The real point of contention was the underlying principle of "transparency" (i.e., openness and accessibility in arms-control talks) concerning on-site inspection favored by the South but opposed by the North. This difference in positions was thus insurmountable because of conflict of interests and approaches between the two sides to on-site inspection.

Unification Policy and Politics: Change and Continuity

Reunification policy plans put forward by North Korea and South Korea reflect an attempt to make them sound more flexible and realistic. North Korea, for instance, advocated giving greater authority to "regional governments" under its plan for a proposed confederation, the Democratic Confederal Republic of Koryo (DCRK); the proposal reflects the "one nation, one state, two systems and two regional governments" formula. Although this theme was accentuated by President Kim Il Sung in his 1991 New Year's address, he did not reiterate the same point or raise the DCRK plan in his 1992 New Year's address. In his 1991 address, Kim defended the confederation plan as both "fair" and "the only and quickest way ... to reunify the country peacefully." He then went on to condemn as nonsensical "unification by absorption" or "prevailing over communism" policies attributed to South Korea.[11] According to Kim Il Sung:

> Recently the south Korean authorities, betwitched by the method of amalgamation through absorption adopted by a foreign country, are dreaming a fantastic dream of applying such a method in our country, too, by relying on foreign forces, through entreaty diplomacy, pursuing what they call the "northern policy." They are making requests for interference and intervention of other countries in order to force theirs on the other side, instead of showing sincerity in the talks with the same nation. This is an expression of their sycophant mentality and attitude to keep the country divided forever as well as the replica of the bankrupt policy of "reunification by prevailing over communism."
>
> In our country "reunification by prevailing over communism" is a wild fancy which will never come true. It has already been proved by history that our country cannot be reunified by one side eating away the other, either by war or a peaceful means. The south Korean authorities must understand clearly that the independent stand of our Party and the Government of our Republic is unshakable and that socialism we have built by implementing the Juche idea is unconquerable."[12]

Then Kim Il Sung injected a new element of flexibility or possibility of compromise by stating that "in an effort to make it easier for the whole nation to reach agreement on this [DCRK] proposal, we are ready to consult the matter of gradually and completely effecting reunification through confederation by vesting the regional autonomous governments of the confederal republic with more rights on a tentative basis and then increasing the functions of the central government in the future." This offer was not heeded, however, by the South Korean side.[13]

Because of the rapid and fundamental changes occurring in the external milieu, the leadership of North Korea seems to have resolved to bury the issue of confederation for the time being. Yet it is not quite willing to acknowledge the adoption of a new framework for relations and coexistence between the two systems that the 1991 basic agreement would entail. In reference to the 1991 agreement, Kim Il Sung characterized its adoption as "a great victory" and "a historic event which provided a new landmark in the ways of achieving national reunification."[14] Yet he emphasized its adoption as a reaffirmation of the threefold principles of independence, peaceful reunification, and great national unity as contained in the July 4, 1972, joint communiqué on North-South dialogue.

It is for domestic political reasons, therefore, that North Korea is not prepared or willing to commit to necessary reforms or changes of policy on socialism. Thus, on January 3, 1992, Kim Jong Il made a strong defense of North

Korean policy and strategy for building socialism. In a talk to party cadres and government leaders that was publicized only in February 1992, Kim Jong Il attempted to provide an ideological shield to protect North Korea from external pollution:

> The path to socialism is an untrodden path; it is a thorny path of revolution, an advance along which is faced with relentless confrontation with and an uncompromising struggle against imperialism. Therefore, trials and difficulties are inevitable in the advance of socialism, and unexpected situations may arise. The frustration of socialism and the revival of capitalism in some countries ... is only a temporary, local phenomenon. But we can never regard it as an accidental phenomenon, nor can we consider that it has been brought about only by external factors.[15]

This is a statement of an ideologue, not a pragmatist, who is bent on the course of reform and change in policy that is in trouble. This statement faithfully mirrors the self-righteous worldview of his father, who is bent on defending the system he built at all costs against the whirlwind of change blowing from outside. "The imperialists are clamouring about the end of a cold war and the arrival of the time of peace," observed Kim Il Sung in his 1991 New Year's address, "but the international situation is still tense and complicated and a sharp confrontation and struggle between progress and reaction are going on." Because "they are trying more openly to realize their wild dream of dominating the whole world," Kim insisted, "the world progressive people must not be deceived by the imperialists' honeyed words, pin their hopes on their deceptive 'aid' but forge ahead under the unfurled banner of independence against imperialism."[16]

South Korea has also taken certain "sensible" measures, such as making the proposed Korean National Community (KNC) unification formula—of which establishing the Korean Commonwealth is an integral part—sound more realistic and workable. The newly established Common Fund for Unification was also timely in the light of what transpired in unified Germany. The enormous financial cost incurred following the West German absorption of East Germany has turned out to be unbearably high and almost ruined the German economy. In 1992 the government announced plans to increase the inter-Korean cooperation fund to 100 billion won ($US 137.5 million) from 62.8 billion won.[17]

In June 1991 President Roh Tae Woo presided over the unification policy forum inside his administration to address the hypothetical situation of an emergency that may arise from the collapse of communism in North Korea as in East Germany in 1990. Because this type of contingency planning was vehemently attacked by North Korea, the Roh government subsequently adopted a low-key posture on reunification planning; for example, it issued an unpublicized directive to the ministries for estimating the cost and benefit of the sudden influx of 1 million refugees from North Korea in the hypothetical situation of political turmoil occurring there. The higher economic cost of Korean reunification, in view of the reported experience of Germany, led South

Korea to tone down its initial enthusiasm and rhetoric. The estimated cost of Korean reunification, if North Korea collapses and is absorbed by South Korea, runs anywhere from $300 billion to $700 billion depending on when the reunification would take place.[18]

Apart from this adjustment on a policy level, North Korea and South Korea continue to uphold the strategic position on unification that can be called "hegemonic reunification."[19] Each side desires to bring about reunification of Korea on its own terms—the DCRK scheme for the DPRK or the KNC or Korean Commonwealth plan for the ROK.[20] The signing of the basic agreement in 1991 has not changed fundamental reality: the self-serving character of the unification policy and strategy of the respective Korean states.

In 1992 South Korea dismissed the North Korean demand to abolish the national security law on the ground that it would heighten North Korea's strategy of the "united front campaign" and foster antigovernment forces in South Korea. In 1993 the Kim Young Sam government expressed reluctance to repeal the law. The South Korean proposal for "the challenge inspection"—intended to assure transparency in mutual inspection of suspected nuclear facilities—entails on-site safeguard verification of suspected installations simultaneously and on short notice. The proposal is strenuously opposed by the North. North Korea demands the withdrawal of U.S. troops from Korean soil; South Korea dismisses this demand as being in violation of the terms of noninterference in internal matters as stipulated in the basic agreement.

Underlying these maneuvers are the deep-seated distrust and the long-standing mutual suspicion between the two sides. Despite these charges and countercharges, the important fact is that North Korea and South Korea have come a long way notwithstanding the reality of the stalemate in their relations. It is no mean accomplishment that North Korea has finally come to acknowledge and accept the principle South Korea has insisted on all along: that reunification cannot be achieved overnight, barring revolution and war, and that peaceful coexistence and exchanges must precede any reunification because the latter entails change in the status quo.

How to Manage Political Transition?

Both Koreas have embarked upon the path of political change and transition. Whereas North Korea has been working for a smooth transition of political leadership from President Kim Il Sung to his son, Kim Jong Il, South Korea has completed a peaceful and orderly democratic transition (via the 1992 presidential election) from the Roh Tae Woo era into the postdemocratization era. The factors and forces underlying the dynamics of political change in each Korea and the problems and prospects of the successful democratic transition will be the focus of attention by policymakers and the public alike inside and outside of Korea.

North Korea: Political Succession

North Korea continues to face the task of an orderly transition of power and political succession from Kim Il Sung to Kim Jong Il. What makes North Korea unique as a political system is the cult of personality of President Kim Il Sung, perhaps unsurpassed in the annals of communist states. Kim Il Sung has been the undisputed leader of North Korea since 1948: president of the communist state, general secretary of the Communist Party, de facto supreme commander of the armed forces, and founder of *Juche*, the reigning ideology of North Korea.[21]

What makes the North Korean version of communism distinctive is the hereditary succession of leadership from Kim Il Sung to his son, Kim Jong Il. The ratio of party membership to population, 17 percent, is the highest in the communist world. The ratio was around 4.5 to 5 percent in the former Soviet Union and 11 percent in Romania under Ceauşescu. The change within the party is therefore more difficult in North Korea than it was in other communist countries.[22] The campaign is under way to transfer charisma from father to son by means of building up the cult of Kim Jong Il's personality. For instance, on the occasion of celebrating Kim Jong Il's fiftieth birthday February 16, 1992, the *Pyongyang Times* printed on the front page birthday "best wishes" with the following claims:

> A man with a total knowledge and understanding of the Juche idea founded by President Kim Il Sung, Comrade Kim Jong Il has to its [sic] credit a number of brilliant achievements both ideological and theoretical in enriching this idea. He has rounded President Kim Il Sung's idea into a complete system and developed it in keeping with the demands of the present time and the development of revolution. Particularly to be noted is that he has given perfect answers to the theoretical and practical problems arising in socialist construction, thus showing the way to realize the independent cause of the popular masses.

The propaganda on him continued:

> Comrade Kim Jong Il has a remarkable set of human qualities: he is modest, unaffected and considerate. He takes the people to his all-embracing heart and is responsible for their fate, showing warm care in every way for their living. That is why the Korean people call him "our dear leader" and are advancing along the road indicated by him, entrusting their fate in him.[23]

In these laudatory statements on Kim Jong Il is the sense of the Confucian norm of filial piety of the son toward his father. The "dear leader" (Kim Jong Il) is depicted as a man displaying both loyalty to the "great leader" (Kim Il Sung) and compassion and modesty toward his subjects in the socialist "hermit" kingdom that is now ready to open up slightly. The son's filial piety has taken the form of mastering the *Juche* idea founded by his father and also erecting a series of monuments to his father (the Juche Tower and Arch of Triumph) and deceased mother.

One of the unfulfilled tasks of President Kim, who on April 15, 1992, turned eighty years old, is the reunification of Korea. That this could not be achieved perhaps in his lifetime in accord with the North's confederation scheme has been a rude awakening for President Kim and for many of his followers in North Korea. Realizing that a confederal Korea will not be attained very soon,

President Kim wishes to leave to his son a modus vivendi that is acceptable to North Korea by initiating normalization talks with Japan and the United States and undertaking negotiations with South Korea on reunification.

The succession to power by his son will occur sometime after the seventh congress of the Korean Workers' Party is convened (not yet called into session as of mid-1993). Kim Il Sung then will probably retire and manage the affairs of the party and the state in the background as an elder statesman. He will perhaps create and chair a council of elder statesmen and retired party cadres, as Deng Xiaoping did in China. Kim Il Sung will then exit from power accompanied by some of his faithful followers and senior cadres, such as Pak Sŏng-chŏl, Li Chong-ok, and Oh Jin-wu.[24]

South Korea: Democratic Transition

Under the South Korean constitution, President Roh Tae Woo could not succeed himself after completion of his five-year term in 1993. Before stepping down as president of the Sixth Republic, Roh expressed his desire to leave as his legacy the fact that he was instrumental in bringing reunification of Korea closer to reality. During his tenure, he was credited with three major accomplishments: democratic reforms, the northern policy, and inter-Korean dialogue.[25]

Of these three major policies, Roh's northern policy has been the most successful, although strides also have been made in democratization.[26] Since the reunification of the country has not been achieved, it is in this area of inter-Korean dialogue and negotiation that Roh wished to see further progress made before he stepped down as president in February 1993. Because of stalemated negotiations on the nuclear issue, however, the Roh government was unable to achieve substantive progress in such areas of inter-Korean relations as the Red Cross talks on divided-family reunion, which would allow older Koreans to travel and meet with family members across the border before it is too late for this aging group.

President Roh is no doubt credited with implementing the bold initiative of putting an end to the authoritarian legacy and bringing about the democratic transition in South Korean politics. Although his commitment to the cause of democracy seemed undiminished, he was often criticized by democratic forces as sometimes too slow and hesitant in carrying out the reform measures.[27] Of the eight points in the reform package he announced June 29, 1987, most of them, including freedom of the press, have been implemented. Yet the economic slowdown and rampant corruption, such as deals on money and politics, led his administration to be increasingly subject to severe criticism for indecisive leadership. Consolidation of democracy was slow in coming in the Roh administration in South Korea.

By taking a bold stand on North-South relations, President Roh wanted to find an exit from the stalemated economy and the slowdown in democratic consolidation. Clearly he wished to be remembered in history for being on the front line of inter-Korean relations and Korean reunification, as shown in the successful conclusion of the historic reconciliation and nonaggression pact between North and South.

In his 1992 New Year's address, President Roh said that "1992 will be remembered as the first year of the concentrated efforts of the 70 million Korean people to accomplish the great task of building a single national community.[28] He is clearly the one who took a positive step toward achieving reunification, the nationalist aspiration of the Korean people. He held reunification, like democracy, foremost in his mind, perhaps to the same degree that economic growth and industrialization were the goal-driven obsession of former President Park Chung Hee. The election of Kim Young Sam in December 1992 marked a new beginning for South Korea's postdemocratization politics.

Why Korean Reunification
Is Difficult to Attain

As to the problems and future prospects for Korean unification, there are two preliminary points of analysis to note; these highlight the contrast between the 1991 and the 1972 agreements and the perceptual variance between North Korea and South Korea on the 1991 agreement. First, whereas the July 4, 1972, joint communiqué led North and South to agree on the three principles of Korean unification—independence, peaceful means, and great national unity—the 1991 nonaggression pact provided a legal framework and basis for peace and reunification between the two sides. Whereas the 1972 joint communiqué stipulated the *desired goals* and ideals, the 1991 agreement specified the *necessary means* through which to attain Korean reunification. In 1991 North and South agreed on how to achieve unification rather than on unification itself.

Yet the 1991 agreement also made it obvious how difficult it is to bring about reunification overnight. Reunification as an end product cannot be attained without peaceful coexistence first, achieved via the intermediary step and stage of promoting cooperation and exchanges. The moment the agreement on reconciliation and nonaggression was attained, peace and coexistence rather than unification became the accepted norm and rule of conduct. The reason is that reunification entails change in the status quo. Normalization of relations and institutionalization of the peace process logically precede rather than follow reunification of the divided country if war and revolution are ruled out as the means. The 1991 basic agreement is thus the precondition for an eventual reunification of North and South.

Second, however, one can detect variation between North and South regarding the perception and expectation, at least initially, as to what the 1991 agreement entails. The ultimate strategic goal of North Korea's Kim Il Sung remains the withdrawal of foreign (i.e., U.S.) troops from Korean soil. This basic premise was conveyed by Kim Il Sung to South Korea's visiting delegation during the sixth conference of prime ministers in Pyongyang. When he addressed members of both delegations February 20, 1992, Kim Il Sung expressed his satisfaction with the basic agreement and the joint declaration on denuclearization by calling them "an epochal event that will become a milestone in achieving the country's peace and reunification." He continued: "The time has come when there is no need for foreign troops to stay in the country. The time has come when there are no conditions for foreign military bases in the country. I believe that now is the time for us to make a resolute decision on this matter."[29]

The following conversation between Prime Minister Chung Won-sik and President Kim Il Sung during the closed-door meeting in Kim's office is revealing in its exhibition of how perception varied between the two sides. The text of this conversation was released by the South Korean spokesman on the train during the return trip from Pyongyang to Kaesong:

> *Chung:* Our conviction is that although the country has been divided against our will, unification should be achieved with our own hands.
>
> *Kim:* Cooperation will be realized by itself if only we can unite.
>
> *Chung:* The problem is to dispel mutual distrust at an early date.
>
> *Kim:* Even distrust can be removed if we unite. Now that the issue of nonaggression has been resolved, we should unite and unify independently. We should unite by emptying everything of the past regardless of whether it is Ch'ŏndo-kyo, Christianity, Confucianism, or Marxism.

This exchange obviously reflects differences in perception and expectation between the two sides. Whereas Seoul takes the agreement with caution, Pyongyang takes it with flair. Removing foreign influences from the unification talks is manifest in both sides, although Kim Il Sung is more xenophobic in his reaction.

Roh's desire to hold summit talks with Kim Il Sung failed to materialize even though an ROK press release February 18, 1992, issued on the eve of the scheduled sixth high-level talks in Pyongyang had provided an optimistic note that "an era of rapprochement and cooperation is opened up."

In the light of these perceptual gaps and variance in expectations between North and South, the 1991 agreement will need to be placed in its proper perspective. It is important to stress that in the Korean context, peaceful coexistence is a means to an end rather than an end in itself. What North and South agreed on in 1991 and 1992 is to allow an interim stage to come about—a stage between past confrontation and future reunification. This stage of peaceful coexistence for the interim is something South Korea has insisted upon all along. It is noteworthy that North Korea has finally come to accept reconciliation and détente as both necessary and unavoidable; the North has recognized the changing reality of world politics in the post–Cold War era.

In terms of adjustment and adaptation, North Korea has carried out its diplomacy with skill. Its decision to join the United Nations simultaneously with South Korea in 1991 is a testimonial to North Korean acceptance of realism in diplomacy.[30] In taking this step, North Korea abandoned its longstanding objection to separate membership in favor of joint membership of North Korea and South Korea as a single country. Pyongyang's seeking of diplomatic normalization with Japan is also a strategic move not only to counter Seoul's successful northern policy of reaching out to the socialist countries in Eastern Europe and the former Soviet Union but also to secure "compensation" money from Japan to resuscitate its stagnant economy. North Korea skillfully maneuvered to hold a high-level talk with the United States in New York in June 1993. The main agenda was North Korea's announced withdrawal from the nuclear NPT regime. These are telling examples of North Korean acceptance of the dictates of political realism in diplomacy.

What Lies Ahead?

The basic agreement was arrived at by the indigenous means of North Korea and South Korea themselves. That the two sides opted for bilateral and direct negotiations without involving a third party or an intermediary is important. It shows a posture of independence and self-reliance in the settlement of longstanding disputes between North and South. Although this is a positive development from the standpoint of Korean nationalism, the multilateral approach sometimes works better when the parties to a dispute are hopelessly stalemated and unable to resolve the conflict directly. This is precisely what is happening in the unification politics between North and South Korea.

Many problems and difficulties therefore lie ahead on the path toward Korean reunification. Clearly, an agreement is one thing, but its implementation is another matter. Within one month after exchange of final documents, three separate committees were established in the political, military, and exchange and cooperation spheres, although the work of these committees has been meager thus far. This was followed by the establishment of a South-North liaison office, a joint commission on economic exchanges and cooperation, and other working-level groups; their function is to implement the terms of the basic agreement.[31]

Moreover, the subsequent talks between prime ministers in Pyongyang and in Seoul have not been evaluated positively. Except for an exchange of ratified documents during the February 1992 meeting in Pyongyang, no substantive progress has been made in resolving the pending issues. During a meeting in Pyongyang with Prime Minister Chung Won-sik, President Kim Il Sung was rather formalistic and rigid, repeating the familiar demand for withdrawal of foreign troops from Korean soil. No breakthrough was forthcoming on the nuclear issue or on the Roh-Kim summitry.

From Pyongyang's perspective, President Roh's successor will be better suited as a counterpart in the summitry. In fact, a summit between Kim Il Sung and Kim Young Sam, South Korea's newly elected president, was floated as a possibility in 1993; this summit could possibly provide a means of breaking the deadlock in inter-Korean relations. Whereas the democratization process in South Korea has thus injected a new element into the equation of Korea's reunification politics, the anticipated seventh congress of the Korean Workers' Party may likewise affect the outcome of North Korea's policy on Korea's future reunification. Before the possible summit, however, there will likely be a series of moves and maneuvers.

In 1993, as far as South Korea's "new democratic" government was concerned, the Korean Commonwealth plan remained as the key component of its official unification policy. In a major foreign policy address on May 24, 1993, President Kim Young Sam proclaimed "a new diplomacy" for Korea, one that would incorporate "a future-oriented policy" on the unification issue.[32] His government, he continued, "will move from the initial step of reconciliation and cooperation to the next phase of a Korean Commonwealth, and to a final stage of a united nation of one people and one state."[33] This statement clearly indicated that the newly elected "democratic" government did not necessarily deviate from the KNC unification policy of its predecessor regime in the Sixth Republic. Under the KNC formula, the Korean Commonwealth (Nambuk Yŏnhap) is not the ultimate form but only an interim stage or a transitional system that is deemed essential and necessary before reaching the final destination of creating a "Unified Democratic Republic" of Korea.

As for North Korea in 1993, its leader Kim Il Sung unveiled a new ten-point program for reunification, which was subsequently adopted by its parliament during the fifth session of the ninth Supreme People's Assembly on April 7, 1993.[34] In presenting this measure to the parliament, DPRK Premier Kang Sŏng-san mentioned ROK President Kim Young Sam's "alleged" reference in his inaugural address that "no ally is better than the nation."[35] Yet he also presented four preconditions for resuming inter-Korean dialogue, ones politically almost impossible for the Seoul government to accept:

1. The south must give up its policy of reliance on foreign powers. It must not rely on the United States and Japan politically, militarily and economically; instead, it must regard solidarity between the same ethnic group as more important.
2. The south must express its determination to oust U.S. troops from the south.
3. The south must suspend forever joint military exercises with foreign (U.S.) troops.
4. The south must pull itself out from under the U.S. nuclear umbrella.[36]

The timing of Pyongyang's peace gesture, however, was suspected by some observers. According to this view, Pyongyang's desire was to create a favorable impression internationally so as to conclude successfully the scheduled high-level talks with the United States in New York. In June 1993 the United States and North Korea opened a dialogue, and North Korea suspended on June 11 its announced withdrawal from the nuclear nonproliferation treaty regime. Earlier in May, DPRK Premier Kang Sŏng-san had indicated a favorable reaction to the ROK's proposal for resuming the suspended inter-Korean dialogue. Again, the targeted audience was interpreted to be the United States, not South Korea. The speculation was that an exchange of special envoys between the two Koreas might take place so as to prepare for a possible summit between presidents of the two sides.

The purpose of Pyongyang's latest move on unification, according to the Korean Central News Agency report on April 7, 1993, was "to put a period to the nearly half a century long history of division and confrontation and to re-unify the country … [by] transcending all differences, and pave together the way for national reunification.[37] In this way North Korea wanted to reaffirm the July 4, 1972, joint communiqué of South-North dialogue and negotiation on Korean unification—that is, the threefold principles of independence, peace, and great national unity.

In short, North Korea continued to adhere to the policy of hegemonic reunification of Korea, although the tone of its proclamation was rather moderate yet self-righteous. Included in the ten-point platform were the following:

1. A unified state, independent, peaceful and neutral, should be founded through the great unity of the whole nation.
2. Unity should be based on patriotism and the spirit of national independence.
3. Unity should be achieved on the principle of promoting coexistence, coprosperity and common interests and subordinating everything to the cause of national reunification.
4. All manner of political disputes that foment division and confrontation between the fellow countrymen should be stopped and unity be achieved.
5. They should dispel fears of invasion from the South and from the North, prevailing over communism and communization altogether and believe in and [have] unity with each other.
6. They should set store by democracy and join hands on the road to national reunification, not rejecting each other for the difference in isms and principles.
7. They should protect material and spiritual wealth of individual persons and organizations and encourage them to be used favorably for the promotion of great national unity.
8. The whole nation should understand, trust and unite with one another through contacts, travels and dialogues.
9. The whole nation in the North and the South and overseas should strengthen solidarity with one another on the way to national reunification.
10. Those who have contributed to the great unity of the nation and to the cause of national reunification should be highly estimated.

The overall impression one gets from reading Pyongyang's ten-point proclamation is mixed. A moderate and reasoning tone and self-righteous and self-defensive rhetoric were combined in the pronouncement. The latter used to be the prevailing tone that characterized earlier pronouncements on Korean reunification.

Some of the old themes Pyongyang repeated in its 1993 proclamation included "the unity of the whole nation," "the spirit of national independence," practicing "democracy," and strengthening "solidarity" among Koreans in the North, South, and abroad. Appearing afresh were such eye-catching themes as to promote "coexistence, coprosperity, and common interests" (point 3), to "dispel fears of invasion from the South and from the North" (point 5), and to "trust and unite with one another through contacts, travels and dialogue" (point 8) instead of "dialogue, contacts and travels" in that order.

Conspicuously lacking in the 1993 proclamation—the absence might signify a new approach and new thinking on Korea's future by the DPRK leadership—were the accent on "urgency" and the counsel on "immediate" moves and actions toward reunification of the country.

Conclusion

As the initial enthusiasm and euphoria die down over the historic inter-Korean agreement on nonaggression, the cold facts have to be faced: separate existence of and confrontation between the two rival systems. Whether and how long this state of skepticism will reign—at a time when pressures are mounting on North Korea to abandon its ambitious nuclear weapons program—is not clear. The high expectations South Korean business has about North Korean trade and investment (as articulated by Daewoo's president, Kim Woo-choong, in 1992) will also need to be cooled to the level of realism. North Korea has a long way to go before it is ready to deal with the outside world meaningfully. Internal economic and institutional reforms must be implemented before it will be ready to entertain foreign business and joint ventures. Political opening and liberalization are needed, but for domestic political reasons, the Kim regime is not likely to institute needed reform measures.

Nevertheless, there is reason for a more positive and hopeful expectation for the future of Korea. North and South have come a long way, and they are headed in the right direction, thanks to the breakthrough of the inter-Korean agreement on reconciliation and nonaggression in 1991. It will take a long time for the two Korean states to reach the proper stage ready for reunification by way of inter-Korean exchanges and cooperation. The agenda of Korean reunification has not been shortened by the parties' latest agreement. Until there is progress on inter-Korean exchanges and cooperation, the peaceful reunification of North and South will remain a theoretical possibility rather than a realistic and attainable alternative. Nonetheless, just as Rome was not built overnight, so too will the edifice of Korean reunification require the painstaking nurturing of an architectural work. It is hoped that the nationalist dream and aspiration of the Korean people for reunification of their divided country will be realized before too long, perhaps not beyond the close of the twentieth century.

Notes

1. Northern policy, or Nordpolitik, refers to the foreign policy initiative of President Roh Tae Woo's government in 1988 to normalize diplomatic relations with the communist countries in Eastern Europe, the Soviet Union, and China. By 1992 Seoul had successfully established diplomatic ties with all but Castro's Cuba.

2. Young Whan Kihl, "North Korea's Foreign Relations: Diplomacy of Promotive Adaptation," *Journal of Northeast Asian Studies*, Vol. 10, No. 3 (Fall 1991), pp. 30–45.

3. Bruce Cumings, *The Origins of the Korean War*, 2 vols. (Princeton, NJ: Princeton University Press, 1981 and 1990).

4. Andrew Mack, "North Korea and the Bomb," *Foreign Policy*, Vol. 83 (Summer 1991), pp. 87–104; Leonard S. Spector and Jacqueline S. Smith, "North Korea: The Next Nuclear Nightmare?" *Arms Control Today*, March 1991, pp. 8–13.

5. Young Whan Kihl, *The 1990 Prime Ministers' Meeting Between North and South Korea: An Analysis*, Asian Update Series (New York: The Asia Society, 1990).

6. *Korea Newsreview*, September 14, 1992, p. 4.

7. For the text of the joint declaration, see Appendix C. Also see *Korea and World Affairs*, Vol. 16, No. 1 (Spring 1992), p. 149.

8. The details of the discussion at the various meetings of the South-North nuclear control commission appear in *South-North Dialogue in Korea*, No. 55 (July 1992), pp. 85–96, and No. 56 (October 1992), pp. 95–102.

9. Ibid., No. 57 (April 1993), pp. 57–58.

10. Ibid.

11. *Pyongyang Times*, January 1, 1991.

12. Ibid.

13. Ibid.

14. *Pyongyang Times*, January 1, 1992.

15. *Rodong Sinmun*, February 4, 1992; *Pyongyang Times*, February 8, 1992, p. 1.

16. *Pyongyang Times*, January 1, 1991.

17. *FBIS Daily Report–East Asia*, January 13, 1992, pp. 36–37.

18. Australian National Korean Studies Center, *Korea to the Year 2000: Implications for Australia* (Canberra, Australia: East Asia Analytical Unit, Department of Foreign Affairs and Trade, 1992), p. 101.

19. The expression is borrowed from B. C. Koh, who characterized the unification policy of all six republics of South Korea as "hegemonic unification." This applies also to the unification policy of North Korea. See B. C. Koh, "South Korea's Unification Policy," paper prepared for the conference Prospects for Korean Reunification, Claremont McKenna College, Claremont, CA, February 7, 1992, p. 2.

20. On comparison of the unification plans of North and South, see B. C. Koh, "A Comparative Study of Unification Plans: The Korean National Community Versus the Koryo Confederation," *Korea Observer*, Vol. 21, No. 4 (Winter 1990), pp. 437–455.

21. In December 1991, Kim Jong Il was made marshal of the Korean People's Army and named to succeed his father as the supreme commander of the armed forces.

22. Dae-Sook Suh, "Political Change in North Korea and Inter-Korean Relations," speech to Harvard University's Korea colloquium, March 10, 1992.

23. *Pyongyang Times*, February 16, 1992.

24. On scenarios for political change in North Korea, see Young Koo Cha and Tae-ho Kim, "Prospects for Political Change and Liberalization in North Korea," paper presented at the 1991 annual meeting of the American Political Science Association, Washington, DC, August 29–September 1, 1991.

25. "ROK Celebrates Achievements of 6th Republic," *Korea Update*, Vol. 3, No. 4 (February 17, 1992).

26. Young Whan Kihl, "South Korea's Foreign Relations: Diplomatic Activism and Policy Dilemma," in Donald Clark, ed., *Korea Briefing, 1991* (New York: The Asia Society; Boulder, CO: Westview Press, 1991), pp. 57–84.

27. Young Whan Kihl, "South Korea in 1989: Slow Progress Toward Democracy," *Asian Survey*, Vol. 30, No. 1 (January 1990), pp. 67–73.

28. Press release, Korean Information Service, New York, February 1992.

29. *FBIS Daily Report–East Asia*, February 20, 1992, p. 17.

30. Kihl, "North Korea's Foreign Relations."

31. *New York Times*, March 15, 1992.

32. This address was delivered to the Seoul meeting of the Pacific Basin Economic Council (PBEC), May 24, 1993, which was convened on a theme of "Open Regionalism: A New Basis for Globalism?" In the speech, President Kim accentuated the theme of "open and global diplomacy" and upholding universal values of "democracy, liberty, welfare and human rights" as components of his "new diplomacy." *Korea Newsreview*, May 29, 1993, p. 5.

33. Ibid.

34. "DPRK President Proposes 10-Point Platform for Great Unity of Korean Nation," *Korean Report* (Tokyo), No. 272 (April 1993), pp. 1–6; Also see *North Korea News* (Seoul), No. 679 (April 19, 1993), pp. 1–2.

35. This reference does not appear in the English-language text of Kim Young Sam's inaugural address. See the text in *Korea Times*, February 26, 1993, p. 2, as reprinted in *Korea and World Affairs*, Vol. 17, No. 1 (Spring 1993), pp. 141–145.

36. *Vantage Point* (Seoul), Vol. 16, No. 4 (April 1993), p. 13.

37. *Korean Report*, p. 4.

9 ✓

A Comparison of Unification Policies

B. C. Koh

The principal lesson of the breathtaking changes that swept the world in the late 1980s and early 1990s is that the outer limits of what is feasible have been pushed beyond the ken of conventional wisdom. This can only be good news for the Korean people, who have suffered so much for so long due to the partition of their land and nation at the end of World War II. The reunification of the Korean peninsula has now moved from the realm of wishful thinking to that of an attainable goal.

No one who is familiar with the turbulent history of inter-Korean relations, however, needs to be reminded that the road to Korean unity will be neither short nor smooth. Although external factors and actors will continue to be major variables in the equation, the pivotal roles will be played by the parties directly concerned—the governments of North and South Korea. Their policies toward each other will help determine whether, when, and how unification will materialize on the peninsula.

It is therefore worthwhile to assess how the two Koreas have dealt with the issue of unification thus far. Specifically, this chapter presents a preliminary comparison of the unification policies of the Democratic People's Republic of Korea (DPRK) and the Republic of Korea (ROK) with emphasis on four dimensions: (1) the salience of unification policy, (2) strategic objectives, (3) operational direction and tactical behavior, and (4) the efficacy of unification policy.

Salience of Unification as a Policy Goal

Unification emerged as a key policy goal of both the DPRK and the ROK as soon as they were established as two separate states in 1948, but its salience has not remained the same. In terms of rhetoric and behavior alike, the DPRK has clearly displayed a higher degree of commitment to the goal than has the

ROK. In the latter, moreover, the importance attached to unification has varied over time, depending upon the needs and capabilities of the regime in
power.

The longevity of Kim Il Sung's rule goes a long way toward explaining the
persistence with which North Korea has pursued the goal. In the words of former Congressman Stephen J. Solarz, then chairman of the Subcommittee on
Asian and Pacific Affairs of the U.S. House of Representatives, Kim Il Sung's
"commitment to reunification [is] not just verbal but visceral."[1] A logical corollary of such a "visceral" commitment is that North Korea under Kim Il Sung
will make unceasing efforts to attain the goal. The abortive invasion of the
South, multifaceted attempts to destabilize the ROK government, the intermittent dialogue with the latter, overtures toward Washington, and the unceasing campaign to drum up support for the DPRK's positions in the world
arena—all of these reflect not only Kim Il Sung's unwavering commitment to
his elusive goal but also his willingness to use whatever means he deems necessary to achieve it.

In Kim's view, only reunification would enable the Korean people to eradicate all the vestiges of colonialism, to regain national sovereignty, and to attain a full measure of independence. As he put it in his report to the sixth
congress of the Korean Workers' Party (KWP) in October 1980, "division is
the road to slavery and national ruin; reunification alone will lead us to independence and prosperity."[2] The aging North Korean leader (born in 1912)
does not seem to have abandoned the hope that unification will come within
his lifetime; in a talk with delegates to the sixth high-level (or prime ministerial) talks between North and South in Pyongyang on February 20, 1992, he
expressed his "conviction" that Korean unification will occur within the decade of the 1990s provided that both sides faithfully implement the two agreements that were signed in December 1991 and entered into force on February
19, 1992.[3]

In contrast to North Korea, South Korea has not elevated unification to its
foremost objective. Nor has Seoul been willing to use all available means to
hasten its realization. Syngman Rhee, the first ROK president, it is true, did
use militant rhetoric vis-à-vis the North, threatening to unify the peninsula by
force. Coping with domestic challenges to his rule by opposition politicians as
well as by the agents and sympathizers of the North, however, commanded a
higher priority than carrying out his threat against the North. That he lacked
the capability to conquer the North, moreover, could only undercut the credibility of his threat.

The outbreak of the war triggered by the North Korean invasion on June 25,
1950, particularly the intervention of the United States and other UN member
states on behalf of the ROK, did provide Rhee with a chance to attain his goal,
but the Chinese intervention on behalf of the DPRK helped to banish that
chance. In the postarmistice period, Rhee found himself preoccupied with
other tasks—notably, rehabilitating the war-torn economy and coping once
again with political opposition that was becoming increasingly bold and popular. Unification receded into the background.[4]

Although the arrival of democratic rule under Chang Myon (John Chang) in the wake of Rhee's downfall in a student-led revolution helped to catapult the unification issue to the forefront of national debate, the short-lived Chang government was saddled with too many pressing problems to pay serious attention to unification. It did, however, reaffirm the policy of the caretaker government of Hŏ Chŏng, which had renounced force as a means of unification. In a sense, then, what occurred during Chang's brief rule was an anomaly: The salience of unification rose sharply as an issue, but it failed to galvanize the government.[5]

The initiation of the first phase of dialogue with the North by the Park Chung Hee regime in the early 1970s did not necessarily signal the rise of unification to the top of its agenda. At best, it represented Park's grudging tactical response to a dramatic change in Korea's strategic environment; at worst, it bespoke his cynical manuever to pave the way to the aggrandizement of his power at home.[6]

Although unification clearly received higher priority in the Chun Doo Hwan regime than it did during the Park Chung Hee era, it never became a top policy goal. It is instructive to recall that an opposition politician was harshly penalized by the Chun regime for suggesting that unification, not anticommunism, should be the principal national objective (*kuksi*) of the ROK government. It was not until the advent of the Sixth Republic under Roh Tae Woo that unification was elevated to a top policy goal, albeit not the top one. Roh not only pursued the goal of achieving a breakthrough in inter-Korean relations with a vigor unmatched by any of his predecessors but also succeeded in producing tangible results.

Strategic Objectives

Stripped to their core, the strategic objectives of the two Koreas pertaining to unification have remained remarkably similar. Both have pursued what can be described as "hegemonic unification"—unification in which one side prevails over the other. To North Korea, that has meant the communization of the South or the forging of an integrated political system in which North Korean–style socialism eclipses any other competing ideology or structure. As for South Korea, the only acceptable form of unification is one in which either the South Korean political system or a system embodying democratic values prevails over the North Korean system.

A discrepancy between the preceding view and the official positions of the two Koreas needs to be noted. Actually, both Seoul and Pyongyang concur in part with the view. Seoul continues to harbor the suspicion that Pyongyang has not yet jettisoned its goal of communizing the South yet disavows any intention to prevail over the North. Pyongyang, in contrast, is openly apprehensive about Seoul's alleged desire to emulate the German formula of unification by absorption. As for its own policy, Pyongyang has publicly substituted "confederation" for "systemic unification."[7]

Whether the adoption of the confederation plan—establishment of a Democratic Confederal Republic of Koryo (DCRK)—signals a change in North Korea's strategic objective, however, is debatable. My interpretation is that the DCRK proposal has undergone change since it was first unveiled at the KWP's sixth congress in October 1980 and now embodies a new strategy of unification.

Briefly, the DCRK proposal has evolved through three stages: (1) the propaganda stage, (2) the proposal stage, and (3) the adjustment stage. During the first stage, October 1980 to January 1983, the DCRK proposal served primarily as a propaganda tool, for North Korea effectively nullified its central premise by openly inciting an overthrow of the Chun Doo Hwan regime. On one hand professing to pursue the policy of forging a confederation of the two divergent systems in Korea, leaving the idiosyncrasies of the Chun regime intact, Pyongyang on the other hand sought radically to transform the complexion of the South Korean system.

In January 1983, however, North Korea reversed its policy and indicated a willingness to engage in a dialogue with the Chun government, thereby ushering in a new stage in the life of the DCRK proposal. The policy reversal was reflected in Pyongyang's proposal for tripartite talks involving the two Koreas and the United States. In a sense, this marked a dual reversal: Pyongyang had reversed not only its previous policy of refusing to deal with the Chun regime but also its previous opposition to the idea of tripartite talks. The idea originated in the summit meeting between Presidents Jimmy Carter and Park Chung Hee in summer 1979, but Pyongyang had promptly turned down a joint proposal by Carter and Park. It was now Seoul's and Washington's turn to reject Pyongyang's overtures. The timing of the latter could not have been worse, for they came in the aftermath of the Rangoon bombing incident in which North Korean agents killed four South Korean cabinet ministers, two top presidential aides, and others in an apparent attempt to assassinate Chun Doo Hwan.[8] Nonetheless, the significance of Pyongyang's policy reversal was that the DCRK proposal had entered a new stage, a stage in which it became amenable to negotiation between the two Koreas for the first time.

Finally, in January 1991, North Korea began to hint that it was willing to give more power to the "regional governments" of the two halves of Korea under the DCRK rubric. They would exercise control over foreign and defense policies and legislation. In practical terms, the two Korean governments would retain their full autonomy within their respective domains while coordinating their internal and external policies. In a word, the DCRK would resemble the Korean Commonwealth envisioned by Roh Tae Woo's Korean National Community (KNC) unification formula.[9]

If North Korea's strategic objective regarding unification has indeed been downgraded from hegemony to parity, which the DCRK proposal in its 1991 incarnation is designed to attain, that reflects a pragmatic adaptation on Kim Il Sung's part. If hegemony is unattainable, then North Korea is prepared to settle for the next best thing—the institutionalization of parity between itself and South Korea.

Has South Korea also lowered its sights? Or does it remain committed at heart to hegemonic unification notwithstanding its conciliatory rhetoric? To the extent that South Korea or the Kim Young Sam government truly wants unification, it has no intention of extending parity to North Korea in the final stage. Only in the interim stage of the Korean Commonwealth is Seoul willing to grant equality to Pyongyang. The implementation of the proportional-representation (one person, one vote) formula in the establishment of the unified government will ensure that the latter will embody democratic principles and values.

It is worthwhile to compare the principal proposals of North and South that form the centerpiece of their respective unification policies—the DCRK and the KNC proposals—to note their salient similiarities and differences.[10]

The principal similarities appear to be the following:

First, both plans recognize not only the pressing necessity of reunification but also its ultimate inevitability.

Second, both plans recognize that the long duration of division has widened the gap in ideology, ideas, and systems between North and South.

Third, both plans accept or profess to accept the proposition that strengthening the bonds of the Korean nation is more urgent than achieving a political union and that it would be easier to attain "national reunification" (*minjokjŏk t'ong'il*) than to realize "systemic reunification" (*chedojŏk t'ong'il*).

Fourth, both plans affirm the importance of honoring the principle of regional representation or equality of North and South in moving toward reunification.

Finally, both plans subscribe or profess to subscribe to the three principles of reunification embodied in the North-South joint statement of July 4, 1972, namely (1) independence, (2) peace, and (3) great national unity. They also embrace the goals of social welfare for all citizens, democracy, and peaceful foreign policy.

These common denominators are counterbalanced or even eclipsed by some profound differences between the two plans, of which the following seem noteworthy:

First, whereas the KNC plan adopts an incremental approach, the DCRK plan adopts an approach that would tackle and solve all problems at once. Under the KNC plan, an interim stage of the Korean Commonwealth (Nambuk Yŏnhap) will pave the way for reunification by fostering a sense of national community (*minjok kongdongch'e*) through dialogue and multifaceted cooperation and exchanges between North and South. The DCRK plan, by contrast, calls for the attainment of "national reunification" without any intermediate or preparatory period.

Second, whereas the ultimate goal of the KNC plan is to establish a single nation-state in Korea, that of the DCRK plan is to substitute "national reunification" for "systemic reunification" on the ground that the latter is unattainable under existing conditions. The DCRK plan does not explicitly entertain the possibility that improvement of conditions under the DCRK would make systemic reunification possible at a later date.

Third, even though both plans are said to be based on the acceptance of the three principles of reunification, Seoul and Pyongyang are poles apart in their interpretations of two of the three principles: independence and great national unity. According to Pyongyang, the former requires the elimination of the U.S. military presence from South Korea, and the latter mandates the repeal by Seoul of its national security law and the adoption of a policy of tolerating all political ideas and activities, including those that support North Korea. Seoul rejects both of these interpretations.

Fourth, whereas the DCRK plan initially had preconditions, the KNC plan never had any. Pyongyang's preconditions were the replacement of the "military fascist" government in Seoul by a "progressive" one and the withdrawal of U.S. troops from South Korea. These preconditions have subsequently been modified. The first has been implicitly jettisoned; the second has ceased to be an abolute barrier, even though it still remains an important component of the DCRK plan in terms of goals to be attained.

Finally, even though both plans endorse the principle of equal representation of North and South, the KNC plan also incorporates the principle of proportional representation (PR). Given the two-to-one advantage in population South Korea enjoys over North Korea, the PR principle benefits the former at the expense of the latter. It would be naive to expect that Pyongyang would voluntarily accept such a principle initially, even if it is combined with the equality principle.

Operational Direction and Tactical Behavior

In the preceding section, the focus was on the strategic dimension of unification policy. To round out the discussion, examined here are operational directions and tactics. The differences among these three concepts need to be explained briefly. *Strategy* refers to a long-term plan of action, whereas *tactics* encompass short-term adaptations of behavior within the overall context of strategy. *Operational direction* is an intermediate concept; it "is subordinate to strategy and concerns the direction and unification of tactical episodes. It is more flexible than strategy, but less so than tactics. Its range of duration is shorter than strategy; it changes with new clusters of tactics, which it funnels along the lines established by strategy."[11]

If war, revolution, and confederation are treated as manifestations of North Korea's unification strategy, then their respective component parts become either operational directions or tactics. If the Korean War context is excluded—it represented North Korea's first strategic instrument in its quest for unification—there are three operational directions identifable in each of the remaining strategies. The strategy of revolution thus encompassed the three interrelated operational directions of (1) building a revolutionary base in the North, (2) fostering revolution in the South, and (3) building support in the international arena.[12] The three stages through which the DCRK proposal has evolved can be equated with operational directions.

Other examples of Pyongyang's operational direction are also noteworthy. Dialogue is a case in point. Its realization in 1971 was in part a function of the Sino-U.S. rapprochement and the convergence of tactical responses by the two Koreas to that momentous development. It did not, however, signify either a jettisoning or a significant modification of strategy on the part of either Seoul or Pyongyang.

As far as Pyongyang was concerned, dialogue represented but a change in or an addition of operational direction. Its operational direction of fostering revolutionary forces in the South had proved to be sterile in the face of South Korea's effective countermeasures against North Korean subversion. Dialogue with Seoul, however, could conceivably open up legitimate channels of communication and contact with the South Korean people. Additionally, there was a distinct possibility that dialogue, by reducing tensions and dispelling Seoul's fear of Pyongyang's aggressive designs, might help achieve the foremost intermediate goal in North Korea's strategy of unification—withdrawal of U.S. troops.

From Pyongyang's standpoint, the July 4, 1972, North-South joint statement (see Appendix A) vastly improved the chances that the preceding might actually materialize. What Pyongyang seemed to have overlooked, however, was that neither Seoul's strategy nor its distrust of Pyongyang had undergone an iota of change. Nor did Pyongyang foresee the domestic political uses to which Park Chung Hee would put the dialogue. After trying to maneuver Seoul into unwittingly creating conditions favorable to North Korea's unification strategy, Pyongyang found itself outmaneuvered by Seoul.

The failure of the first phase of the inter-Korean dialogue to produce the desired outcome led Pyongyang to adopt another operational direction: an active quest for direct negotiations with the United States. Notwithstanding unremitting efforts, however, the new operational direction proved to be no more productive than its predecessor. Fourteen years were to elapse before North Korea finally got a chance to engage in direct bilateral negotiations with the United States. The breakthrough, if it can be so described, was the result not of Pyongyang's diplomacy but of a change in Washington's policy, which in turn had been triggered by a change in Seoul's policy. Roh Tae Woo's special declaration on July 7, 1988, had paved the way for Washington's decision to adjust its North Korea policy; in December of that year, U.S.–North Korea talks began in Beijing at the embassy political counselor level.[13]

Roh's July 7 declaration was also instrumental in inducing change in Japan's policy toward North Korea; the shift eventually led to the initiation of Tokyo-Pyongyang negotiations for diplomatic normalization. Pyongyang's decision to seek relations, in fact, marked a notable departure from its previous policy—hence the beginning of a new operational direction. Change in its operational environment, both internal and external, helps to explain Pyongyang's behavior. The single most important factor perhaps was the persistence of economic difficulties, compounded by the transformation of Soviet policy; the stunning speed with which Seoul and Moscow established full diplomatic relations may have been the last straw for Pyongyang. The need to find ways to compensate for the virtual disappearance of its principal aid donor and trading partner was so compelling as to banish any reservations about "cross recognition."

The initiation of high-level talks between North and South in September 1990 also reflected a new operational direction on the part of both parties. The developments previously noted provided the same backdrop against which Pyongyang changed its policy. In addition to the new reality of growing

Seoul-Moscow bonds, Pyongyang had to ponder the implications of German unification. It could ill afford to miss any new opportunities that might develop. The conduct of the high-level talks, however, was affected by tactical considerations by both sides, as was true of all previous cases of inter-Korean dialogue.

The signing of two agreements in December 1991—one on reconciliation, nonaggression, and exchanges and cooperation (Appendix B) and another on denuclearization (Appendix C)—symbolized the convergence of both sides' operational directions and tactical calculations. The two agreements entered into force in February 1992. Should they be fully implemented, the agreements would usher in a new era in inter-Korean relations. Of the myriad factors that must have entered into the respective calculi of North and South, Pyongyang's need to expedite its normalization talks with Tokyo and Roh Tae Woo's desire to achieve a breakthrough of historic dimensions before his term of office expired seem most noteworthy.

Seoul's decision to formulate a comprehensive proposal on unification in 1982 and to reformulate it in 1989 falls under the rubric of operational direction.[14] The 1982 proposal appeared aimed at countering North Korea's DCRK proposal and bolstering Chun Doo Hwan's shaky legitimacy; the 1989 proposal was emblematic of Roh Tae Woo's determination to open a new era in inter-Korean relations. (The latter proposal is discussed in the next section in connection with the efficacy of unification policy.)

At the tactical level, both North and South have displayed a mixture of rigidity and flexibility. In the case of North Korea, tactical rigidity manifests itself in the form of a duality of behavior and a refusal to make concessions. By a duality of behavior is meant the coupling of an overture with an invective against the party with whom Pyongyang ostensibly seeks a dialogue; duality is also seen in Pyongyang's use of a united-front tactic while conducting a dialogue with Seoul. The ideological and structural rigidity of North Korea's political system helps to explain such behavior.

Ideologically, the apotheosis of *Juche* (self-reliance) has spawned an excessive amount of national pride and an obsessive concern for national dignity. These in turn place severe constraints on Pyongyang's ability to empathize and compromise with its adversaries. Structurally, the North Korean political system is bedeviled by compartmentalization and a sluggish decisionmaking apparatus. Its propaganda machinery, although a tool of the state, may have its own vested interests to protect and its own agenda to pursue. If nothing else, entrenched bureaucratic routines and sheer inertia may help sustain more or less the same level of vituperation against traditional enemies in the absence of explicit guidelines from the top to the contrary.

None of this, however, has prevented Pyongyang from displaying tactical realism from time to time. It has shown that it is capable of making tactical adjustments should expediency dictate, of switching operational direction, and even of reappraising strategy in the face of compelling necessity. Change in North Korean operational directions and tactics has occurred innumerable times, most though not all of which can be cited to illustrate Pyongyang's ability to behave flexibly when the stakes are high.

South Korea has clearly displayed more flexibility than its northern rival. When Seoul shows rigidity, however, it is frequently intentional. Had Seoul been consistently flexible, for example, the "breakthrough" in the high-level talks could have occurred a year earlier—at the third round of the talks held in Seoul in December 1990, because the gap between the two sides had become narrower than at any time since the beginning of the talks. Nonetheless, Seoul seems to have opted for a hard-line posture of trying to compel Pyongyang to make further concessions.

Not to be minimized, however, is the rigidity stemming from "cognitive closure"—a propensity to dismiss as a ploy evidence of change in the adversary's behavior—which is a function of a bitter experience, coupled with deep-seated mutual distrust. Empathy is as scarce as it is necessary in inter-Korean relations.

Efficacy of Unification Policy

Against what yardstick should the efficacy of unification policy be evaluated? If efficacy is construed as the extent to which policy has produced its intended results, then these plainly provide a convenient yardstick. Identifying the intended results of unification policy, however, may not be as easy as it may appear at first glance. It is therefore necessary to use both the manifest and latent goals of unification policy as criteria of assessment but to keep in mind that the latter, by definition, can only be surmised.

The first point to note is the foremost latent objective of hegemonic unification. If the assumption is made for the moment that neither side has lowered its sights, plainly the goal has eluded North and South alike. Is either side closer to attaining it than the other? Theoretically, the simplest way to achieve hegemonic unification is military conquest. Apart from legal constraints, which have arguably become more onerous for both the DPRK and the ROK since they joined the United Nations as full-fledged members in September 1991, the military balance on the Korean peninsula militates against its use.

Peaceful methods, which appear to be the only realistic and sensible options, may give an edge to a party with superior economic capability. The German experience suggests, however, that superiority must be overwhelming—on the order of five to one in gross national product and ten to one in per capita GNP. Although a strict comparison is hazardous, South Korea does seem to enjoy such an overwhelming superiority over North Korea in terms of ratios alone. What the German experience also shows, however, is that absolute economic power plays a crucial role in economic integration of two disparate economic systems. It is on this score that the two Korean states fall short: Just as South Korea has a long way to go before it can rival West Germany on the eve of unification, so too does North Korea not even begin to compare with the former East Germany.[15]

An additional consideration in applying the German analogy is the solidity or fragility of political systems. If the North Korean economy is incomparably weaker than the East German economy in the preunification era, the obverse is true with respect to the strength of political systems. Although the boast by the North Korean heir apparent, Kim Jong Il, that "the people-centered social-ism" in the North is "invincible" may be grossly exaggerated, there is little doubt that the political system forged there over four decades has awesome powers to sustain itself for some time to come. It has but a slim chance of dis-integrating itself. Should the regime fail to "solve adequately the problem of feeding, clothing, and housing" its people for a prolonged period of time, however, one should not rule out the possibility of a popular uprising of the type that occurred in Romania in late 1989.[16]

The regime has a number of options in its repertoire that can sharply curtail an imminent threat to its survival. One choice is to accelerate economic ex-changes and cooperation with South Korea by agreeing to implement the agreement on mutual inspections of nuclear facilities. Another option is to re-move all the obstacles impeding progress in its negotiations with Japan on diplomatic normalization, which Pyongyang has the capability if not the incli-nation to do at the moment (as of mid-1993).

When analysis shifts from strategy to operational direction, however, the picture changes markedly. A key latent goal of both sides on the level of operational direction seems to have been to create conditions conducive to the attainment of such other goals as reaching early conclusion of a normalization agreement with Japan; paving the way for the influx of much-needed foreign exchange, technology, and direct investment; and winning a place in history for a president who opened a new era in inter-Korean relations. All of these goals have yet to be attained, but the signing and entry into force of the two inter-Korean agreements indicate that the necessary groundwork has been laid.

What of manifest goals of unification policy? If North Korea's DCRK pro-posal can be taken seriously, what it wants is to persuade South Korea to ac-cept a confederal form of government. As has already been argued, the pro-posal has been transformed to such an extent that it now resembles the Korean Commonwealth in Seoul's KNC unification formula. What is more, should all the structures envisaged by the two inter-Korean agreements come into being and key provisions be implemented, something approximating the Korean Commonwealth would materialize. In order for all this to happen and, especially, in order for the DCRK proposal in its modified form to see the light of the day, however, both sides need to exercise restraint, to respect each other (which has never happened before), and to manifest an even higher de-gree of pragamatism than they have thus far.

Implicit in the preceding discussion is the suggestion that Seoul's KNC for-mula also has a chance of being partially implemented. The South's blueprint for the second and ultimate stage of unification, however, will remain just that—a blueprint—for some time to come. Nevertheless, the only form of uni-fication acceptable to the two-thirds of the Korean people who live in the southern half of the Korean peninsula is plainly the establishment of a unified government based on democratic principles and proportional representation (at least in one house of the projected bicameral parliament). In other words, the KNC formula does seem to contain irreducible conditions.

In overall terms, can it be said that one side's unification policy has been more efficacious than the other side's? As far as tactical pragmatism is concerned, South Korea arguably has outperformed North Korea. On the one hand, agreements between the two sides, large and small, have typically embodied or stemmed from Seoul's somewhat greater willingness to compromise than Pyongyang. On the other hand, North Korea has always retained and frequently exercised a retroactive veto on inter-Korean agreements by either dragging its feet in the implementation phase or renouncing them outright, citing Seoul's insincerity or perfidy, alleged or real.

In the realm of operational direction, however, Seoul has scored some conspicuous victories. The success of its northern diplomacy has enabled Seoul to achieve what may be its greatest triumph vis-à-vis Pyongyang: their joint admission to the United Nations.

Conclusion

In sum, the unification policies of the two Koreas turn out to be amalgams of wishful thinking and attainable goals, of rigidity and flexibility, and of successes and failures. What is encouraging is that although failure has thus far been the fate of the ultimate goal, small successes have nonetheless occurred, thus helping to keep the dream of Korean unification alive—a dream shared by all Koreans regardless of their ideologies or relative positions in the socioeconomic or political hierarchy.

Since the entry into force of what may well turn out to be historic agreements between the two Koreas, unification no longer seems so distant. Should the impasse over the issue of mutual inspections of nuclear facilities be resolved, the door to economic, cultural, and humanitarian exchanges will be opened. With the institutionalization of peace and the acceleration of exchanges and cooperation that the inter-Korean agreements envisage, an era of creeping unification may dawn on the Korean peninsula—a new era in which the pains of division will gradually be alleviated and the threshold to unification will eventually be crossed.

Notes

1. U.S. Congress, House of Representatives, Committee on Foreign Affairs, *The Korean Conundrum: A Conversation with Kim Il Sung,* Report of a Study Mission to South Korea, Japan, the People's Republic of Korea, and North Korea, July 12–21, 1980, August 1981, 97th Congress, 1st Session (Washington, DC: U.S. Government Printing Office, 1981), p. 6. Solarz had a four-hour conversation with Kim Il Sung.

2. Kim Il Sung, *Report to the Sixth Congress of the Workers' Party of Korea on the Work of the Central Committee* (Pyongyang: Foreign Languages Publishing House, 1980), p. 65.

3. *Rodong Sinmun,* February 21, 1992.

4. On the politics of this period, consult John Kie-Chiang Oh, *Korea: Democracy on Trial* (Ithaca, NY: Cornell University Press, 1968).

5. For an incisive analysis of the politics of this period, see Sung-joo Han, *The Failure of Democracy in South Korea* (Berkeley: University of California Press, 1974).

6. For an elaboration of this view, see Byung Chul Koh, *The Foreign Policy Systems of North and South Korea* (Berkeley: University of California Press, 1984), pp. 156–160.

7. Choguk P'yonghwa T'ong'il Wiwonhoe, *Koryo Minju Yonbang Konghwaguk ch'angnip pang'an kwa 10 tae sijŏng pangch'im e taehayo* (On the proposal for the establishment of the Democratic Confederal Republic of Koryo and the ten-point program) (Pyongyang: Choguk P'yonghasa T'ong'il Wiwonhoe, June 1981).

8. Although Pyongyang officially unveiled the tripartite proposal in January 1984, it reportedly broached the idea to Washington through Chinese intermediaries in October 1983. According to Young C. Kim, "North Korea asked China to transmit the DPRK's willingness to hold talks with the United States shortly before the bombing in Rangoon. The message, however, reached the United States after the incident, and the public announcement of the proposal was not made until January 1984." See his article, "North Korean Foreign Policy," *Problems of Communism* 34, 1 (January-February 1985), pp. 10–11.

9. The hint was first contained in Kim Il Sung's New Year's address. See *Rodong Sinmun,* January 1, 1991. For an elaboration of this interpretation, see B. C. Koh, "Pukhan 'Koryo yonbangje an' ui chongch'e wa unmyong" (The Identity and Fate of North Korea's "Koryo confederation proposal"), *Sin Tong'a,* August 1991, pp. 148–157.

10. For the contents of the DCRK proposal, see Kim Il Sung, *Report to the Sixth Congress;* for the Korean-language text, see *Choguk ŭi chajujŏk p'yonghwa t'ong'il ŭl irukhaja* (Let us attain the independent and peaceful reunification of our fatherland) (Pyongyang: Chosŏn Rodongdang Ch'ulp'ansa, 1980). For the contents of the KNC proposal, see *Hanminjok kongdongch'e t'ong'il pang'an: Kibon haesŏl charyo* (The Korean National Community unification formula: Basic expository materials) (Seoul: Kukt'o T'ong'ilwon, September 1989).

11. Jan F. Triska, "A Model for Study of Soviet Foreign Policy," *American Political Science Review* 52, 1 (March 1958), pp. 67–69.

12. For Kim Il Sung's articulation of the strategy of revolution encompassing the three operational directions, see his speech to the eighth plenum of the fourth Central Committee of the Workers' Party of Korea on February 27, 1964, "Choguk t'ong'il wiwŏp ŭl silhyon hagi wihayo hyongmyong yongnyang ŭl paekpang ŭro kanghwa haja" (Let us strengthen revolutionary forces with all the means at our disposal in order to accomplish the great task of the reunification of our fatherland) in *Kim Il Sung chŏjak sŏnjip* (Selected works of Kim Il Sung), Vol. 4 (Pyongyang: Chosŏn Rodongdang Ch'ulp'ansa, 1968), pp. 77–96. Note that neither phrase "strategy of revolution" nor "operational direction" appears in Kim's speech. These are analytic terms employed by outside observers such as myself.

13. On October 31, 1988, the U.S. government "announced changes in [U.S.] policy toward North Korea in three areas: trade, people-to-people diplomacy, and diplomatic contact policy." Washington made it plain that the impetus for its move had been Roh Tae Woo's declaration on July 7, 1988, encouraging Seoul's allies to have contacts with Pyongyang. Thomas P. H. Dunlop, "The United States, the Republic of Korea, and Reunification," speech at Western Michigan University, Kalamazoo, MI, April 27, 1989. Dunlop was director of the Office of Korean Affairs, the Bureau of East Asian and Pacific Affairs of the U.S. Department of State at the time.

14. For the text of the 1982 proposal, see Kukt'o T'ong'il-won, *Nambuk taehwa paeksŏ* (White paper on the South-North dialogue) (Seoul: Kukt'o T'ong'il-won, Nambuk Taehwa Samuguk, 1988), pp. 481–485; for the text of and commentary on the 1989 proposal, see Kukt'o T'ong'il-won, *Hanminjok kongdongch'e t'ong'il pang'an: irŏk'e t'ongil hajanŭn kosida* (The Korean National Community unification formula: This is how we can attain unification) (Seoul: National Unification Board, 1989).

15. For the relevance of German unification for the Korean peninsula, see the excellent study, Pak Song-jo and Yang Song-ch'ol (Sung Chul Yang), *Togil t'ong'il kwa pundan Han'guk* (German unification and the divided Korea) (Seoul: Kyongnam Taehakkyo Kuktong Munje Yŏn'guso, 1991).

16. Kim Il Sung mentioned the need to solve the problem of "feeding, clothing, and housing the people" for the second time in as many years in his New Year's speech in 1992. See *Rodong Sinmun,* January 1, 1992.

10

Domestic Politics and Unification: Seoul's Perspective

Manwoo Lee

Although there is ample evidence of positive developments in inter-Korean relations during the 1988–1993 tenure of the Roh Tae Woo government, the unresolved nuclear issue threatens the credibility of the 1991–1992 inter-Korean accord on reconciliation, nonaggression, cooperation, and exchanges between the two Koreas (Appendix B). At the annual security consultative meeting in Seoul in October 1992, Seoul and Washington announced that they would restart the Team Spirit joint military exercise in spring 1993 unless the two Koreas implemented bilateral nuclear inspections by then. North Korea virtually called off the ninth round of the South-North high-level talks. A deadlock in inter-Korean dialogue may last for some time, even under the new administration of Kim Young Sam.

At the moment, the prospect for reunification is uncertain at best as both Koreas are in deep domestic trouble. The South is undergoing a painful and very difficult period of transition from authoritarianism to democracy. Kim Young Sam, who was elected president with 42 percent of the vote on December 18, 1992, faces the monumental task of curing what he calls the "Korean disease"—rampant corruption, lawlessness, and lack of authority—and creating a "new Korea." In the North, the survival of the system itself, the "paradise" of Kim Il Sung and his son, is threatened as its allies have one by one abandoned it and its economy approaches bankruptcy.

The purpose of this chapter is to put the inter-Korean relationship in perspective by focusing on a number of important domestic factors. First, it examines whether or not the two Koreas have abandoned the game of unification politics, which they have engaged in for five decades. Second, it analyzes

how South Korea's unification policy evolved during the Sixth Republic under Roh within the context of South Korea's internal problems—political, social, and economic—and how these factors affected debates on unification.
Third, it examines why South Korea shows reluctance in accepting the German style of unification known as "absorption." Finally, it assesses North Korea, which is becoming increasingly petrified as a nation, evaluates the 1991
inter-Korean agreement, and questions the motives of the two regimes for entering into it.

The Game of Unification Politics

Korea, liberated from Japanese colonial rule for thirty-six years (1910–1945),
did not deserve division, but chaotic internal political conditions, compounded by the rivalry between the United States and the Soviet Union,
made it virtually impossible for a united Korea to emerge. In the South,
Syngman Rhee, backed by conservative and reactionary elements and the
United States, chose "real politics" over a united Korea and decided to set up
a separate regime. In the North, Kim Il Sung too, backed by fanatic communist revolutionaries and the Soviet Union, established a separate regime a few
weeks later. Other Korean leaders, who desperately sought to avoid division,
were assassinated. As soon as the two separate regimes with incompatible
ideologies and credentials were established in 1948, they began the game of
unification politics.

In the early days, Syngman Rhee, South Korea's first president (1948–1960),
openly called for marching to the North. Then, on June 25, 1950, North Korea
struck first and invaded South Korea in an attempt to unify the peninsula by
means of war. The Korean War (1950–1953) failed to unify the peninsula but
had far-reaching results: First, it established deep distrust between the two
Koreas that is likely to remain well beyond this century. Second, it contributed
to the buildup on both sides of a large military arsenal, greatly out of proportion to the size and population of the two countries; the escalation transformed the two Koreas into formidable military powers. Third, both Koreas
established security regimes resembling garrison states. Finally, the war retarded the development of democracy in South Korea until the late 1980s and
accelerated the growth of an Orwellian state in the North.

Both Koreas have thrived on using the other side for political gain. Hence,
the unification issue has been transformed into a powerful political tool to
serve each regime's security and interests. In this process, unification, its rhetoric notwithstanding, has ceased to become the highest national priority. The
two Koreas have become less and less interested in normalizing relations, but
their commitment to hostility has achieved "the status of an elevated moral
principle.[1] In both Koreas, political values and institutions have been molded
by the assumption of a demonological perspective of the other side. Hostility
toward each other is reflected in both Korean governments' structures, particularly in the various bureaucracies.

In South Korea, the Blue House (the presidential palace), the NSPA (the National Security Planning Agency, formerly the Korean Central Intelligence

Agency), the police, the Ministry of Defense, the Ministry of Foreign Affairs, and the National Unification Board have all carved out a privileged position in playing the game of unification politics. These bureaucracies, not the people, determine where the true national interests lie, and the political reward structure has been developed to punish anyone who tries to play a different kind of game in unification politics.[2]

Of course, this situation is even more discouraging in North Korea where the game of unification politics is a complete monopoly of Kim Il Sung and Kim Jong Il and their Korean Workers' Party bureaucracy. The interests of the 10 million victims of the division were never taken seriously because they interfered with the game of unification politics.

The nature of the game is such that each regime in the two Koreas tries to create the illusion for its respective people that it is doing its best to achieve unification, but in reality the illusion maximizes the security and well-being of each regime. Therefore, the game has been essentially antiunification-oriented.

The politicization of the unification issue by both sides and the inability to deal with the problem have made the goal of achieving unification more difficult. The division of the Korean peninsula was itself tragic, but North Korea's refusal to recognize and accept the reality of the division has compounded the tragedy and has compelled each side to channel its political, economic, military, and diplomatic resources into causing pain and injury to the other.

As the game of unification politics has been transformed into a powerful political tool in each Korea to defend its system or to attack the other's, people in both Koreas have become pawns, and unification itself has been held hostage to the following functional dimensions of an essentially antiunification-oriented political game.

1. *Legitimizing function:* By developing a highly nationalistic doctrine known as *Juche* (self-reliance)—a foundation of political legitimacy for the moral supremacy of North Korea on the Korean peninsula—North Korea has continuously portrayed South Korea as a puppet of the United States and Japan and its regime as a fascist gang that seeks a permanent division of the peninsula.[3] Because of the image that the successive governments in the South have lacked legitimacy to govern, North Korean leaders have undermined the legitimacy of the South Korean authorities with impunity.

The South Korean leadership, thus put on the defensive, has sought to overcome its inferiority complex by outpacing North Korea in all sectors of the economy. As a result, South Korea takes pride in having defeated North Korea's *Juche*. The Asian and the Olympic games held in Seoul in 1986 and 1988 respectively symbolized South Korea's victory over North Korea without war.

However, the successive South Korean governments since the founding of the republic have been at war with their own people and with North Korea. This situation makes North Korea extremely reluctant to take the views of the South Korean leaders seriously. North Korea delights in exploiting the tension between the South Korean government and its people.

Thus, until political stability is firmly rooted in South Korea, it cannot confront North Korea with strength and credibility. There is no guarantee that North Korea will accept the Kim Young Sam government as legitimate even though Kim is viewed by Korean voters as the first legitimate civilian president since 1961.

2. *Governing function:* Although South Korea has been politically freer than North Korea, in both Koreas unification policies are set forth by the government. In North Korea no one dares to contradict Kim Il Sung's unification policy. In South Korea the harsh national security law defines North Korea as an antistate organization and mandates severe punishment for anyone who praises or sympathizes with North Korea.

3. *Propaganda function:* Proposals, schemes, gestures, and ideas advanced by the two Koreas for unification tend to be ploys for the two systems to strengthen themselves.

North Korea mobilizes its mass media, both foreign and domestic, to extol the "great achievements" of Kim Il Sung and paints its system as a socialist "paradise." South Korea depicts North Korea as a prison and a savage nation that exports terrorism and engages in a personality cult, nepotism, inhumanity, and political brutality. South Korea advertises itself as an economically dynamic and politically free nation.

Kim Il Sung's unification plan, known as the DCRK (the Democratic Confederal Republic of Koryo, proposed by Kim in 1980), Chun Doo Hwan's UDRK (the Unified Democratic Republic of Korea, 1982), and Roh Tae Woo's KNC (Korean National Community) and Korean Commonwealth formula (1989) all belong in the realm of propaganda aimed at satisfying the domestic audience and the international community.[4]

4. *Liberation function:* Although North Korea appears to have abandoned revolutionary efforts to liberate South Korea, it continues to encourage revolution in the South by siding with radical dissidents. In October 1992 the South Korean government revealed a North Korean espionage network, which has penetrated deep into South Korean society. The radical elements in South Korea, however, have lost much influence in politics because of the dramatic changes in the former Soviet Union and elsewhere. South Korea has been less successful in penetrating North Korea because of its tight control, but it hopes to open up the North by exposing it to South Korea—the ultimate goal being liberation of the North.

5. *National security function:* Talks between the two Koreas were often stalled because North Korea persisted in demanding removal of U.S. troops and nuclear weapons from South Korea and discontinuation of the annual U.S.–South Korean Team Spirit military exercises. South Korea saw that North Korea's ultimate intention in this demand was to disarm the South, launch an attack, and unify the peninsula by force.

For its part, North Korea, surrounded by three hostile powers—South Korea, Japan, and the United States—and two unreliable allies—the former Soviet Union and China—has developed a siege mentality.[5] Thus, North Korea's insistence that unification be achieved without foreign interference is rooted in its national security need. What Kim Il Sung has been asking is simple:

"Disarm yourself and come to the negotiating table." The December 1991 accord between the two Koreas was made possible partly because South Korea's major concessions to the North included some of the most contentious elements aggravating inter-Korean relations: removal of nuclear weapons and discontinuation of Team Spirit.

6. *Indoctrination and mobilization function:* Both Koreas have preferred indoctrination to education as the means of educating their citizens about the reality of the Korean peninsula. South Korea's rigid anticommunist campaigns have led to serious confrontations between the government and its people, and North Korea always has been eager to exploit the tension. North Korea has perceived South Korea so much through its *Juche* lenses that the South Korean reality is completely lost to it.

A brief review of these functional dimensions of unification politics indicates that the past five decades have been a history of both Koreas endeavoring desperately to mold and socialize their respective citizens to ensure the preservation of the separate system despite their claim that unification is the supreme national task. The separate state, the separate regime, and the separate leadership role have been given a higher value and priority than the people they were to serve.[6] I have argued elsewhere that the greatest lesson of the postdivision period for both Koreas should be that depoliticizing the unification issue and accepting the reality of the division would help the goal of achieving eventual unification.[7] This means that both Koreas would serve their people better by abandoning the usual game of unification politics and avoiding use of the unification issue for the self-promoting functions outlined in this section.

Domestic Politics and
Roh's Unification Formula

During its first year in office, the Roh government faced a serious challenge from dissident forces known as the *jaeya* (consisting of many who had opposed the regimes of Park Chung Hee and Chun Doo Hwan). After gaining great confidence from their success in forcing President Chun Doo Hwan to accept democratic reforms in summer 1987 (the June 29 declaration), they literally forced the Roh government to improve relations with North Korea. Thus, the first major challenge the Roh government faced was politicization of the unification issue. Roh was under enormous pressure to put forth more accurate information about the North, and the dissidents and liberal elements within South Korea rejected the promotion of diabolical images of North Korea.

Roh swiftly responded to this pressure by making available more information about North Korea. For the first time, the major television networks showed films about Pyongyang, and Kim Il Sung's picture appeared on magazine covers and on television screens. In 1990 a weekly government television series started showing selected clips from North Korean television broadcasts. This was a revolutionary change—one that made South Koreans less afraid of North Korea. *Rodong Sinmun*, North Korea's major propaganda newspaper, which the public had never been allowed to read, became available in selected places. The government diluted its anticommunist education and instead promoted reunification education. Thus, the Roh government went out of its way to sensitize itself to the shifting mood of the nation and began to play a different game not only to stay in power but also to bolster the regime's image. It appears that there was a definite correlation between democratization and the government's sudden demonstration of interest in promoting unification of the peninsula. Hence, the speed and success of democratization may very well determine the future course of unification as well as improve inter-Korean relations.

Faced with the challenge from the Left, the Roh regime was desperate to impress upon the public its sincerity about both reunification and democratization. It hurriedly devised a new policy to normalize inter-Korean relations, and Roh surprised the nation with his July 7 declaration in 1988.[8] In a major policy reversal, Roh declared that North Korea would no longer be regarded as an enemy and promised the possibility of exchanges between the two Koreas. He also called for South Korea's allies to cooperate and improve relations with North Korea. But most important, the declaration acknowledged that North Korea's efforts to be included in the international community would no longer pose a threat to the South.

In addition, the Roh government launched its northern policy, asserting that participation by the Soviet Union, China, and other former Warsaw Pact nations in the 1988 Seoul Olympic Games helped dismantle East-West barriers and usher in a new era of international reconciliation and cooperation. The former Soviet Union and other communist nations ended their hostile relations with South Korea. In sum, Roh moved quickly to improve his image and answer *jaeya's* challenge.

Roh's July 7 declaration and his northern policy presented him with a major dilemma. His northern policy and the nation's curiosity about North Korea weakened South Korea's long-standing anticommunist creed. Many conservatives felt this endangered South Korea's national identity, if not its national security. Thus, Roh alienated the bulk of his own constituency. People who had spent their lives monitoring North Korea became ineffective as the flirtation with South Korea's northern neighbors picked up steam.

As *jaeya* forces began to play an increasingly important role as generators of policy discussion, conservative elements as well as the general public began to have second thoughts about Roh's attempts to accommodate *jaeya* wishes. Roh was shocked to learn that on the pretext of promoting reunification, radical students tried to undermine the government and disrupt the Olympic Games. Students unsuccessfully tried to march to the North on several occasions and demanded that they be allowed to take part in North Korea's highly publicized World Youth and Student Festival held July 1, 1989.

The South Korean government, fearing North Korea's attempt to pit South Korean students against their government, repeatedly denied the students' requests to go to the North. One of the student leaders, Yim Su-kyŏng, managed to travel to Pyongyang to participate in the festival and received a rousing welcome from North Koreans. Radical students wanted to test Roh's sincerity, as expressed in his July 7 declaration, and used the unification issue to undermine the Roh government. In a sense, the students' reunification drive was a continuation of their struggle against what they called the "Roh dictatorship"—an extension of the Park and Chun regimes. Thus, despite a liberal policy toward North Korea, Roh faced the same twin challenges from North Korea and his own people that bedeviled Park and Chun.

As a result, Roh was suspect in the eyes of both Right and Left. Questioning his sincerity and distrusting him, the Left viewed President Roh's July declaration and northern policy as a propaganda offensive undertaken to improve his image, whereas the right saw the danger in President Roh's premature initiatives toward South Korea's northern neighbors.

As if to present the Roh government with a suitable pretext to crack down on the leftist elements and discredit the *jaeya* forces, Rev. Mun Ik-hwan, a prominent dissident, visited North Korea without permission of the government in March 1989. Security officers stormed Mun's plane upon his return in April and arrested him. To make matters worse for the opposition and the *jaeya* forces, South Korea was stunned to learn in late June 1989 that Sŏ Kyŏng-won, an opposition National Assembly member of Kim Dae-Jung's party, had traveled secretly to North Korea in August 1988, met with Kim Il Sung, and even received money from North Korea. Roh's national security politics jolted both Kim Dae-Jung and his party. In early August, Kim Dae-Jung underwent a twenty-two-hour marathon interrogation by security agents for his alleged role in Sŏ's clandestine trip.

Roh viewed the nation as divided into two groups—the conservatives and the radical Left. He revived the much-dreaded joint investigation agencies ((Hapsubu) consisting of the National Security Planning Agency, the Military Security Command, the police, and the prosecution. The government jailed prominent dissidents who tried to contact North Korea. Opposition parties were in disarray and distanced themselves from the *jaeya* forces. Nevertheless, actions of the *jaeya* forces, including the visits by Mun, Yim, and Sŏ to Pyongyang, played an instrumental role in pushing the Roh government to improve relations with North Korea. Ironically, the government borrowed many progressive ideas regarding unification from the *jaeya* forces.

Roh clearly gained the upper hand in the confrontation between the Right and the Left, thanks to the unauthorized visits by several dissidents to North Korea. After discrediting the progressive *jaeya* forces, Roh was free to develop his own formula for reunification. On September 11, 1989, he outlined the Korean National Community (KNC) unification formula.[9] This was intended to effectively counter the North's DCRK formula Kim Il Sung introduced in October 1980.

Under the KNC formula, any other unification plan is unacceptable unless it is based on the principles of independence, peace, and democracy. The proposal embodies the concept of a Korean Commonwealth as an interim stage toward Korean unification.

In spirit and substance, the KNC unification formula is not that different from President Park Chung Hee's unification policy, announced on August

15, 1974. Park's plan was based on the idea of peace first and unification later. President Chun Doo Hwan restated this in 1982 in his UDRK formula, which proposed normalization of relations between the two Koreas. The only difference is that the Roh formula accentuates the importance of the process of unification through stages.

Under Roh's plan, the first stage of unification would involve exchanges and visits between the two Koreas in order to unify separated families. This stage could be called "one people, two nations" or "two governments and two systems." The second stage would involve a loose federation combining both governments that could deal with military, diplomatic, and trade matters. This stage could be termed "one people, one government, two systems." The final stage would see the dissolving of differences between the two different social and economic systems and realization of "one people, one government, one system."

Rejection of Hasty Unification

In 1990, South Koreans watched emotionally as West Germany absorbed East Germany, thinking that perhaps the two Koreas would also be soon unified. Initially, many South Koreans wanted to believe that the Korean case was similar to that of Germany and that South Korea could somehow absorb North Korea. This "German syndrome" did not last long, however. Through public discussions at numerous seminars and symposiums dealing with the unification issue, South Koreans began to assess similarities and differences in the German and Korean cases.

There were more differences than similarities between the two cases.[10] First, East Germany and other East European regimes were completely dependent on the Soviet Union and collapsed when the USSR abandoned them. Obviously, Asian communist nations—especially China and North Korea—are much different in that nationalism played a bigger role in their establishment. North Korea has been able to hold out against the forces of glasnost and perestroika because it does not depend on a superpower patron for its existence, as East Germany did. East Germany tumbled into reunification "because there was nothing—neither a viable dictatorship nor a separate nationhood nor a decent economy—to stave off collapse."[11]

Second, East European nations, including the most oppressive country, Romania, were exposed to Western newspapers and radio. Their citizens were allowed to travel and meet foreign tourists; this is not so in North Korea. In 1989 alone there were exchanges and visits of more than ten million people between the two German states. Article 16 of chapter three of the inter-Korean accords, signed in December 1991, deals with exchanges and cooperation in various fields and is one of the biggest concerns for North Korea. Hence, it will try to avoid giving practical effect to the provision by not allowing massive exchanges of people between the two Koreas. In the case of Germany, the implementation of such a provision was one of the major factors leading to unification. Undoubtedly, the North Korean leadership believes that East Germany made a major mistake in permitting such exchanges and visits.

Third, it is not clear whether South Korea could manage the consequences of a DPRK collapse. South Koreans are disturbed, if not frightened, at the prospect of massive movements of people, uncontrollable demands for economic aid, and the legal, administrative, and political problems of absorbing a large and economically backward nation. South Korea's fear of losing control over the situation once the unification process starts is real.

Sobered by the staggering costs of German unification, the deep domestic problems of South Korea, and the serious economic problems of North Korea, the Roh regime had second thoughts about hasty unification. Talk of unification by absorption suddenly stopped, and fear of quick unification surfaced in public discussions.

The Korea Development Institute (KDI) and other government agencies working on the costs of unification by absorption estimate that if South Korea adopts the German formula of absorption to even out the two economies of North Korea and South Korea, it would cost more than $250 billion.[12] South Koreans see the danger of unemployment, bankruptcies, rising taxes, and the prospect of one or two million refugees as costs to be borne by Seoul alone. Thus, unification has become less a matter of moral imperative than a practical problem—the economics of unification—and South Koreans have begun to talk more about taking care of their internal problems and gaining greater confidence at home before applying the South Korean system to the North.

South Korea's Domestic Problems and Loss of Confidence

South Koreans have become extremely critical of themselves. There is a significant gap between foreign and domestic perceptions of Korea. South Korea is referred to as "Asia's beacon of freedom." In early 1992, President George Bush told the Korean National Assembly that "South Korea is at peace, free, and prosperous."[13] In reality, however, South Koreans are increasingly apprehensive about their domestic political, economic, and social troubles. As a result, they are not only losing confidence but doubt their ability to join the ranks of the advanced nations. During the 1992 December presidential election, all major candidates—Kim Young Sam, Kim Dae-Jung, and Chung Ju-Yung—promised to do something about South Korea's maladies.

The Roh government was adversely affected by a number of problems, including pervasive political distrust between political leaders and the people, regional antipathy between the Honam and Yŏngnam regions, the breakdown of social and ethical norms in society, class conflict, and a sagging economy. These domestic problems raise quesitons about whether South Korea is indeed ready to absorb North Korea if it ever collapsed.

Roh's leadership was often questioned by the public, and he was sometimes portrayed as incompetent. It is possible that Roh was harshly criticized because people were able to question his leadership more freely than under the repressive Fifth Republic. The Sixth Republic allowed freedom of speech and press in an unprecedented way, and as a result, the number of publications, often very critical of the government's performance, sharply increased. This gave the impression that more problems existed under the Sixth Republic than under the previous regime.

Issues South Koreans most frequently complain about include (1) uncontrolled growth of Seoul; (2) problems of unearned income; (3) conspicuous consumption and declining economy; (4) crime; (5) corruption; and (6) political distrust.

South Korea's population in 1992 was about 44 million, and Seoul and its vicinity, constituting 41.5 percent of the national population, was one of the most densely populated places in the world. South Korea's rural areas are practically deserted, but Seoul faces enormous housing shortages and skyrocketing housing costs (often five to ten times higher than in the United States), daily traffic jams, serious air pollution, shocking crimes, disorderly conduct of many people, and unsanitary public and private facilities.

The vast majority of the people living in Seoul are rural people with premodern habits and parochial behavioral patterns that do not reflect a sense of public responsibility and concern. These attitudes are often incompatible with a larger, modern society. Seoul's traffic conditions are so bad that some people think of it as a potential national security nightmare. Most people in Seoul are more concerned about their own problems than about unification.

The Roh regime was criticized heavily for its inability to deal effectively with problems of unearned income. It inadvertently encouraged land speculation by promising to build a large number of apartment units. During the Sixth Republic, land prices increased four to five times. Although the government tried to curb land speculation by placing a tax on unused land and promising to lower land prices by 30 percent within a year or two, land prices in 1992 were still extremely high.[14]

The problem of unearned income has caused a number of social ills, such as a declining work ethic, frequent labor disputes, and a tendency to shy away from dirty, dangerous, or difficult jobs (known as "3-Ds").[15] Above all, a widening economic gap is causing rising enmity between the rich and the poor. One source indicates that 67.3 percent of private land is owned by only 540,000 people, or 5 percent of the nation's total landowners. This group garnered an unearned profit of some 800 trillion won ($1 trillion) due to land price increases since the beginning of the Sixth Republic.[16] The total wages earned by Korea's 10 million workers 1988–1992 pale in comparison. This phenomenon has seriously undermined the morale of the working people and has destroyed incentives to work hard.

The year 1991 was disastrous for the Korean economy. The 9 percent growth in GNP stemmed mainly from domestic consumption rather than investment and merchandise exports. Matters were even worse in 1992; 95,000 small- and medium-sized enterprises went bankrupt and several businessmen killed themselves in despair over their business failures. Also, in 1990 and 1991, the consumption spree touched off brisk imports, and South Koreans began living beyond their means.

South Korea's economy is mired in a "one-two-three" economy, the "three highs," and the "four shortages."[17] *One* means a single-digit figure of growth; *two*, double-digit inflation; and *three*, a triple digit trade deficit. In 1991, the trade deficit was nearly $10 billion, a negative mirror image of the $10 billion surplus in 1988. The *three highs* refer to high wages, high interest rates, and high exchange rates between the Korean won and foreign currencies. The *four shortages* include labor, funds, technology, and social infrastructure. These have been responsible for soaring prices, sagging exports, growing balance-of-payment deficits, and stock market doldrums. The effects of all these will have far-reaching implications in terms of sustaining South Korea's fragile democracy and achieving unification.

Under the Sixth Republic, freedom increased and overt repression diminished. At the same time, law and order broke down in almost every sector of society. The Roh government declared a war against criminals in October 1990. But the results of the "war" were not believed to be sufficient for ordinary citizens to feel safe. Kidnapping, robbery, theft, and violence of all kinds horrified the people.[18]

Corruption is nothing new in Korean society. But the Roh regime suffered revelations of increasing corruption. In 1991, several scandals involving the purchase of university admissions for large sums of money erupted in succession. Also in 1991, the Roh administration was hit by the Susŏ land scandal, which implicated the presidential office, the ruling and opposition parties, the National Assembly, and Seoul's city administration in illegal housing construction.[19] In 1992 the secret sale of the ruling Democratic Liberal Party's training center, allegedly to raise political funds, and another huge land fraud scandal involving a retired army officer and a leading insurance company jolted the nation, resulting in a bitter feud among rival political parties.

The problem of corruption in Korea is serious enough to warrant a warning that the moral fabric of Korean society is on the verge of disintegration. In every sector of society, people are habitually infected by bribe giving and taking. It is widely known that reporters and editorial staff of the print media receive money known as *ch'onji* from politicians on a regular basis, the amount ranging from several hundred to several thousand dollars. In November 1991, the *Han'gyŏre Sinmun,* read by the dissident and liberal elements, ran a series of articles graphically explaining the extent of corruption among Korean reporters and editors.[20]

The 1987 presidential election, the 1988 National Assembly elections, the March and June 1991 local elections, the March 1992 general elections, and even the 1992 presidential election, which was considered the cleanest ever, were all tainted with "dirty" political money. The retired chairman of the Hyundai Group, Chung Ju-Yung, who founded his own political party, the United People's Party (UPP), revealed that he gave Roh some $40 million. On January 10, 1992, during his New Year's press conference, Roh himself admitted that he had received money from business interests. Several days later the opposition leader, Kim Dae-Jung, admitted that he had also.

Political Instability Under the Sixth Republic

As soon as Roh was sworn in as president of the Sixth Republic, political battles over parliamentary elections erupted, testing the leadership of Roh and the three Kims. The results of the April 1988 general elections were totally unexpected because they produced *yeo-so ya-dae*—a ruling minority and combined opposition majority. This was a new phenomenon in Korean politics. The April elections showed that all four parties in effect had become regional parties: the Honam party (Kim Dae-Jung's Party for Peace and Democracy), the Taegu party (President Roh's Democratic Justice Party), the Pusan party (Kim Young Sam's Reunification Democratic Party), and the Ch'ungch'ong party (Kim Jong-Pil's New Democratic Republican Party).

Because it lacked a majority in the National Assembly, the Roh regime had difficulty coping with political problems. In November and December 1988, the nation was consumed with the frustrating investigation of President Chun's abuse of powr and the Kwangju massacre. As a result, Chun was internally exiled, and this created a deep rift between Roh and his mentor, Chun.

In early 1989, the nation was rocked by the issue of whether to hold a plebiscite on Roh's performance. Warning that such a plebiscite could result in a repetition of the confusion and violence of 1987 and 1988, he canceled it altogether. The *jaeya* forces accused President Roh of deceiving the people. The two opposition leaders (the two Kims), however, accepted President Roh's decision, fearing that Korean democracy was too fragile to withstand another tumultuous political campaign. Also, the two Kims were not sure whether they could defeat President Roh if a referendum were held.

The Korean public in general rated Roh's performance negatively, largely because of his inability to resolve difficult national problems. In addition to his failure to satisfactorily resolve the issue of liquidating the legacies of the Fifth Republic and the Kwangju probe, the public was impatient and frustrated over labor unrest, the deteriorating national economy, and crime. Roh blamed all these problems on the fact that the ruling party was a minority and the combined opposition had a majority.

Then, on January 22, 1990, an unprecedented event in Korean politics occurred. President Roh, Kim Young Sam, and Kim Jong-Pil announced that their parties would merge into a grand conservative majority party. This merger was ostensibly to end a two-year political deadlock caused by the entrenchment of the major parties in their four regional bases. Thus, South Korea's political landscape changed overnight, and the political scales tipped sharply. Risking his reputation, Kim Young Sam joined with his past enemies and became part of the establishment, hoping to succeed President Roh after he stepped down in 1993. This was a great surprise to the nation.

The new megaparty was rocked by major intraparty squabbles within a few weeks of its establishment. Because it consisted of incongruous groups with different intentions and ambitions, this new party, the Democratic Liberal Party (DLP), had difficulty operating smoothly. The ensuing controversy threatened its very existence. In October 1990 Kim Young Sam, seriously considering quitting the party, refused to carry out his duty as the executive chairman of the DLP for ten days.[21] Until May 1992 the nation was engrossed in speculation as to whether President Roh would pick Kim Young Sam as his successor. The public engaged in futile discussions regarding the politics of succession. The issue became a national obsession.

The stark reality of Korean politics is that one powerful region dominates all aspects of national life—at least this seems to be the perception of the people. This dominant group is known as the TK group, an acronym for Roh's home town, Taegu, in north Kyongsang province, which is synonymous with power and wealth. This group, though by no means cohesive, was perceived to dominate high-level government positions as well as key posts in financial and business circles and the military. The president, the chairman of the National Assembly, the head of the National Security Planning Agency, and a host of other important political, bureaucratic, and military people were TKs. This group was extremely hostile to the two Kims, even though one of them joined the establishment. TKs were divided into two groups—the old and the new. The former believed it could continue to wield power by making Kim Young Sam the next president. The latter feared that Kim Young Sam's presidency could mean the end of the privileged position they had held since the military coup of 1961.

Also, there was the so-called SK group—Seoul and Kyong-ki province—seeking to end TK domination and prevent Kim Young Sam from becoming president. In May 1992 Lee Chong-chan—four-term lawmaker (DLP), presidential contender, and vocal critic of the 1990 party merger—refused to accept Kim Young Sam's presidential nomination, alleging that the nomination process was essentially unfair. Proclaiming himself to be the leader of the new generation, Lee even defied Roh for mishandling the nomination process—a sign of a serious crack within the ruling party.

Under Presidents Park, Chun, and Roh, regionalism became an important factor in the choice of personnel in the ruling elite. As of December 1991, Roh had appoitned eighty-six cabinet members, their terms in office lasting about eleven to thirteen months. Only 12 percent came from the Honam region, Kim Dae-Jung's power base. Six of the eight who headed the prosecutor's office, the National Security Planning Agency, and the National Tax Administration—agencies most feared by the people—came from the TK region. A Gallup survey showed that nearly 90 percent of the people saw regional animosity as one of the most serious problems.[22] Some Koreans worry that South Korea, badly divided regionally, may not be able to withstand the vortex of national unification.

The performance of the opposition parties was viewed just as negatively as that of the ruling party by the public. One of the most interesting developments in Korean politics during the Sixth Republic was that traditional respect and sympathy accorded to the opposition parties were significantly eroded. The South Korean electorate was disappointed when the two Kims failed to unite during the 1987 presidential election. Voters were disappointed again when the two Kims failed to join together after the election. The split between the two only helped the ruling party. One of the two Kims joined the ruling party, and Kim Dae-Jung was often criticized by his own followers for prolonging his grip on power. Kim Dae-Jung's party failed to overcome its image as a narrow regional party even though in September 1991 it merged with a small splinter party consisting of several lawmakers who refused to go along with Kim Young Sam when he joined the ruling party.

Besides Kim Dae-Jung's Democratic Party (DP) (the new name of Party for Peace and Democracy), several other minor parties emerged. Of these, the only noteworthy one was the Unification National Party (UNP); its founding by the Hyundai Group's Chung Ju-Yung signalled an uneasy relationship between South Korea's *chaebŏl* (business conglomerates) and the government. In the March 1992 general elections, the ruling DLP performed poorly, falling short of winning a majority in the 299-seat National Assembly. The opposition DP emerged stronger, gaining a total of 97 seats. The UNP, barely two months old, obtained 17 percent of the total votes and gained 31 seats. The UPP (a new name for UNP) phenomenon was a new factor in South Korean politics and was the eye of the short-lived political hurricane during the December presidential election.

Also unprecedented in South Korean politics was that the ruling party was characterized by its multifactional instability involving a bitter intraparty struggle for hegemony among its leaders. The ruling party was extremely unstable because of unsettling succession politics, and the opposition was hardly united. This raised a serious question about the country's chronic inability to stabilize party politics. One of South Korea's major dailies, *Chosŏn Ilbo*, characterized the National Assembly as being of "low quality, anachronistic, having dirty factional fights, blindly obedient to bosses, corrupt, and a rubber stamp."[23]

Nevertheless, South Korea successfully managed to hold the presidential election in December 1992. On September 18, 1992, Roh divorced himself from the ruling party and later appointed a neutral cabinet to oversee a fair presidential election. As a result, the election became a contest between major and minor parties. None of the contenders had a military background. The conservative South Korean voters chose stability over drastic reforms. Kim Young Sam, whose main campaign theme was "reform amidst stability," defeated Kim Dae-Jung and Chung Ju-Yung. Bitter regional animosity and ideological controversy failed to elect Kim Dae-Jung president, his third bid. Billionaire Chung's attempt to buy the presidency also failed. Although South Koreans are generally happy with the election of Kim Young Sam as the first legitimate civilian president since 1961, serious and difficult tests for Korean democracy lie ahead. These include the elimination of corruption, the first local election contests for mayors and governors, and the possibility of a constitutional revision battle calling for a parliamentary system. In February 1993 Kim Dae-Jung resigned as leader of the DP. This was followed by Chung Ju-Yung's resignation from the UPP. Kim Young Sam's popularity reached a high 85 percent approval rating because of his bold reform and anticorruption campaign, but his administration faces the likelihood of factionalism in the majority party, the severe problem of a sagging economy, and the intractable problem of inter-Korean relations.

Petrified North Korea

If South Koreans have a generally bleak view of their own situation, their assessment of North Korea is even bleaker. This gives some comfort to South

Koreans, and it is because of this realization that they are relatively better off, despite enormous domestic problems, and that South Korea thrives.

South Koreans as a whole believe that a number of factors have steered Pyongyang toward finding ways to preserve its system rather than scheming to communize the whole peninsula. These include the disintegration of the Soviet Union, Romania's tragedy, China's positive attitude toward South Korea, the impact of the Gulf war, South Korea's relative strength, and U.S. efforts to mobilize world public opinion against North Korea's nuclear program.

South Koreans also know that independence of North Korea, despite its *Juche* rhetoric, has always been compromised by its dependence on the former Soviet Union for oil and other necessities. Kim Il Sung's trip to China in October 1991 was viewed in the South as a desperate attempt to seek financial and material aid to compensate for the cutoff of aid from the dying Soviet Union.[24]

Clearly, North Korea faces a systemic crisis. High-ranking officials in the North are finding out about the outside world through "secret communications," which circulate among the party cadres. They watch South Korean television, read South Korean newspapers, and even talk about the possibility of reforms after Kim Il Sung dies.[25]

South Koreans are told that North Korea's economy is in shambles—the North's GNP being about one-tenth of South Korea's $238 billion. There have been reports of North Koreans breaking into state-run warehouses and of chronic crop failures resulting in serious hunger.[26] The huge difference in economic performance between the two Koreas began when President Park Chung Hee challenged Kim Il Sung on August 15, 1970, by posing a question:

> Are the North Korean Communists interested in participating in a competition—a bonafide competition in development, in construction and in creativity—to prove which system, democracy or Communist totalitarian, can provide better living for the people, and which society is a better place in which to live, instead of continuing to commit the crime of war preparations at the sacrifice of our innocent brethren in the North?[27]

This spirit still constitutes the keystone of South Korea's approach to North Korea. President Park, driven by his economic development policy, suppressed his people harshly. This in turn created dissidents and political turmoil; the atmosphere gave Kim an illusion that South Korea was governed by a madman. Kim did not understand Park and ignored Park's economic development policy. This was Kim's fatal mistake. Of course, given his *Juche* philosophy, he was intellectually ill-prepared to understand Park's development strategy. The gap between the two Koreas has since widened exponentially.

North Korea's military spending is a drag on the economy; it accounts for roughly 21.4 percent of GNP, compared with 4.5 percent in the South. North Korea has persistently demanded the discontinuation of the joint U.S.-ROK Team Spirit military exercises because it has to respond by placing its military on alert, which wastes expensive fuel and valuable personnel. Also, the North Korean system cannot function unless the whole population is constantly mobilized to defend the Kim dynasty and its cult. North Korea's regime-maintenance costs are extremely high. For example, it spent lavishly on giant monuments and other unproductive investments designed mainly to glorify the Kim dynasty. The 1989 World Youth and Students Festival cost $4.7 billion, or 23 percent of GNP.[28]

North Korea has also launched massive propaganda efforts to counter the effects of the rapid changes in the former Soviet Union and other socialist nations. To preserve its system, North Korea must first discard the myth of a lifelong struggle against Japanese imperialism because it has turned to Japan for help—a sign of real desperation. Also, the survival imperative has at times compelled the North to join hands with the South to deal with its economic troubles. Inter-Korean trade rose nearly twentyfold between 1988 and 1991; by the end of 1991 it amounted to over $100 million.[29] Kim Il Sung received Kim Woo-choong, chairman of Daewoo Business Group, in January 1992; earlier he had even met with perhaps the most anticommunist religious leader and business tycoon, Rev. Moon Sun-Myung of the Unification Church.

Thus, it is obvious to South Koreans that North Korea is trying to avoid collapse by slowly normalizing relations with previous enemies—South Korea, Japan, and the United States—while avoiding the danger of overexposing its people to the outside world.

North Korea under the Kim dynasty has no choice but to defend its system. The rigidity of the system is so great that it has very little room for any immediate meaningful reforms. To concede that the revolution or North Korea's socialist experiment has failed would be a blow so devastating to the efforts North Koreans have made toward creating an "ideal society" that, psychologically, it would be unbearable to admit such failure. To sustain the illusion, it is absolutely necessary to put on blinders about the outside world. North Korea's isolation is a crucial requirement for its short-term survival. The Kim dynasty must reassure the party faithful and maintain that the Pyongyang system is infinitely superior to Seoul's "bourgeois fascist" system. It also feels that it must gain the upper hand in inter-Korean relations, the management of which is crucial to the survival of the North Korean system itself.

It is interesting to note North Korea's view that "our party has infinite greatness which no one can totally measure" and its pronouncement extolling "the most superior socialism in the world."[30] Accordingly, disarray, confusion, and social and economic breakdown in the former Soviet Union and elsewhere are viewed as proof of the wisdom of North Korea's version of socialism. The Kim dynasty admits that "socialism has suffered a setback and capitalism has revived in some countries in recent years." But it insists that North Korea is the successor to Marxism—that is the *Juche* idea—and laments the fact that less fortunate countries (often unnamed) are castigated for various sins that led to their downfall: revisionism, flunkyism, dogmatism, and bureaucratism.[31] Kim Jong Il once saw the problems in the former Soviet Union and Eastern Europe in terms of external influence, but he came to see them in light of internally defective elements. Thus, he finds the North Korean system has been managed correctly. He believes the Soviet system collapsed because of failure to recognize *Juche* philosophy and relate it to the masses, a fatal error stemming from the absence of the firm guidance of a great leader and by an erosion of ideology.

North Korea has used the nuclear card for some time for domestic as well as foreign consumption. Regardless of its strategic value, if any, the card has positive political value for regime security in North Korea. It has induced the United States to enter into a dialogue. North Korea is seen engaged in important exchanges with world powers because of the prominence of the issue. Also, the nuclear card is used to manipulate the population into believing that hostile outside imperialists are interfering with and subverting North Korea: It is a pretext to mobilize and unite the people and intensify nationalist sentiment. This trick works because North Korea's civil society is primitive at best.

North Korea's nuclear card may be valuable for its political purpose, but at the same time it contains North Korea's "catch-22." As long as that card is used, North Korea cannot hope to improve relations with South Korea, Japan, and the United States. If North Korea gives it up, the country loses prestige and political advantage and must face implementation of the 1991 inter-Korean agreement, which in turn may pave the way for North Korea's demise in the long run.

The Kims in the North do not possess the knowledge of external conditions necessary to choose the right policy, and North Korea's bureaucratic reality militates against bold experimentation. Those who understand the dynamics of South Korea or the U.S. or international environment are not in a position to decide. The best informed must tailor their advice and think about their own survival. In the meantime, the best North Korea can do is to adopt policies for procrastination—pretending to open up, pretending to abide by the rules of the IAEA mutual inspection regime, and pretending to have serious talks with South Korea. It will no doubt also continue to dream that the new world order led by the United States will collapse.

Perhaps the North Korean system can survive in the post–Kim Il Sung era because its civil society is not ready for the kind of massive transformation that occurred in Eastern Europe. A clear distinction between political society (army, police, bureaucracy) and civil society (media, trade unions, religious groups, schools) must emerge in North Korea. There may be limited, intermittent riots in North Korea, but these will give the ruling elite an excuse to crack down. Also, two conditions are necessary for a meaningful regime change in North Korea: the spread of new values (liberalism, market economy, human rights) among elites and the loss of the will to continue to rule on the part of the old elites. These two conditions do not exist in North Korea.

The 1991 Inter-Korean Accord

On December 10, 1991, North Korean Prime Minister Yon Hyong-muk arrived in Seoul for high-level talks, hoping to rescue his troubled communist dynasty. By manipulating the nuclear card and taking advantage of the Roh government's eagerness to improve relations with the North, he succeeded in taking back with him a historic accord on reconciliation, nonaggression, cooperation, and exchanges between the two Koreas.

South Korea took a huge risk in endorsing the accord without resolving the potentially most dangerous issue: Pyongyang's nuclear program. In the face of enormous domestic problems, the Roh government had to demonstrate at least one substantial accomplishment—improvement in North-South relations. Thus, Roh went out of his way to accommodate North Korean demands, such as denuclearization of the Korean peninsula and an inter-Korean nonaggression pact. The *Korea Herald,* an English daily usually friendly to the views of the government, even suspected the inter-Korean accord was "a product of overlapping political interests of the ruling elites of the two Koreas" and suggested that a summit with Kim Il Sung was a major motive for President Roh to hasten the signing of the accord.[32]

In January 1992, South Korean Prime Minister Chung Won-sik and his northern counterpart formally exchanged instruments of ratification in Pyongyang, ostensibly defining the relationship between the two parts of Korea for the first time since their division in 1945. This should have resulted in celebrations in both capitals, but neither showed any excitement over the historic accords. Also, as soon as the document was exchanged, North Korean leaders reverted to their old habits, calling for the withdrawal of U.S. troops from South Korea, the termination of South Korean–U.S. joint military exercises, and the release of political dissidents jailed for visiting the North without permission. Furthermore, Kim Il Sung refused to clear the air regarding his nuclear program by denying its existence. Deeply disappointed, the South Korean delegation returned home wondering about the future of inter-Korean relations.

The two Koreas have different things in mind even as they use the same terminology—reconciliation, nonaggression, exchanges, cooperation. In a July 4, 1972, communiqué (see Appendix A), the two Koreas had agreed on principles for unification. North Korea's primary aim was to use the communiqué to force the removal of U.S. ground forces from the South, whereas President Park regarded it as nothing more than a limited agreement between himself and his northern counterpart that would allow him to manage his own domain unimpeded.

In fairness, one should acknowledge that the 1991 agreement is more promising than its 1972 antecedent, but one must also be cautious about predicting a bright future for relations between the two Koreas. Because the political clocks of the two Koreas are set so differently, North and South face different needs and problems and are thus bound to interpret the accords differently. Particularly because both Koreas were in a hurry to finalize the agreement, one must question the motives of their two competing elites. One can easily find the true motivations in the domestic problems facing both Koreas.

Conclusion

In a broad sense, there are three main groups in South Korea that articulate views on inter-Korean relations and the unification issue. The right wing believes that despite changes in the former Soviet Union and Eastern Europe, North Korea has not changed at all. Unless and until North Korea opens up its system and abandons its communization scheme, this group contends that the hard-line policy toward North Korea should be maintained. Rightists believe that radical left-wing groups in South Korea are no different from North Korean communists and that moderate elements in the South are dangerously naive about North Korea. The right wing, out of power, was extremely unhappy with what it saw as Roh's appeasement policy toward North Korea.

The radical left wing, although small in number, believes that the root cause of the "mess" in South Korea is the supposed division of Korea by the United States.[33] Radicals claim that this division has caused South Korea's external dependency and dictatorship and the exploitation of the people. They feel that in order to overcome these problems, unification must be hastened. They also insist that the prime movers of the unification drive must be the *minjung* (people), not the government, which they view as an antiunification-oriented institution. They portray Rev. Mun Ik-hwan and Yim Su-kyŏng, who visited North Korea without government permission, as true patriots. In May 1992, radical students claimed that the national security laws run counter to the spirit of the inter-Korean accord; they vowed to exchange letters with North Korean students, show North Korean films, sing North Korean songs, and read banned books on North Korea. Recently, the South Korean government as well as the public expressed concern about radical students waving North Korean flags on campuses.

Moderates, perhaps the largest in number, reject both extremes. They perceive the right-wing view as rigid and anachronistic and dismiss the radical view as harebrained and dangerous. Moderate elements think that North Korea is changing, albeit slowly, and that sooner or later North Koreans will come to appreciate the achievements of South Korea's market economy and pluralistic democracy. The most important step that can be taken toward unification, they insist, is to begin exchanges and contacts between the two Koreas, as occurred between the two German states for twenty years before their unification. Moderates are well aware of South Korea's internal turmoil, and they feel that improving inter-Korean relations is less pressing than dealing with South Korea's economic, social, and political problems. In a 1992 survey, only 4 percent of the respondents believed in the urgency of reunification.[34]

These different positions reveal that only the Roh government and the radical elements, albeit for different reasons, were eager to improve relations with North Korea. The important thing is that the bulk of South Korean people do not seem to desire hasty unification.

Although Seoul and Pyongyang have designated 1995 as the target year for achievement of reunification, such is not likely in this decade unless forced by war or an internal collapse of one or both parts of Korea. There is a simple reason for such a pessimistic appraisal: A society in trouble cannot cooperate harmoniously with its enemy. A close examination of the internal conditions of both Koreas reveals that each is beset by enormous problems. South Korea's economic miracle is past history. Its state is not as strongly democratic as many people think. For its part, North Korea is a fragile socialist state. The principal distinguishing feature of weak states is their high level of concern with domestically generated problems.[35] Although South Korea's GNP is roughly ten times that of North Korea, the South's weakness lies in the social and political sectors, which in turn adversely affect economic performance. North Korea's Orwellian socialist state is weak because of its bankruptcy, and it can only keep itself going by deliberately preventing its people from knowing about the defects of their system.

The Sixth Republic under Roh failed to create a domestic consensus of sufficient strength to deal effectively with the unification issue. The Roh regime was pushed into improving relations with North Korea by the *jaeya* forces and international circumstances. Its venture into the northern policy and unification politics was largely an attempt to divert attention from domestic difficulties. Given that the Roh regime enjoyed little public confidence and the people generally felt the nation was in a state of crisis, the government was strongly motivated to turn the 1991 inter-Korean agreement into a political boon. Very few Koreans seriously believe that the pact can solve the most pressing problems between the two Koreas in the near future. Terming the agreement a historic milestone in inter-Korean relations was a bit premature. Rather, it was something that a regime facing difficult domestic problems could point to as progress on paper.

During the seventh round of South-North high-level talks May 5–8, 1992, the North was quick to agree to set up liaison offices and three joint commissions (military matters, economic exchanges, and social and cultural exchanges) to implement the inter-Korean accord. When these joint mechanisms were activated to resolve the real issues of unification, the truly difficult task began and the inter-Korean dialogue again became deadlocked. What the two Koreas must accomplish sooner or later should include the following:

- Institutionalizing peaceful coexistence
- Opening postal and telephone connections between the two Koreas
- Allowing exchange of people to visit relatives
- Pulling troops away from the demilitarized zone
- Letting North Korea divert its military spending for economic growth
- Letting South Korean businesses invest in North Korean factories, thus tapping a pool of cheap labor
- Establishing a European Community–style free-trade zone
- Unifying Korea under a free-market system near the end of the 1990s[36]

Given the internal conditions of both Koreas and their different motives for agreeing to the 1991 pact, the prospects for realizing these tasks remain murky. For North Korea, permitting direct interchange of its citizens with South Koreans is too risky for the system.

Under the Kim Young Sam administration, we will find out if the agreement will simply be a piece of paper like the July 1972 communiqué. The true test of whether the pact will have any meaning will come only when North Korea allows its citizens to have direct exchanges with the people of the South.

I would like to end this chapter with a personal note. If reunification of the Korean peninsula means the merging of the two systems, then I do not believe it is possible, short of a war or a collapse of either the North or the South or both. But there is another way of achieving the practical effects of reunification by keeping the two Koreas in peace. My personal vision for the future Korean peninsula draws its inspiration from contemporary U.S.-Canadian relations. The countries maintain undefended borders and belong to the Atlantic community; both Canadians and Americans speak the same language and share a similar culture and way of life. Both people can travel to the other side freely and yet maintain their separate identities. A sense of a united Korean community or commonwealth can be promoted without territorial and political integration. It can be accomplished through multiple transactions and exchanges. What is really needed is to rethink the old concept of reunification. The most urgent task of reunification is to alleviate the suffering of the ten million separated families. Therefore, the ruling elites of both Koreas must accept much of the blame for perpetuating tensions in the Korean peninsula. Democratic dynamism and changes in South Korea are bound to have a significant impact in creating attitudes in North Korea that would be a bit more compatible with South Korea's worldview. This gives hope for reassociation between the same people of the two Koreas, if not for reunification.

Notes

1. Miroslav Nincic, *The Anatomy of Hostility: The U.S.-Soviet Rivalry in Perspective* (New York: Harcourt Brace Jovanovich, 1989), p. 255.

2. See ibid., pp. 146–154. Nincic explains how international conflict is often held hostage to a biased structure of political rewards.

3. *Pyongyang Times* in 1992 charged that the United States still dictated to the South Korean ruler and called for withdrawal of U.S. troops from South Korea, abolishment of the national security laws, and release of the "patriots" jailed for visiting North Korea. See *Pyongyang Times*, March 28, 1992.

4. See Manwoo Lee, "Domestic Factors Influencing the Korean Unification Process," *Asian Perspective*, Spring-Summer 1986, pp. 46–47.

5. See Manwoo Lee, "How North Korea Sees Itself," in C. I. Eugene Kim and B. C. Koh, eds., *Journey To North Korea: Personal Perceptions* (Berkeley: Institute of East Asian Studies, University of California, 1983), pp. 135–138.

6. See John W. Burton, "North and South Korea: Shared and Separate Values," *Korea and World Affairs*, Vol. 8, No. 1 (Spring 1984), p. 51.

7. Lee, "Domestic Factors Influencing the Korean Unification Process," p. 54.

8. See *South-North Dialogue* (Seoul: International Cultural Society of Korea, December 1988), pp. 7–93.

9. See *Democratic Unification Theory* (in Korean) (Seoul: Ministry of National Unification, 1991), pp. 70–96.

10. See *Comparative Analysis of German Unification and the Korean Case* (Seoul: International Cultural Society of Korea, 1991), p. 70; Sung Chul Yang and Sung-jo Park, *German Unification and the Korean Division* (in Korean) (Seoul: Institute for Far Eastern Studies, Kyungnam University, 1991).

11. *Comparative Analysis of German Unification and the Korean Case*, p. 70.

12. *Korea Times*, August 17, 1991.

13. *Korea Herald*, February 25, 1992, and January 7, 1992.

14. *Korea Times*, January 1, 1992.

15. Ibid.

16. Ibid.

17. *Korea Times,* December 24, 1991.

18. *Korea Newsreview,* October 19, 1991.

19. *Dong-A Ilbo,* February 12, 15, 16, 21, 1991.

20. See *Han'gyore Sinmun,* November 7–14, 1991.

21. An opinion survey showed that 66.6 percent regarded the merger of the three parties in 1990 as a mistake and 77 percent disapproved of the ruling party's performance. See *Dong-A Ilbo,* December 27, 1990.

22. *Korea Times,* November 24, 1991; *Chosŏn Ilbo,* November 23, 1991.

23. *Chosŏn Ilbo,* December 19, 1991.

24. *Korea Times,* October 15, 1991.

25. *Chosŏn Ilbo,* June 13, 1991.

26. *Korea Times,* November 8, 16, 1991.

27. Park Chung Hee, *Toward Peaceful Unification* (Seoul: Kwangmyong Publishing Co., 1976), p. 22.

28. *Asian Wall Street Journal,* January 9, 1991.

29. *Korea Herald,* December 14, 1991.

30. *Rodong Sinmun,* February 11, 1991, quoted in Rinn-sup Shinn, "North Korea: Squaring Reality with Orthodoxy," in Donald N. Clark, ed., *Korea Briefing, 1991* (Boulder, CO: Westview Press, 1991), p. 85.

31. "China, North Korea," *The Economist Intelligence Unit* No. 1, 1992, pp. 32–33.

32. *Korea Herald,* December 14, 1991.

33. See Manwoo Lee, Ronald McLaurin, and Chung-in Moon, *Alliance Under Tension: The Evolution of South Korea–U.S. Relations* (Boulder, CO: Westview Press, 1988), pp. 12–16.

34. *Korea Herald,* March 3, 1992.

35. George Sorensen, "Revised Paradigm for International Relations: The Old Images and the Post-Modernist Challenge," *Cooperation and Conflict,* June 1991, p. 106.

36. Adapted from Damon Darlin, "Koreas Closer Than Ever to Unification," *Asian Wall Street Journal,* December 27, 1991.

11

Economic Factors in Korean Reunification

Hy Sang Lee

This chapter focuses on the economies of North Korea and South Korea and analyzes their impact on the prospects for reunification. The ailing communist economy in the North features dimensions that will sustain the socialist state for a protracted period in its struggle for unification on its own terms; the prosperous capitalist economy in the South suffers from serious economic inequality and radicalized labor factions that stand in the way of sensible approaches to reunification. Given these economic factors that conspire to delay reunification, the chapter ends with a discussion of their implications for South Korea's unification policies for the future.

North Korea

How long is North Korea likely to stay viable as an assertive state in the face of grave economic difficulties engendered by the collapse of communism? In the absence of available quantitative economic data, published speeches of Kim Il Sung yield both descriptive information and isolated numbers that reveal broad contours of movements in the economic sphere. The emerging picture is of an economy that is deeply troubled but capable of weathering its difficulties at near-subsistence standards, to which the people are accustomed.

Agriculture

Frequent outside reports of food crisis in North Korea suggest that agriculture may serve as the trigger for destabilizing North Korea. North Korea is a mountainous country located in the upper Northern Hemisphere and has relatively short summers—natural conditions not well suited for agriculture. Before the partition of Korea in 1945, the North imported rice from the South or coarse grains from northeastern China. Until the early 1980s, however, socialist North Korea made extraordinary efforts to achieve self-sufficiency in food

under a philosophy of governance called *Juche* (self-reliance). Food self-sufficiency was apparently achieved in the 1970s. However, conditions have deteriorated in recent years due to the loss of socialist trade. The basic inquiry here
is to determine how bad the food situation is and will be in North Korea. The
conclusion is that although grain production is not sufficient to provide for a
steady margin over minimum subsistence, it is not bad enough to create large
shortages that could not be offset by modest imports and that would destabilize the country.

   Subteam System. A review of agricultural performance in any socialist
country involves the central question of how the institutions of collectiviza-
tion there fared. North Korea collectivized agriculture in the 1950s mostly in
the form of cooperative farms.[1] A cooperative farm coincided with the basic
rural administrative unit (*ri*), consisting of several natural villages. Each village comprised a work team involving several dozen peasants. All members
of the work team constituted a single pool of labor from which individuals
were dispatched in the morning to fields by the work team leader.[2] Because
each peasant worked many different fields over time, the traditional ties
farmers had toward their land and crops were severed. Low incentives for
food production were thus set to operate in North Korea as in other socialist
countries.

   By the early 1960s, production failures became serious. Kim Il Sung responded by proclaiming a farm management technique (Ch'ongsanri
method) to improve work practices, but production failures continued. At
this point, North Korea acted to institute a reform of some significance in
terms of incentives. A subteam management system was introduced in 1966
in which fifteen to twenty peasants became the basic unit of operation. The
work team became an intermediary management unit. The significance of the
subteam reform was partially related to the reduction in size of the accounting unit within which individual income shares were mostly determined. Of
greater significance, however, was a restoration of ties between peasants and
the land they worked. The subteam of a small group of farmers was permanently assigned to a given area of land and an assortment of tools.[3] How
much of a role the subteam system played in dealing with production declines is difficult to quantify because Pyongyang stopped publishing production statistics during this period of economic difficulties. In a speech in early
1968, two years after the introduction of subteams, Kim Il Sung announced
that grain production in 1967 was 16 percent greater than in 1966; he indicated
that instituting the subteam system in all cooperative farms was the central
factor in the increase.[4]

   The subteam system represented a concession to individualism in a retreat
from the collectivism that informed the establishment of cooperative farms.
By restoring at least physical ties between peasants and the land, it provided
minimal levels of incentives and productivity for socialized agriculture.
There has been no other institutional reform of any kind in North Korean cooperative farms. A continuity in the collectivized system endowed with some
individualistic incentives appears to have provided for minimal levels of
peasant productivity in North Korea.

Two-Crop System. The central strategy adopted by North Korea from the outset toward the goal of food self-sufficiency was a virtual two-crop system, rice and maize (corn). Rice paddies were expanded by means of irrigating part of dry fields, and dry fields, extending onto the hills, were planted with maize to the exclusion of other traditional and more preferred grains. Under the slogan "maize is the king of dry fields," the acreage for maize was expanded for its potential for high yield, as experienced in advanced countries.[5] By the mid-1960s, the acreage had been increased to approximately 700,000 hectares each for rice and maize, from 382,000 hectares and 283,000 hectares respectively in 1949. In order to pursue high yields with rice and maize, North Korea extended its irrigation network vigorously. Irrigation for rice paddies was virtually complete in the 1960s, and a sprinkler system began to cover dry fields by the 1970s.

The sight of green belts of maize standing in terraced fields blanketing steep hill after hill is one of the sea changes wrought by *Juche* socialism in North Korea since partition. Another remarkable aspect of maize growing in North Korea is the practice of transplanting seedlings, a well-established technique in rice cultivation for high yield. North Korea transferred the practice to maize cultivation in the 1970s, raising maize seedlings in early spring in protected humus fields and transplanting them one by one in late spring to extend the growing period for higher yields.[6] Labor intensity involved in the practice is monumental, but it is a price readily paid for raising crop yields.

Input Improvements. Concerted efforts were made in the 1970s to increase fertilizer application and mechanization. Although claimed increases in fertilizer tonnage per hectare and the number of tractors per 100 hectares are not necessarily evidence of proportionally higher output, major strides were made in food production in the 1970s when many varieties of input improvements were made.[7] Among other improvements, the most significant was the development of high-yielding strains. North Korea began to plant new strains of maize and rice in the 1970s.[8]

The institutional and agronomic improvements described here have been described qualitatively to establish the presumption that there were significant increases in grain production in North Korea through the 1970s. Quantitatively, however, the increases cannot be ascertained by outsiders with reasonable accuracy; because of lack of data, some production figures are derived from the speeches of Kim Il Sung.

Historical Estimates of Output. In 1961, the year before North Korea stopped publishing most economic statistics, Kim Il Sung made a speech at a party congress indicating that grain production reached 3.8 million tons in 1960 for an increase of 32 percent from 1956.[9] This claim represented an average annual growth of 8 percent, an unusually high rate for agricultural production. Then, after a period, he addressed the national congress of agricultural officials in 1967 and 1968 and gave isolated numbers relating to grain production but not production totals. When the two speeches are juxtaposed, however, it is possible to calculate the unrevealed numbers.

In his February 1967 speech, Kim stated that his goal for 1967 was to increase grain production by 1 million tons:

If we produce two tons of maize per chongbo [approximately a hectare], we can harvest 1,400,000 tons of maize on 700,000 chongbo, and if we produce four tons of rice per chongbo, we can harvest 2,800,000 tons of rice from 700,000 chongbo. ... If, in addition, we produced approximately 350,000 to 400,000 tons of soybeans, and a bit more of some other grains, we could harvest one million tons more grain than last year. ... If we succeed, we could not only do without the 500,000 tons imported annually, but sell approximately 500,000 tons to other countries, and even store reserves.[10]

Grain output for 1966 was omitted even for agricultural officials or was deleted from the speech when it was published later to keep it from the public. In any case, if the figure can be deduced, the production number for 1966 can be identified and the consumption level approximated. The speech does reveal something about grain consumption in 1966, which was the unknown production level plus 500,000 tons imported.

Interestingly, the speech Kim delivered in the following year contained this brief statement: Thanks to our energetic campaign to increase output per chongbo by 500 kilograms, grain production increased by 16 percent [in 1967] over 1966."[11] If these numbers are related to those given in the 1967 speech, production data can be approximated (see Table 11.1). Because one speech gives the per hectare output goals for 1967 (for rice and maize each), whereas

TABLE 11.1   Planned and Actual Production of Grains, 1966 and 1967

1967 Planned Production per Ha	*1967 Planned Total*
Rice 4 tons per ha	$4 \times .7 = 2.8$ million tons
Maize 2 tons per ha	$2 \times .7 = 1.4$ million tons
Soybean	.4 million tons
Other grains	.6 million tons
1967 planned total for all grains	5.2 million tons

1966 Actual Output per Ha	*1966 Actual Total*
Rice $4 - .5 = 3.5$ tons per ha	$3.5 \times .7 = 2.45$ million tons
Maize $2 - .5 = 1.5$ tons per ha	$1.5 \times .7 = 1.05$ million tons
Soybean	.30 million tons
Other grains	.40 million tons
1966 actual total for all grains	4.2 million tons

1967 actual total for all grains	$4.2 + (4.2 \times .16) = 4.87$ million tons
1966 actual grain consumption	$4.2 + .5 = 4.7$ million tons

SOURCES: Kim Il Sung, "On Revolutionizing the Peasants and Carrying Through the Party Conference Decisions in the Field of Agriculture," speech at a national congress of agricultural functionaries, February 21, 1967, *Selected Works*, Vol. 4 (Pyongyang: Foreign Languages Publishing House, 1971), p. 485; Kim Il Sung, "On Correctly Introducing the Sub-Work Team Management System and on Effecting a New Upsurge in Agricultural Production," speech at the national conference of agricultural workers, February 14, 1968, *Jojakjib* (Works), Vol. 22 (Pyongyang: Workers' Party of Korea Publishing House, 1983), p. 11.

the other address specifies the amount needed above 1966 levels to reach the 1967 goals, it is possible to calculate the 1966 outputs per hectare by subtracting the needed increases from the 1967 goals. From there, a multiplication by the acreage of each crop gives the 1966 output total for rice and maize. For other crops, rough backtracking calculations from the 1967 goal figures provide 1966 production estimates for soybeans and other grains. A total of 4.2 million tons for 1966 ultimately emerges, 1 million tons less than the 5.2 million ton goal for 1967.

The 4.2 million figure for 1966 represented a growth of 10.5 percent in six years, or an average annual rate of 1.75 percent. Such a growth rate is common in many countries but would have been disappointing and thus not publishable for a country such as North Korea. Especially significant is that the 1966 production figure is accompanied by a consumption number that includes about 500,000 tons more imported—that is, 4.7 million tons.

There are built-in exaggerations in the North Korean grain production figures even when they are reported straightforwardly. A major source of exaggeration is the sample harvesting method—taken from fields showing high yields—used in the estimation of production. An additional source of exaggeration is the propensity of cooperative farms and higher-level officials to inflate output estimates markedly during special campaigns, as occurred in 1974. In 1973 Kim Il Sung launched "three-revolution" teams (political, technical, and cultural) to shake up the stagnant bureaucracy and a stagnating economy. Young party cadres and college students were organized in small groups and dispatched to cooperative farms and factories to prod and lead enterprise cadres and workers to redouble their efforts on the political, technical, and cultural revolutions. Politically, this program coincided with the rise of Kim Jong Il as heir designate, and he was put in charge of it. In the economic realm, the program was shock therapy to enterprises to increase innovation and production.

The impact on reported output was dramatic. Early in 1975, Kim Il Sung announced that grain production in 1974 had reached 7 million tons, an increase of 30 percent over 1973; further, it was claimed that output per hectare for rice and maize reached 5.9 tons and 5 tons respectively. Exaggerations were contained in these numbers, discovered by none other than Kim Il Sung. The discovery occurred at a cooperative farm where Kim visited. The farm had sent to the supervising county a rice output report of 7.4 tons per hectare for 1974. A county official suggested that the reported figure was too low. Consequently, the cooperative farm drew new harvest samples from higher-yielding fields and reported a yield of 8.2 tons per hectare. Actual harvest of all rice fields gave an average yield of 6.8 tons per hectare.[12]

Although this case of exaggeration is not necessarily typical of all cooperative farms, it can provide a rule of thumb for the purpose of discounting announced production because of inflated figures: a 9 percent padding as a norm and an additional 12 percent (total of 21 percent) during a special production campaign. Under this rule of thumb, the announced output of 7 million tons for 1974 can be discounted by a full 21 percent to 5.8 million tons; this was the early period of the three-revolution team program. The 1966 production of 4.2 millions tons can be discounted by 9 percent to 3.9 million tons; only the normal padding is applied because the subteam management system being introduced in 1966 had little expectation of immediate effects.

The last officially reported production of 10 million tons of grain for 1984 also can be discounted. The number is especially suspicious because it matches the output level targeted in the Second Seven-Year Plan for its final year—1984.[13] However, it is proposed that the same rule of thumb at its maximum discount rate be applied here. Discounted by 21 percent, the 10 million figure shrinks to 8.3 million tons. How can this be interpreted? An 8.3 million ton production in 1984 represents a growth of 2.5 million tons from the discounted 1974 level of 5.8 million tons. It indicates an average annual growth rate of 4.3 percent during the ten-year period. This is a fairly high sustained rate for agriculture, but not out of line for North Korea in the 1970s during its burst of productivity-boosting accomplishments.

Grain production after 1984 must have been disappointing in view of the absence of any output announcement. A reasonable approach would be to take the (discounted) 1984 level for 1989, the last normal year before the crumbling of socialism in Eastern Europe. For 1990, 1991, and 1992, there was a progresively declining production, probably at an average annual drop of 3 percent, a total of 9 percent in three years. Thus, output for 1992 can be fixed at 7.6 million tons (the 1989 level of 8.3 million tons reduced by 9 percent).

What do these discussions suggest about food conditions for North Korea in the 1990s? Grain consumption in 1966 was fairly plausibly indicated as equaling production plus imports of 500,000 tons. After 1966 production is discounted to 3.9 million tons, total consumption works out to be 4.4 million tons. From 1966 to 1992, the population of North Korea increased from 12.5 million to 22.5 million, for a growth of 80 percent. Meanwhile, the same system of food rationing, in grains and meat, was in force throughout the period. In other words, grain consumption per capita, both directly and through meat, remained virtually constant. Therefore, the need for grain in 1992 would have been approximately 7.9 million tons (180 percent of the 1966 level of 4.4 million tons).

Because the 1992 output is fixed at 7.6 million tons, there would have been a shortage of approximately 300,000 tons. This shortage could have been met through imports at a cost of about $70 million, a sum North Korea can handle. Only if grain output were to fall for several more years at the recent rate would import costs for offsetting ballooning shortages become very burdensome. Otherwise, a stabilization of production at current levels or even further declines for a few more years could be managed by North Korea without undue difficulty.

Industry and Finance

As in agriculture, North Korea started to modify its socialist structure of industry and finance early in its statehood. It maintained an unquestioned continuity of core socialist institutions—state ownership and centralized planning and control—and made system modifications of modest proportions directed toward a structure of a high degree of localized self-sufficiency in consumer goods.[14] An initial move in that direction was made in 1958. During the preceding five years since the Korean War, North Korea had directed its investment programs decidedly toward heavy industry. Production of consumer goods had been left largely to the handicraft and cottage industries supervised by local officials under the direction of the provinces. Lack of investable resources and the remoteness of provincial offices from the widely scattered petty producers kept production languishing. In 1958 the shortage of consumer goods reached crisis proportions.[15] At this point, Pyongyang made a critical decision not to direct part of its investable resources toward consumer industries but to restructure local economies to better respond to their own needs. The idea of local self-sufficiency in consumer goods was thus born early as a product of ruthless single-mindedness in the political goals Pyongyang had set for itself.

The initial move was a decision of the party Central Committee at the June 1958 plenary meeting involving three main points: First, the search for raw materials and the production of consumer goods were to be conducted on the basis of mass movement in each county, city, or city district of larger cities. Second, at least one local industry factory was to be built in each county or its city equivalent. Third, new factories were to be staffed with idle members of households of workers and officials in the county seats and city districts.[16]

This decision embodied a structural shift in the focus of local government decisionmaking from the province to the county. A system of local industries to produce goods to meet the basic needs of local people on the basis of raw materials acquired from local areas was to be developed under the auspices of county officials who were closest to the scene of needs and resources.

There were economic and security justifications for the strategy of local self-provision. Kim Il Sung pointed to transport economy, urban growth limitation, development of the countryside, and the dispersion of production facilities conducive to wartime needs.[17] The response to the local self-reliance program was enthusiastic. Encouraged to be creative and to look after their own needs, local citizens responded with a degree of good sense and energy. Within a few months, 1,000 local factories appeared—an average of five factories per county.[18] Only one or two per county had been anticipated for starters by policymakers. More remarkable is that local factories grew by 1961 to account for 50 percent of total consumer goods produced.

At the August 1962 joint conference of local party and economic officials at Changsong (north Pyongan province) called to discuss further development of local industry, Kim Il Sung stated that an average of ten local factories in each county had been built and that the output value of local industry amounted to "more than one-half" of the consumer goods produced in North Korea.[19] To reach an average of ten factories by 1962, the growth of local industry must have been substantial by 1961.

According to another source published virtually at the same time as Kim's Changsong speech, output of local factories was reported to have reached 56 percent of all consumer goods produced by 1962. It also was reported to have accounted for 39 percent of total gross industrial production; local industry output grew from an index of 100 in 1957 to 171 in 1958, 340 in 1959, 423 in 1960, and 500 in 1961.[20]

Despite the vigor and perhaps because of it, the expanding system of local self-sufficiency was reined in by ideologues during the 1960s. Many local factories of larger size were turned over to central industry under the direct control of the central ministries. Local factories in food processing and manufacturing of daily necessities were placed under the direction of the newly established Ministry of Food and Daily Necessities Industries. Kim Il Sung indicated that functionaries in this field merged one factory with another at random, in a subjective way, without taking the specific conditions into consideration on the pretext of specialized production. As a result, many locally run factories disappeared, and the variety of goods was considerably cut."[21]

Kim Il Sung likes to blame functionaries for things that go wrong. But it was he who led the assault on local industry with a perfectionist approach to socialist planning. In 1965, Kim Il Sung launched a campaign for what he called unified and detailed planning.[22] It was Stalinist planning in the extreme. During this campaign, many thriving local factories were brought under the direct control of central ministries. In addition, a planning section was established in 1969 in each county and city district under the direct control of the State Planning Commission.[23] That local industry as well as industry in general (except ordnance plants under the 1966 party conference line of "simultaneously building up the economy and defenses") languished soon after the Changsong conference is no surprise. Kim Il Sung failed to achieve socialism and productivity in tandem and eventually made a modest retreat from central planning.

In the retreat, Kim Il Sung saved face by holding on to the notion of unified planning but enabling county governments to draw up their own plans for local industry.[24] Thus, North Korea is able to and regularly does claim that its entire economy is under unified and detailed socialist planning. In effect, however, local industries have been released from the yoke of central planners since 1974. The seriousness Kim Il Sung brought to the 1974 reform for revival of the local self-sufficiency system was underlined by a related financial reform carried out a year earlier in 1973.

Until the early 1970s, North Korea operated on a centralized finance system whereby the revenues and expenditures of local governments were all part of a single government budget controlled by the center. Because local industries were an economic extension of county governments, the single budget system left little room for local initiatives. With this system in place, a reform in the planning sector alone would not have released the energies of local factories to a meaningful degree. Thus, Kim Il Sung instituted a finance reform in concert with a reform on planning and applied the concept of an independent accounting system to local governments. This concept had long been under promotion for production enterprises (all socialist countries have required their factories and farms to stand on their own feet, financially, without necessarily succeeding), but Kim Il Sung decided to make local governments financially independent, too, with the 1973 introduction of what he called the local budget system. All local government units—counties, cities and city districts, and provinces—were instructed to earn incomes to meet expenses (administration, education, services) and to secure budget surpluses to turn over to the central treasury.[25] The original idea of setting up a structure of local self-reliance in the 1950s was to avoid spending central funds for consumer goods production to offset a critical shortage. In introducing the so-called local budget system, Kim Il Sung turned socialist county governments into a string of business conglomerates that happened to perform educational and other public functions and that could finance part of the political activities of the central government. It was a manifestation of high political pragmatism designed to preserve socialism at the core at the expense of peripheral reforms.

The carefully coordinated and calibrated introduction of a local budget system and planning reform in the early 1970s has resulted in a decisive revival of localized self-sufficiency in consumer goods. Today there are twenty to thirty local factories—typically producing furniture, utensils, containers, ornaments, apparel, building materials, paper, and processed foods—in each county (regularly mentioned in the press, especially around the anniversary of the 1958 plenum decision). Local governments have worked to expand production of daily necessities for their citizens and to fulfill their new obligation of earning enough budget surpluses to turn over to the center. By 1977, Kim Il Sung was pleased to announce that local revenue surpluses received by the treasury had reached 1 billion won.[26]

However, local enthusiasm and innovation never seemed to reach the levels Kim Il Sung desired. In 1980 he complained that local governments ceased working hard to expand local industry once their incomes met expenses with something left over.[27] Consequently, in order to infuse creativity into local economies to increase self-reliance, the Kim regime removed another socialist barrier to local creativity by establishing direct sales stores for a new category of locally produced goods. These are known as "August 3 people's consumer goods," so named for the 1984 reform date.

Until 1984, locally fabricated consumer goods had no established distribution channels other than the state commerce network. Large central factories that produced a few consumer items aside from their regular assigned products used to open factory outlets called direct sales stores to dispose of the consumer products. When an increasing number of small local factories began to turn out a variety of goods in small lots, however, a need arose for a flexible collection and distribution mechanism that the state stores operating under central plans could not offer. Hence, it was decided to allow county governments to establish and operate their own direct sales stores outside the state commerce network for August 3 goods. The program constituted the final institutional reform carried out to build a system of localized self-sufficiency in daily necessities.

The August 3 reform has a number of attributes other than its direct sales stores.[28] It signaled the personal involvement of Kim Jong Il in the welfare of North Korean consumers; it was launched by him. The program attribute most emphasized by Pyongyang is reliance on the use of local reserves—waste materials, idle labor, industrial by-products, scrap, wild fruits, and crops raised on unused land.

The significant aspect of the reform is the direct sales store. It represents a systemic change in that a class of manufactured goods is formally allowed to circulate outside the planned distribution network. However, it is this attribute that Pyongyang has been discreet about. In fact, Pyongyang has consistently avoided acknowledging any reform measures instituted; the clear message sent is that its brand of socialism is here to stay and requires no reforms.

The August 3 program has progressed substantially in quantity, variety, and quality. Clothes are no longer popular items. Chinaware and furniture sell well. Even electrical products have begun to be manufactured.[29] The supposed use of by-products and scrap increasingly seems to be stretched to include new raw materials and parts fit for the production of regular goods. By 1989, the number of workers engaged in the production of August 3 goods had grown to "several hundred thousand." Sales proceeds of direct sales stores nationwide grew at an average annual rate of 20.8 percent, reaching 9.5 percent of total sales value of retail stores operated under central planning (*kukyong sangŏpmang*) in 1989.[30] There also was a report that nationwide output under the program increased further to equal 13 percent of total sales of state stores in 1991.[31] Because state stores under planning continue to distribute the products of both central industry and local industry, the weight of the August 3 program is in the 20–30 percent range in relation to either central industry or local industry.

As previously noted, output value of local industry accounted for 56 percent of all consumer goods produced in the early 1960s. Because of the subsequent blackout on information, it is not possible to cite an updated number. In all probability, however, the 56 percent number declined but thereafter recovered to at least that level. It may easily have gone higher but is fixed at that level for purposes of this discussion.

If the 56 percent weight of local industry is added to the 13 percent of August 3 goods in relation to state store sales, which include both central and local industry goods, the adjusted combined weight (adjusted by dividing both percentages by 1.13) of local industry and August 3 goods as a percentage of all consumer goods sold works out to be 61 percent. In other words, approximately 61 percent of manufactured goods consumed by North Koreans is provided locally by local people, and 39 percent comes from the center. The significance of a 60 percent range in local self-sufficiency is that North Koreans are protected for a majority of their minimal needs on a sustainable basis even if the national economy encounters production setbacks from time to time. Moreover, the relatively light role of the center in people's consumption enables the center to continue producing minimal amounts of such essential supplies as cloth and shoes to supplement locally produced goods.

North Korea is famous for its claim of economic self-reliance. The concept is meant to pertain to the national economy. However, setbacks in production in the wake of the upheaval in the socialist world have demonstrated the shallowness of *Juche* in terms of the national economy. Despite national-level exposure to external shocks, North Korea does have a certain self-reliance. In food, the system is capable of balancing (or close to balancing) production and consumption albeit at steady though minimal levels. For consumer goods, there is a subnational layer of self-sufficiency of considerable degree and sustainability. Virtual self-sufficiency in food and localized self-reliance in daily necessities constitute domestic economic realities of the North that should be taken into account when the prospects of Korean reunification are considered.

These economic factors will remain sustainable as long as North Korean society remains essentially closed to the outside world. If it opens up widely, the domestic system of minimal provisions will readily become unacceptable to the people because the human sense of well-being is relative. But North Korea needs to earn foreign currencies if it is to offset the losses of subsidized trade with socialist countries and to import grain from time to time. Foreign exchange is needed only partly for domestic needs, however. The low levels of domestic consumption and the essentially localized system of self-sufficiency imply that the needs for foreign exchange are considerably for military procurement and foreign policy activities. These needs can be both immense and flexible, but the latter aspect enables Pyongyang to be discriminating in its trade openings to the free world. Indeed, its external openings have persistently been restricted to narrow and veiled kinds.

External Economic Sector

North Korea commenced external sector reforms of opening in 1984. As with the domestic August 3 reform, the opening to the free world has been instituted slowly and carefully to pursue the same goal—sustenance of a socialist base in the northern half of Korea. The essential characteristic common to all measures of opening has been an element of concealment designed to minimize damage to North Koreans' faith in the viability of socialism.

The Joint Venture Program. North Korea sought to attract outside capital.[32] It inaugurated an external opening in the form of a foreign investment inducement program with the joint venture law of September 8, 1984.[33] Unlike the companion August 3 reform, the joint venture program had to be publicized worldwide in order to attract investors. At home, however, the program has been kept at minimal visibility because it flies in the face of the ideology of self-reliance. Efforts to institute a hidden opening have evolved into two principal approaches to capital inducement: a reliance on Ch'ongryŏn Korean investors and a pattern of consignment production with other investors.

According to an official announcement, North Korea attracted approximately 100 joint ventures by mid-1989[34] and apparently a few more thereafter. About 70 of them were with procommunist Koreans residing in Japan— those belonging to Ch'ongryŏn, the General Association of Korean Residents. The rest were with other foreign nationals—from a few Western and mostly socialist countries. Ch'ongryŏn Koreans who invest in North Korea are loyal to the North Korean system and the ruling Kims. Hence, the reliance on them for external capital can be construed to deviate little from the ideology of self-reliance.

The situation differs for capitalist world investors, including South Koreans. Pyongyang has had considerable difficulty in absorbing them because their presence in North Korea would produce ideological damage. Hence, not many of them have actually established operations in North Korea. Those who have eventually have fallen into a pattern of consignment production, staying overseas and sending processed materials, product designs, equipment, and technical personnel to North Korea. In return, they receive finished products at prices compensating for the risk and costs involved in furnishing the inputs.

Cases of consignment production represent an evolving pattern in which North Korea has shaped its joint venture program. The process in evolution has a considerable range of potential variations. Since the inter-Korean accord was signed December 13, 1991, a flood of proposals has been put forward by Pyongyang for the expansion of the joint venture program. All of the proposals, however, fall within the framework of the eight-year experience of managing the program on the *Juche* principles of self-reliance and self-control. They entail keeping foreign intrusions to the lowest possible visibility and projecting overseas Korean involvement (including South Korean) in terms of loyalty to the fatherland.

North Korea announced on December 30, 1991, that it would create free zones in Sŏnbong, Rajin, and Ch'ŏngjin, three adjacent port cities in the northeastern corner of North Korea, south of the Tumen River bordering both China and Russia. Officially designated as economic and free trade zones, they will offer foreign investors customs reductions, tax incentives, and capital protection for production and trade in the zones.[35] This plan is part of a larger, long-term Tumen River basin development project involving about 10,000 square kilometers of North Korea, China, and Russia being studied under sponsorship of the United Nations Development Program (UNDP).[36]

Although the planned free trade zones will widen the openings somewhat, one characteristic of the zones can be expected to conform to the essentially hidden scheme of the joint venture program that has evolved. It relates to how North Koreans working and residing in the zones will communicate with those in the rest of the country. The mode of communication between the two segments will affect how much information about foreign intrusion in the zones would reach the rest of the country. There are few private telephones and automobiles in North Korea. Thus, the primary channel of communication will be through people entering and leaving the zones by mass transit. In addition, North Koreans need an official permit to travel outside their city or village. All these factors can be expected to enable North Korea to limit travel across zone boundaries and contain the thought-contamination effects of the free trade zones.

On October 5, 1992, North Korea proclaimed what could be seen as measures to widen considerably the openings to the free world. It overhauled the joint venture law by adopting three new laws on outside investment governing foreigners' investment, contractual joint ventures, and foreign enterprises.[37] The law on contractual ventures in effect formalizes the consignment production pattern discussed in this section. A contractual joint venture is defined as a joint venture in which "production and management are assumed by the host partner" and the foreign partner "is redeemed" in accordance with the provisions of the joint venture contract. This arrangement best accords with the notion of *Juche*.

The law on foreign enterprises allows the establishment of wholly foreign-owned enterprises in North Korea, a provision lacking in the joint venture law of 1984. However, they will be confined to the free economic and trade zones. Thus, the veiling characteristic of the zones will remain effective with wholly foreign-owned firms. The final law is a set of general principles and rules governing foreign investment in North Korea, including provisions covered in detail in the other two laws. The three laws of 1992 will thus continue to provide the framework for an essentially veiled scheme of foreign-capital inducement.

In December 1991, Rev. Moon Sun-Myung of the Unification Church visited North Korea as president of the World Peace Federation. He issued a joint statement with the government of North Korea calling for, among other things, economic, cultural, and humanitarian cooperation between the two parties. What is noteworthy is that the joint statement referred to the willingness of Rev. Moon to invest in North Korea in the context of welcoming any overseas Korean contributions made "in influence by those who have influence, knowledge by those who have knowledge, and money by those with money."[38] This phrase—which resembles the socialist labor contribution formula "from each according to ability" used by Kim Il Sung in the early years of Korean partition in connection with his united-front strategy,[39]—signaled that Pyongyang was prepared to portray all investments by Koreans outside the North in terms of loyalty to the fatherland or united front.

How tightly Pyongyang intends to monitor and contain the ideological contamination effects of intrusive investments from abroad has been revealed in a deal it struck with a South Korean conglomerate. Kim Woo-choong, the founder of the Daewoo Group, visited the North in January 1992. He returned with a package of agreements to invest in the North and to employ North Korean workers in Daewoo's construction and industrial projects abroad. Investment agreements amounting to tens of millions of dollars for nine industrial plants involved the production of blouses, shirts, jackets, shoes, luggage, toys, utensils, televisions, refrigerators, and other items.[40] These products are simple enough for North Koreans to take charge of production once plants are installed. Daewoo agreed to send equipment, designs, materials, and technical personnel in the construction phase and to provide materials, designs, and its overseas marketing network for export of the output upon commencement of production. In short, the investment agreements fell within the framework of consignment production.

International Tourism. Keeping foreign intrusions to minimum visibility also applies to international tourism.[41] North Korea has acted as if it can develop a tourist industry capable of generating hard currencies. Notwithstanding, it has not been prepared to accept free contact between foreign tourists and local inhabitants. A well-established technique of shielding foreign travelers from the inhabitants has been the deployment of tour guides; these are attached to travelers in groups or one to one for single travelers. Guides accompany all travelers like a shadow, including overseas Koreans individually visiting their native places. The *Pyongyang Times* reported in 1991 that Chang Chŏl-gu University has a faculty of tourism and trains "tourist workers."[42]

North Korea has revealed a stronger measure to separate willful visitors from local residents. In October 1991, South Korean reporters accompanied their prime minister to Pyongyang for a high-level conference. A reporter eluded his guide and slipped away from the conference site. When he walked into a store, he found himself immediately surrounded by what appeared to be shoppers. They took turns asking him why things were so bad in the South. They argued back in increasingly hostile tones. They would not let up for what seemed hours. Finally, in fear, he begged his way out of the store. Back in the hotel, he found that a number of his colleagues had suffered the same kind of experience. Whenever a reporter freed himself to accost a person in the street or a store, the person initiated conversation by saying, "I have a question to ask you." Quickly, other people nearby joined him, encircling the reporter and throwing out a barrage of argumentative questions. At an evening banquet, a reporter recounted the experience to a host official sitting next to him. The official casually responded, "Ah, we call it a *bongbyon* [humiliation encounter]."[43] The *bongbyon* technique was devised to block the work of South Korean reporters who after previous rounds of conferences had brought back reports generally unflattering to the North. It also clearly can be applied to ordinary travelers tending to be inquisitive; trained people can be deployed around designated tourist spots.

Economic Opening to South Korea. Pyongyang has instituted economic opening to South Korea.[44] This opening has two avenues—merchandise trade and capital transfer. The latter was discussed in conjunction with the joint venture program. Here the focus is on trade opening, the predominant characteristic of which has been concealment from average North Koreans.

Inter-Korean trade began November 21, 1988. A package containing forty kilograms of North Korean clams arrived in Pusan, South Korea, on that historic day.[45] The excitable South Koreans exploded in emotion upon the outbreak of the news about the clams. Pyongyang immediately condemned the news as a fabrication and a conspiracy against Korean reunification perpetrated by Seoul. In the conspiracy theory, the news was designed to perpetuate the division by "idling away the time while appearing to conduct trade."[46] So began the campaign to institute and yet hide a trade opening to South Korea.

While denouncing the clam trade as a fabrication, North Koreans proceeded to negotiate for additional transactions. On January 3, 1989, a second inter-Korean trade was consummated when a shipment of 612 pieces of North Korean art products—paintings and industrial artworks—arrived in Pusan.[47] As in the first incidence of trade, however, the art transaction was conducted through a third-country party in Hong Kong, and the shipment made a detour to Hong Kong before heading for South Korea. When a subsequent shipment was bulky—it was coal—and expensive to detour, the concealment tactic involved hiring a third-country vessel to sail the short distance between the two Koreas.[48]

Despite frustrations engendered by Pyongyang's insistence on disguising the trade, Seoul pushed for more trade as a means of interacting with and opening up the North. In 1990, South Korea established the Inter-Korean Economic Cooperation Fund designed, in part, to reimburse companies for losses incurred in transacting with the North.[49] On March 29, 1991, the Ch'onji Trading Company of South Korea and the Kŭmgangsan International Trade Company based in the North concluded an agreement to exchange 5,000 tons of southern rice for northern coal and cement. Shortly thereafter, Seoul announced that the Inter-Korean Economic Cooperation Fund would be activated to reimburse Ch'onji for the full amount of loss from the transaction, loss stemming from use of the lower international market value for the rice rather lower than the domestic agricultural support price.[50]

Both the government and the press in South Korea applauded the agreement as the first case of direct trade allowed by North Korea to be conducted openly. But the openness pertained only to South Koreans because even the government announcement of the agreement mentioned the stipulation that the rice was to be shipped to the North by a freighter of a third-country flag. The dock workers in North Korea were not supposed to know that the loaded vessel sailed from South Korea. Furthermore, the government failed to mention that the South Korean rice was to be packed in a way not to show its place of origin.[51] From the beginning of inter-Korean trade, North Korea has insisted on removing place-of-origin marks from South Korean products. On July 29, 1991, 5,000 tons of Southern rice, contained in plain unmarked bags, arrived at Rajin, North Korea, on board a Grenada vessel.[52]

The insistence on hiding inter-Korean trade is in part aimed at South Koreans, some of whom may want to hear Pyongyang say that it does not need to trade with the South. Primarily, however, it is designed to keep average North Koreans from seeing that the South has something useful to sell, in contradiction to their lifelong belief that deprivation is the rule there. As time blunts the sharpness of new realization and as trade volume grows, Pyongyang can be expected to find it permissible to ease the requirement of masking the trade. Thus, the requirement of involving a third party can eventually be expected to be dropped. The demand for removal of place-of-origin marks has already been waived for some imports, such as products intended for use in tourist hotels (color televisions, refrigerators)[53] and equipment to be handled by limited numbers of workers.[54] However, made-in–South Korea labels will continue to be removed from imports destined to reach average North Koreans.

United-Front Strategy

The underlying theme of the economic realities and associated institutional reforms of North Korea has been a historically persistent drive for the sustenance of socialism. What higher political goal would justify continuation of such a consistent economic policy? In a historically and ethnically singular Korea, what future can a sustaining but poor socialist state in the northern half see for itself in an era of withering socialism and in the face of a thriving capitalist state in the South?

This question has led many observers to conclude that North Korea will soon inevitably open up and restructure the system. However, a possible alternative course, one consistent with the North's long-standing economic policy, is discernible in new strategy of united front that Pyongyang has been pursuing both openly and underground. Campaigning for the formation of a united front of antigovernment forces in South Korea has been a consistent strategy of North Korea toward reunification—a strategy that has shifted tactics among violence, peaceful means, and dialogue, depending on changing circumstances.[55] The essential purpose has been to replace the existing government of South Korea with a united-front regime. The united-front strategy involves the following characteristics: (1) dialogue, (2) nonviolence, (3) a worldwide surface organization, and (4) underground organizations. Of these components, the third entails something new and an open articulation.

The worldwide group was launched when the Pan-National Alliance for Reunification of the Fatherland (Pŏmminryon) was formed in the wake of a Rally held in Panmunjom on August 15, 1990, the forty-fifth anniversary of national liberation. The rally was originally proposed by South Korean dissidents in August 1988 and gained the support of North Korea's Committee for the Peaceful Reunification of the Fatherland (CPRF or Chop'yongt'ong) in December 1988. Delegates from the North and abroad participated in the rally, but those from the South were blocked from attending by Seoul authorities. The rally participants proposed formation of Pŏmminryon, to be organized along regional and branch headquarters for North, South, and overseas and coordinated by a co-presidium consisting of four representatives each from North and South and five from overseas. The importance of Pŏmminryon was underscored by the fact that North Korean members of the co-presidium included Hŏ Dam, the party official in charge of South Korean affairs, and Yun Ki-bok, Hŏ Dam's deputy and his replacement after his death.[56]

Pŏmminryon is conceived by Pyongyang as "a voluntary association of our compatriots of all strata in the north, south, and abroad." It is "a patriotic organization for the reunification movement whose mission it is to reunify the country on the three principles of independence, peaceful reunification, and great national unity." It will seek reunification through a "confederation based on one nation, one state, two systems, and two governments." These quotations describing the mission of Pŏmminryon come from a speech delivered by Kim Il Sung on August 1, 1991, at a joint meeting of officials of the North side's headquarters of Pŏmminryon and the CPRF.[57] In the same address, Kim emphasized the importance of building "great national unity"—a term Kim uses in place of or in proximity to "united front"—by incorporating (p'osŏp) all compatriots, excluding only national traitors but including religionists. A confirmed atheist, Kim provided a rationale for welcoming religionists: "We cannot say that religionists are bad. Bad are anti-people politicians who make people suffer fatalistically in this life and yearn to find happiness at least in the next world."[58]

Branch headquarters of Pŏmminryon have been established in the United States, Canada, Europe, Australia–New Zealand, Japan, China, and the former Soviet Union.[59] Regional headquarters for the overseas side, originally in

Berlin, are in Japan and for the North Korean side in Pyongyang. In South Korea, Pŏmminryon has been moot in view of the national security law under which dissident movements in general and pro–North Korean activities in particular have been reined in; this dormancy will continue as long as the law remains in force.

A second component of the new united-front strategy was revealed when Seoul's Agency for National Security Planning (ANSP) uncovered a string of underground networks in fall 1992. On September 7, ANSP announced the existence of underground activity involving Kim Nak-jung, a professor and leader of the defunct Popular Party. The announcement indicated that Kim had been connected with North Korea since 1957 and that he received a total of $2.1 million in 1990 and 1991 from Pyongyang to support leftist politicians in elections, of which $1 million was uncovered in a cache in his residence.[60] ANSP announced on October 6 another discovery of underground activities involving 400 persons, of whom 62 had been arrested. They were charged with organizing a Workers' Party chapter in South Korea, a patriotic league, and an underground guidance department in the defunct Popular Party. These underground organizations have regularly been referred to in Seoul as spy rings, but they are best viewed as part of Pyongyang's new strategy. Although some small arms were reportedly uncovered in the caches, participants seem to have pursued nonviolent political means toward their goals. The large number of intellectuals involved in these episodes points to the kind of hope that Pyongyang can conjure up for its future to justify continuation of a socialist state in the North.

The dialogue aspect of the united-front strategy has taken the form of high-level talks and agreements signed, an approach in keeping with the post–Cold War era. There are some peripheral goals, such as economic gains from trade and investment with South Korea and its allies, but the main objective of the dialogue is creation of conditions in South Korea for the ultimate establishment of a government favoring a unification formula acceptable to Pyongyang. This point can be seen in Pyongyang's demand in early 1992 in the wake of the December 1991 North-South agreement. North Korean newspapers carried a series of signed articles all of which articulated one simple logic: Activation of the inter-Korean agreement meant that Seoul must abolish the national security law and ANSP, the mechanisms used to deem the North a hostile state.[61]

Recent ideological developments show what North Korea is trying to achieve. Most noteworthy is that Kim Jong Il, who has been the chief ideologue for North Koreans for some time, has stepped forward to take the leading role in the ideological formulation for the world communist movement. In "The Historical Lesson in Building Socialism and the General Line of Our Party," issued on January 3, 1992, Kim Jong Il reviewed the reasons for the collapse of ruling socialist parties in Europe and the Soviet Union: "One-step concession and retreat from the socialist principles has resulted in ten and a hundred step concessions and retreat, and, finally, invited the grave consequence of ruining the working class parties themselves."[62] The progressive concessions, of course, referred to revisionism, reform, and restructuring—three words Kim cited in quotation marks.

Kim Jong Il has not only issued major treatises on contemporary communism but also has organized a new structure of international communism aimed at the solidarity of all surviving socialist movements. During the April 1992 celebrations of his father's eightieth birthday, he persuaded visiting delegations of socialist parties to sign a Pyongyang declaration pledging to defend and advance the cause of socialism. The declaration calls for the solidarity of all "political parties from different countries of the world who are striving for the victory of socialism" and offers this slogan: "Let us all fight it out to open up the future of mankind with a firm conviction in the cause of socialism." Forty-eight parties, ranging from the Workers' Party of Bangladesh and the Russian Communist Workers' Party to the Communist Party of the United States, signed the declaration on April 20, 1992.[63] Significantly, none of the other ruling communist parties from China, Vietnam, or Cuba joined in the signing. Yet North Korea has pressed on to expand socialist solidarity into all corners of the world. By December 1992, there were 151 signatories to the Pyongyang declaration, still not including the three major ruling parties. This effort has involved a constant flow of party delegations in and out of North Korea and entailed major expenditures of work and funds to place North Korea at the center of the renewed international communist movement.

On the forty-seventh anniversary of the founding of the Korean Workers' Party, October 10, 1992, Kim Jong Il published another major treatise, "On the Fundamentals of Revolutionary Party Building." It concluded: "The resurgence of socialism is the only way out of the political, economic, ideological and moral confusion and crisis which are becoming more serious with every passing day in the countries where capitalism has revived."[64]

Thus, in the ideological perspective of North Korea, a revival of socialism is inevitable in the former Soviet Union, and the retreat of socialism is a temporary phenomenon. Meanwhile, Pyongyang is positioning to be the center of a second Communist International. It is in this context that the unreal aspects of the united-front strategy of North Korea toward the South must be understood. Pyongyang's persistent targeting of the national security law reveals its belief that in the absence of the law, the internal weaknesses of South Korea kept under control by means of legal instruments would be exposed and would create conditions favorable to North Korea. Is there any conceivable basis for such a belief with respect to conditions in South Korea? This question shifts the focus to South Korea.

South Korea

Conditions in South Korea seem favorable enough to warrant policies toward the North to encourage its power structure to seek alternatives to its course of domestic sustenance and a united-front line toward the South. In the economic sphere, South Korea's GNP of $238 billion in 1990 was approximately ten times North Korea's $23 billion. In terms of GNP per person, the South's $5,569 stood at more than five times the North's $1,064.[65] On the political front, South Korea held free elections in 1992 to elect a civilian leader for the third consecutive one-term presidency. Looking deeper, however, one finds that suppression is continuing to play a role for internal stability, especially on the labor scene.

For a quarter of a century until 1987, South Korea rushed to catch up with and then overwhelmingly surpass the North in economic power and well-being. The policy adopted for the high-growth strategy consisted of market and other liberal institutions subject to authoritarian control over investment, labor movement, and political dissent. Authoritarianism, which became harsher in the late 1960s and enshrined in a new constitution in 1972,[66] helped to bring about a widely recognized economic miracle but at the expense of civil rights, labor rights, and economic justice.

With democratization since 1987, civil rights have been substantially restored, and the support base for political dissidence has declined rapidly. The problems of workers' rights to free unionism and of economic inequality have been carried over, however.

Economic Inequality

During the authoritarian era, control over investment was carried out primarily through "policy loans"—bank loans to businesses chosen to invest in industries specified in five-year development plans. In a rush to build up industries, South Korea favored big companies able to benefit from mass production and capable of penetrating distant overseas markets. Policy loans thus accentuated the market tendency toward economic inequality because they were channeled to the already aggrandizing enterprises and because they were virtually interest-free (interest rates were often negative in real terms discounting inflation).[67] A result has been the rise of giant conglomerates (*chaebŏl*) within South Korea; the top thirty conglomerates accounted for over 33 percent of manufacturing sales by 1985.[68]

Despite the rise of the conglomerates, the South Korean case of economic growth regularly was cited as one of the most equitable among the developing countries. In 1979, for example, the World Bank reported statistics showing that South Korea had the second most equitable income distribution among middle-income nonsocialist countries. The poorest 40 percent of households in South Korea received 16.9 percent of national income, only slightly below the high of 17.8 percent reported for Spain.[69] The income share of South Korea's poorest 40 percent further improved to 19.7 percent by 1988. Under this measure, then, lower-income groups in South Korea have improved their lot compared with their fellow citizens and with their counterparts in other developing countries. But the key words in this statement are "incomes" (not wealth) and "reported" (not left unrealized or unreported).

In the context of South Korea, income distribution statistics are grossly misleading as an indicator of overall economic equality because they exclude incomes not reported and incomes gained in property appreciation but left unrealized in a country where housing supply is low. In a rush to build industries, South Korea allowed the housing-supply ratio (the number of

housing units available in proportion to family units) to decline from 83 percent in 1960, to 78 percent in 1970, to 75 percent in 1980, and to 70 percent in
1985.[70] The proportion of families living in single rooms rented from others
increased from 17 percent in 1960 to 30 percent in 1985. In South Korea, where
rental apartments are scarce and where workers toil close to fifty hours a
week to save for an apartment purchase, the deteriorating ratio of housing
supply has represented a more appropriate indicator of economic inequality
than income distribution numbers. The absolute and worsening shortage of
housing, aggravated by land price speculation, pushed apartments further
out of reach of worker families; by 1988 alone, the price of a modest apartment approached $100,000.[71]

One of the promises made by candidate Roh Tae Woo during the presidential campaign of 1987 was to build 2 million homes during the five-year presidential term (1988–1992)—a pledge fulfilled one year early in late 1991. This
success reversed the declining housing-supply ratio, but it also raised housing expenditures as a share of GNP from 4.2 percent in 1987 to as much as 8.5
percent in 1991 and triggered inflation.[72] This enraged workers who had been
saving to buy apartments. They readily resorted to strikes, often exceeding
the limits of their newly gained rights.

Radicalized Workers

Until Roh Tae Woo's democracy declaration of June 29, 1987, oppressive labor
laws and practices had been in force for much of the history of South Korea
dating back to the Japanese colonial period. Even existing labor laws include
three key provisions generally known as "poisonous" clauses: (1) no more
than one labor organization at each level (company, region, and nation); (2)
no third-party participation in labor disputes; and (3) no political activities by
labor organizations.[73] Under the one-union rule, companies with friendly
unions are safe from any autonomous unions. Under the no-third-party rule,
anyone not employed by an enterprise cannot assist a union in dispute with
the enterprise.[74] The net result of these provisions is to criminalize free-union-
ist activities for organizing and bargaining.[75]

Until 1987, unions operating under the harsh environment were mostly
controlled by enterprises at the local unit level and by the government at the
national level. At the end of 1986, 940,000 dues-paying members belonged to
2,263 local unions that were affiliated with 16 national unions and the Federation of Korean Trade Unions (FKTU).[76] From the onset of democratization in
mid-1987 through 1988, the first year of the Roh administration, the harsh labor laws were ignored, and the government practiced a laissez-faire policy on
labor dispute. Then major conflict erupted: During August 1987 alone, there
were 2,552 labor disputes, most involving strikes, compared with 276 in all of
1986 and 265 in 1985. For all of 1987, there were 3,749 labor disputes, more
than in all previous years combined.[77]

Arising from the massive wave of strikes in 1987 were a large number of
new local unions. Many of them joined the FKTU, but a significant number remained outside as "free" or "democratic" unions. The free unions, which

grew to represent about 15–20 percent of all organized workers, began coordinating at regional and national levels. Eventually, two national coalitions were formed. Organized first in January 1990 was the National Labor Union Alliance (abbreviated in Korean as Chŏnnohyŏp). Initially, it claimed a membership of 700 unions representing 200,000 workers, most of them in small and medium-sized enterprises. The second free union grouping, the Solidarity Conference of Large Company Unions, was formed in November 1990. Its members unions came from 16 large industrial firms and represented at least 1,000 workers and up to over 10,000.[78]

The early hands-off posture of the Roh government toward labor disputes allowed both free and traditional unions to experience organizational expansion and collective bargaining for the first time. Not surprisingly, many of them, especially the democratic ones, pushed their actions to excesses, including violence. In late 1988, worker-management confrontation intensified as wildcat and sit-in strikes lengthened in duration and the incidence of violence increased on both sides.[79]

In early 1989, the Roh administration abandoned its laissez-faire stance and started to employ the police to break up strikes. The poisonous labor-legislation clauses were brought back into full force. Strike leaders were sentenced to prison terms. Up to 1,500 teachers were fired for refusing to renounce their new union, prohibited as a public-sector union. According to Chŏnnohyŏp, 364 workers were arrested during the first five months of 1990 alone, and another 134 were on the police-wanted list.[80] The resumption of the practice of jailing free unionists for violating rules stacked against them served to restore labor peace in South Korea.

The incarceration of free unionists has created greater numbers of dissident workers who see social and personal interest coincide as they continue to fight. The endurance of the large pool of dissident unionists in South Korea results in part from a peculiar Korean phenomenon—the disguised student worker. During the 1980s, thousands of college students quit school and joined the ranks of industrial workers by falsely presenting themselves as having only a high school education on their job applications. Consciousness-raising among the workers was their goal, first to gain confidence of fellow workers and then to transform them into activist workers. Eventually, many student workers were fired and arrested for falsified personal identification and forgery.

The number of students who have become disguised workers, discovered or undiscovered, is not something that can be easily counted. A foreign author who has connections to the dissident community has ventured an estimate of as many as 3,000.[81] In any case, the potential magnitude of the pool of discovered student workers and other radicalized workers was revealed in September 1991 when a blacklist was discovered in the employment office of a shoe manufacturer in Pusan. The list contained some 8,000 names; listed for each were seven items on personal background, including dismissal history, college attended, circle activities in college, and church activities. This computer-updated list had been used since 1986 by forty shoe manufacturers in the Pusan area.[82]

In sum, the existence of thousands of radicalized unionists who lack regular means of livelihood and who live to sensitize and organize fellow workers represents a destabilizing force bottled up under the peaceful surface of the South Korean labor scene. The labor peace of 1992 was bought at the expense of suppression and an economic slowdown of the worst kind since 1981. As the economy revives in the coming years under President Kim Young Sam, the first civilian democratic (*munmin*) administration in thirty years, the bottled-up force will need to be diffused peacefully if the economy is to grow and mature. Until that tension is diffused, South Korea's confidence in its ability to finance unification costs will remain low, and North Korea's hope for a successful united-front strategy will remain high.

Conclusion: Implications for Seoul's Unification Strategy

North Korea has long been positioned to sustain itself economically for a protracted period and is fielding a new strategy of united front against South Korea in the hope that internal weaknesses will create conditions for an acceptable reunification. It does not matter that, on objective grounds, such a stance fails to make sense. What matters is that it seems to make sense to Pyongyang. The fundamental implication of these political and economic realities of the North for unification policies of the South is that Seoul must develop a long-term unification strategy of its own. Too often, Seoul has proclaimed unification policies designed for transient advantages or tactics. Seoul must institute a reunification plan that successive administrations (should national partition outlast an administration) would feel advised to inherit and carry out.

A long-term strategy of this nature must be long term in two different but often confused meanings. First, the plan should be sensible for the long pull as well as for the day. It should not be for only or primarily short-term logic or popularity, but it should be sensible for today. At the same time, the strategy must remain sensible and compelling five or ten years later, should partition persist so long. The plan must be long term in that the government can hold to it without changes or defensiveness for as long as the protracted strategy of united front pursued by Pyongyang assaults the airwaves and democratic cohesion of the South.

Second, the unification plan should be long term in the sense of containing concrete measures that are sensible prerequisites for a viable reunification and that would clearly take time to be accomplished. To be a credible long-term strategy, one that can overcome impatient demands for quick unification, the contained measures must have time to be implemented, not merely because they are sequential conceptually.

The central policy lesson drawn from this study is the need for and clarification of the nature of a long-term strategy for unification. What concrete measures are to be contained in the strategy is a question that requires careful research and a synthesis of various perspectives. For example, reduction in military tension is a prerequisite measure. Offered here are two measures deemed sensible from an economic perspective, one of which would provide an adequate time frame within which other strategy components can be placed.

It is proposed that Seoul institute a program of accumulating a unification fund of $20–30 billion to be placed in overseas banks or bonds. The function of the fund will be to finance expenses during the initial period of economic reunion with the North. Funds should be in foreign exchanges, not in South Korean currency, for the accumulation of noninflationary purchasing power. South Korea should plainly acknowledge that it is unable to enter into economic union—the essence of reunification—before a targeted fund is accumulated. For too long, the South Korean government has acted as if it really wants reunification as soon as possible without saving a dollar in noninflationary funds.

The proposed program will entail reforms to streamline the economy to generate export surpluses on a steady basis. It is accordingly a proposal to integrate unification strategy with domestic policies. Any unification proposal not integrated with domestic capabilities cannot stay relevant for long. Reforms will involve the conglomerates and taxation. But the most critical and difficult one will pertain to labor movement. It will be morally and politically indefensible to force workers to comply with a program of generating export surpluses for the sake of national unification. Labor movement must be freed first. Then, a social compact will need to be forged among free labor, the conglomerates, taxpayers, and the government.

The time and activities necessary to carry out the proposed program of accumulating a dollar fund can provide the time framework of a long-term unification plan. One measure that can be included in the plan and pursued commencing immediately relates to a need to build a political house over North and South under which trade on special terms can be expanded without violating GATT rules on tariffs. Before an economic union is consummated, living standards in the North must be raised appreciably in order to avoid pressures of massive population movement that would destabilize both sides. Needed is a period of expanding trade and investment designed to raise consumption in the North without involving labor migration to the South. However, GATT rules will impede aid through trade under the current relationship. Under the second element of the proposed long-term strategy, Seoul would negotiate with Pyongyang for a transitional relationship, perhaps a Commonwealth of Korean States, which would enable resource transfers through trade and investment while a dollar fund is built up and other components of the unification plan are negotiated.

There are advantages in the proposed two elements of a long-term unification plan. It endows South Korea with a coherent plan of its own to pursue negotiations. At the same time, the negotiation agenda has a built-in go-slow stance timed with the progress of the unification fund. It contains a compelling argument to overcome pressures for quick actions from both the North and impatient groups in the South. It is a self-blaming argument that the South is honestly unprepared to assume the expenses of unification costs, costs that are plainly associated with the disparity in wealth of the two sides.

The South is wealthier but not well organized internally; all impatient groups on both sides should be kept reminded of this reality.

Notes

1. Joseph Sang-hoon Chung, *The North Korean Economy* (Stanford, CA: Hoover Institution Press, 1974), pp. 12–17.
2. Kim Il Sung, "On Correctly Introducing the Sub-Workteam Management System and on Effecting a New Upsurge in Agricultural Production," speech at the national conference of agricultural workers, February 14, 1968, *On the Management of the Socialist Economy* (Pyongyang: Foreign Languages Publishing House, 1992), p. 248.
3. Ibid., pp. 245–248.
4. Ibid., p. 236.
5. Kim Il Sung, "On Some Problems for Future Development of Agriculture," speech at a meeting of managerial workers of agricultural cooperatives in south Pyongan province, January 21, 1957, *Works*, Vol. 11 (Pyongyang: Foreign Languages Publishing House, 1982), pp. 2–7.
The volumes of *Works* and *Selected Works* of Kim Il Sung are published in English by the Foreign Languages Publishing House in Pyongyang, and in Korean by the Workers' Party of Korea Publishing House in Pyongyang. Due to frequent references to these books, the publisher and location are hereafter omitted. When speech titles in Korean are quoted, only their English translation is given; book titles are cited in Korean accompanied by translation.
6. For a picture of maize-seedling transplanting, see *Rodong Sinmun*, April 29, 1992, p. 3.
7. "Epoch-Making Change Brought About by the Great Rural Theses," *Foreign Trade of the Democratic People's Republic of Korea*, February 1992, p. 30.
8. International Rice Research Institute, "Rice Research and Production in the Democratic People's Republic of Korea," report based on the visit of M. S. Swaminathan, G. S. Khush, and B. S. Vergara to the Democratic People's Republic of Korea, October 1–8, 1985, Manila, Philippines, December, 1985, p. 3; Kim Il Sung, "Speech Delivered at a Consultative Meeting of Agricultural Officials," June 17, 1975, *Works*, Vol. 30, 1987, p. 333.
9. Kim Il Sung, "Report on the Work of the Central Committee to the Fourth Congress of the Workers' Party of Korea," September 11, 1961, *Selected Works*, Vol. 3, 1971, p. 82.
10. Kim Il Sung, "On Revolutionizing the Peasants and Carrying Through the Party Conference Decisions in the Field of Agriculture," speech at a national congress of agricultural functionaries, February 21, 1967, *Selected Works*, Vol. 4, 1971, p. 485.
11. Kim Il Sung, "On Correctly Introducing the Sub-Work Team Management System and on Effecting a New Upsurge in Agricultural Production," speech at the national conference of agricultural workers, February 14, 1968, *Jŏjakjib* (Works), Vol. 22, 1983, p. 11.
12. Kim Il Sung, "On Some Immediate Tasks in the Rural Economy of Pyongyang City and South Pyongyang Province," speech to agricultural workers of Pyongyang city and south Pyongyang province, March 31, 1972, *Jŏjakjib* (Works), Vol. 30, 1985, pp. 184–185.
13. Kim Il Sung, "On the Second Seven-Year Plan (1978–1984) for the Development of the National Economy of the Democratic People's Republic of Korea," adopted at the first session of the sixth Supreme People's Assembly, December 17, 1977, *Works*, Vol. 32, 1988, pp. 516–535.

14. The notion of localized self-sufficiency in consumer goods was discussed by the author in "Economic Reforms of North Korea: Sustaining Through Restricted System Modifications for Localized Self-Sufficiency," paper presented at the workshop The Future of North Korea, Keck Center for Strategic and International Studies, Claremont McKenna College, Claremont, CA, December 5, 1992.

15. Robert A. Scalapino and Chong-sik Lee, *Communism in Korea, Part 2: The Society* (Berkeley: University of California Press, 1972), p. 1212.

16. North Korea Research Institute, *Bukhan Ch'ongram* (North Korea comprehensive review (Seoul: North Korea Research Institute, 1983), p. 832.

17. Kim Il Sung, "Let Us Radically Improve the People's Living Standards by Strengthening the Role of the County and Further Developing Local Industries and Agriculture," concluding speech at the Changsong joint conference of local party and economic functionaries, August 8, 1962, *Selected Works*, Vol. 3, 1971, pp. 341–345.

18. Kim Il Sung, "Report on the Work of the Central Committee to the Fourth Congress of the Workers' Party of Korea," September 11, 1961, *Selected Works*, Vol. 3, 1971, p. 78.

19. Kim Il Sung, "Let Us Radically Improve the People's Living Standards," *Selected Works*, Vol. 3, 1971, p. 344.

20. Pak Yong-song, "The Formation of a Firm Foundation of Local Industry and Its New Stage of Development," *Kulloja*, No. 15, September 20, 1962, p. 18, quoted in Scalapino and Lee, *Communism*, p. 1227.

21. Kim Il Sung, "Let Us Develop Local Industry and Bring About a Fresh Upswing in the Production of Mass Consumer Goods," speech at the national conference of workers in local industry, February 27, 1970, *Selected Works*, Vol. 5, 1972, pp. 384–385.

22. Kim Il Sung, "To Give Full Play to the Great Vitality of the Unified and Detailed Planning of the National Economy," speech to a general meeting of the party organization of the State Planning Commission, September 23, 1965, *On the Management of the Socialist Economy* (Pyongyang: Foreign Languages Publishing House, 1992), pp. 200–226.

23. Kim Il Sung, "For Further Development of the Unified Planning System," speech to officials in the planning sector, July 2, 1969, *Works*, Vol. 24, 1986, pp. 96–97.

24. Kim Il Sung, "On the Direction of Drafting a Second Seven-Year Plan," speech at a meeting of planning officials, July 10-11, 1974, *Works*, Vol. 29, January–December 1974, 1987, pp. 297–298.

25. Kim Il Sung, "On Developing a Local Budget System," speech to the fifth session of the fifth Supreme People's Assembly, April 8, 1975, *Works*, Vol. 30, 1987, pp. 187–200.

26. Kim Il Sung, "Let Us Further Accelerate Socialist Construction Through Efficient Financial Management," speech at a conference of financial and banking workers, December 23, 1978, *On the Management of the Socialist Economy*, 1992, p. 362.

27. Kim Il Sung, "On Drafting an Accurage State Budget for This Year," speech at a meeting of the Political Committee of the Central Committee of the Workers' Party of Korea, March 26, 1980, *Works*, Vol. 35, 1989, p. 66.

28. Part of this segment is based on Hy Sang Lee, "The August Third Program of North Korea: A Partial Rollback of Central Planning," *Korea Observer*, Vol. 21, No. 4 (Winter 1990), pp. 457–474.

29. *Rodong Sinmun*, November 10, 1991.

30. Choe In-duk, "Our District Party Committee's Political Organization Works for the Increased Production of People's Consumer Goods Through a Mass Movement," *Kulloja*, No. 1, January 1990, pp. 80–85.

31. *Rodong Sinmun*, February 3, 1992.

32. Part of this section is based on Hy Sang Lee, "North Korea's Closed Economy: The Hidden Opening," *Asian Survey*, Vol. 28, No. 12 (December 1988), pp. 1271–1279.

33. Chin Kim, "North Korea Joint Venture Law," *California Western International Law Journal*, Vol. 19, No. 2 (1988–89), p. 206.

34. *Choong-Ang Ilbo*, July 28, 1989.

35. *Wall Street Journal*, December 31, 1991.

36. *People's Korea*, November 21, 1991.

37. *People's Korea*, October 31, 1992.

38. *Rodong Sinmun*, December 6, 1991.

39. Kim Il Sung, *Selected Works*, Vol. 5, 1972, p. 361.

40. *Han'guk Ilbo*, January 28, 1992.

41. See Hy Sang Lee, "Inter-Korean Economic Cooperation: Realities and Possibilities," paper presented at conference Korea in the 1990s: Prospects for Reunification, co-sponsored by the Claremont Institute and the Industrial Research Institute for Pacific Nations at California State Polytechnic University, Pomona, California, February 24, 1990, for the early development of tourist programs in North Korea.

42. *Pyongyang Times*, July 6, 1991.

43. *Han'guk Ilbo*, October 30, 1991.

44. See Hy Sang Lee, "Patterns of North Korea's Economic Transactions with the South," *Asian Pacific Review*, Vol. 1, No. 1 (Spring 1989), pp. 119–123, for a history of Inter-Korean trade up to February 1989.

45. *Wall Street Journal*, November 23, 1988.

46. *People's Korea*, July 23, 1988.

47. *Korean Newsreview*, January 11, 1989, p. 13.

48. *Choong-Ang Ilbo*, February 4, 1989.

49. *Han'guk Ilbo*, February 6, 1990. The present author is the originator of the proposal to establish the Inter-Korean Economic Cooperation Fund. See Hy Sang Lee, "Economic Dimensions of Inter-Korean Interactions and Cooperation," in Republic of Korea, National Unification Board, *The Korean National Community and the Question of Unification*, compendium of papers presented to the fifth international conference on Korean reunification, Los Angeles, California, July 6–9, 1989 (Seoul: National Unification Board, 1989), pp. 103–121.

50. *Han'guk Ilbo*, April 15, 1991.

51. *North Korea News*, No. 575, April 22, 1991, p. 4.

52. *Han'guk Ilbo*, August 5, 1991.

53. *Han'guk Ilbo*, October 15, 1991.

54. *Choong-Ang Ilbo*, January 5, 1991.

55. For a review of the united-front strategy of North Korea, see Ilpyong J. Kim, "The United Front Policy of North Korea," *Korea Observer*, Vol. 22, No. 4 (Winter 1991), pp. 519–535.

56. *People's Korea*, September 1, 1990.

57. *Minju Chosŏn*, August 6, 1991.

58. Ibid.

59. *The Committee for the Peaceful Reunification of the Fatherland: Secretariat Report*, No. 108 (Pyongyang: CPRF, December 1991), p. 6.

60. *North Korea News*, No. 649, September 21, 1992, p. 4.

61. See *Rodong Sinmun*, January 15, 1992.

62. *People's Korea*, February 15, 1992.

63. *People's Korea*, May 2–9, 1992.

64. *Pyongyang Times*, November 7, 1992.

65. National Unification Board, *Overall Evaluation of the North Korean Economy* (Seoul: National Unification Board, August 1992), p. 3.

66. For a political-economic analysis focused on the emergence of the Yushin constitution, see Hyug Baeg Im, "The Rise of Bureaucratic Authoritarianism in South Korea," *World Politics*, Vol. 29, No. 2 (January 1987), pp. 231–257.

67. Jung-en Woo, *Race to the Swift: State and Finance in Korean Industrialization* (New York: Columbia University Press, 1991), p. 198.

68. Byung-Nak Song, *The Rise of the Korean Economy* (Hong Kong: Oxford University Press, 1990), p. 115.

69. World Bank, *World Development Report 1979* (New York: Oxford University Press, 1979), p. 173.

70. Korean Statistical Association (KSA), *Major Statistics of Korean Economy 1992* (Seoul: KSA 1992), p. 246.

71. *Han'guk Ilbo*, January 17, 1990.

72. KSA, *Major Statistics*.

73. U.S. Department of Labor, *Foreign Labor Trends: Korea, 1987* (Washington, DC: U.S. Government Printing Office, 1987), p. 10.

74. The FKTU and its industrial affiliates are removed from the category of third parties, but free unions are not.

75. *Han'gyore Sinmun*, April 16, 1990.

76. U.S. Department of Labor, *Foreign Labor Trends: Korea, 1986* (Washington, DC: U.S. Government Printing Office, 1986), p. 16.

77. Ministry of Labor, *White Paper on Labor* (Seoul: Ministry of Labor, 1991), p. 486.

78. U.S. Department of Labor, *Foreign Labor Trends: Korea, 1990–1991* (Washington, DC: U.S. Government Printing Office, 1991), pp. 3–4.

79. U.S. Department of Labor, *Foreign Labor Trends: Korea, 1988–1989* (Washington, DC: U.S. Government Printing Office, 1989), p. 7.

80. U.S. Department of State, *Country Reports on Human Rights Practices for 1990*, report submitted to the Committee on Foreign Relations, U.S. Senate, and the Committee on Foreign Affairs, House of Representatives (Washington, DC: U.S. Government Printing Office, February 1991), p. 940.

81. George E. Ogle, *South Korea: Dissent Within the Economic Miracle* (London: Zed Books, 1990), p. 99.

82. *Choong-Ang Ilbo*, September 18, 1991.

12

Improving Military Security Relations

Tong Whan Park

A genuine detente between two adversaries is impossible without the stabilization of their military security relations. Nowhere is this maxim more relevant than on the Korean peninsula, which remains armed to the teeth despite the end of the Cold War. In effect, the bilateral talks and exchanges across the demilitarized zone (DMZ) will bear only limited fruit for the process of integration unless they are accompanied by a reduction in military tensions.

What measures will be necessary to bring about military reconciliation between Pyongyang and Seoul? Or, more fundamentally, will it ever be possible to transform the structure of confrontation into one of coexistence and cooperation? Answers to these questions will be a first stepping-stone to the eventual unification of the two Koreas.

Common sense dictates that the answers will depend first upon the threat perceptions of each Korea, as the most natural starting point of détente should be a decreased sense of danger from without. Thus, this chapter begins with a survey of the dominant security concerns facing the Korean peninsula. Because the security of the two Koreas is not only determined by their bilateral rivalry but is also affected by both global and regional developments, three different levels of analysis are employed. First, structural shifts in the global system are examined as they affect Northeast Asia in general and the two Koreas in particular. Second, future developments in the four major powers are investigated in the context of their involvement in Korean affairs. Third, the future of inter-Korean relations is analyzed as a focal point in the Northeast Asian international system.

The investigation of the dominant security matters of the two Koreas from these three perspectives then leads to an exposition of the major military security issues pending between them and likely to figure prominently in the future. In the final section of this chapter, an attempt is made to synthesize the various arguments presented and to analyze the prospect of change in the military security relationship between Pyongyang and Seoul.

Dominant Security Concerns
Facing the Two Koreas

Trends in Global Systemic Changes

Probably the most critical global systemic changes affecting the Korean peninsula are the changing polarity and hegemonic instability caused by the demise of the Leninist systems. During the last half century, Northeast Asia has largely been under a bipolar international structure in which the two blocs played out the politics of confrontation. Surely, the nature of bipolarity has undergone modifications, especially since the early 1970s when the United States began to downgrade its role in the doctrine of extended deterrence. The rise of cooperative ties linking Washington, Tokyo, and Beijing also was instrumental in loosening the bipolar makeup in the region. But even after Gorbachev's *glasnost*, Northeast Asia remained an arena of competition and contest between the two rival camps. Now that the Soviet Union has disappeared from the map and Russia appears to be unable or unwilling to sustain a bipolar structure, regional politics is suddenly thrown into unknown territory.

Needless to say, the only surviving hegemon, the United States, is expected to provide strong leadership in the international relations of Northeast Asia as either a unitary pole or a component of a multipolar structure. But is the United States capable of leading the region in which its military dominance is not matched by a corresponding economic superiority? Likewise, are other regional actors ready to accept the United States as a single hegemon of Northeast Asia? For now, it appears that nobody can answer these questions positively. And it can be supposed that the hegemonic instability, when combined with a changing polarity, could become a source of conflict in the region.

Four Major Powers in Search of New Regional Roles

To many South Koreans, no less important than the global systemic changes for their security calculus are developments within the four major powers—the United States, Japan, China, and Russia. Although interactions among these powers may span the globe, the Korean peninsula is one focal point where their interests are intertwined in a complex manner. It is critical to understand the main directions of transition in each of these four powers and how the trends would affect the political-military environment of the Korean peninsula.

The United States and Its Changing Regional Security Posture. Despite ongoing debates on the decline of the United States as a global power, it is difficult to foresee any fundamental changes in U.S. foreign policy goals in Northeast Asia. This is because the twin objectives of preserving U.S. security interests in the region and promoting the political-economic development of the nations within it will remain the bedrock of U.S. policies. The key question is, however, which of the two goals will be given a higher priority in the coming decade? Will Washington be able to harmonize the needs of the international system with its national interests? Or will the United States attempt to shape the new international order so as to maximize its own gains? Many observers believe that Washington is likely to lean toward the second option and, therefore, that its foreign policy changes will materialize not in the expressed goals themselves but in the instruments with which they are to be implemented. The time will soon come, if it is not already here, when the United States can no longer play godfather to its former client states in Northeast Asia. Instead, it will provide its Northeast Asian allies with indirect leadership in which the primary responsibility of maintaining security would fall on the latter's shoulders. Simply put, the U.S. role will become more supportive than directive: Allies will be expected to fend for themselves and receive U.S. assistance only when needed.[1]

Adding more credibility to this observation is the change of guard in the White House after twelve years of Republican control. Judging from his campaign platform, President Clinton is expected to keep his promise of "maintaining U.S. troop presence in Northeast Asia as long as there remains tension on the Korean peninsula." In addition, he has been extremely critical of the possible nuclear threat from North Korea as well as its violation of human rights. Nevertheless, many South Koreans fear that the Democrats will become less hesitant than their predecessors to reduce U.S. forces stationed overseas as part of their program to cut financial deficits.

Japan's Search for a Higher Political-Military Profile. In contrast to the apparent neoisolationist U.S. stance, Japan will most likely continue to upgrade its international involvement as seen in the use of its Self-Defense Forces (SDF) for UN peacekeeping operations (PKO) and in the public debate on possible revision of its "Peace Constitution." In a sense, it may be natural for Japan to seek a political-military status commensurate with its high economic achievement. But those who feel uneasy with Japan's remilitarization have made a persuasive argument about its military strength. Tokyo's annual defense budget—about 1 percent of Japan's GNP—has been about $35 billion. Japan's overall high commodity price index notwithstanding, this is indeed a staggering figure that makes the SDF an elite military force equipped with high-tech weaponry. Given the small size of the SDF (about a quarter of a million), it may be no match for the Chinese or Russian armed forces. Nevertheless, many Asians remember the days when the Japanese military controlled a huge chunk of the world in the name of "Greater East Asian Co-Prosperity Sphere." If Japan were to spend 4 to 5 percent of its rapidly growing GNP on defense, it would be natural for Tokyo's neighbors to show apprehension about the resurrection of Japan's "military ghost."[2]

What will be the impact of Japan's rising military stature on the security environment of the Korean peninsula? There are two plausible speculations about this question. One is that a militarized Japan would heighten instability in Northeast Asia; the other is that the opposite would occur. The rationale for the former position is the fact that the militarization would mean Japan's be-coming a superpower. With money in the left hand and a gun in the right, Ja-pan could wield enormous influence in Northeast Asia. It would inevitably disturb the status quo in the region and, in particular, upset the precarious balance between the two Koreas.

On the other hand, it may be argued with equal potency that Japan's grow-ing military strength would serve as a contributing factor to stabilization of Northeast Asia. According to this view, Japan would prevent abrupt changes in the regional balance of power by gradually filling the void to be created by the decreasing involvement of the United States and Russia. Proponents of this position further claim that other members of the Northeast Asian theater would keep a keen eye on Tokyo lest it fall back into the anachronistic trap of military hegemonism.

Both of these opposing scenarios contain some elements of truth and a high probability of occurrence. From Tokyo's perspective, it should be politically expedient to hold onto both options. From the standpoint of the two Koreas, however, it is critical that any Japanese militarization be used as a stabilizing force in the region. Because Japan's militarization appears to be an irrevers-ible trend, it is counterproductive to worry solely about the "Japanization of Asia." Instead, it is far more important for all nations in Northeast Asia to help Japan become not a malevolent hegemon but a superpower with a sense of commitment to regional peace and harmony.

China's Continued Drive Toward Modernization. Despite a temporary set-back following the 1989 Tiananmen Square incident, China appears to be firmly back on the course toward modernization. Just as Japan's militariza-tion is seen to have both a positive and negative effect on the stability of Northeast Asia, China's growth would be a mixed blessing to the nations in the region. On one hand, China needs a peaceful environment in which to pursue economic reforms and hence would adopt more cooperative policies toward its neighbors. On the other hand, as China's modernization continues to accelerate, its national power may rise to a point at which its foreign policy would become increasingly assertive in the management of regional affairs.

Combined with its desire to maintain influence over Pyongyang, Beijing's pursuit of a new status as a regional power will make its relationship with Seoul a mixed bag of activism and passivism. As shown in the phenomenal rise in bilateral trading, China will exploit South Korea's friendly attitude to maximize its economic gains. As far as political relations are concerned, how-ever, Beijing seems to be in no hurry to beef up cooperative ties with Seoul, even though the latter had to take the risk of estranging Taipei. Despite the es-tablishment of formal diplomatic relations in August 1992 and the subsequent state visit by the South Korean president to China, Beijing's attitude toward Seoul remains far from enthusiastic. By remaining relatively passive in politi-cal dealings with Seoul, Beijing could kill two birds with one stone: not only continuing to enjoy favorable terms of trade with Seoul but also being able to hold Pyongyang on a short leash by playing it off against Seoul.

Russia's Emergence as a Pacific Power. Unlike the European theater, North-east Asia is the region where Russia can maintain and expand its international stature by participating in the formation of a new order. Consequently, Russia is expected to show its interest in developments on the Korean peninsula. Knowing that it does not have as much leverage over Pyongyang as Beijing does, however, Moscow may not emulate Beijing's strategy of "divide and conquer." Instead, it will seek to upgrade its interactions with South Korea both economically and politically.

The Two Koreas Locked in a Security Dilemma

Although global systemic changes and domestic transitions in the four major powers would strongly influence Korea's security environment, developments on the Korean peninsula itself would have an even stronger impact on the future of inter-Korean relations. Of special importance is that the two Koreas are nowhere near the threshold of détente. Despite the flurry of talks and exchanges between the two Koreas, there has been little substantive progress in their security relationship.

Indeed, there was a tremendous amount of activities in inter-Korean security dialogue in the early 1990s. The critical turning point was, undoubtedly, the signing on December 13, 1991, of the agreement on reconciliation, nonaggression, and exchanges and cooperation (hereafter "basic agreement," see Appendix B), which took effect the following February. Both sides agreed to work together to transform the 1953 armistice into a solid state of peace between the South and the North, to observe the military demarcation line with mutual nonaggression, to take proper steps to build military confidence, and to undertake exchanges in various fields.

At the sixth high-level talks held in Pyongyang February 18–21, 1992, two additional documents were put into effect: the joint declaration on denuclearization of the peninsula signed December 31, 1991, and an agreement on formation of subcommittees of the high-level talks. At the seventh round of talks held in Seoul May 7, 1992, the two sides agreed to form a liaison office and three joint commissions on military matters, economic exchanges and cooperation, and sociocultural exchanges and cooperation. Even after this protocol, no substantive progress was made until September 17 when the two sides decided to put it into effect at the eighth high-level talks held in Pyongyang. By officially linking the protocol to the basic agreement, the two Koreas finally agreed to activate in mid-November the three commissions and a fourth one on reconciliation.

After the eighth prime-ministerial talk, inter-Korean relations cooled a great deal for three reasons. One was the revelation of a massive North Korean spy network that had been operating in the South for ten years. Although 62 suspects were apprehended and some 300 were under pursuit, what made this case truly astounding was that Pyongyang had been running this operation in violation of the letter and spirit of the inter-Korean dialogue.[3] The second reason was a decision made by U.S. and South Korean military leaders at the annual security consultative meeting (SCM) held in Washington, D.C., October 7–8 to suspend the second phase of reduction in U.S. forces in Korea and to resume the annual joint Team Spirit military exercises. The last reason is the possible calculation by North Korean leaders that they have gone far enough to exploit the appearance of détente with the South. North Korea has since refused to convene any of the joint commissions and the ninth high-level talks, which were originally scheduled for December 1992.

In a similar vein, there has not been much progress toward settlement of the denuclearization issue despite the fact that the North, at long last, accepted the inspections of the International Atomic Energy Agency (IAEA). If anything, the IAEA's demand for special inspections following a series of ad hoc inspections and Pyongyang's threat to withdraw from the international nonproliferation regime have generated more questions than answers about North Korean intentions.[4]

Why does it appear so difficult for the two Koreas to follow through with the terms of the basic agreement? Why is pessimism prevalent regarding the future activities of the joint committees? In my opinion, the main stumbling block is the fact that each Korea is facing its own "security dilemma."[5]

First, Pyongyang has been under heavy pressure from China and Russia to respond favorably to Seoul's cooperative gestures. At the same time, it badly needs assistance from Japan and the United States to save its faltering economy. Unfortunately, however, North Korea faces the dilemma of executing its version of economic reforms without "contaminating" its society with Western ideas of freedom and democracy.

Second, Seoul has been faced with the task of managing its security dilemma in which it needs to promote détente with Pyongyang but not lower its guard against the unthinkable—another Korean war. North Korea's track record leaves no doubt that it is not hesitant to use violence to settle disputes if necessary. Nevertheless, Seoul cannot but knock on Pyongyang's door for rapprochement because there is no better way to pursue peace than through dialogue. Moreover, what leaves Seoul with no alternative to talks is that it is neither capable of nor necessarily desirous of a German-style unification by absorption. In the unlikely event of an implosion in the North, some even argue that Seoul may have to contain the southward migration of northerners across the DMZ while conducting food drops on villages in the North.[6]

Issues of High Priority in
Military Security Relations

Military security issues pending between the two Koreas have their origins in all three levels of interaction previously discussed: global, regional, and peninsular. Global and regional security concerns affect inter-Korean relations, but the most immediate source of bilateral tension is the fact that Pyongyang and Seoul have fundamentally different outlooks on prospects for détente on the Korean peninsula. The North is pursuing what is to it a highly rational policy: "Leave us alone politically but supply economic aid." In contrast, the most sensible choice of action for the South is a functionalistic approach to integration in which both sides would gradually build mutual trust through the establishment of many overlapping linkages. To South Koreans, unification is a goal to strive for, but the process leading to it is as important as the goal itself. They would like to see unification in which their well-being will not be threatened.

Although there are many critical issues underlying the inter-Korean security relationship, five have been selected for examination in this chapter; the first four issues reflect the difference in perspectives on rapprochement. They are (1) conflicting approaches to arms control and reduction; (2) the balancing of troop reduction with military modernization; (3) the structural adjustment to U.S. forces in Korea; (4) the threat of nuclear weapons on the Korean peninsula; and (5) changes in civil-military relations.[7]

Conflicting Approaches to Arms Control and Reduction

Arms reduction or disarmament is aimed at reducing military capabilities, whereas arms control represents a mechanism that produces agreements on the use of military forces and weapons—type, how and where they are deployed, their characteristics, and safety conditions to prevent accidents. The primary objective of arms control is hence to stabilize the military relationship between the adversaries. Because arms control and reduction are considered to be closely related in both theory and practice, the two are sometimes combined in the same conceptual category of arms control; the former is called *operational* arms control and the latter *structural*. The European experience has shown that progress in the operational aspect tends to pave the way for structural arms control.

Unfortunately, the relationship between arms control and reduction has become a focal point of contention between the two Koreas. Seoul's functionalistic stance has naturally led to a linear approach that progresses from operational arms control and confidence-building measures to the eventual arms-reduction agreement. In contrast, Pyongyang has advocated the importance of structural arms control, including the withdrawal of U.S. troops from the Korean peninsula. South Koreans believe that the North-South confrontation is the product of mistrust accumulated over several decades and, therefore, that bilateral tensions can be lowered by increasing mutual confidence through political, economic, and military talks. For their part, Pyongyang's leaders appear to be extremely sensitive to the negative side effects of operational arms control: Transparency and military confidence-building measures may hasten the opening of North Korean society to the "unhealthy" ideas of the Westernized South, and the credo "socialism according to our style" may be jeopardized. As a result, Pyongyang is likely to maintain its posture that reduction of military capability would provide a setting of decreased physical threats and would hence enable the two sides to start building confidence in each other.

This is why the exercise of comparing the proposals for arms control and reduction advanced by the two Koreas would have only limited utility.[8] Surely, the two sets of proposals contain an array of components for both operational and structural arms control, and the proposals from the two Koreas have many elements that are identical or strikingly similar. But the history of inter-Korean negotiations suggests that the two sides can hardly be expected to work from them to enlarge the area of common interest. Lest there be any misunderstanding, it should be clarified that military policy-makers in Seoul and Pyongyang should continue to monitor any subtle changes in nuances of the multitude of arms-control proposals presented by the opposite side. More important, however, is for them to see a larger political picture that shapes the relationship between the operational and structural aspects of arms control. As it stands now, there is little convergence in the approaches taken by the two Koreas on this most fundamental issue of military relations.

Troop Reduction Versus Military Modernization

The second issue deals with the thorniest of all problems in military negotiations between adversaries: how to bring about balance while reducing total military outlay. Today, the Korean peninsula is one of the most heavily armed areas in the world. The North maintains a total of 1.01 million troops in uniform; they outnumber those in the South by the ratio of 1.5 to 1. The combined force size of 1.66 million in the two Koreas, not counting various types of reserves, represents 2.5 percent of the total population—far above the 1 percent level that may be considered average. Given such disproportionately large numbers serving in the military, it is not surprising that the two Koreas face shortages in the labor force, though the problem is far more serious in the North than the South. The question is how to proceed with force reduction so that each side's deterrence capability remains at a level of "reasonable sufficiency."

At the same time, it must be noted that the two Koreas need to modernize their respective military forces by streamlining the organizational structure and acquiring conventional high-tech weapons. If one were to assign a relatively low probability to another inter-Korean war, the primary roles of the Korean armed forces—North and/or South—would become regional. Evidently, it cannot be expected for either force to carry out a full-scale war against China, Russia, or Japan. Nevertheless, both Koreas need to possess a level of military capability strong enough to make them regional players. Should the two Koreas (or the unified Korea) be armed with high-tech elite forces, the major powers in the region would have to think twice before attempting to expand their spheres of influence on the peninsula.

The problem is that the North appears to have virtually no surplus capital to modernize its military. Having to spend about 22 percent of its total output for military purposes must be truly burdensome, especially for an economy known to be in deep trouble. In contrast, the South has been allocating close to 4 percent of its GNP to defense, and Seoul's annual defense budget, which is almost twice that of Pyongyang's, is likely to increase further due to the sustained growth of the South Korean economy. The task at hand for Seoul is to convince Pyongyang that its force modernization program would be for the common good of the Korean nation and for the purpose of a "porcupine-style" defense against potential enemies from outside the peninsula.

One may question the plausibility of such an idea—it appears to resemble the hypothetical argument that North Korean nuclear bombs will be beneficial to the South because they will remain the Korean people's assets. However, there exists a definite difference between nuclear and conventional weapons in terms of potential destructive power and the chances of deployment with little warning. As long as South Korea's force modernization program does not become excessive, Seoul may be able to combine it with arms control with the North. To do so, the Seoul government may have to show its willingness to adopt, even unilaterally, some transparency measures to assure the defensive nature of its force structure.

The Future of U.S. Forces in Korea

The issue of U.S. troops in Korea has always been the primary weapon in Pyongyang's propaganda warfare. In fact, Pyongyang may have had a hard time justifying its dictatorial rule had it not been for the U.S. soldiers stationed in Korea. After the fall of the Eastern bloc and Seoul's somewhat overzealous attempt to please Pyongyang, North Korea once again raised the issue.

Originally designed to serve as a tripwire along the DMZ, U.S. troops—especially the ground component—have become a type of peacekeeping force in Northeast Asia charged with the mission of maintaining the status quo. As such, they serve as a buffer between the two Koreas, a check against Japan's military expansion, and a messenger to China and Russia that the United States will remain a Pacific power. In a sense, they are the most visible evidence of U.S. resolve to protect U.S. economic interests in the region. Hence, the United States will try to continue its military presence on the peninsula even after Korean unification, although the size and form of deployment will certainly undergo substantial change.[9]

From the standpoint of South Korea, the U.S. intention to stay in Korea for as long as possible can be used as an "ace in the hole" in dealing with Washington and, to a lesser extent, Pyongyang. From the United States, the Seoul government could win such concessions as the supply and co-production of high-tech weaponry in return for continued financial support for stationing U.S. soldiers. It might even be able to link the question of U.S. troops with such nonmilitary issues as trade, technology transfer, and cooperation in international forums. With regard to North Korea, the South can utilize this card in negotiating both structural and operational arms control. For example, the phased withdrawal of U.S. troops from Korea could be tied to a matching reduction in North Korea's standing armed forces. And a redeployment of U.S. forces some distance away from the DMZ could be linked to a demand that the North pull back a sizable portion of its forward-deployed troops to north of the Wonsan-Pyongyang line.

It must be pointed out, however, that Seoul's leaders may have been reluctant to use U.S. troops as a bargaining chip in the triangular relationship with Pyongyang and Washington. South Korea's leaders have had special ties with the U.S. military—from early socialization to the maintenance of the regime—and therefore the attitudinal independence required for such a move would not have been possible during the military regimes. Given that a truly civilian government took office in 1993 after thirty-one years of military rule, one may cautiously predict that U.S.-Korean military relations will be conducted on a more equal footing.

Nuclear Weapons on the Korean Peninsula

In the post–Cold War era, nothing has raised more controversy in Northeast Asia than Pyongyang's alleged nuclear weapons development. Whereas South Koreans feel that "the North Korean bomb" poses the ultimate threat to their existence, the four surrounding powers view it as a dangerous source of instability in the region. As such, Russia and China have been pressuring North Korea to give up its nuclear weapons program, and the United States and Japan demand resolution of the nuclear issue as a precondition for economic and political exchanges. Of the four powers, Washington appears to be most sensitive to the issue of nuclear proliferation in Northeast Asia. For example, the drafts of the Pentagon's defense planning guide for fiscal years 1994–1999 included North Korea in two of the seven scenarios of post–Cold War conflicts in which the United States may become involved.

The critical question is whether the North has the capability of fabricating crude nuclear devices as the U.S. Central Intelligence Agency has claimed or if the whole issue is a hoax aimed at gaining political and economic trade-offs from Japan and the United States. According to the IAEA, a detailed 100-page document submitted by North Korea on May 4, 1992, described the mysterious site in Yongbyon as a "radiochemical laboratory" designed for research on separating very small amounts of uranium and plutonium as a way of controlling nuclear waste. Although the IAEA's inspection team found a partially finished structure, the true nature of the laboratory still remains unclear. But the same building was said to house far more than a small lab by U.S. intelligence sources: a nearly completed plutonium reprocessing center capable of producing a large volume of weapons-grade plutonium.

The North Korean report identified four nuclear reactors as in operation or under construction: (1) an aging, small research reactor under IAEA inspection for fifteen years; (2) a 5-megawatt experimental nuclear power reactor at Yongbyon using natural uranium—available in North Korea—and modified by graphite rather than expensive, imported "heavy water"; (3) nearby, a 50-megawatt reactor under construction; (4) a 200-megawatt reactor under construction in north Pyongan province. North Koreans also had hoped to build three 635-megawatt plants along the eastern coast. Those are believed to be power plants Pyongyang previously agreed to buy from the former Soviet Union. But their purchase has been delayed for years apparently because of the fears of weapons development and because Russia demands payment in hard currency.

To South Korea, what matters a great deal is not only the exact magnitude of Pyongyang's capability of developing nuclear weapons but also the fact that the nuclear card has elevated North Korea's status in the international system as an equal partner or adversary of the major powers. To add insult to injury, Seoul has been forced to abandon its own nuclear option, including the development of technologies for uranium enrichment and spent-fuel reprocessing, mostly because of pressures from Washington. In a sense, nuclear politics has left Seoul in the cold, whereas Pyongyang has been enjoying the international limelight.

Although the IAEA has concluded a number of ad hoc inspections of North Korean facilities, the nuclear mystery is far from being solved. For example, the IAEA believes that Pyongyang must have extracted far more plutonium than reported and would like to inspect two sites in Yongbyon suspected of storing nuclear wastes. Pyongyang has so far refused to accept such special inspections and even threatened to withdraw from the nuclear nonproliferation treaty (NPT). But the especially thorny problem is bilateral inspection between the two Koreas. Seoul and Washington maintain that IAEA inspections will not uncover the entire scope of Pyongyang's nuclear weapons program because of various institutional constraints. Although bilateral inspection cannot guarantee 100 percent disclosure, they believe it represents a giant leap forward from IAEA inspections. But the main stumbling block is Pyongyang's refusal to accept any form of bilateral inspection proposed by Seoul. Why is North Korea so adamantly opposed to bilateral inspection? There are two possible answers to this question. One is based on the assumption that the North has an ongoing nuclear weapons program hidden away in one or more of its 11,000 underground tunnels. In that case, Pyongyang would not want to risk the chance of having such facilities discovered by the South, which has insisted on "short-notice suspect-site challenge inspections." The other possibility is that the Pyongyang government may not be close to completion of its nuclear weapons program and that the whole affair has been a setup to earn time and boost its internal and external prestige. By refusing to accept bilateral inspection, the North will be able to continue its bluff in the game of nuclear poker. Unfortunately, nobody knows exactly where the truth lies between these two possibilities.[10]

Furthermore, bilateral inspection is an issue that appears to split Seoul from Washington, and Pyongyang therefore would have an advantage in playing one off against the other. The United States and South Korea are in agreement that bilateral inspection is a must because IAEA inspections would have only limited effect. What differentiates the United States from South Korea is the former's insistence that all suspected military installations in the North be included in bilateral inspection. Because U.S. military bases in Korea no longer house any nuclear devices, it is a no-loss position to Washington; some would even claim that conservative elements in the U.S. government may not like to see an early settlement of the nuclear issue in the Korean peninsula. The Seoul government does not disagree with Washington's position in principle, but it is worried that such a demand will surely kill any hope of bilateral inspections. It believes the North would never allow South Korean experts to inspect any military bases the South chooses to visit.

The worst possible scenario is thus for Seoul to grope and agonize in the dark as Pyongyang and Washington stretch this nuclear game for as long as it is beneficial for domestic and external consumption. It is no wonder that there is a growing voice of nuclear nationalism in South Korea, albeit limited to a very small number of experts and conservatives.

Changes in the Civil-Military Relationship

A potential but important obstacle in reducing tensions across the DMZ is the changing civil-military relationship in the two Koreas. It can be supposed that some military leaders in each Korea may be hesitant to accept an arms-control regime, especially because the reality of bilateral confrontation has not changed in substance. To further complicate the situation, they seem to be under pressure for internal reforms. The North Korean armed forces are expected to have a crucial political function in the transfer of power from the elder to the younger Kim, but the national economy is stagnating in large part because of the heavy defense burden. In contrast, the South Korean armed forces are facing a challenge of a different type—the adjustment to a society rapidly becoming civilian.

Pressure on the military for change must be far greater for the South than the North. In the North, the state's viability would continue to depend upon the unquestionable support of the military, and unless a crisis broke out, the military would find it difficult to oppose the political leadership. In the South, however, the civil-military balance is shifting rather dramatically and hence deserves close scrutiny of its impact on military security policies. Of particular import is a form of "Messianic complex" that has prevailed among some military leaders. As successive military regimes used national security as a political ideology to support their legitimacy, the South Korean military may have been spoiled in thinking that the military's interest was beyond the realm of civilian control. Furthermore, the military at times may have felt justified to intervene, directly or indirectly, in civilian politics under the pretext of preserving national integrity.[11] As a result, a "reactionary" response might be expected from the military to the aspect of political democratization that calls for civilianization of national security decisionmaking. Because the military could erroneously interpret increased civilianization as a sign of a less hawkish attitude toward Pyongyang, civilian planners need to compromise with the military as they inch ahead with inter-Korean détente.

Prospects of Change in
Inter-Korean Military Relations

A broad sketch of the dominant security concerns and outstanding military security issues reveals that there is no royal road to improving the military relationship between the two Koreas. In fact, the two governments and peoples on the Korean peninsula are being asked to discard old ways of conducting inter-Korean business and to develop new thinking and behavior. The transition is doubly hard because the politics of confrontation has served the needs of the two governments rather well. At home, the existence of a hostile regime on the other side of the border has been used as a convenient excuse in maintaining authoritarian rule. Abroad, the division of the peninsula has enabled the two sides to gain political, military, and economic favors from their respective patrons.

Now all these established rules of the game have disappeared, and the two Koreas are being asked to respond to the new post–Cold War international order. What really troubles them is that the new world order contains conflicting implications on the politics of Northeast Asia. On one hand, there is the trend toward global détente and the destruction of ideological barriers; the shift demands that the two Koreas reconcile their differences and develop a system of peaceful cooperation. On the other hand, one cannot deny the lingering sentiment among the major powers in the region; they seem to favor the status quo on the Korean peninsula. Because of Korea's strategic location, the surrounding major powers have tried throughout history to maintain some control over it. Today's powers are no exception to this rule. Why else would it become news in Tokyo, for instance, when some observers comment that a unified Korea may not severely endanger Japan's national interests? Likewise, why would Washington hint at its desire to maintain its military presence in Korea even after unification if U.S. troops were intended purely for the deterrence of North Korean aggression? It can also be presumed that China and Russia would be reluctant to see Korean unification, especially in the form of absorption by the South.

These contradicting signals from the international environment are challenges that the two Koreas will have to overcome. With patience and some luck, they may be able to turn them into opportunities. Compared to the bipolar world of confrontation, there seems to be more room for Seoul and Pyongyang to maneuver in the fluid regional environment. As seen in the case of nuclear weapons, the major powers will surely try to intervene in the inter-Korean talks in order to protect their interests. What the two Koreas should endeavor to achieve at this juncture is a tacit understanding of cooperation so as to play one outside power off against another. In a world where nationalism is resurgent the two Koreas should also become more assertive in promoting their national interests. Unlike the major powers with disparate interests, the two Koreas should be able to find wider areas of commonality once they establish mutual trust and a code of conduct in inter-Korean relations.

Arms control and disarmament are prime candidates for building such an area of common interest between the two Koreas. Neither side would want or could afford another war of attrition, and rapprochement will immensely boost the security of the peninsula as a whole. At the same time, the maintenance of a small modern force by each Korea will help prepare for the day when the Korean peninsula becomes a truly important nucleus in the Northeast Asian theater. After all, there is no reason why Koreans cannot become citizens of a major power, and inter-Korean arms control and reduction could very well be the first stepping-stone toward the rebuilding of the great Korean nation. The two Koreas should no longer wage a battle of wasteful confrontation but should invest the peace dividends in productive enterprises.

Notes

1. For a more detailed look at U.S. military posture toward Asia, see U.S. Department of Defense, *A Strategic Framework for the Asian Pacific Rim: Report to Congress 1992* (Washington, DC: Department of Defense, 1992).

2. Understandably, many Japanese advocate the international role that their country has been called upon to play as shown in the 1991 Gulf war. To them, Pax Nipponica will simply complement Pax Americana but not supersede it the way the latter replaced Pax Britannica. For a fuller exposition of this perspective, see Yuzi Suzuki, "Japan's New Leadership in East Asia: From Hegemony Towards Equal Partnership Among Unequals," paper presented at the international conference New Asian-Pacific Era and Korea, sponsored by the Korean Association of International Studies (KAIS), Seoul, August 20–22, 1992.

3. The entire operation had been controlled by Lee Sun-sil, a seventy-year-old woman who ranks twenty-second in power as a candidate member of the Politburo in the Korean Workers' Party. She reportedly escaped to Pyongyang just prior to the arrest. The purpose of this spy network was to build the "South Korean Chosŏn Workers' Party," which one day would become a catalyst in revolutionizing South Korean society. See *Chosŏn-Ilbo*, Chicago edition, October 7, 1992.

4. A more detailed discussion of North Korea's nuclear program appears in the chapter section headed "Nuclear Weapons on the Korean Penisula."

5. The term *security dilemma* is used here in a context not dissimilar to Robert Jervis's original formulation. According to Jervis, two adversaries end up with a security dilemma in which the security of both is endangered when each party is undertaking rational actions to improve its security (arms buildup) in mutual competition toward an arms race. In the case of the two Koreas, the action of each country to maximize its security through military and economic means tends to increase tension between the two, thus creating a security dilemma. For more details, see Robert Jervis, "Cooperation Under the Security Dilemma," *World Politics*, Vol. 30, No. 2 (January 1978), pp. 169–170.

6. Speech by Donald P. Gregg, U.S. ambassador to Korea, at the Chicago Council on Foreign Relations, Chicago, June 4, 1992.

7. The analysis of the issues presented here is an updated version of the arguments presented in Tong Whan Park, "Issues of Arms Control Between the Two Koreas," *Asian Survey*, Vol. 32, No. 4 (April 1992), pp. 350–365.

8. For a systematic comparison of the proposals for arms control and disarmament by the two Koreas, see Kwan Chi Oh, "The Inter-Korean Arms Control Negotiation: The Present State of Affairs," in *Proceedings*, KIDA/CSIS (Center for Strategic and International Studies) workshop, *Tension Reduction and Arms Control on the Korean Peninsula*, Seoul, November 8–9, 1990 (Seoul: Korea Institute for Defense Analyses), pp. 1–19.

9. In this context, one should note that Washington has been lowering the profile of its forces stationed in Korea in order not to irritate the North and the radical elements in the South. Evidence of this new posture includes the suspension of Team Spirit exercises in 1992 and agreements with South Korea to make it the primary actor in common defense and to move some facilities of the U.S. Eighth Army headquarters out of the heart of Seoul.

10. According to Leonard S. Spector, who visited Pyongyang April 28–May 4, 1992, as a member of a Carnegie endowment delegation, the North has a laboratory-scale reprocessing plant and has produced some plutonium, and a larger facility is partially completed. See Selig S. Harrison, Leonard S. Spector, and James F. Leonard, "Report of a Carnegie Endowment Delegation Just Back from Pyongyang with Important New

Findings on North Korea's Nuclear Program," in Carnegie Endowment for International Peace (Washington, DC), *News from the Carnegie Endowment,* May 5, 1992. On the critical question of whether North Korea has the capability to design, fabricate, and test the nonnuclear component of the weapon, Spector's answer was "Don't know, even though other achievements suggest that this [implosion package needed to trigger a nuclear device] is easily within North Korean capabilities." Leonard S. Spector, "The U.S. and the Nuclear Issue," speech at conference Rethinking the Korean Peninsula: Arms Control, Nuclear Issues, Economic Reformation, Georgetown University, Washington, DC, May 27, 1992.

11. In 1990, South Koreans were truly shocked to learn that the Defense Security Command (the counterintelligence unit) had been charged with the illegal surveillance of several hundred civilians for political reasons. This was indeed a troublesome revelation because nobody expected the continuation of such a practice in the Sixth Republic, which was vigorously pushing democratizing reforms.

13

North Korea's Nuclear Program

Kongdan Oh and Ralph C. Hassig

The Democratic People's Republic of Korea (DPRK) vigorously denies having the intention or capability of developing nuclear weapons, but the denial is unconvincing. After belatedly signing the International Atomic Energy Agency's (IAEA) nuclear safeguards accord (NSA) in early 1992, the North hosted several ad hoc inspections of its declared nuclear facilities in preparation for regular inspections. These preliminary inspections have not satisfied the IAEA that the North Koreans are fully disclosing their nuclear capabilities. In the light of both past North Korean aggressions and continuing North Korean hostile rhetoric toward South Korea, Pyongyang's delay in signing the NSA and refusal to allow IAEA inspection of two suspicious sites have placed North Korea under a dark cloud of suspicion.

North Korea's secrecy about its nuclear capabilities is only a symptom of more basic problems. North Korean society is closed and isolated. The totalitarian government in Pyongyang has long outlived its usefulness. The nation's aging president, Kim Il Sung, has ruled since the North and South were separated at the end of World War II. In recent years the bulk of political power has passed to Kim's son, Kim Jong Il, who—unlike his father—has done little to earn the respect or gratitude of the North Korean people and who has rarely traveled abroad. The junior Kim appears to have a tight hold on the reins of power, and the likelihood of a popular uprising against his dynastic succession seems remote.

The authors would like to thank William R. Harris and Dean A. Wilkening of RAND and Robert Swartz of the Los Alamos Nuclear Laboratory for valuable discussions on nuclear matters. The views expressed in this chapter are those of the authors and do not necessarily represent those of RAND or its clients.

Meanwhile, the North Korean economy, cut adrift from the support of China and the former Soviet Union, experienced declines in GNP in 1990, 1991, and 1992. Although statistical measures of North Korea's economic ills are unavailable to outsiders (and perhaps even to the North Korean leadership), foreign reports of food riots paint a grim picture of the standard of living in the North.

On the diplomatic front, the North Koreans not only have lost the close backing of their Chinese and Russian allies but have painfully witnessed all the former communist states (except Cuba) extend diplomatic recognition to Seoul, Pyongyang's archrival. After a brief springtime of warming relations in 1991 and 1992, relations between North and South cooled. In the face of international pressure to open their society to outside scrutiny, the North Koreans have resisted, going so far as to announce their intention to withdraw from the nuclear nonproliferation treaty (NPT).

Has the world been fair to the North Koreans? Or have they been made a scapegoat of the Cold War, persecuted by an international community that is manipulated by the United States? This chapter first examines the evidence for the assertion that North Korea has both the intention and capability to develop nuclear weapons. Then the more practical question of what policy might be adopted to deal with the North Korean regime is addressed.

North Korea's Nuclear Capabilities

Information about North Korean society is difficult to come by.[1] The totalitarian regime is able to manipulate information for its own purposes. Disinformation is routinely used to implement both domestic and foreign policy. Most ordinary North Korean citizens have little knowledge of the workings of their government, much less of the reality of the outside world. Until the regime adopts a policy of Soviet-style *glasnost*, outsiders—including IAEA inspectors—can only speculate about the extent of North Korea's nuclear capabilities. In regard to intentions, if past history is any indication, little credence can be given to Pyongyang's repeated disavowals of interest in nuclear weapons.

North Korea's nuclear program has its roots in the late 1950s, when Pyongyang and Moscow agreed to establish a joint nuclear research institute. North Koreans were sent to the Soviet Union to study nuclear science, and in 1964 the Research Institute of Atomic Energy was established. In the 1970s nuclear science departments were set up at Kimilsung University and Kimchaek Engineering College.

North Korea's first nuclear facility was a small 1,000 kilowatt (KW) "critical assembly." The next, in 1964 or 1965, was a larger 2–4 megawatt (MW) research reactor fueled with low-enriched uranium. Both facilities were supplied by the former Soviet Union. The two reactors were installed at Yongbyon, 90 kilometers north of Pyongyang, and were opened to regular IAEA inspection in 1977.

In 1980 the North Koreans began construction of a 5 MW reactor fueled with natural uranium and moderated with graphite.[2] The reactor design was similar to early Western and Soviet models of the 1950s. Although a natural-uranium (in contrast to an enriched-uranium) type of reactor is relatively inefficient, it does have the advantage that the technology is relatively simple (as nuclear reactors go), and the uranium fuel and graphite are available in abundance in North Korea. One of the obvious uses of this type of reactor is to produce plutonium that can be reprocessed into weapons-grade material. Because the reactor was developed without major Soviet assistance, the North Koreans were not obligated by the Soviets to place it under IAEA surveillance. This reactor began operation in early 1986, but the North Koreans claim that it has been operating only intermittently. If the reactor has indeed been running since 1986, it should by now have generated enough plutonium to make at least one nuclear weapon.

Work on a second indigenously constructed natural-uranium reactor was begun in 1984. This reactor, with a capacity of 50–200 MW, is considered to be inordinately large for research purposes, but like the smaller reactor, it is capable of producing plutonium. The North Koreans' target date for completion is 1995, and they claim that the reactor will be used for electrical generation, although there are conflicting reports as to whether an associated power grid is being put in place. A 200 MW reactor planned for completion in 1996 is also under construction in Taech'on.

With Soviet assistance, North Korea reportedly planned construction of three or four enriched-uranium reactors for power generation. The reactors, to be located at Sinp'o on the east coast—distant from the Yongbyon area—have not progressed beyond the planning stage now that Russian assistance has been withdrawn.

Whatever other nuclear facilities the North may have, the most worrisome is the spent-fuel reprocessing plant at Yongbyon. This plant was shown to Hans Blix, the IAEA's director general, in his initial visit in May 1992 (of which more later). Published reports based on U.S. satellite surveillance had it that there was unusually heavy traffic of large trucks coming and going from the reprocessing building shortly before Blix arrived, but whether to move equipment in or out was not reported.

North Korea and the IAEA

In December 1985 North Korea signed the IAEA's nuclear nonproliferation treaty, presumably as a condition for receiving Soviet nuclear assistance. Signatories of the NPT are required to sign the safeguards accord (NSA) within eighteen months. This accord provides for the regular inspection of declared nuclear facilities to ensure that they are not used for weapons production. All peaceful uses of nuclear facilities are permitted, including plutonium production under IAEA surveillance.

North Korea failed to sign the NSA within the allotted time, first citing IAEA procedural discrepancies (the wrong document was sent to be signed) and then protesting that the signing would jeopardize North Korea's security unless three preconditions were met. First, the United States must remove its alleged nuclear weapons from South Korea. Second, the annual U.S.–South

Korean Team Spirit military exercises (which the North Koreans term a "nuclear war game") must be discontinued. Third, the North Koreans would reserve the right to abrogate their NSA responsibilities depending on their evaluation of the attitudes of the nuclear powers toward their country.[3]

In 1990, four and a half years after signing the NPT, Pyongyang's Foreign Ministry announced that the safeguards accord would be signed if the United States removed its "nuclear threat."[4] One year later, in the face of mounting international pressure (in which the United States played a leading role), the North Koreans said they would sign the document at the IAEA's September meeting. However, when the time came they refused to sign, claiming that at the meeting the United States, Japan, and unspecified other nations had adopted an "unjustified resolution unilaterally urging us to sign the nuclear safeguards accord and ratify it as quickly as possible, thereby putting up an artificial obstacle to our signing the safeguards accord."[5] In Korea, this type of behavior is said to be characteristic of a "green frog"—which won't do what it is asked to do but will do what it isn't. It is tempting to speculate that the North Koreans intended to use their signing as a bargaining chip to extract promises from the United States, Japan, and/or South Korea, and that in the absence of such promises, they withheld their signature.

In late September 1991 President Bush announced that the United States would withdraw all its overseas land- and sea-based tactical nuclear weapons, although the traditional U.S. "neither confirm nor deny" (NCND) policy prevented the president from specifying whether any withdrawals would be made from South Korea. It is widely believed that some tactical nuclear weapons had been based in South Korea, and in that regard South Korean President Roh Tae Woo subsequently announced that no nuclear weapons were presently located on South Korean soil.

Two months later—on December 31, 1991—South and North initialed a joint declaration for denuclearization of the Korean peninsula (Appendix C), in which the two sides agreed not only to renounce the possession and use of nuclear weapons and facilities for nuclear fuel reprocessing and uranium enrichment but also to institute mutual inspections of each other's suspected nuclear sites.

To reward North Korea for its cooperative efforts, South Korea announced on January 7, 1992, that its annual Team Spirit exercise with the United States would be canceled. This primarily defensive exercise, which pulls in troops from the continental United States, has consistently been regarded by North Korea as a serious threat to national security. The South Koreans also urged that several "pilot" nuclear inspections be made to fill in the gap before the regular South-North and IAEA inspections began, but nothing ever came of the suggestion. On January 30, 1992, North Korea finally signed the IAEA's safeguards accord, agreeing to accept inspections after the accord had been ratified by its legislative assembly. The IAEA Board of Governors in February decided to request a "special inspection" of North Korean facilities pending North Korea's ratification of the accord. This request was intended to speed up the ratification process (at the time, some experts feared that the North might be only months away from developing a nuclear weapon).[6] The accord was ratified by North Korea's rubber-stamp Supreme People's Assembly on April 9, and the North Koreans entered into negotiations with the IAEA to arrange for the preliminary ad hoc inspections that would prepare the stage for regular inspections.

As a first step, North Korea submitted a list of its nuclear facilities to the IAEA on May 4. This list is significant because IAEA regular inspections can only be made of sites declared by the host government. However, the host government is required by IAEA rules to list all of its nuclear sites. On May 12, Hans Blix made a five-day visit to North Korea to familiarize himself with the scope of the Korean nuclear program. The IAEA's first ad hoc inspection followed on May 12. This inspection, as well as most of the subsequent six inspections (to July 1993), lasted from one to two weeks.[7]

Results of IAEA inspections are not released to the public, but in response to intense media interest, Blix held a press conference on his return from the North. He said he was shown all the sites that he had requested to see, including the 5 MW research reactor and the 50 MW and 200 MW facilities under construction.

Of greatest interest was his visit to the "radiochemical laboratory," which U.S. satellite photographs had identified as a fuel reprocessing plant capable of transforming spent fuel from operating reactors into plutonium. In fact, the satellite intelligence was correct: Although the North Koreans said the facility was only 80 percent complete and only 40 percent furnished, they did admit to having processed a "tiny quantity" (a few grams) of plutonium at the facility (far less than the approximately five to ten kilograms required to make a bomb). The North Koreans, however, insisted on calling the facility a "radiochemical laboratory" rather than a plutonium reprocessing plant. Hans Blix said that "If it were in operation and complete, then certainly, in our terminology, we would call it a reprocessing plant."[8]

The North Koreans said they built the reprocessing facility to experiment with plutonium extraction in case they should choose to use plutonium to fuel a breeder reactor (a highly sophisticated device that would lie many years in the North's future) or to make mixed oxide fuel to power a light-water reactor, the type of reactor that has largely replaced the old natural-uranium reactors the North has built so far. They explained that they did not wish to depend on other nations for a supply of plutonium or enriched uranium and so were experimenting with the early stages of domestic production.

At his press conference, Blix was cautious in expressing his opinion about the purpose of the reprocessing facility. He said he was impressed with the level of nuclear technology he had observed during his trip, and he applauded the North Koreans for their openness. He admitted that—as in the Iraqi case—IAEA inspections cannot uncover nuclear facilities if the host government is determined to hide them, and he urged Pyongyang to complete arrangements with Seoul for a mutual inspection regime to parallel IAEA inspections.

In testimony before a U.S. congressional hearing in July 1992, Blix said he saw no good reason why North Korea would need plutonium for its nuclear program. And he remained skeptical that the North Koreans had disclosed the existence of all their nuclear facilities, noting in particular that it was "unusual, not to say exceptional, that a country can build a fairly large plant for reprocessing without going through a pilot project." (The North Koreans have not admitted the existence of a smaller pilot reprocessing facility.) His conclusion for U.S. lawmakers was that "We are neither giving a clean bill of health nor wanting to sound an alarm."[9]

As the IAEA inspections got under way, the North Koreans boasted that their "nuclear problem" with the international community had been successfully resolved and that their claim to nuclear "innocence" had been vindicated. They blamed both the United States and Japan for insisting on mutual South-North nuclear inspections as a precondition for improved political relations, asserting that the nuclear question involved only North Korea and the IAEA.

The North Koreans' optimism, whether feigned or real, was blighted by continued suspicions that they were hiding something. IAEA analysis of documents and nuclear materials (including a small amount of plutonium) provided by North Korea disclosed apparent discrepancies between North Korean claims and IAEA estimates regarding the number of times nulcear fuel had been removed and reprocessed and consequently the amount that had been reprocessed into weapons-grade plutonium. North Korea declared that fuel had been removed only once and reprocessed into "a few grams" of plutonium as an experiment. The IAEA is adamant that reprocessing occurred on at least three occasions, leading to speculation by outside observers that North Korea might have reprocessed enough plutonium to make at least one nuclear weapon.[10]

Immediately after the fourth ad hoc inspection in November, Blix proposed to North Korea that the IAEA send several officials to clear up the discrepancies. North Korea's minister of nuclear energy, Ch'oe Hak-kun, and several other officials met with Blix in Vienna and assured him that the inconsistencies would be resolved during an upcoming inspection scheduled for January 1993.[11] At the same time, the North Koreans were sending conflicting signals as to whether they would permit continued inspections if the United States and South Korea resumed their Team Spirit exercises in 1993.

The inconsistencies were not resolved during the fifth or sixth ad hoc inspections, and in late January 1993 senior IAEA officials visited North Korea to discuss the discrepancies and urge that inspectors be given access to two unreported sites that U.S. intelligence sources suspect of being storage sites for nuclear waste. One of these facilities, adjacent to the nuclear complex, was two stories high during construction but was subsequently landscaped to look like a one-story building. When IAEA officials paid a brief visit to the building in September 1992, the North Koreans denied there was a first (now a basement) level. It is this basement that is suspected of holding the nuclear waste.[12] The North Koreans claim that this building is a military warehouse having nothing to do with the nuclear program. During the sixth ad hoc inspection, which began in late January 1993, access to these sites was denied, and the North Koreans were unable to resolve the discrepancies to the IAEA's satisfaction. On February 9 Hans Blix cabled a request to the North Koreans that they accept a special inspection of these sites.

The North Koreans, through their ambassadors in Russia and the United Nations, strongly hinted that they would withdraw from the NPT if these inspections were forced on them. They continued to maintain that the sites were military in nature and had nothing to do with nuclear energy. Furthermore, they charged the IAEA with "illegally" using information obtained from Western intelligence sources and of being a tool of the enemies of North Korea.[13]

On February 25 special meeting of the IAEA Board of Governors delivered an ultimatum to North Korea: Either open the sites to inspection within one month or the issue would be referred to the UN Security Council. The North Koreans continued to make threats concerning what they would do, ranging from the general threat of "taking appropriate self-defense measures to safeguard the nations's sovereignty and security"[14] to the more ominous "If any special inspection or sanctions are forced upon us, encroaching on our sacred land, it will bring about a dangerous situation to throw the whole peninsula into the ravages of war."[15]

On March 12, 1993, the North Korean government announced its intention to "withdraw unavoidably" from the NPT, attributing the withdrawal to the alleged nuclear threats of the United States (especially the Team Spirit exercises, which had begun three days earlier) and to the "unfair demands" of the IAEA for special inspections of the two North Korean "military" facilities. But the withdrawal statement left open the door to Pyongyang's return to the treaty: "The DPRK's principled stand will remain unchanged until the United States stops its nuclear threats against the DPRK and the IAEA secretariat returns to its principle of independence and impartiality."[16]

Article ten of the NPT stipulates that a signatory may withdraw from the agreement "if it decides that extraordinary events, related to the subject matter of [the NPT], have jeopardized the supreme interests of its country." Before the withdrawal takes effect, the country must notify the UN Security Council and the other signatory nations (now numbering 155) ninety days in advance of its withdrawal. Obviously, once a nation has withdrawn from the treaty, it is no longer subject to UN sanctions for violating that treaty.

The withdrawal announcement set the stage for North Korea's next diplomatic act: negotiations for returning to the NPT. The North Koreans wisely cast the NPT dispute in terms of a disagreement not with the international community but only with the United States. Within a week of making the withdrawal announcement, North Korea's deputy ambassador to the UN, Ho Chong, was quoted as saying that North Korea–U.S. negotiations could solve the NPT issue. He suggested that the preconditions for North Korea's return would include (1) a U.S. guarantee not to launch an attack on North Korea; (2) a permanent cancellation of Team Spirit; (3) the opening of U.S. military bases in South Korea to nuclear inspection; and (4) IAEA respect for the independence of member nations.

The IAEA's possible responses to a withdrawal threat are severely limited. On March 18 the twenty-five-member Board of Governors adopted a resolution of "concern" over the withdrawal. China urged its fellow members not to immediately refer the issue to the UN Security Council in order to allow more time for dialogue with North Korea. But two weeks later, with no positive response forthcoming from Pyongyang, the board found North Korea to be in noncompliance with the NPT and referred the matter to the Security Council. China and Libya opposed the resolution, and India, Pakistan, Syria, and Vietnam abstained. In the Security Council, a resolution was subsequently passed (with China and Pakistan abstaining) calling for North Korea to return to the NPT.

In the ensuing weeks, North Korea continued to insist that the nuclear problem could be resolved in bilateral talks with the United States. Washington agreed to the talks, which were held from June 2 to June 11, 1993. On the last day of the talks—one day before North Korea's NPT withdrawal would become official—the two sides reached an agreement on several basic principles:

> Assurances against the threat and use of force, including nuclear weapons
> Impartial application of fullscope [nuclear] safeguards
> Mutual respect for each other's sovereignty and noninterference in each other's internal affairs
> Support for the peaceful reunification of Korea

In the communiqué, Washington and Pyongyang agreed to continue their dialogue, and "in this respect the government of the DPRK has decided unilaterally ["and temporarily" in the Korean-language version] to suspend the effectuation of the withdrawal from the NPT as long as it considers it necessary."[17]

In this agreement the United States was only reiterating guarantees toward North Korea that it has made before and that are extended to all members of the United Nations. For its part, North Korea agreed to return to the NPT of its own volition. The key issue of special inspections, which prompted the withdrawal in the first place, was left unresolved. North Korea's agreement to "fullscope" inspections appears to commit it to accept the special inspections it had vowed never to accept, but the stipulation that such inspections be "impartial" could easily be used to resist such first-ever inspections.

The U.S. side did little boasting about the agreement. Assistant secretary of state for political-military affairs Robert L. Gallucci, who headed up the U.S. delegation, called North Korea's return "a step in the right direction."[18] The North Koreans gave the agreement heavy press coverage, characterizing it as the "first-ever historic document" signed by the two governments and a "turning point" in their relationship. The principles of agreement were interpreted as a pledge on the part of the United States to remove its protective strategic nuclear umbrella from South Korea, respect the Kim Il Sung–Kim Jong Il government, and work toward the signing of an armistice to replace the technical state of war that exists between the two governments.[19] Finally, the agreement set the stage for a long series of talks between the two governments. Whatever the outcome of these talks, North Korea is likely to escape most international pressure for inspections as long as it continues with the dialogue.

Nuclear Negotiations Between South and North

North Korea has been advocating a nuclear-free Korean peninsula at least since 1976. In 1975 South Korean President Park Chung Hee had threatened to develop nuclear weapons if the United States implemented proposed force reductions in Korea, even though Seoul had signed the NPT in 1975.[20] It was widely assumed, however, that notwithstanding South Korea's NPT membership and the U.S. NCND policy, U.S. tactical nuclear weapons were based in South Korea.[21] In June 1986 the North Koreans proposed a denuclearization agreement with the United States to make the peninsula nuclear-free. In September 1986 North Korea hosted an international conference for denuclearization and peace on the Korean peninsula.

When a Japanese news service reported in November 1990 that the U.S. government had presented Tokyo with photos and other evidence strongly suggesting that North Korea was developing nuclear weapons at Yongbyon, South Koreans became sensitized to the nuclear issue, and the U.S. and South Korean governments launched a two-pronged campaign to prevent the North from pursuing nuclear weapons development. On the one hand, renewed emphasis was placed on forcing North Korea to live up to its international obligations by signing the safeguards accord and permitting IAEA inspections. On the other hand, as part of South Korean President Roh's "northern policy," progress continued on a wide-ranging dialogue between the North and the South to ease tensions and make nuclear weapons unnecessary as a deterrent in the North-South arms race.

From North Korea's vantage point, signing the safeguards accord would not gain the removal of U.S. nuclear weapons from South Korea because Washington insisted that the signing was an obligation North Korea had undertaken with the IAEA and not an issue involving the United States. Thus, North Korea took another tack by proposing on July 30, 1991, that North and South sign a declaration that would guarantee a nuclear-free Korean peninsula.

The Cold War was ending, and the South Koreans felt that there was hope of improving relations with the North and perhaps even opening up the border between the two sides to permit social and economic intercourse for the first time in forty years. But despite this optimism, the United States and South Korea were increasingly concerned that the North was on the brink of developing a nuclear weapon. Because the North refused to sign the safeguards accord while "under nuclear threat from the United States" (usually taken to refer to the threat posed by the alleged U.S. nuclear weapons based in

South Korea), the obvious solution was to remove any such weapons in exchange for a promise from North Korea to abandon its nuclear weapons program and accept inspections.

The logjam was broken serendipitously in September 1991 when President Bush announced the worldwide withdrawal of U.S. land- and sea-based tactical nuclear weapons. Although this withdrawal was not made to accommodate North Korean concerns (it had to do with U.S.-Soviet détente), it gave the North what it wanted, and within short order a South-North nonnuclear agreement, a South-North reconciliation agreement, and the nuclear safeguards accord had been signed. All that remained was to implement these three agreements.

The joint declaration on denuclearization contained six provisions, including a prohibition on possession of nuclear weapons and nuclear reprocessing facilities. A joint nuclear control commission (JNCC) was to be set up to implement the agreement, and South and North would conduct inspections of designated "objects" (as agreed upon by both sides) for purposes of verification.[22] A separate agreement to implement the JNCC was signed by the two sides on March 18, 1992, following seven rounds of preliminary negotiations.

In the course of subsequent JNCC meetings, a number of issues were raised concerning how the mutual inspections were to be conducted and how the nuclear agreement was to be implemented in the context of broader South-North issues.[23] First, the South wanted quid pro quo inspections—one inspection in the North for one in the South. The North wanted inspections according to the principle of "simultaneous dispelling of misgivings"—that is, whatever inspections of either side that would be necessary to convince the other side that the agreement was being upheld. This issue was related to a second issue concerning what was to be inspected. The South wanted the freedom to inspect any suspicious sites. The North insisted that it be allowed to inspect U.S. and South Korean military bases (which at least in the past had presumably housed nuclear weapons), and the North would open up its nuclear facilities at Yongbyon but not its military bases (which the North Koreans claimed had nothing to do with nuclear weapons). A third disagreement arose concerning the surprise challenge inspections demanded by the South but unacceptable to the North, which wanted at least a ten-day notice period.

Before any of these issues could be resolved, South Korea and the United States agreed at their annual security consultative meeting in September 1992 to resume the Team Spirit military exercises in March 1993 unless progress was made in the JNCC talks. This decision created an impasse: The North Koreans refused to engage in further nuclear discussions unless Team Spirit was canceled; the South Koreans refused to cancel Team Spirit unless the North Koreans agreed to at least one mutual inspection. Neither side budged, and all contacts ceased between North and South—with the exception of the fruitless JNCC meetings, which at least provided a channel of communication. Seoul and Pyongyang did not even begin to talk about talking until May 1993, when both sides realized the importance of avoiding an international conflict related to North Korea's impending withdrawal from the NPT.

Choosing a North Korea Policy

The controversy surrounding North Korea's nuclear capability and intentions has generated more heat than light. It is time to consider whether the right questions are being asked. Questions such as "How much plutonium do the North Koreans have?" "Where is it hidden?" and "Are they making a bomb?" are ultimately unanswerable given the nature of the current North Korean regime. Perhaps some incontrovertible evidence of a nuclear weapons program will come to light. Almost certainly not all of the evidence will be discovered. (And even if everything is discovered, how will outsiders ever know what "everything" is?) There will always linger a suspicion that something has been hidden in one of North Korea's thousands of tunnels. A broad and well-implemented inspection regime, whether administered by the IAEA or by South Korea, may impede North Korea's nuclear weapons program but not necessarily eliminate it. In this sense, the North Korean nuclear problem can never be fully resolved to the satisfaction of a skeptical world.

Despite their adamant denials, it seems likely that the North Koreans have been and perhaps still are engaged in nuclear weapons development. For them not to be thus involved would be almost criminally negligent, given the circumstances.

Short of a dramatic reversal of fortunes for democratic forces in China and the former Soviet Union, North Korea's only hope of economic and political survival is to change its political and economic system, which would be political suicide for the Kim regime, or to rely on its own resources to preserve its national security. Not surprisingly, Pyongyang has continued to stress the second option in the form of its national ideology of *Juche:* independence and self-sufficiency. As it becomes necessary for the North Koreans to "circle the wagons," an indigenous nuclear deterrent becomes increasingly attractive as a means of maintaining political autonomy.

It is a moot point whether the North Koreans have yet managed to make a bomb.[24] What is not so moot is the likelihood that, given time, they will be able to acquire sufficient plutonium (either by processing it themselves or acquiring it from another nation) to make at least a few weapons that could count as a deterrent, even if the weapons turn out to be duds. After all, for the sake of deterrence, a bomb does not have to explode—it need only make other nations suspect that it might explode. A nuclear NCND policy, such as the United States has followed in South Korea, would suit North Korea's needs for a deterrent very nicely. In fact, Pyongyang already seems to have established the equivalent of such a policy.

Perhaps it would be more fruitful to sidestep the "do they or don't they?" issue and seek to answer questions that might illuminate how North Korea perceives its nuclear program in terms of its security in the region and its position as a proud nation in the international community. That is, the focus should shift to intention and away from capability, for assuredly if the North Koreans have the intention of securing nuclear weapons, they will sooner or later acquire the capability.

Admittedly, the workings of the policymaking apparatus in Pyongyang are hidden from outside observers, so the following is little more than speculation based on the presumption that North Korea could easily recognize the value in developing nuclear weapons.[25] In order to limit the scope of this speculation, only three questions relating to nuclear matters are considered:

1. Why did the North Koreans sign the NPT and safeguards accord?
2. Why did they then undertake to renounce the accord?
3. What should the international community do about this?

Why Did the North Sign?

As previously suggested, North Korea presumably signed the NPT in 1985 in order to secure Soviet assistance with its nuclear program. The North Koreans may have had little intention of implementing the agreement. Certainly they seem to have been in no hurry to do so. But whatever was North Korea thinking when it agreed in late 1991 and early 1992 to South Korean and IAEA inspections? There are several possible answers. Of course, the basic answer is that at the time, signing the agreements appeared to be the best way to obtain what North Korea needed: improved relations with Japan and the United States.

That the IAEA discovered serious discrepancies in Pyongyang's nuclear story may have come as a surprise to the North Koreans. Perhaps they did not realize how sophisticated international nuclear technology has become and believed they could continue their secret weapons program in spite of international inspection. Or perhaps North Korea's nuclear scientists were aware of the possibility—even the certainty—of discovery but were unable to communicate this danger to decisionmakers in Pyongyang. Or perhaps the danger was communicated to Kim Jong Il and company, who decided to go ahead anyway and deal with the situation as it developed.

In any case, signatures of North Koreans are now on the documents, obligating them to do things they do not want to do. What is worse, by dragging their feet on implementing the NSA and the South-North agreement, and then by threatening to withdraw from the NPT, they have gained an even worse reputation in the international community without getting any closer to their goal of improved relations with the United States and Japan.

Why Did the North Announce Its Withdrawal from the NPT?

If the assumption is that the North Koreans have something nuclear to hide, their subsequent withdrawal announcement could be explained in several ways.

The North Koreans themselves attribute their announcement to a principled stand against foreign meddling in their national security affairs. Granted that this is true, the extreme nature of their response may suggest that there are other concerns involved.

For example, the threat to withdraw may be a desperate attempt to save face. Certainly North Korea's withdrawal decision is extremely damaging to its reputation—such as it is. But the alternatives, at least as seen in Pyongyang, may look worse. It is altogether probable that IAEA special inspections would uncover at least some of North Korea's undeclared nuclear capability, catching the North Koreans in a lie. So far they have tried to put the best face on the lies or near-lies that have been revealed—for example, by referring to a reprocessing facility as a "radiochemical laboratory" and claiming that the amount of plutonium they have already reprocessed is negligble. But now they have gone on record as saying that there are no unreported nuclear facilities in North Korea, which is highly unlikely. If only one such facility is discovered, they are caught in another lie. This reflects badly not only on the North Korean government but also and more importantly on their godlike leader Kim Il Sung, who has personally declared that his nation has neither the intention nor the capability to develop nuclear weapons.

Moreover, effective IAEA or South Korean inspections will undoubtedly peek into many dark corners of North Korea, for that is where secrets are most likely to be hidden. A nation that does not even permit its citizens to speak with outsiders is unlikely to tolerate that level of curiosity.

Another intriguing possibility is that having failed to obtain maximum advantage with minimum effort, the North Koreans are broadening their bargaining game. Because they were unsuccessful in gaining diplomatic recognition from the United States and Japan by doing a bit of something "good"— talking to the South Koreans and letting IAEA inspectors into some sites— they may be trying to secure the same gains by promising not to do something "bad"—promising not to go through with their threatened NPT withdrawal. If their return to the international nonproliferation fold could be traded for promised recognition from Japan and the United States or increased support from China, then perhaps even if they were later caught in a lie, they would feel the gambit had been justified. They would in any case be trading a bird in the hand for a bird the IAEA has yet to find in the bush.

What Should the International Community Do?

Military Action. One school of thought concerning an international response to North Korea's refusal to accept fullscope nuclear inspections is to take a page from the Iraqi casebook and bomb North Korea's known nuclear facilities. It is hard to imagine that this could be done with the support of the UN. More likely, it would have to be carried out by U.S. forces, perhaps with the support of South Korea. Apart from the appalling political consequences for the United States and South Korea, this course of action is impractical from a military standpoint. North Korea is not Iraq—as the North Koreans have frequently warned. The likelihood of successfully eliminating all of North Korea's nuclear weapons capability is extremely low, but the likelihood of triggering an armed response against South Korea (which along with Japan is considered by the North Koreans to be a "shock brigade" for U.S.-orchestrated persecution) is very high. Moreover, resorting to violence would be engaging in precisely what critics accuse the North Koreans of doing and would confirm them in their worst fears about the threats they face in their environment.

Economic and Political Sanctions. As long as North Korea chooses to remain in the NPT, any sanctions for noncompliance have a quasi-legal basis, although the IAEA and the UN will be treading on new ground. Should North Korea choose to withdraw from the NPT, it is hard to see how it can legally be treated differently from other non-NPT nations such as Israel, India, and Pakistan, which have an undeclared nuclear weapons capability. In this case, sanctions would have to be imposed by a "coalition of concerned nations." Although North Korea is relatively independent—both politically and economically—from the rest of the world, it has few reserves to draw on, and a reduction in or embargo of trade with Japan, China, Russia, and South Korea would undoubtedly be a serious blow to a North Korean economy already on its knees.

The North Koreans could survive such an embargo (at least for several years), but despite their brave talk, the regime in Pyongyang is becoming increasingly vulnerable as it faces three grave crises: (1) the ideological crisis of the demise of worldwide socialism; (2) the political crisis of legitimating the junior Kim's succession to his father; (3) the economic crisis resulting from years of misguided economic policies.

The application of UN-mandated sanctions on North Korea is not without certain risks. Because little is known about North Korean policymaking, it is difficult to predict how the North Koreans would respond. Pyongyang might choose to increase the threat level on the Korean peninsula by going on a war footing. During Team Spirit, which was being played at the time the North Koreans announced their NPT withdrawal, the country was already on a "semiwar" footing. Low-intensity conflict is certainly not out of the question.

The North might also gain sympathy and support from other Third World nations (it has already made a bid for this in the context of the IAEA inspections); for example, it might look to its weapons customers in the Mideast. It is also possible that China, unwilling to abandon its sometime friend and fellow communist, would either veto a Security Council resolution on sanctions or surreptitiously break a UN-imposed embargo.

Finally, an embargo would hurt the ordinary Korean people, who are already suffering from severe shortages. It might even serve to rally the populace behind the Kim regime and make the junior Kim a heroic figure of the "new resistance"—just as his father was a hero of the Japanese wartime resistance.

Noncommittal Dialogue. A third possible international response would be to change the rules of the game. Instead of using either threats or inducements to get North Korea to play by (more or less) accepted international rules, the international community might simply ignore North Korea. As it is, North Korea is dying on the vine. In their own interest, the North Koreans should be seeking solutions to problems, not creating them. If lines of communication were kept open to the North, perhaps the North Koreans themselves would come up with some suggestions for solving the "nuclear problem." Suggestions that did not warrant serious consideration could be gracefully ignored. The world could out-wait the North Koreans, for whom time is an enemy.

Of course, this approach would not do anything for the reputation of the IAEA, which took a beating in the Iraqi case.[26] But the temptation to make North Korea a "test case" to prove the viability of the IAEA is shortsighted. North Korea is its own case, not someone else's test case.

Nor would this approach necessarily address a very basic concern of much of the international community, which is to prevent nuclear proliferation. A new Asian domino theory asserts that if North Korea is allowed to go nuclear, then South Korea and Japan will follow, all of which would create serious strains on Asian stability. The effort to prevent this proliferation of nuclear as well as chemical and biological weapons of mass destruction is undoubtedly a worthy cause, but the risks involved in the North Korean case should not be ignored in the service of a nonproliferation principle that seems to have received less than whole-hearted international acceptance.[27]

Whether sanctions are imposed on the North Koreans, or whether their apparent nuclear weapons game is ignored, the North Koreans as a people should not be ignored. The regime in Pyongyang has had little high-level contact with the Western world during its almost fifty years of existence. The Kims seem to be running the nation according to an Orwellian script written many years ago. Through continued high-level dialogue, the West should communicate disagreement with and disapproval of Pyongyang's totalitarian policies without resorting to threats that would jeopardize the political existence of the present regime, regardless of how anachronistic it may appear to the outside world.

Postscript: No End in Sight

Since threatening to withdraw from the NPT, the DPRK has performed a high-wire act designed to extract concessions from a hostile world. Pyongyang left the June talks in New York with broad negative-security assurances from Washington and the promise of more dialogue. The United States thought it had secured a DPRK promise to remain in the NPT and ultimately accept full-scope safeguards.

In July 1993, U.S. and DPRK negotiators met in Geneva, but the DPRK still refused to accept full-scope inspections. Frustrated by DPRK recalcitrance, the IAEA voted on October 1 to urge the DPRK to accept IAEA inspections. The DPRK minister of atomic energy then charged the IAEA with "political intrigue" against his country and concluded that "the IAEA has lost its qualification and face to have further negotiations with the DPRK."

U.S. options for ensuring denuclearization of the DPRK were limited. Military action against DPRK nuclear targets was judged too risky and seemed unlikely to take out all DPRK nuclear sites. Economic sanctions were also unattractive, given the independent nature of the DPRK economy and the reluctance of China and Japan to cooperate. The South Koreans wanted at all costs to avoid isolating and antagonizing the North. Offering the DPRK inducements to fulfill its obligations to the IAEA and to South Korea was unpalatable but at least seemed to hold out hope of an eventual solution to the nuclear problem.

President Clinton insisted that "North Korea cannot be allowed to develop a nuclear bomb," but the administration quickly backed away from the statement. U.S. intelligence had concluded that there was a better than even chance that the DPRK already had one or two crude nuclear weapons.

By year's end, the DPRK considered that it was no longer "completely" in the NPT but offered to return and accept at least one more inspection of its previously declared nuclear sites in return for a "package" of U.S.-offered concessions. Regarding inspections, the DPRK said the IAEA would first have to prove its "impartiality," presumably a reference to the IAEA's demand for special inspections. Since this demand had driven the DPRK out of the NPT, the North Korean offer seemed in no way to resolve the original problem.

The United States was impatient for results, and the Clinton administration appeared willing to allow North Korea to retain whatever nuclear weapons it already had in return for DPRK acceptance of a modified safeguards regime that would provide a fair chance of preventing the further diversion of domestically reprocessed plutonium.

Even the modest goal of achieving what Vice President Gore termed "some reasonable degree of certainty that [the North Koreans] are not making nuclear weapons" seemed elusive at the end of 1993. North Korea had found that the threat of nuclear weapons was a goose that might lay much-needed future golden eggs. Ironically, if inspections confirm that North Korea *has* been telling the truth and has not built nuclear weapons, North Korea will again face a bleak economic and political future with little hope of support from an indifferent world.

Notes

1. The following overview of North Korea's nuclear capability relies primarily on these sources:

Leonard S. Spector and Jacqueline R. Smith, "North Korea: The Next Nuclear Nightmare?" *Arms Control Today,* Vol. 21, No. 2 (March 1991), pp. 8–13.

Song Yong-sun, "North Korea's Potential to Develop Nuclear Weapons," *Vantage Point,* Vol. 14, No. 8 (August 1991), pp. 1–10.

Joseph S. Bermudez, Jr., "North Korea's Nuclear Program," *Jane's Intelligence Review,* September 1991, pp. 404–411.

Andrew Mack, "North Korea and the Bomb," *Foreign Policy,* No. 83, Fall 1991, pp. 87–104.

Kim Min-sok, "North Korea's Nukes—Their Urgent Examination," *Sindong-A,* July 1992, pp. 262–284; translated by the Foreign Broadcast Information Service, *Daily Report, East Asia (FBIS-EAS),* September 25, 1992, pp. 14–21.

Yu Yong-won, "Top Secret Intelligence—The Three Riddles of North Korea's Nuclear Facilities," *Wolgan Chosŏn,* August 1992, pp. 254–271; translated by *FBIS-EAS,* November 3, 1992, pp. 28–36.

2. This reactor has been rated by foreign observers as generating 30 MW of thermal power. Most experts would consider the reactor to be too large for "research" purposes and assume that its main purpose is the production of plutonium. See Yu Yong-won, "Top Secret Intelligence—The Three Riddles of North Korea's Nuclear Facilities."

3. *FBIS–EAS*, September 1, 1990, p. 29.

4. *Korean Report*, October 1990, p. 3.

5. Press statement issued by a North Korean Foreign Ministry spokesman, Pyong-yang, September 14, 1991; quoted by Pyongyang Central Broadcasting Network on the same date; cited in translation by *FBIS–EAS*, September 16, 1991, p. 10.

6. Yŏnhap News Service, Seoul, February 27, 1992; cited in *FBIS–EAS* on the same date, p. 19.

7. In 1992, the following inspections were conducted: (1) May 25 to June 6; (2) July 7 to 17; (3) August 31 to September 15; (4) November 2 to 15; and (5) December 14 to 21. As of July 1993, (6) January 1 to February 6.

8. Transcript from press briefing by Dr. Hans Blix, director general of the IAEA, Beijing Hotel, Beijing, May 16, 1992. The "laboratory" is the size of two football fields.

9. Lindsay Griffiths, "N.K. May Be Hiding Secrets: IAEA Chief," *Korea Herald*, July 24, 1992, p. 1.

10. The North Koreans themselves have admitted to discrepancies but claim that through discussion they can be resolved: "Of course, there are some problems yet to be solved by inspectors. However it is not 'inconsistency' as claimed by the agency side but a mistake coming from a hasty interpretation of the results of inspection not taking into detailed consideration the characteristic features of our facilities operation condition and nuclear activities." See "DPRK Ministry of Atomic Energy Industry Opens to Public Truth of Ad Hoc Inspection by IAEA," Korean Central News Agency (KCNA), February 21, 1993; cited by *FBIS–EAS*, February 22, 1993, p. 10. See also the North Korean report entitled "DPRK Ministry of Atomic Energy Issues Detailed Report on Problems in Implementation of Safeguards Agreement," KCNA, February 22, 1993; cited by *FBIS–EAS* on the same date, pp. 13–19.

R. Jeffrey Smith presented a detailed account of the discrepancies and the reasons the IAEA, acting on U.S. intelligence, suspects that two structures adjacent to the Yongbyon nuclear complex are undeclared nuclear waste disposal sites. "North Korea and the Bomb: High-Tech Hide-and-Seek," *Washington Post*, April 27, 1992, p. 1.

11. As reported by KBS-1 Television Network (Seoul), December 1, 1992; translated by *FBIS–EAS* on the same date, p. 19.

12. Smith, "North Korea and the Bomb."

13. "It is entirely unjustifiable for the IAEA to call for a 'special inspection' of the DPRK. It is because some quarters of the IAEA have complied with a [sic] false 'information' provided by the United States, bowing to pressure at expanding the inspection by the IAEA to military bases of the DPRK, which have nothing to do with nuclear activities and thus disarming the country." From KCNA, February 20, 1993; cited in *FBIS–EAS*, February 22, 1993, pp. 10–11.

14. See "DPRK Ministry of Atomic Energy Industry Opens to Public Truth."

15. "We Should Not Fall Prey to the Big Powers," *Rodong Sinmun* commentary of February 21, 1993; translated by *North Korea News*, March 1, 1993, pp. 3–4.

16. "DPRK Pulls Out of NPT Condemning U.S. N-War Threats and IAEA's Unjust Resolution: Statement of the DPRK Government," *People's Korea*, No. 1596, March 20, 1993, pp. 3–4.

17. For the English-language version, see "U.S. Pledges Non-Threat, Non-Use of Nuclear Force Against DPRK: Joint Statement," *People's Korea*, No. 1608, June 19, 1993, p. 1.

For the Korean-language version, see Pyongyang Central Broadcasting Network, June 12, 1993, translated by *FBIS–EAS,* June 14, 1993, p. 13.

18. Douglas Jehl, "North Korea Says It Won't Pull Out of Arms Pact Now," *New York Times,* June 12, 1993, p. 1.

19. "U.S. Pledges Non-Threat," p. 1.

20. However, the South Korean nuclear weapons program may have continued in secret until 1979. See "South Korea Planned Nuclear Weapons," *Jane's Defense Weekly,* Vol. 19, No. 9 (February 27, 1993), p. 6.

21. For North Korea's official view of South Korea's nuclear program, see the memorandum from its Foreign Ministry read on Pyongyang's Korean Central Broadcasting Network, January 30, 1993; translated by *FBIS–EAS,* February 1, 1993, pp. 10–16.

22. National Unification Board, *Intra-Korean Agreements* (Seoul: Republic of Korea, 1992), p. 49.

23. See, for example, Yi Kye-song and Sin Hyo-sop, the "Monday Forum" column in *Han'guk Ilbo,* June 8, 1992, p. 3; translated by *FBIS–EAS,* June 10, 1992, pp. 15–17.

24. President Clinton's appointee as CIA director, James Woolsey, during testimony before Congress in early 1993, weighed in with the opinion that there is a "real possibility that North Korea has already manufactured enough fissile material for at least one nuclear weapon and is hiding this from the IAEA." See U.S. Senate Governmental Affairs Committee Hearing, February 24, 1993; News Transcripts, Inc.

Estimates from the CIA and other U.S. governmental departments ebb and flow. In February 1992 Robert M. Gates, Woolsey's predecessor at the CIA, estimated that North Korea could have a nuclear weapon from within a few months to a couple of years. This pessimistic view was disputed by the State Department, which estimated that a North Korean bomb was at least two years away. See Elaine Sciolino, "U.S. Agencies Split over North Korea," *New York Times,* March 10, 1992, p. 1. Gates himself became less pessimistic in May 1992 after the IAEA inspections began.

25. Discussion of North Korea's nuclear motivations can be found in a variety of sources. See, for example, Kongdan Oh, "Nuclear Proliferation in North Korea," in W. Thomas Wander and Eric H. Arnett, Eds., *The Proliferation of Advanced Weaponry: Technology, Motivations, and Responses* (Washington, DC:. American Association for the Advancement of Science, 1992); Andrew Mack, "The Nuclear Crisis on the Korean Peninsula," *Asian Survey,* Vol. 33, No. 4 (April 1993), pp. 339–359.

26. See, for example, the severe critique of the IAEA made by Gary Milhollin, "The Iraqi Bomb," *New Yorker,* February 1, 1993, pp. 47–56.

27. In his congressional testimony, CIA Director Woolsey estimated that "more than 25 countries, many of them hostile to the U.S. and our friends and allies, may have or may be developing nuclear and biological and chemical weapons, so-called weapons of mass destruction, and the means to deliver them." U.S. Senate Governmental Affairs Committee Hearing, February 24, 1993.

PART FOUR

Future Prospects

14

Prospects for
Korean Reunification:
An Assessment

Young C. Kim

No longer does one risk becoming an object of ridicule or being labeled as suffering from delusion when speaking of a reunified Korea. It is even becoming fashionable to assume that reunification of Korea will occur in the near future. One of the leading 1992 presidential candidates in South Korea expressed his firm conviction to this author in the summer of 1992 that we will see a reunified Korea within five years.

Such beliefs are echoed by many Korean leaders in government, academia, and the mass media. Foreign observers, too, often express a similar belief. Zbigniew Brzezinski's prediction that reunification will take place before the end of this century is a case in point.

Recent revolutionary changes sweeping through the former Soviet Union and Eastern Europe appear to have profoundly shaped the perceptions and thinking of Korean affairs analysts. Everyone seems readier than before to concede that reunification is possible in the near future. The dominant scenario these analysts envisage is one involving the collapse of the North Korean regime along the lines of the collapse of Eastern Europe. Gone are the days when their dominant concern is a Korea reunified through North Korea's military conquest of the South. How realistic is this belief about an early disintegration of the North Korean regime leading to "reunification by absorption"? This chapter is an attempt to specify and assess the likelihood of a variety of scenarios leading to the reunification of Korea.

A conventional classification of various scenarios for reunification is based on the criterion of whether reunification occurs by war or by peaceful means. It is useful to keep two additional criteria or dimensions in mind: (1) whether the process of reunification is accompanied by domestic violence and (2) whether prior consent of the existing authorities was obtained. These dimensions often but not always overlap. If war is the means chosen by a party (either by the North or the South) to accomplish reunification, it is evident that such a case would be classified as not meeting either prior consent or the presence of domestic violence. A distinction is made here between war—which necessarily involves inter-Korea violence—and the case of reunification accompanied by domestic violence in either or both Koreas. Suppose one Korea's existing government is overthrown by force and the new revolutionary government agrees through negotiations to be merged or absorbed into the other Korea. Such a process of reunification may be characterized as one accompanied by domestic violence, not by war.

Type I: Reunification by War

There are two general variants of the war scenario. Type I(a) refers to a process whereby war is deliberately chosen from the beginning as the means to achieve reunification. Reunification by war was attempted by North Korea (1950–1953); had it been successful, the Korean War would have been a case in point of this strategy. The type I(b) scenario refers to those cases in which the use of force for limited objectives by paramilitary or regular units escalates into all-out war that leads to a reunified Korea. Several variations are conceivable:

In type I(b)(1), terrorist activities such as the Rangoon bombing or the KAL airliner bombing lead to retaliations by the South; the conflict escalates into a full-scale war that eventually culminates in a reunified Korea under the auspices of either Korea.

Unless terrorist acts are extraordinary in terms of scale or target, South Korea is unlikely to retaliate with military actions on a level that would lead to full-scale war between the two Koreas. This judgment is based on four assumptions, which seem warranted: First, the South Korean government will not have been taken over by militant, extreme right-wing forces. Second, South Korea will not face the magnitude of domestic instability that might predispose or compel the government to respond militarily to external events. Third, the international environment (particularly South Korea's relations with major powers) will continue to be perceived as hospitable to South Korea, thus raising the level of its tolerance for North Korea's provocations. Finally, the U.S. military presence will continue, albeit at a reduced level, and the United States will exert a constraining influence.

In a second variation of the escalation scenario, Type I(b)(2), North Korea's military operations are aimed at occupation of a limited portion of South Korea's territory (e.g., five islands off the west coast); the action provokes full-scale war that results in a reunified Korea by either Korea.

This scenario poses the hypothetical situation of North Korea first successfully occupying a part of South Korean territory (whether the islands, the area north of Seoul, or even Seoul), then stopping military operations and calling for a cease-fire. Some Korean analysts assume the United States might be inclined to explore the possibility of a negotiated settlement rather than commit to war automatically. However, North Korea is more likely to opt for a blitz-krieg type of all-out war rather than to halt after the capture of a part of South Korean territory. In any event, it is a virtual certainty that South Korea would respond militarily and that the conflict would lead to all-out war.

In the type I(b)(3) scenario, North Korea's imminent success in developing a nuclear weapons capability prompts South Korea to undertake preemptive strikes against North Korea's targets; this action in turn leads to war resulting in a reunified Korea. In a slight variation of this, North Korea suddenly announces its successful development of nuclear weapons, and subsequent military action by South Korea and/or the United States leads to full-scale war and eventual reunification by either side.

Of these two variations, the former (facilities suspected) presents greater probability of preventive strikes than the latter (weapons capabilities confirmed). However, in either case the probability of the use of force to destroy North Korea's nuclear facilities by either the United States or South Korea is low. This conclusion is based on the following assessments: First, such a military action would be certain to provoke North Korea's military operations against South Korea and lead to all-out war. The South Korean government would be opposed to the use of force against North Korean nuclear facilities for that reason and would instead opt to seek its own nuclear weapons capability. Second, because of domestic constraints and likely adverse international repercussions, the U.S. administration would probably lack the political will to initiate military attacks on North Korean targets.

In any event, the type I(b)(3) scenario presupposes that IAEA inspections of North Korea's nuclear facilities proved inadequate and further that bilateral inspections between the North and South—even if agreed upon and implemented—also were insufficient to detect or prevent North Korea's clandestine development of nuclear arms capabilities.

Type II: Reunification by Mutual Consent

The premise in type II scenarios is that reunification is brought about by prior consent of the existing authorities in North and South. The process comes closest to what is conventionally called peaceful reunification and is to be distinguished from scenarios involving war or substantial domestic violence. There are three subtypes.

In type II(a), both parties agree in advance on the procedure whereby reunification is to be achieved. For example, by mutual consent a joint committee is established to draft a constitution, and the formula for unification is accepted by the existing authorities. An example of such a formula might be general nationwide elections based on population to elect a chief executive and/or to compose a national assembly. In any event, the emergence of a single state under international law is envisaged.

The type II(b) scenario involves both parties agreeing to establish a confederation in the technical sense of the term but to call it a reunified Korea. Two constituent parts would exercise all the rights normally given to sovereign states under international law. However, as a symbol of a "unified nation," an all-Korean council composed of the representatives of both sides may be set up.

In type II(c), the government of one side agrees to be integrated into the political system of the other. For example, an extralegal seizure of power might occur in either part of Korea—necessarily involving substantial violence— and be followed within a relatively short time by a decision of the new revolutionary government to accept reunification of a type posed in scenarios II(a) or II(b). (If either side decides to take advantage of a revolutionary situation on the other side and resorts to military operations, it would be a variation of type I.)

One manifestation of the type II(c) scenario might involve the process of a so-called southern revolution that results in the establishment of a people's government, which subsequently accepts essentially the terms of reunification offered by North Korea. A comparable case would be the emergence of a new North Korean political leadership—for instance, one dominated by a coalition of technocrats, moderate pragmatic party leaders, and a segment of the military—that would lead to North Korea's acceptance of reunification by consent of type II(a) or II(b). A similar variation involves the establishment of a new government in the South formed by a new party or coalition of parties in accordance with existing constitutional procedures and the subsequent acceptance by the new government of reunification by consent of type II(a) or II(b).

The probability of an extraconstitutional transfer of power in North Korea such as a military coup is very low. A number of factors are likely to sustain the current leadership and the system of elite recruitment and transformation: over four decades of intensive political indoctrination; an elaborate system of controls of the entire society through a mixture of reward and punishment; and the presence of elites with sufficient resources, vested interests, perceived threat to their common interests, and a sense of solidarity.

The scenario involving a southern revolution is of course the one the orthodox doctrine of the North Korean regime has long called for. The underlying assumptions are that (1) the discontent in the South would erupt into a serious political crisis; (2) the South Korean government would be unable to cope with the magnitude of turmoil effectively and in a timely fashion; (3) the counterelite would successfully carry out a revolution in which the existing political elite is overthrown and replaced by forces favorable to the interests of workers and peasants; and (4) the new people's government would then accept North Korean terms for unification, thus realizing "peaceful unification."

Assumptions two through four seem unwarranted. It is true that South Korea has been subjected to a series of serious political crises, including instances of coups d'état during the past several decades. However, a revolution led by left-wing forces has not taken place, and it is highly unlikely that one will occur in the midrange period. Note the demonstrated capacity of the South Korean government to withstand and manage major crises, as it did in

1979 after the assassination of President Park and in 1987 during the transition from President Chun to President Roh.

The formation of a confederation of the kind described under the type II(b) scenario is akin to the one that has long been advocated by North Korea, although specific details have varied over the years. If the North Korean proposal in effect envisages the existence of two independent sovereign states under international law as a transition phase, its feasibility does not pose a major problem because it would then depend on affirmative action by South Korea. A new government in South Korea may emerge in the midrange period to accept essentially such a system of confederation.

South Korea may even be willing to call it "Yŏnbangje" in Korean, an expression the North Koreans are fond of using but one that has long been politically taboo in South Korea. The South Korean government could at the same time claim that such a confederal system is virtually identical with a system of commonwealth—an interim stage of its own formula of "national community reunification"—that could lead to eventual integration of the two political systems of North and South.

The emergence of a "pragmatic/moderate" leadership in North Korea would facilitate movement toward constitution engineering and unification by consent (type II(a)), but the probability of such a development occurring in North Korea is small.

Type III: Reunification by Default

Type III reunification, which has three subtypes, entails collapse of the regime of one side when it becomes unable to perform the most essential government functions; the disintegration enables the other side to extend effective control to the collapsing side. The basic scenario is to be distinguished from type I in which absorption by the other side involves at some point the use of military means. It is also to be distinguished from type II in which consent is given by the existing government of the side being absorbed. The type III scenario involves what is popularly known as unification by absorption—the pattern occurring in Eastern Europe.

In some cases involving a regime on the verge of collapse, the existing government may successfully resort to violence to suppress the would-be counterelite. Or there may be cases when an attempt at suppression fails and the counterelite emerges to form a new government, which in turn initiates a policy of reunification of either type I or II.

The absorption scenario cited most often, type III(a), foresees a serious economic dislocation in North Korea involving acute and widespread shortages of food and other basic necessities of life. The result would be a severe loss of legitimacy in the political system and the leadership. Many manifestations of nationwide turmoil—riots, demonstrations, strikes, and other forms of illegitimate collective behavior—would occur with increasing frequency and intensity, but the government would be unable to manage the crisis because of lack of political will. Under the circumstances, acts of open rebellion would accelerate the breakdown of the semblance of public order, and a mass exodus of

North Koreans into South Korea would follow. The disintegration of the political system in the North thus would pave the way for the South to extend its system to the North by default.

The type III(b) scenario—which is suggested sometimes in conjunction with or independently of grave economic crisis—emphasizes the adverse impact of political succession on political stability. According to this view, President Kim Il Sung's demise would be followed by the highly unstable coercive rule of his son, Kim Jong Il. Many analysts argue that with the charisma, legitimacy, and authority of the senior Kim gone, and given the inexperience and limited capabilities of the successor and his close associates, North Korea would enter a period of turbulence, repression, unpredictability, and intense power struggle. A dominant view among Korean analysts is that Kim Jong Il would be incapable of maintaining the present regime for any length of time. The view also holds that he would be susceptible to pursuing adventurous policies toward the South and his rule would eventually cause massive economic and societal dislocations, resulting in extensive repression and the ultimate disintegration of his system of rule.

The type III(c) variation of the scenario leading to reunification by default is that North Korea may be compelled to subject its society to corrosive external influences as it pursues a policy of economic reforms and foreign economic interactions. Foreign ideas and practices and information about the reality of the external world would be certain to undermine the legitimacy of the regime, eventually contributing to the disintegration of the present political system.

What are the chances that reunification by default will occur in the mid-range? For several reasons, the probability of any of the three subtypes materializing is low. First, despite the severity of the economic situation, North Korea will have resources available to provide the minimum level of basic necessities for the people. (It bears noting that the threshold at which popular discontent might explode into an uprising is probably higher than Western analysts think.) Second, the various mechanisms of control exercised by the authorities will be effective in neutralizing manifestations of illegitimacy. Third, the myth surrounding the leadership and the regime will not ebb because it is sustained by prolonged indoctrination and the demonstrated performance of socialist construction in the eyes of the North Korean people. Fourth, the will of the leadership to safeguard the existing regime at all costs will remain undiminished, and it will not hesitate to use all instruments of power to avert absorption by the South. It would be unrealistic to expect the North Korean leadership to replicate the behavior its East European counterparts showed during the process of disintegration of their political power.

The fifth factor relates to an assumption underlying the anticipated fragility of the Kim Jong Il regime: that unlike his father, the junior Kim does not enjoy legitimacy or support among the elites as well as the people. This view underestimates the result of meticulous planning and preparation extending over a twenty-year period that the North Korean leadership undertook to install Kim Jong Il as successor to President Kim Il Sung. When this is compounded by the elaborate system of controls at the junior Kim's disposal, his capacity for survival following his father's death will be considerably greater than Western analysts are prepared to concede. In the long run, his performance will affect whatever level of legitimacy he enjoys in the eyes of power elites and in turn presumably have a bearing on his durability.

Even if Kim Jong Il's rule is overthrown, that would not necessarily signify the collapse of a North Korean regime. The new leadership may be able to sustain North Korea as a separate entity.

It will be recalled that one scenario envisions North Korea pursuing a policy of opening and reforms, thereby exposing itself to a destabilizing impact from without. The North Korean leadership is indeed acutely aware of such a danger of contamination and therefore has been and will remain extremely cautious with regard to both the types and the speed of foreign involvement to be allowed. However, one must recognize that once foreign influences begin penetrating into North Korean society, their corrosive impact would come in greater degree and at greater speed than anticipated by North Korean planners. The North Korean leadership must adapt its system flexibly to the new social forces, or it is likely to face major manifestations of illegitimacy, which would contribute to the process of disintegration of power.

Probability Assessment

Of the various scenarios leading to a reunified Korea reviewed in this chapter, reunification by mutual consent (type IIb) would be the easiest to attain, but it would not necessarily be most likely in the short run. In the midterm, trends in the domestic and international environment may induce greater realism, enabling the leadership of both Koreas to accept a confederal arrangement but to claim the semblance of a reunified Korea in form. The ideological and political ingredients to such a course have been gradually losing ground.

The scenarios regarding reunification by war appear least likely of all the scenarios examined. The scenarios leading to reunification by default—collapse of the North Korean regime followed by absorption of the North by the South—are only slightly likely. As compared with reunification by war, reunification by default is relatively more likely. However, if it occurs, it is likely to be transformed into reunification by war, thus elevating the likelihood of reunification by war to slightly likely.

15

The Lessons of United Germany for Divided Korea

Sung Chul Yang

This chapter first identifies some problems and difficulties stemming from the swift realization of united Germany. Korea, still a divided land, should maximize the so-called advantages of the latecomer by learning from the German experiences and encounters. Next, on the basis of the German experience, a new approach to the Korean question is proposed here as an alternative to the currently existing official and unofficial models and formulas for Korean unification.

Learning from German Unification

Contrasts and Similarities

Before the problems and pitfalls of German unification are identified and examined briefly, a few salient differences between the former two Germanys and the two Koreas are worth noting. Two propositions can be formulated for clarifying the present discussion. First, it is posited here that both Kim Il Sung of North Korea and Fidel Castro of Cuba, the two last remaining communist revolutionary dinosaurs,[1] will not be exceptions to the general trend of communist demise.

Second, South Korea may face a similar situation to that of West Germany, both controllable and uncontrollable, if the one-party father-son regime in

This chapter is a condensed and revised version of Sung Chul Yang, "United Germany for Divided Korea: Learning from Euphoria and Dysphoria," *Korea and World Affairs,* Vol. 16, No. 3 (Fall 1992), pp. 436–462. Used with permission of *Korea and World Affairs.*

North Korea collapses. The question, then, immediately arises: Is South Korea, like West Germany, politically stable and secure, economically strong and sound, and socially fair and equitable enough to absorb North Korea? The answer is more likely to be in the negative. South Korea is not West Germany. Nor is North Korea East Germany, for that matter. The reality of their internal political and economic conditions and the complexity of their external relations and alliances are sharply contrasting.

The Federal Republic of Germany (FRG), or West Germany, is a decentralized federal government founded by local governments (*Laenders*). Furthermore, the rise in popularity of federalism over centralism has been impressive.[2] By contrast, the Republic of Korea (ROK), or South Korea, is a highly centralized typical unitary government. The ROK's central government is wrestling with the timetable of when and how to form local governments. The local and provincial legislative assemblies have been formed and in operation only since 1991. In short, West Germany has had (and the current unified Germany has) a firmly rooted local autonomy, but South Korea has just begun its political experiments of local autonomy.[3]

Above all, the FRG has been one of the most stable and efficient democratic nations in the postwar world. Thus far, it has experienced two interparty transfers of power—from the Christian Democratic Union (CDU) coalition to the Social Democratic Party (SPD) coalition in 1969 and from the SPD coalition back to the one led by the CDU and the CSU (Christian Social Union) in 1982. During this period, the FRG had five presidents and thirteen cabinets of which eight were formed by CDU-led coalitions and five by SPD-led coalitions.[4]

By contrast, the ROK has been marked by political instability during the same period. It had six republics with nine constitutional revisions, not to mention two military coups (1961 and 1979), three major student and popular uprisings (1960, 1980, and 1986) and twelve declarations of martial laws and emergency decrees. Since its founding, the ROK has experienced only two peaceful transfers of power—in 1988 and 1993. Even then, the power succession did not occur between parties but only within a ruling party. Thus, South Korea has yet to experience a peaceful transfer of power from the ruling party to an opposition party. All in all, South Korea is in the midst of an early phase of democratization at best, or it is still being plagued by political instability and infantile political paralysis.[5]

Noteworthy also is the fact that West Germany is a typical cabinet-responsible system, whereas South Korea's Sixth Republic is a presidential system. The West German legislature is bicameral, the Bundestag and the Bundesrat, that of South Korea is unicameral, the National Assembly. The powers and authority of German local governments are strong and growing, but the newly created South Korean local assemblies are inherently weak. They are dependent upon and subject to the control of the central government.[6] Worse, former President Roh in 1992 unilaterally postponed the mayoral and the provincial gubernatorial elections until 1995. In fact, this move violated the local autonomy laws that, among other things, prescribed such elections by June 1992.

The FRG's and the ROK's legal or constitutional provisions for unification, too, are in stark contrast. The FRG's basic law was temporary in nature, as its preamble stipulates: "desiring to give a new order to political life *for a transitional period,* has enacted, by virtue of its constituent power, this Basic Law of the Federal Republic of Germany." The irony is that the FRG's basic law has remained virtually intact (albeit with two revisions over forty years) despite its "transitional" character, whereas the ROK's constitution, its seemingly permanent nature notwithstanding, was revised nine times with six substantial changes.

The FRG's basic law had two legal provisions enabling unification (articles 23 and 146); the ROK's current constitution has six provisions dealing with unification. Unlike the West German law, however, the South Korean constitution claims the territory covering both the present South Korea and North Korea (article 3). Most important, not only the German framers of the basic law but also key political leaders placed the task of national unity above and before politics. German politicians of both the ruling and opposition parties seldom resorted to the basic law as an instrument of perpetuating or strengthening their partisan power. By contrast, South Korean politicians have often misused or abused the constitution as if it were a personal political tool to rationalize or perpetuate their power.[7]

Glaring differences in international and external dimensions also exist between Germany and Korea. For example, the German people did not experience the fratricidal proxy war in the early 1950s that victimized the Korean people and others. As a result, the Korean people both in the North and the South still have a deep-seated and lingering mutual distrust; similar feelings are virtually absent in the minds of the German people.

Germany's center-stage position also contrasts sharply with Korea's peripheral—or, at best, middle-power—status: Germany, the claimant of the traditional Mittel Europa, the principal actor ("culprit") of both World Wars, and the main locomotive of European integration; Korea, the principal victim of the Sino-Japanese (1894–1895) and the Russo-Japanese (1904–1905) wars, World War II, the Korean War, and even the Cold War.

In post–World War II alliance and integration frameworks, Germany has been involved in multilateral arrangements such as the North Atlantic Treaty Organization (NATO), the European Community (EC), and the Conference on Security and Cooperation in Europe (CSCE). In contrast, South Korea's security alliances and external relations have been primarily bilateral—for example, the 1954 U.S.-ROK mutual defense treaty. In recent years, some multilateral arrangements have been in the offing, but they are still embryonic. The launching of the Asia-Pacific Economic Cooperation (APEC) group and the proposal of the Conference on Security and Cooperation in Asia (CSCA), as a counterpart of the CSCE, are cases in point.[8]

The economic dimensions of the former FRG vis-à-vis the former German Democratic Republic (GDR) and of South Korea vis-à-vis North Korea seem to resemble each other on the surface, but at a closer look their differences are more glaring than the similarities. Before unification, the size of the FRG economy in terms of GNP was about ten times greater than that of the GDR economy. According to the federal government's statistical office, in the last half of 1990, that is, the first six months after unification, East German GNP was estimated at 105.3 billion deutsche marks (DM) ($60.2 billion), whereas West German GNP was approximately DM 1.28 trillion. Thus, East German economic size was only 8.3 percent of West German.[9] Meanwhile, it was reported that South Korean GNP ($237.9 billion) in 1990 was roughly nine to ten times bigger than North Korean GNP ($23.1 billion).[10]

The similarities between the two nations, however, end quickly there. Structurally, the Federal Republic is one of the fully developed and leading high-tech nations; South Korea is a mid-tech newly industrializing country at best, and its 1990 per capita income of $5,569 was still one-third or one-fourth the size of the advanced nations. For example, workers in the FRG have had the right to participate in and organize political parties from the inception of the country. Furthermore, the 1951 law on worker participation stipulated workers' right to equal representation in industrial management, although it was limited to coal and steel industries. A new law passed in March 1976 provided equal representation of workers on workers' councils in all large-scale companies, although representation of shareholders remains dominant in the event of a conflict. As early as 1957, provisions of the pension law tied pension increases to wage increases, and the five-day-forty-hour workweek has now been achieved.[11] In this area and in other social and economic egalitarian measures, the Federal Republic is substantially ahead of South Korea.

The FRG-GDR treaty on economic, monetary, and social union, which was signed May 18 and implemented July 1, 1990, is one primary example. The economic union reaffirmed the Federal Republic's social market economy (*soziale Markwirtschaft*). The specific elements included private property, the free market system, principles of economic competition, introduction of free commerce and industry, free movement of goods, capital, and labor, and introduction of tax, finance, and budget systems compatible with the free market system. Stipulations in the monetary union included the DM as the official currency, the Federal Republic's Deutsche Bundesbank as the only official central bank, and a differential exchange rate of DM for OM (ostmark). For example, a one-to-one ratio was applied to wages, salaries, pensions, monthly rent, and scholarships. The same ratio was applied to individual savings up to a certain amount (OM 2,000 for those fifteen years old or younger, OM 4,000 for ages sixteen to sixty, and OM 6,000 for those sixty or older). A ratio of two OM to one DM was applied to all other monetary claims except debts.

Most important, the social union meant the GDR's wholesale adoption of the Federal Republic's social measures, including its pension, health, unemployment, and accident insurance systems and the low-income assistance programs. In addition, the GDR was compelled to adopt the FRG's far superior social measures and programs for its workers—the autonomy of worker-management, collective bargaining, the right to organize, the management of strikes, the practice of codetermination, democracy within industry, and the law to prohibit arbitrary dismissal.[12]

Can South Korea offer North Korea such social measures as the FRG's, which were attractive and sound enough to absorb the GDR's system? Unfortunately, at the present time, the answer cannot be in the affirmative.

German Unification: From Euphoria to Dysphoria

On October 3, 1990, divided German states were reunited. Of three major divided states in the aftermath of World War II, Vietnam (by force) and Germany (by political settlement) have been reunified; only Korea remains divided with much rancor and little reconciliation.

"The German people are the happiest people in the world!" This remark was made by the mayor of West Berlin at the mass rally on November 10, 1989, one day after the Berlin Wall was removed. The German people's euphoria reached its height on October 3, 1990, when two Germanys were reunited after forty-five years of externally imposed partition. In a way, unification is like a marriage. After the excitement of premarital courtship, formal engagement, marriage ceremony, and honeymoon, the real life of the newlyweds must begin. The real life, however, is unlike the honeymoon, which was filled with honey and happiness. It often requires trials and hardship. In a similar vein, the preunification euphoria could not and would not last forever. The German people came to the realization soon into the postunification period that in the short run at least, the cost of unification, both monetary and mental, far outweighs its benefits. As Edward Roby pointed out, things are likely to get worse before they get better: The economies, life-styles, and mentalities of the two regions have not yet grown together, and the rebuilding of the GDR's decrepit transportation, telecommunications, and governmental infrastructure alone will cost more than half a trillion deutsche marks in coming years.[13] Thus, preunification euphoria has been quickly replaced by postunification dysphoria. The political and economic union was relatively quick and easy, but what German President Richard von Weisaecker called the "human union" will be harder to achieve.[14] Stephen Kinzer reported that when Germans talk of bringing the two sides of their country to economic equality, they speak in terms of years, but when asked how long it will take to achieve "inner unity," they often speak of generations. A Leipzig University professor's lament quoted by Kinzer is noteworthy in this connection:

> Not only did their [people in eastern Germany] political system change completely, but so did the material basis of their lives—administrative structures, social relationships, self-image, the meaning of their past, their present and their future, and with it the very point of their existence. Even the familiar smells of their homeland are different, from cleaning fluids to gasoline. With unification came not only a falling away of everything familiar, but also implantation in a completely new world.[15]

Only fools would have believed, of course, there could be painless birth of a united state out of a long and mutually hostile and separated existence. Still, the costs and pangs of German unification have turned out to be far more serious than expected. In mid-1992, Chancellor Helmut Kohl acknowledged that the economic upswing in the former East Germany would take longer and cost more than he originally thought: "Many expectations have been filled in this time, but there have also been disappointments and setbacks. ... Some things will take longer than we assumed in the autumn of 1990, and transfer of payments from West to East are higher."[16] To save space, it suffices to list some of the salient problems that united Germany is confronting.

1. There is an exorbitant unification cost,[17] including the Federal Republic's subsidy for the withdrawal of Soviet troops and their dependents from the former GDR (370,000 troops and 230,000 dependents). For example, outstanding German public-sector debt in 1991 was DM 1.2 trillion, 46 percent of GNP. It could soar to DM 1.8 trillion (over 51 percent of GNP) by 1995. West German transfer of money to the eastern sector in 1991 was DM 170 billion, and in 1992 the transfers were around DM 212 billion with DM 35 billion paid in eastern taxes. The net shift, thus, was DM 180 billion—more than 6 percent of GNP, or roughly a quarter of total public spending.[18]

2. The process of economic adjustment is slow—both to privatize some 45,000 decaying communist factories and faltering businesses in eastern Germany by Treuhandanstalt, the German state-run privatization agency, in particular and to transform a state-planned economy into a market economy in general.[19]

3. East German workers face worsening unemployment. For example, unemployment in western Germany rose to 7 percent in January 1992 from 6.5 percent in December of the previous year; unemployment in eastern Germany bolted to 17 percent from 11.8 percent during the same period.[20]

4. Another concern is the treatment of the East German secret police (Stasi) and its informants (according to one source, there are 4,000 spies in the NATO member nations and 85,000 formal employees and thousands of unknown informants). A more general problem is the restructuring (dismantling) of the former East German political system. The remarks of Joachim Lehmann, a Lutheran clergyman in eastern Germany, are illustrative:

> I have never lived in freedom. Never before have I been allowed to say what I believed. Like all citizens of East Germany, I lived a schizophrenic life. There are certain things you could say only at home, and then very different things you had to say at school or at work. My parents taught me to live that way, and that's what I taught my kids. In East Germany, life consisted mainly of waiting to be told what to do, and then doing it. I'm never going to be able to break away from this conditioning. I will always be an Ossie—an easterner. Maybe my children will be able to adjust to the new situation. But only the generation of my grandson, who is now one year old, will grow up like normal Germans and Europeans. ... Naturally I want to see evil people punished, but why focus on every Stasi informer and forget the party officials? If we can put the whole politburo and regime on trial, then I'd be for it. ... You can't just be a revolutionary for 40 or 50 years. You have to live with the power structure and that means compromising. ... People desperately want this moment, unification, to end well. I believe it will. We're dis-

appointed with some things, but at heart we're satisfied. I've never met anyone who wants to go back to the old days.[21]

5. Deportation of foreign workers in the former East Germany (estimated to be around 100,000, including some 50,000 Vietnamese workers) is an issue. Worse, the flow of refugees, including asylum seekers and ethnic Germans, which in 1991 was running at 1,600 a day, poses a serious problem.

6. An overburdened and understaffed bureaucracy must handle property claims, the GDR's national debts, and industries' liabilities. For example, there were 40,000 claims on 16,000 properties in Leipzig alone.

7. Efforts must be made to narrow the language differences between the two Germanys.

8. There is concern about upward inflationary pressure and downward economic growth. *The Economist* (May 2, 1992), for example, reported that Germany's trade deficits for the preceding twelve months amounted to $23.3 billion, but signs of favorable trade balance were evident. So was its GNP improving after the negative growth rate in 1991. Its unemployment rate is also steady at 6.2 percent.

9. An intractable task is to narrow the significant differences in both Germanys' wage, pension, and living standards in particular and quality of life in general. For example, in 1991 western Germany's 61 million people enjoyed a GDP per person of DM 38,000 ($23,500) a year; the figure for their 17 million eastern brethren was only DM 13,000.[22] In addition, there were disparate average monthly wages for postal workers ($2,317 west, $1,390 east), bus drivers ($2,378 west, $1,464 east), and white-collar workers ($3,219 west, $1,290 east). In other words, postal workers or bus drivers in the East earn just 60 percent of what their western counterparts make. Pensions are also unequal—retired people in the East receive about one-third less than those in the West. The German government plans to equalize wages and pensions by the end of the 1990s.[23] The west German workers also feel economically pinched. The public-sector strikes that began April 27, 1992, were the first of their kind in nearly twenty years. Roughly 100,000 workers in transport, postal, and refuse-collection services began the action demanding a pay raise of 9.5 percent.[24]

10. There is the so-called mental disunity between East and West Germans—the easterners' mental depression and feeling of being second-class citizens in united Germany. As already noted, the political and economic changes of reunification are insufficient to repair the psychic damage done by forty years of socialism. According to one report, nine of every ten easterners feel they have second-class status in the united country.[25]

11. A major problem is air, water, and soil pollution in eastern Germany. For example, dirty brown coal has provided 70 percent of its primary energy needs and 85 percent of its electricity.[26]

The postunification elections have in fact evinced the German people's changing mood. West Germans are angry and weary of their increasing monetary and social burden, and easterners are frustrated by their relative misery and misfortunes. In the all-German election on December 2, 1990, the CDU-

TABLE 15.1   German Party Seat Distribution, December 2, 1990, General Election

Party	Seats
CDU	268
CSU	50
FDP	79
Total government coalition	397
SPD	239
Greens (eastern)	8
Former Communists	17
Independent	1
Total	662

CSU coalition obtained 43.8 percent of the vote, a slight increase over the results of the 1987 general election (42.3 percent). The opposition SPD, on the other hand, received only 33.5 percent of the vote, a significant loss as compared with 1987 results (37.0 percent). The Free Democratic Party (FDP) acquired 79 seats in the Bundestag (for distribution of party seats, see Table 15.1).

After the December general election, however, the CDU-CSU coalition lost in the various local elections. It lost not only in Schleswig-Holstein, Lower Saxony, and Hesse but also in such traditionally CDU-CSU strongholds as Rhineland-Palatinate. As of 1992, the SPD controlled 10 out of 16 *Laenders,* and the CDU-CSU holds a majority only in two *Laenders*—Bavaria and Baden-Wuertemberg. In Hamburg on June 2, 1991, the SPD took 48 percent of the vote, a 3 percent gain over the 1987 election; the CDU received only 35.1 percent of the vote as compared with 40.5 percent it garnered in 1987. Of the 121 total seats in the Hamburg parliament, the SPD took 61 (previously 55), the CDU 44 (49), the FDP 7 (8), and the Greens 9 (8). Technically, Kohl's chancellorship can last until 1994, but his coalition may collapse suddenly, depending on political developments in united Germany. One thing is clear, nevertheless. Helmut Kohl, like Mikhail Gorbachev, has already secured a high place in history as a statesman who successfully led and realized the unification of Germany, but again like Gorbachev, Kohl too can be a victim of his own political success. History is fair in the end, but people are inherently gullible and politics is thus fickle.

A New Approach to Korean Unification

In the light of the foregoing brief accounts of German unification experiences, what can the Korean people and the South Korean government do specifically in realizing the united country?

First, in dealing with North Korea, an interest-based bargaining strategy instead of the heretofore used position-based strategy needs to be adopted. The interest-based bargaining strategy, predicated upon four basic objectives, employs a much different set of negotiating behaviors that are nonadversarial and mutually supportive. Its elements are (1) attempts to separate the people involved in the negotiation from the problem the process is intended to resolve; (2) parties who focus their attention on the interests brought to the negotiation by each side and not on the positions of each player; (3) participants who work together to devise options that might represent mutually satisfying solutions; and (4) negotiators who agree to employ objective criteria in their decisionmaking.[27]

Second, in South Korea's use of policymaking as a tool to create regional and global environments conducive to the ultimate realization of united Korea, both the creative foreign policy model[28] and the middle-power role model[29] can be fully utilized. For example, in their case analysis of determinants of creativity in foreign policy, Sylvan, Voss, and Beasley found the tendency among foreign policy scholars and the psychologists "to attribute creativity to individuals rather than groups."[30] This finding about individual creativity is not a new discovery but a reconfirmation. According to their preliminary hypothesis, "the presence of a group leader, open discussion, contingency planning and the freedom from formally mandated group support as a prerequisite for a decision are more likely to foster creativity in foreign policy."[31] This premise is relevant to my proposal that South Korea should adopt a new approach to North Korea and the four powers in the region.

Likewise, South Korea fits the concept of middle-power leadership, which Cooper and Higgot conceptualized as a three-stage pattern: (1) entrepreneurial leadership, in which the middle power's role is as a catalyst providing the intellectual and political energy to trigger an initiative with respect to a diplomatic effort; (2) agenda setting, which entails the role of facilitator for some form of collaborative or coalitional activity (organizing and hosting formative meetings, setting priorities for future activities, drafting declarations, and so on); and (3) institution building, in which the actor functions as manager in creating formal organizations and regimes and developing conventions and norms. Central to institution building is a work program that includes a division of labor, the development of monitoring activity, and possibly but not necessarily the establishment of a secretariat or bureaucracy. This managerial stage also requires the development of confidence-building measures and facilities for dispute resolution as means through which trust and credibility are built up and misunderstandings and misperceptions alleviated; techniques include liaison efforts, shuttle diplomacy, the use of alternative formal and informal forums, the creation of transparency, and other means to push a given process forward.[32]

From a somewhat different perspective, Stephen Walker conceptualized diverse foreign policy roles—conciliationist, mediator, recruiter/promoter[33]—that are also pertinent to the new approach I am proposing here. Namely, South Korea's creative leadership role as a catalyst, a facilitator, a manager, a conciliationist, and a promoter in building a common peace and prosperity in the region cannot be overemphasized. Of significance is that U.S. policymakers and Asian specialists have failed to see the potential implications of South Korea assuming such a role, although they have acknowledged the political and economic success story of South Korea and other Asian countries in the region.[34]

Nevertheless, two trilateral alliance systems—North Korea vis-à-vis the former Soviet Union and the People's Republic of China, and South Korea vis-à-vis the United States and Japan, both of which have been functioning on the Korean peninsula since World War II—are in the process of rapid transformation and reformulation. South Korea's Nordpolitik has been successful on the whole in this regard, and North Korea, too, though belatedly and reluctantly, began to follow suit under the garb of its own Sudpolitik.[35]

Third, it is posited here that the Korean unification process can be divided into three aspects: the uncontrollable, the controllable, and the mixture of the two. If uncontrollable, deliberate efforts and preparations, including preventive measures, should be made to respond to and minimize negative consequences resulting from unanticipated political events.

If controllable, two main tasks must be pursued relentlessly. One is comprehensive research and planning to deal with the "deconstruction" of North Korea's father-son communist totalitarian system. The other is in-depth study and preparation for "deprogramming" the North Korean people's brainwashed mind-set. In addition, the German unification process should be intensively and extensively studied to minimize the negative consequences and problems of Korean unification and maximize its comparable benefits and positive outcomes.

If the unification process is under control, three prerequisites must also be satisfied. First, the full and uninhibited inspection of North Korean nuclear facilities, sites, and materials by the International Atomic Energy Agency (IAEA) and the simultaneous mutual inspections (including short-notice challenge inspections) by North Korean and South Korean teams as agreed upon by the December 1991 denuclearization declaration must be realized. South Korea has proposed four regular and twelve special inspections per year for each party. Up to fifty-six sites in each Korea would be covered. The inspecting party would unilaterally initiate the special inspections, giving the host government twenty-four hours' notice and a schedule of sites six hours prior to inspection. South Korea has also called for the installation of sealed surveillance equipment at sites.[36]

In addition, if suspected nuclear reprocessing plants or nuclear materials are uncovered, they must be removed, destroyed, or dismantled.[37] North Korea must also halt the sale of ballistic missiles, especially to Middle Eastern countries, and eventually abandon missile development projects, including the so-called No-Dong 1, a liquid fuel missile believed to have a range of more than 600 miles.[38]

Several points are in order in this regard. Ever since North Korea's nuclear issue became Korean and international concerns, Kim Il Sung has steadfastly upheld the position that "North Korea has neither intentions nor capabilities of developing nuclear weapons." But in April and May 1992 when the IAEA inspections of North Korean nuclear facilities and sites became inevitable, North Korea, through various official channels, began to acknowledge that "a little bit of plutonium for experimental purposes" had been extracted at a "radiochemical laboratory" at Yongbyon—the facility cited in U.S. intelligence estimates as a likely plutonium reprocessing plant. But news reporting about the Yongbyon facilities was rather conflicting, if not confusing. On the one hand, it was reported that the facilities were "extremely primitive" and "a long way from being finished," although they fit "the definition of a reprocessing plant," which appeared to be about 80 percent complete.[39] Countering Blix's estimate, Gary Milhollin, for example, contended in his *New York Times* column that "North Korea now has enough nuclear weapon materials for six to eight atomic bombs."[40] In March 1992, the Russian newspaper *Arguments and Facts* reprinted a classified KGB report of February 1990 to the Soviet Communist Party Central Committee that according to a reliable source, "the first North Korean atomic explosive device has been completed ... in the city of Yongbyon."[41]

In sum, it looks as though the IAEA is more concerned about potential North Korean nuclear disasters (such as the 1986 Chernobyl incident in the USSR) stemming from the mishandling of its rather primitive facilities, whereas the United States is very suspicious of its crude bomb-making. But the Korean people will be the primary victims of either a nuclear accident or a bomb. What can be done if North Korea does not fully satisfy either the IAEA investigations or the South Korean, U.S., and Japanese demands? Above all, close coordination and concerted actions of South Korea, the United States, and Japan are vital in persuading or coercing North Korea to comply with such demands. Essential is an adroit and sophisticated use of both carrots and sticks, rewards and punishments, and persuasion and coercion. The UNDP (United Nations Development Program) Tumen River delta project and North Korea's urgent need for better and new relations with and economic aid from South Korea, Japan, and the United States are some positive enticements. For example, Li Sam-ro, chief of the North Korean delegation to the Pyongyang-Tokyo normalization negotiations, reportedly stated that his government would accept inter-Korean inspection because it had signed a joint declaration. Further, he remarked that "if the United States supports Korean reunification, and if it continues to argue about North Korean threats, its troops may remain in South Korea until it has confirmed the non-existence of those threats." Coincidentally, this rather positive statement by one of North Korea's senior officials resulted in positive U.S. and South Korean military actions. The formal dismantling of the ROK-U.S. combined field army on June 26, 1992, which was activated on March 14, 1980, provides concrete evidence.[42] Actions through the UN Security Council, the G-7 meetings, and other international and regional organizations, a resumption of Team Spirit exercises, and a reintroduction of U.S. nuclear weapons may be invoked as negative sanctions against North Korean noncompliance.

A point needs to be raised here: Between the peaceful approaches and the military actions in dealing with North Korea exists a host of intermediate options, such as trade embargo, financial sanctions, arms embargo, naval blockade and quarantine, travel restrictions, and freezing of assets and financial transactions, as the UN Security Council resolutions on the Iraqi invasion of Kuwait amply demonstrated.[43] Hence, any premature and hasty military action against North Korean nuclear sites and facilities is an absolute taboo. The military option can be justifiable only as the last resort after all means and forms of nonmilitary methods and mechanisms are exhausted and have failed.[44]

Most important, if North Korea's nuclear weapons development project is proved to be true, it is against every conceivable interest; against the spirit of the new global current of a denuclearized world; against the genuine interests of the North Korean people and the Korean people as a whole; and against the people in the region.

The second prerequisite is that North Korea and South Korea should remain as two separate states for the time being. During this transitional period, the North should transform itself and go through political liberalization and democratization as Eastern Europe and the former Soviet Union did. The process must include launching marketization and privatization, price, financial, and trade reforms, and corresponding institution building. This is indeed a tall order to fulfill, but without such self-transformation, any premature unification attempt will bring forth nothing but disaster and misery to the Korean people on both sides of the demilitarized zone.

Third, the North-South control and coordination commission composed of representatives from both sides must be created to deal with common external and international affairs and bilateral questions. As a result of the 1991 North-South reconciliation agreement and denuclearization declaration, four joint committees (political, military, exchanges and cooperation, and nuclear control) are now in operation. The launching of these commissions notwithstanding, the forty-year-old glacier between North and South would not and could not be melted away overnight. The bitter lessons learned from the July 4, 1972, joint communiqué and the subsequent disappointments of the short-lived North-South Coordinating Committee should be remembered. Only patience, prudence, and persistence with the firm goal of mutually beneficial national reunification will remove the glacier bit by bit.

Finally, the format for maintaining the two separate states should be a confederation—not the North Korean version of confederation but a confederation of two independent sovereign states. The American Confederacy under the Articles of Confederation (1776–1787) or the Southern Confederacy (1860–1864) during the American Civil War are closer to the present definition,[45] but it should be a new formulation rather than a replica of historical examples. Kim Il Sung's so-called confederation idea(s)[46] is, at best, a Soviet-type central-local political arrangement such as the erstwhile union or autonomous republics (which are now undergoing a rapid transformation) or a Chinese-type central-local political structure such as the autonomous regions. The important point is that both the Soviet and Chinese central-local political and governmental arrangements (which are often called the socialist federation)[47] are federal or confederal only in form and highly centralized in actual operation. The current North Korean political system does follow form, and in fact it represents one of the most extreme cases of a centralized totalitarian communist state.[48] From this standpoint, it supports confederation only in name or as propaganda with little or no feasibility for realization. Worse, since his initial pronouncement of the confederation idea in August 1960, Kim himself has changed its meaning(s) so many times over the years that a huge discrepancy exists between the earliest version and the latest proposal; the different versions are confusing and self-contradictory.[49] In any case, during the temporary confederate period under the present proposal, the borders between the two should be maintained and controlled, although legitimate travel, mutual investments, joint ventures, and other economic development projects and sociocultural exchange programs must be encouraged and expanded. During this border-control period, democratization and liberalization—in particular, decentralization and creation of local autonomy—in North Korea should be actively and aggressively pursued. Likewise, South Korea must continue its policy of liberalization, democratization, civilianizatior , and socialization. In addition, it must pursue further decentralization and strengthen local autonomy.

A plain truth is that until and unless the two political and economic systems presently persisting in the Korean peninsula become more comparable and compatible, it is not only inconceivable but unwise for government policy-planners or others to contemplate a genuine and bloodless unification in a hasty fashion.

Notes

1. See Sung Chul Yang, "The 'Revolutionary Dinosaur' in the North and the Expanding Relations Between Seoul and Moscow," *Sino-Soviet Affairs* (Seoul), Vol. 14, No. 3 (Fall 1990), pp. 77–91.

2. According to a long-running Allenbach survey, 60 percent of respondents in 1952 said they favored "centralism" and only 17 percent "federalism." By 1960, 41 percent of the population called themselves federalists and 25 percent centralists, and by 1988 the number favoring federalism soared to 71 percent versus only 8 percent for centralism. See David Marsh, *The New Germany at the Crossroads* (London: Century, 1989), p. 79.

3. The Republic of Korea's original 1948 constitution stipulated the implementation of local autonomy, but it was not realized during the First Republic (1948–1960) under Syngman Rhee. During the short-lived Second Republic (1960–1961), town, municipal, and provincial elections were held, but local autonomy was suspended immediately after the military coup in May 1961. During the Third Republic, the constitution (article 7, section 3) stipulated local autonomy, but it was never implemented. But during the Fourth Republic (1972–1979) an appendix (article 10) of the constitution specified that local autonomy elections would be held only after the realization of Korean unification, thereby de facto abandoning even the constitutional pledge of local autonomy. During the Fifth Republic (1980–1988), the revised constitution once again pledged local autonomy (articles 118 and 119) and even specified the timetables for elections (appendix, article 10), but autonomy was never realized. After the launching of the Sixth Republic (1988–), for the second time in the electoral history of the ROK, elections for both the so-called basic-level legislative assembly (*kich'o eihoe*) and the county and city at large (*kwangyok eihoe*) were held in February and June 1991, respectively (the pledges for local autonomy are found in the present constitution in articles 117 and 118). For details, see Koo Byong-sak, *The Principles of New Constitution* (in Korean) (Seoul: Pak Yong-sa, 1989), pp. 1000–1022.

4. Marsh, *The New Germany*, pp. 64–88.

5. See Sung Chul Yang, "The Implications of German Unification for Korea: Legal, Political, and International Dimensions," *Korea Journal*, Vol. 31, No. 1 (Spring 1991), pp. 41–50, and also his "Two 'Democracies' in Korea," *Korea Journal*, Vol. 30, No. 1 (January 1990), pp. 4–16.

6. Marsh, *The New Germany*, p. 79.

7. Sung Chul Yang, "The Implications," p. 43.

8. Ibid., pp. 43–48.

9. For details, see Sung-jo Park and Sung Chul Yang, *German Unification and Korean Division* (Seoul: Kyungnam University Press, 1991).

10. Ibid. See also *North and South Korean Social and Cultural Indicators* (in Korean) (Seoul: Ministry of Unification Board, 1991), p. 54.

11. For details, see "Questions on German History, Ideas, Forces, Decisions from 1800 to the Present" (historical exhibition in the Berlin Reichstag Catalogue, 2d updated ed., 1984).

12. For a detailed analysis of this subject, see Sung-jo Park and Sung Chul Yang, *German Unification.*

13. See Edward Roby, "A Painful Healing Process," special advertising section, *Asian Wall Street Journal*, November 21, 1991.

14. Quoted in Gunter Hofmann, interview, "Billy Brandt: Europe Is the Future of the New Germany," *Lufthansa Bordbuch* 11/12 (1990), p. 50.

15. Stephen Kinzer, "As Euphoria of Unity Fades, Eastern Germans Feel Scorned and Excluded," *New York Times*, April 18, 1992, p. L-3.

16. *International Herald Tribune*, June 18, 1992, p. 2.

17. Cost estimates vary greatly among different sources. For details, see Sung-jo Park and Sung Chul Yang, *German Unification.* One estimate in 1991 was that the German unification would cost DM 1 trillion over the next decade; see *Newsweek*, April 1, 1991, p. 9).

18. For details, see *The Economist*, May 23, 1992, "Germany Survey," p. 5.

19. The weak competitiveness and the dismally low level of productivity of the former East German economy stem from a number of reasons: (1) The capital stock in industry is largely obsolete, technology has been outdated, and the quality of commodities is generally low; (2) social overhead capital in transportation and communication is deficient; (3) the market structure is monopolistic or oligopolistic—Kombinates and cooperatives have enjoyed market protection, so that no competition prevails in the whole economy; (4) the central planning system provides no incentives to individuals and management to increase productivity; (5) the autarchical trade structure, bound to the Council for Mutual Economic Assistance (COMECON), allows no signal function of market price, so that the supply of commodities does not reflect the demand of the consumers. For details, see Ahn Doo Soon, "Economic Burden of the National Unification: German Unification and the Lessons for Korea," paper delivered at symposium sponsored by the Institute for Northeast Asian Studies, Kyung Hee University, June 24, 1991.

20. *Asian Wall Street Journal*, February 6, 1992.

21. Stephen Kinzer, "Conversations/Joachim Lehmann," *New York Times*, May 3, 1992.

22. *Economist*, May 23, 1992, "Germany Survey," pp. 3, 59.

23. Kinzer, "As Euphoria of Unity Fades."

24. *Economist*, May 2, 1992, p. 13.

25. See, for instance, *Newsweek*, April 1, 1991, pp. 11, 13; *Economist*, February 23, 1991, p. 45.

26. *Economist*, June 23, 1990.

27. For a detailed analysis of the interest-based bargaining strategy, see Max O. Stephenson, Jr., and Gerald M. Pops, "Conflict Resolution Methods and the Policy Process," *Public Administration Review,* Vol. 49, No. 5 (September/October 1989), pp. 463–473.

28. For an excellent analysis of creativity in foreign policy, see Donald A. Sylvan, James G. Voss, and Ryan Beasley, "Determinants of Creativity in Foreign Policy," paper delivered at the annual meeting of the International Studies Association, Vancouver, British Columbia, March 19–23, 1991.

29. For a discussion of middle-power concepts, see Andrew Fenton Cooper and Richard Higgot, "Middle-Power Leadership in the International Order: A Reformulated Theory for the 1990s," paper delivered at the annual meeting of the International Studies Association, Vancouver, British Columbia, March 19–23, 1991.

30. Sylvan, Voss, and Beasley, "Determinants," p. 21.

31. Ibid., p. 22.

32. For details, see Cooper and Higgot, "Middle-Power Leadership," pp. 4–9.

33. Stephen G. Walker, ed., *Role Theory and Foreign Policy Analysis* (Durham, NC: Duke University Press, especially pp. 282–289.

34. Chinworth and Cheng, for example, in a 1991 article emphasized the traditional postwar role of the United States as an honest broker in Asia. I am emphasizing here that South Korea, too, can be the best candidate for such a role in the region. For details, see Michael W. Chinworth and Dean Cheng, "The United States and Asia in the Post–Cold War World," *SAIS,* Spring 1991, pp. 73–91. See also Bernard K. Gordon, "The Asian-Pacific Rim: Success at a Price," *Foreign Affairs,* Vol. 70, No. 1 (Winter 1990-91), pp. 142–155; William J. Crowe, Jr., and Alan D. Romberg, "Rethinking Security in the Pacific," *Foreign Affairs,* Vol. 70, No. 2 (Spring 1991), pp. 123–140.

35. For further details, see Sung Chul Yang, "On the Trilateral Relations of North Korea, South Korea, and the Soviet Union," paper delivered at conference The Current Situation of the Asian-Pacific Region and Soviet–South Korean Relations," cosponsored by the Institute for Sino-Soviet Studies, Hanyang University, Korea, and the Institute of Far Eastern Studies, Academy of Sciences of the USSR, Kazan, June 1–10, 1991.

36. Kim Chin-kuk, "Contents of the Draft Regulations on South-North Nuclear Inspection," *Choong-Ang Ilbo,* April 5, 1992, p. 2, quoted in Larry Niksch, "Beyond the June Nuclear Weapons 'Showdown': The Turn to South Korea," paper delivered at the Korea-American workshop The Trilateral Relationship Among South Korea, North Korea, and the United States, sponsored by the Korean Association of International Studies, June 1–2, 1992, Seoul, p. 9.

37. Reginald Bartholomew, undersecretary of state for international security affairs, U.S. Department of State, in his mid-1991 visit to South Korea, stated the three-point policy of the U.S. administration on international inspection of North Korean nuclear facilities: First, North Korea should honor its nuclear nonproliferation treaty (NPT) obligation without any reservation to the IAEA safeguards agreement; second, North Korea should faithfully implement the safeguards agreement after signing it; and third, Pyongyang should also forgo nuclear reprocessing capability. See *Korea Times,* June 21, 1991. Noteworthy in this connection is the report that Kim Yong-Nam, North Korea's foreign minister, reportedly demanded two preconditions—a simultaneous inspection of U.S-possessed nuclear weapons in South Korea (the U.S government neither confirms nor denies policy on this issue) and the U.S. promise of no nuclear attacks on North Korea—before North Korea would sign the NPT safeguards agreement. The report by the *Washington Post* (June 21, 1991) was quoted in *Han'guk Ilbo* on June 21, 1991.

U.S. State Department press officer David Denny rejected Kim's demands, however. See *Korea Times*, June 22, 1991.

38. For details, see Kenneth R. Timmerman, "North Korea Arms the Mideast," *Asian Wall Street Journal*, June 9, 1992.

39. Don Oberdorfer, "N. Korea Release[s] Extensive Data on Nuclear Effort," *Washington Post*, May 6, 1992. Oberdorfer quoted David Kyd, information director of the IAEA, that the nuclear facilities seen in mid-May 1992 by Hans Blix, IAEA director general, were about the length of two football fields but were "extremely primitive" and appeared a long way from being finished. For details, see his news article, *International Herald Tribune*, June 5, 1992. See also T. R. Reid, "North Korean Plutonium Plant Cited," *Washington Post*, May 17, 1992, p. A1; Michael Breen, "South Korea Wary After Pyongyang's Nuclear Disclosure," *Washington Times*, May 19, 1992, p. A7. The last two articles are quoted in Niksch, "Beyond the June 'Showdown.'"

40. Gary Milhollin, "North Korea's Bomb," *New York Times*, June 4, 1992.

41. Quoted in Niksch, "Beyond the June 'Showdown,'" p. 6.

42. *Korea Times*, June 27, 1992, p. 3.

43. The UN Security Council resolutions are found in *Resolutions and Decisions of the Security Council 1990* (New York: United Nations, 1991), pp. 19–28. See also American Society of International Law, *Proceedings, The Gulf War: The Law of International Sanctions*, 85th annual meeting, Washington, DC, April 17–20, 1991, pp. 169–190; and Young Dahl Oh, "The Legal Role of the United Nations in the Gulf Crisis of 1990–1991," M.A. thesis, Graduate Institute of Peace Studies, Kyung Hee University, May 1992.

44. For example, at the Senate's Subcommittee on East Asian and Pacific Affairs hearing, Joseph Churba, president of the International Security Council, contended that as its ultimate recourse, it would be folly for the United States not to consider a contingent policy of "assertive (or preemptive) disarmament" to support its other non-proliferation efforts. At the same hearing, Gary Milhollin, director of the Wisconsin Project on Nuclear Arms Control, stated that if all else fails, one is left with the military option. All indications are that this would be costly. The North Korean army is strong; one cannot expect a replay of operation Desert Storm. As reported in *Korea Times*, November 27, 1991.

45. Karl Deutsch, for example, distinguishes a federal government from a confederacy in four main respects: First, a federal government is relatively strong in regard to organization, personnel, budget, and jurisdiction; in a confederacy, the common institutions are weak or nearly nonexistent in some or all of these respects. Second, whereas federal governments act directly upon individuals in all matters within the scope of the national government, the government of confederacy ordinarily deals with individuals only indirectly. A federal government collects taxes, raises armies, and enforces its own decisions, but a confederacy depends for all these matters on what the states will do for it or what resources the states will give it. Third, states may secede from a confederacy if their governments or voters so desire, whereas such secession is not permitted in a federal union. Fourth, within the sphere of federal jurisdiction, the laws of a federal union usually prevail over those of the states, and the state governments are expected to obey them and carry them out. In a confederacy, however, a law or decision of the confederal authorities becomes valid in a state only if the state government endorses it or at least does not exercise its right to veto its application within the state. For details, see Karl Deutsch, *Politics and Government: How People Decide Their Fate*, 2d ed. (Boston: Houghton Mifflin Co., 1974), pp. 211–212.

46. It is interesting to note that V. P. Tkatchenko, head of the Korean desk, Central Committee of the CPSU, and a longtime North Korea hand, made a casual remark that Kim Il Sung's confederation proposal was Khrushchev's idea and it was the latter who

urged Kim to propose it in August 1960. According to Tkatchenko, Kim proposed the confederation idea without even knowing its meaning(s). My informal conversation with Tkatchenko on June 5, 1991, Kazan, USSR.

47. For a discussion of socialist federation in the USSR, the Czechoslovak Socialist Republic, and the Socialist Federal Republic of Yugoslavia, see Boris N. Topornin, "On the Classification of Socialist Political Systems," in Anton Bebler and Jim Seroka, eds., *Contemporary Political Systems: Classifications and Typologies* (Boulder, CO: Lynne Rienner Publishers, 1990), pp. 117–132.

48. Huang Zhong-Liang calls North Korea, Romania, and Cuba "individual head (socialist) systems." See his commentary in Bebler and Seroka, *Contemporary Political Systems,* p. 137.

49. North Korea's confederal unification formula has changed over the years. The confederation idea was first proposed by Kim Il Sung on August 14, 1960, to exploit South Korean political instability in the wake of the April 19 student uprising, which led to the downfall of the Syngman Rhee regime. Kim made the following statements: (1) There should be free general elections held throughout the North and the South on the basis of democratic principles without any foreign interference for the purpose of peaceful unification of the country; (2) if this should not be acceptable to the South for fear of communist domination, the North would settle for a North-South confederation as a provisional measure to iron out different issues; (3) the confederacy would be maintained by way of setting up a supreme national committee composed of the representatives of the two governments to coordinate the cultural and economic development of the entire Korea, but the two current political systems would be retained intact; (4) if the South Korean authorities still could not accept the confederation, a purely economic commission composed of business representatives of the two governments would be set up to "relieve the South Korean brothers and sisters from hunger and poverty," and political questions would be set aside for the time being; and (5) there would be mutual reduction of armed forces to 100,000 or less after the withdrawal of U.S. troops from the South. On June 24, 1973, Kim Il Sung countered Park Chung Hee's June 23 proposal (the seven-point declaration for peace and unification) by announcing his own five-point proposal: (1) remove military confrontation and lessen tension between North and South; (2) realize a many-sided cooperation and interchange between North and South; (3) convene a national congress composed of representatives from all strata, political parties, and social organizations in North and South; (4) institute a North-South confederation under a single nomenclature of Confederal Republic of Koryo; and (5) join the United Nations under that name. It was, however, at the sixth assembly of North Korea's Workers' Party that Kim Il Sung proposed the so-called Democratic Confederal Republic of Koryo (DCRK) plan as a "permanent" form. But in his 1991 New Year's address, Kim stated that two autonomous governments under the DCRK plan must have more power for the time being. His statement became more concrete when key North Korean officials such as Yun Ki-bok and Son Song-p'il remarked that two local governments may have diplomatic and military powers. These statements were inconsistent with the North's previous insistence of a single-seat entry into the UN. North Korea completely reversed its position on the UN when its Foreign Ministry announced on May 27, 1991, that it would join the UN separately. See Kim Il Sung, *For the Independent Reunification of the Country* (Pyongyang: Foreign Languages Publishing House, 1976). See also Sung Chul Yang, "Korean Reunification—Autism and Realism," *Korea and World Affairs,* Vol. 6, No. 1 (Spring 1982), pp. 57–72.

16

Korean Reunification in a Comparative Perspective

In Kwan Hwang

Today, we are witnessing a historic turning point and momentous events on the Korean peninsula. These include the entry of the two Koreas into the United Nations, the signing of a nonaggression pact between the North and the South, the joint declaration of denuclearization of the Korean peninsula, and the normalization of diplomatic relations between Seoul and Moscow as well as between Seoul and Beijing. The former USSR (now the Commonwealth of Independent States) was the main supplier of money and arms to North Korea. The ramifications of normalization of South Korean–Soviet diplomatic relations were far-reaching. For years North Korea had adroitly played off the Soviet Union and China, its other chief ally, against one another, but that strategy no longer seemed feasible.

The world is entering an age of uncertainty and ambiguity, and we may very well be on the brink of forging a new world order (or disorder). In this uncertain milieu of changing world reality, what is the likelihood of Korean reunification? The purpose of this chapter is to analyze the unification of Yemen, Germany, and Austria, which are all divided countries that have achieved peaceful unification, in a comparative perspective vis-à-vis the future outcome of Korean reunification. Vietnam is excluded in this study because its unification was brought about by violent military force.

Unification of Yemen, 1990

In May 1990, the united Republic of Yemen was formed by merging republican North Yemen with Marxist South Yemen with its new capital in San̊a in North Yemen. Roughly the size of France, the new state is the most populous in the Arabian peninsula, and its creation has radically altered the regional

279

balance of power. For many years unification was the rallying cry of rulers and politicians on both sides of the border, causing years of friction and sporadic border fighting between the two countries. However, the unification issue was given new life by the same historical forces that shook up Eastern Europe. The key factor in breaking the unification impasse was the Soviet Union's radical change of course under Mikhail Gorbachev. As the Cold War wound down, Moscow became anxious to reduce its expensive foreign aid commitments in order to ease the pressures on its dead-end economy. In the period 1986–1988, Soviet aid to South Yemen averaged $133 million per year, but in 1989 the amount was reduced to a mere $50 million.[1]

Much of Yemeni history is a record of kingdoms and dynasties. Located on the ancient land route and more modern sea route between the Indian Ocean and the Mediterranean, Yemen has always been a much-coveted intermediary point. Clashes between the Turks and the British there in the nineteenth century led to the establishment of a border between north and south in 1905.[2]

North Yemen (Yemen Arab Republic)

North Yemen emerged from World War I as an independent kingdom when Turkey's Ottoman Empire was dissolved in 1918. Imam Yahya, leader of the Zaidi community, was left in control. In 1948 Yahya was assassinated in a palace coup when power was seized by forces opposed to his feudal rule. However, Yahya's son, Ahmad, defeated the rebel forces and succeeded his father as imam. During the 1950s Yemen's traditional isolation was eased, and in 1958 Yemen and the United Arab Republic (Egypt and Syria) formed a federation called the United Arab States, although this was dissolved at the end of 1961.[3]

Matters have been complicated by long-running border disputes between Saudi Arabia and both Yemens. The very act of unification has deprived Riyadh of the ability to influence Yemeni affairs by playing off north against south and by fomenting border troubles among the northern tribes. This forced northern Yemenis to improve relations with the Saudis. Riyadh supported the royalists in the 1962–1970 civil war in North Yemen, but it eventually reached an accommodation with the republican victors.[4]

Imam Ahmad died in September 1962 and was succeeded by his son, Muhammed. A week later, army officers led by Col. (later Marshal) Abdullah Saleh staged a coup, declared the imam deposed, and proclaimed the formation of the Yemen Arab Republic (YAR). Civil war broke out between royalist forces, supported by Saudi Arabia, and republicans, aided by Egyptian troops. The republicans gained the upper hand, and Egyptian forces withdrew in 1967. In November, President Saleh was deposed while abroad, and a Republican Council took over. In the early 1970s Saudi Arabia reasserted its influence over the North Yemen government, and the YAR remained a relatively pro-Western republic.[5]

Rigorous nonalignment in the Cold War was another central feature of North Yemen's foreign policies. For Moscow, Aden (the capital of South Yemen and a seaport) was a vital foothold on the Arabian peninsula and a useful backup to the Soviet presence across the Red Sea in Ethiopia. Therefore, it was essential for North Yemen to remain neutral to cultivate its relations with the Soviet Union and move toward unification with South Yemen. San^{c}a received military and economic aid from the USSR as well as from the United States and Europe.[6]

South Yemen (People's Democratic Republic of Yemen)

The history of South Yemen (Aden) is intertwined with that of North Yemen, with which it shares the strategic southwestern corner of the Arabian peninsula. In the early nineteenth century, Egyptian advances toward the region led to the British occupation of Aden in 1839. Aden was administered by Britain's Bombay "presidency" until 1937, when it became a British crown colony with its own governor and protectorate. Claims on Aden by Zaidic imams of North Yemen led to the creation of various tribal federations in the Aden protectorate. In 1959, after several years of planning, Britain organized six of the states nearest Aden, known as the Western Protectorate, into the Federation of the Arab Emirates of the South. Other states gradually joined them, and the Federation of South Arabia was created as a protectorate in 1963. In December of the same year, however, the struggle for independence began in earnest when two nationalist groups—the National Liberation Front (NLF) and the UAR- (United Arab Republic) supported Front for the Liberation of Occupied South Yemen (FLOSY)—waged a guerrilla war against the British and local dynastic rulers.[7]

Meanwhile the British promised independence to South Yemen by 1968. The last British troops left Aden on November 29, 1967, and on the following day the People's Republic of Southern Yemen was proclaimed, comprising Aden and the Protectorate of South Arabia. The two rival factions fought for control. The Marxist NLF eventually won and assumed power as the National Front (NF). In November 1970, on the third anniversary of independence, the country was renamed the People's Democratic Republic of Yemen (PDRY) and received extensive military and economic aid from the Soviet Union. After the postindependence introduction of repressive measures against dissidents by the government, more than 300,000 southern Yemens fled to the YAR. Backed by Saudi Arabia and Libya, many of the refugees joined mercenary organizations, aimed at the overthrow of the Marxist regime in southern Yemen, and carried out raids across the border.[8]

Intermittent fighting began in early 1971 and flared into open warfare between the two Yemens in October 1972, with the YAR receiving aid from Saudi Arabia and the PDRY being supported by Soviet arms. A cease-fire was arranged in the same month under the auspices of the Arab League, and soon afterward both sides agreed to the union of the two Yemens within eighteen months. The union was not implemented, however, until May 1990.[9]

Unification of the Two Yemens

Hopes for uniting the two Yemens continued in both states, but each wanted union on its own terms. The first Yemeni summit was convened in March

1970 in Kuwait to discuss and emphasize the importance of formulating a constitution (which was not drafted until 1981). Subsequently, the Cairo accord was signed on October 28, 1972, to form a united constitution draft commission. This was followed by the Tripoli accord in November, which called for the establishment of one state called the "Republic of Yemen" with Islam the state religion.[10] The proposed unification effort received a severe setback when both Yemeni presidents were assassinated in a two-day period in June 1978 as the two sides were about to work out details of a proposed merger. In February 1979, assisted by the Soviet Union, East Germany, and Cuba, South Yemen invaded North Yemen. Saudi Arabia and the United States responded by rushing arms to North Yemen. In March in Kuwait, the Arab League again arranged a truce calling for Yemeni unity.[11] Meanwhile, in October 1979 the PDRY signed a twenty-year treaty of friendship and cooperation with the USSR, which empowered the USSR to station up to 18,000 troops in the PDRY, the Arab world's only avowed Marxist state. In October 1984 the YAR also signed a twenty-year treaty of friendship and cooperation with the USSR (containing no military clauses).[12]

At a summit held in Kuwait in November 1981, the two Yemeni presidents reached accord on a "noninterference agreement," and a month later in Aden they announced concrete measures to implement unification. These included the formation of the Yemen Council (also known as the Yemeni Supreme Council) headed by the two presidents to oversee the unification process. The council was charged with appointing the Joint Ministerial Committee, consisting of the two states' prime ministers; foreign, interior, supply and planning, and education ministers; and the chiefs of staff of their armed forces. It was agreed that the committee would meet at least once every three months. A secretariat was also established to handle the administrative details of the Yemen Council and the Joint Ministerial Committee. Substantive goals included coordination and integration of social and economic development programs and the formulation of a common foreign policy line based on Arab unity and opposition to foreign interference in the region. Commitments were made to facilitate the movement of citizens between the two states, to integrate school curricula, and to promote the cooperation of the two countries' media.[13]

A 136-article draft constitution for the proposed Republic of Yemen was approved by a joint constitutional committee in January 1982. This document designated Sanᶜa the capital of the new state and Islam the state religion. The constitution was to be approved by the legislatures of the two states and then submitted to the people in a referendum. However, not much was accomplished until 1986—North Yemen feared being absorbed in a single Marxist state—despite the constitutional commitment to Islam.[14]

In 1986 the new government of the PDRY, under Haidar Afu Bakr al-Attas, reaffirmed its commitment to the process of unification. In July, President Ali Abdullah Saleh of the YAR and al-Attas of the PDRY met for the first time in Tripoli, Libya, at the invitation of Col. Muammar Qaddafi, to discuss unification. In early 1987, Kuwait's foreign minister acted as a mediator between the two Yemens in an effort to solve the problem of the thousands of refugees from the PDRY who had sought refuge in the north in the previous year. In July 1987 it was reported that more than one-half of these refugees had returned to the PDRY. In May 1988 the YAR and PDRY governments agreed to withdraw from their mutual border and to create a demilitarized zone of 2,200 square kilometers between Marib and Shabwah where they intended to carry out joint projects involving exploration for petroleum. The movement of citizens between the two states was also to be facilitated. In June 1989, direct telephone links between the YAR and the PDRY were established.[15]

Progress toward unification was accelerated in the second half of 1989. In July a program of wide-ranging political and economic reform was introduced to create a free market economy. In November travel restrictions for PDRY citizens were rescinded, and President Saleh and the secretary-general of the Central Committee of the Yemen Socialist Party (YSP), Ali Salin al-Baid, signed an agreement to unify the two states. On December 1, 1989, a 136-article draft constitution for the united country was published.[16] In April 1990, an accord proclaiming the new republic and organizational principles for the transition period was also signed.

Thus, after years of bitter conflict, pro-Western North Yemen and pro-Soviet South Yemen merged into a single nation on May 22, 1990, as the Republic of Yemen and called for it to become final after a thirty-month transition period followed by a plebiscite on the draft constitution and free elections. On the same date, at a joint session, North Yemen's Consultative Assembly (159 members) and South Yemen's Supreme People's Congress (111 members) elected a five-member Presidential Council. The presidency was taken by the North's president, Saleh; the South's Ali Albeid, former secretary-general of the YSP, became his deputy. Other members of the Presidential Council were Salem Saleh Mohammed, a southerner who had been Albeid's deputy, and two northerners, former premier Abdel-Aziz Abdal Ghami and former parliament speaker Abdel-Karin al-Arsh. A new cabinet was named on May 24 with South Yemen's former head of state, Haydas Abu Bakr al-Atlas, as prime minister. The thirty-nine cabinet members included twenty northerners and nineteen southerners. San^{c}a, the capital of the former North Yemen, became the political capital of the united state, and the port of Aden, the former South Yemen's capital, was proclaimed its economic capital. The northern region has 10 million people, the southern 2 million, and another 2 million Yemeni live abroad. The unification was by no means cosmetic. The army command was unified in the first weeks of the transition period, and diplomatic representation was harmonized.[17]

The merger was said to owe much to the ambitions of Saleh as well as to the economic problems of South Yemen (the only Arab communist state), which had moved to end its isolation in the wake of the democratic reforms sweeping the Soviet bloc. Communist Yemen spent twenty years in the Soviet orbit, and the withdrawal of Soviet aid prompted it to accept an offer to unite with North Yemen. South Yemen was one of the poorest Arab countries. Its economy was based largely on agriculture and light industry, and there was a perpetual budget deficit. After independence from British rule in 1967, all major businesses were nationalized, commercial property declined, and the country became dependent on the Eastern bloc, especially the USSR, for foreign aid.[18]

Unification of Germany, 1990

The unification of Germany was formally achieved October 3, 1990, when the Federal Republic of Germany was established upon the unification of the Federal Republic of Germany (FRG, West Germany) and the German Democratic Republic (GDR, East Germany).[19]

Germany was divided after the defeat of the Third Reich in 1945 into U.S., Soviet, British, and French occupation zones according to the Berlin agreement. Berlin was similarly divided. After the failure of negotiations to establish a unified German administration, the three Western-occupied zones were integrated economically in 1948. A provisional constitution ("basic law") came into force in the three zones in May 1949. The first federal elections were held in August of the same year, and the FRG was established on September 21, 1949, with Theodor Heuss as its first president and Konrad Adenauer as federal chancellor.[20]

In October 1949 the Soviet-occupied zone of Germany declared itself the GDR with the Soviet-occupied zone of Berlin as its capital. This left the remainder of Berlin, known as West Berlin, as an exclave of the FRG in GDR territory. Wilhelm Pieck and Otto Grotewohl were elected president and prime minister, respectively, of the GDR. These two men were joint chairmen of the Socialist Unity Party of Germany (SED), which had been formed in April 1946 by the merger of the Communist Party and the Socialist Democratic Party in the Soviet zone. The USSR granted complete sovereignty to the GDR on March 27, 1954.[21]

After establishment of the FRG, the military occupation there was converted into a contractual defense relationship. The Paris agreement of 1954 gave full sovereign status to the FRG from May 5, 1955, and also gave it membership in NATO. In 1957 the Bundestag (Federal Assembly) declared Berlin the capital of Germany, and the FRG continued to aim for a united Germany. Until such time, the FRG would not recognize the GDR as an independent state and designated Bonn as the seat of the FRG government.[22]

From the time of division, Germany became the battleground for the Cold War. A couple of incidents served to secure the division of the two German nations by the superpowers: the Berlin blockade and the building of the Berlin Wall. The Berlin blockade was Stalin's response to a Western attempt to reorganize the German economy without Moscow's blessing. Stalin decided that Berlin, which was also divided into four zones, would be shut off from the West. By the end of June 1948, all land-based access to Berlin was eliminated. Stalin hoped to slow the re-creation of a united German state and to divide Europe and the United States, which led an airlift to fly in food and other supplies for the city. Finally, after eleven months, the blockade was discontinued, and Berlin was left under four-power administration. By 1960, 200,000 people had left the GDR by way of Berlin. Because many of them were either young or specialist workers, the East German government could not last with emigration of this magnitude. This pattern increased in 1961 to the extent that by August 1,000 to 2,000 East Germans were leaving daily. To stop the exodus, the East German government turned to drastic measures and early in the morning of August 13, 1961, began construction of the Berlin Wall, which eventually surrounded the western part of the city.[23]

With the advance of Ostpolitik (the FRG's opening toward the East) under the chancellorship of Willy Brandt of the Social Democratic Party (SPD), the FRG and the GDR signed a basic treaty in December 1972 agreeing to develop normal relations on the basis of equality of rights and to be guided by the United Nations charter. In September 1973, both the FRG and the GDR joined the United Nations, and in March 1974 a further agreement was signed in Bonn (implementing article 8 of the basic treaty) to install permanent missions in Bonn and East Berlin. As a result, many Western countries (including the United States) were able to establish diplomatic relations with the GDR.[24]

Relations between the two German states were affected dramatically as a result of political upheavals in the GDR in late 1989 and early 1990. In the latter half of 1989, many thousands of dissatisfied GDR citizens emigrated illegally to the FRG via Czechoslovakia, Poland, and Hungary. Many of them had taken refuge in the FRG's embassies in those countries as well as in its permanent mission in East Berlin. The exodus was accelerated by the Hungarian government's decision in early September 1989 to allow GDR citizens to leave Hungary without exit visas. As popular dissent increased in the GDR, an independent citizens' action group, the New Forum, was founded. Its declared aim was to serve as a platform for discussion on democratic reforms, justice, and environmental issues. By late October, more than 100,000 signatures had been collected for a petition supporting the foundation of the New Forum.[25]

In early October 1989, the GDR celebrated its fortieth anniversary, which was attended by the Soviet leader, Mikhail Gorbachev. Demonstrations continued following the celebration in East Berlin and spread to other major cities. In mid-October, as the political situation became increasingly troubled, Erich Honecker resigned as general secretary of the SED, chairman of the Council of State, and chairman of the National Defense Council. Honecker was replaced in all his posts by Egon Krenz, a member of the SED Politburo. Dialogue was initiated with members of the New Forum and with church leaders. An amnesty was announced for all persons who had been imprisoned for attempting to leave the country without authorization, as well as for those who had been detained during the recent demonstrations. However, large-scale demonstrations continued in many towns in support of further reforms. On November 7, 1989, Hans Modrow, a member of the Central Committee of the SED, was elected chairman of the Council of Ministers. In an attempt to quell the growing unrest and the continuing exodus, the Modrow government pledged to introduce comprehensive political and economic reforms and to hold free elections in 1990, abolished restrictions on foreign travel for GDR citizens, and opened border crossings to the FRG. During the weekend of November 10–11, 1989, an estimated 2 million GDR citizens crossed into West Berlin, and the GDR government promptly began to dismantle a section of the Berlin Wall dividing the city. Many new crossing points were opened along the GDR border with the FRG.[26]

In late November 1989, Chancellor Helmut Kohl presented to the Bundestag a ten-point plan for the eventual unification of the FRG and the GDR through a confederal structure. Kohl said his plan was in response to the suggestion by East German Prime Minister Hans Modrow of a "treaty-based community" between the two Germanys. To develop confederative structures between the two states in Germany in order to create a federation, Kohl would begin with medical and other humanitarian aid for East Germany. After the establishment of a freely elected government there, new forms of institutional cooperation could emerge and be developed in stages. The structures proposed by Kohl included a joint committee for permanent consultations and political harmonization, joint technical committees, and a joint parliamentary body. In order to allay the fears of neighboring countries, he stressed that unification would take place within a framework of "pan-European development without affecting the stability of the borders determined at the end of WW II and without jeopardizing the FRG's commitment to the establishment of the EEC's single European market in 1992."[27]

In December 1989, Kohl made his first official visit to the GDR and discussed with Modrow the establishment of joint economic, cultural, and environmental commissions and the development of relations between the two countries at all levels. Kohl also reiterated his plan for confederative structures leading to eventual unification. The GDR leadership was initially insistent that the GDR should remain a sovereign independent state. Modrow visited Moscow at the end of January to discuss German unification. The Soviet leadership had agreed to the principle of unity but apparently only under conditions of neutrality. However, in February 1990, in response to the continuing exodus of GDR citizens to the FRG and to escalating demonstrations in favor of immediate unification, Modrow publicly advocated the creation of a united Germany, proposing a four-point plan that included establishment of joint institutions, such as parliamentary commissions, regional governments, and administrative bodies, as well as elements of confederation in the economic, monetary, and judicial structures of both countries. An important condition stressed by Modrow was the removal of all foreign troops from German territory.[28]

After discussion between Kohl and President Gorbachev in Moscow in mid-February 1990, it was reported that the Soviet leader had endorsed the principle of unification, stating that the two German states should themselves decide the timing and form of an eventual unification but do so within the framework of the Final Act adopted at Helsinki in 1975 by the thirty-five-nation Conference on Security and Cooperation in Europe (CSCE). Shortly afterward, Kohl and Modrow held further consultations in Bonn at which the establishment of a joint commission to elaborate steps toward full economic and monetary union was agreed upon. There was disagreement, however, by the Soviet Union on the issue of NATO membershp for unified Germany. In late February the GDR minister of national defense, Adm. Theodor Hoffmann, proposed the creation of a joint army for a unified Germany, which would be reduced to less than one-third of the combined size of the FRG's and the GDR's armed forces. He also suggested that the two countries should remain in their respective military alliances.[29]

Later in the month, at a meeting at Camp David, Kohl and U.S. President George Bush reaffirmed their commitment to Germany's full membership in NATO following unification. They stressed, however, that the territory formerly constituting the GDR would initially enjoy a "special military status" to protect the security interests of the USSR. Meanwhile the first free legislative elections in the GDR were held on March 18, 1990; more than 93 percent of the electorate participated. The Christian Democratic Union (CDU), which had received considerable financial and technical assistance from its sister party in the FRG, received 40.8 percent of the total votes cast. The newly reestablished Social Democratic Party (SPD), which was also strongly supported by its counterpart in the FRG, obtained only 21.8 percent of the votes. In early April a "grand coalition government" chaired by Lother de Maiziere, the leader of the CDU, pledged its determination to achieve German unity on the basis of article 23 of the FRG's provisional constitution. The SPD favored the slower route of article 146.[30]

In mid-May 1990, the legislative bodies of the FRG and the GDR signed the treaty establishing a monetary, economic, and social union (this treaty came into force July 1). Meanwhile the first round of the so-called two-plus-four talks was held in Bonn to discuss external aspects of the establishment of German unity. Earlier, on April 6 in Washington, Soviet Foreign Minister Eduard Shevardnadze had dropped Moscow's consistent demand that a united Germany be neutral, probably in exchange for large economic assistance to the USSR. At talks between Kohl and Gorbachev in Moscow in mid-July, it was agreed that united Germany would exercise full sovereignty and decide freely to which military alliance it would belong.[31]

On August 31, 1990, the treaty (over 1,000 pages) between the FRG and the GDR on the establishment of German unity was signed in East Berlin. This treaty stipulated, among other provisions, that the GDR was to accede to the FRG on October 3, 1990, in accordance with article 23 of the basic law of the FRG. The united Germany would continue to be known as the Federal Republic of Germany with its capital in Berlin. The last two-plus-four talks in Moscow in early September settled the external aspects of unification and granted united Germany full membership in NATO.[32]

The first all-German elections to the Bundestag since 1933 were held on December 2, 1990, and the unification policy of Kohl and the CDU was confirmed by 43.8 percent of the total votes. The SPD received 33.5 percent. On October 3, the two German states were formally unified to end forty-five years of division. October 3 is now a national holiday.[33]

Austrian Unification, 1955

Austria was formerly the center of the Austrian (later Austro-Hungarian) Empire, which comprised a large part of central Europe. The empire, under the Hapsburg dynasty, was dissolved in 1918 at the end of World War II, and

Austria proper became a republic. The first postwar Council of Ministers was a coalition led by Karl Renner, who remained chancellor until 1920, when a new constitution introduced a federal form of government. Most of Austria's inhabitants favored union with Germany, but this was forbidden by the postwar peace treaties. In March 1938, however, Austria was occupied by Nazi Germany's armed forces and incorporated into the German Reich.[34]

After Austria was liberated by Allied forces, a provisional government under Renner was established in April 1945. In July, after Germany's surrender, Austria was divided into four zones of occupation: Soviet in the east, British in the south, U.S. in the northwest, and French in the west. In addition, the city of Vienna (surrounded by the Soviet zone, thus similar to the situation of Berlin) was divided into five zones: one for every occupying power and an international sector in the center of the city. In May 1955, after occupying Austria for ten years, the four powers signed an Austrian state treaty and withdrew their armies. Austria regained its unified independence by accepting permanent neutrality.[35]

The fact that Austria emerged from the quadripartite occupation neutral and in one piece has proved the usefulness of military neutrality as one way out of the predicament of a small country divided by occupation into two spheres controlled by contending military blocs. Most Austrians welcomed the neutrality solution on the basis of Austria's geographical location, size, and relatively weak military potential.[36]

The authority of the Socialist Karl Renner as chancellor in the Soviet zone was later extended to the western zones when Renner was approved by representatives of the Austrian provinces. Shortly after the West recognized the Renner government, the Russians agreed to free elections under impartial control. The first postwar elections were held on November 25, 1945. Out of the 165 seats in parliament, 85 were won by the Conservative People's Party, 76 by the Socialist Party, and 4 by the Communist party. The People's Party formed a coalition government with the Socialists. In December Renner became the first president of the second Austrian Republic and held office until his death in December 1950.[37]

With parliamentary democracy reestablished and national unity appearing to be secure, the Austrians pressed for complete implementation of the Moscow declaration—free and independent Austria without foreign occupation. The idea of Austrian neutrality or freedom from military alliance as a mechanism of gaining united independence had been recognized by Renner in January 1947. He envisioned a Swiss solution for Austria:

> As Switzerland is situated between the three great nations of Western Europe, likewise Austria's territory is situated between the five peoples of Central Europe, and their connecting thoroughfares lead across this territory. It is the common interest of these five neighbors that this territory which connects them should be and remain free for all, that it should not be monopolized by anyone against the others or even made the springboard of military aggression.[38]

Renner continued to observe that Austria and Switzerland might form a bridge that would connect the peoples of Europe in peace but separate them in war. He thought that a Swiss solution offered Austria the prospect that Austrian people might finally find peace, which Switzerland found after the Congress of Vienna. Similarly, the October 1947 program of the Austrian Socialist Party asked for an international guarantee of Austrian neutrality for the security of its borders, its freedom, and its independence.[39]

The Swiss example seemed attractive to other Austrian statesmen. Renner's successor as president, Theodore Köner, stated in November 1951 that a free and independent Austria—removed from all rivalries, not bound by one-sided ties in any direciton, and devoted only to the cause of peace—would be a gain for Europe and for the world. He also suggested in a letter to the *Journal de Genève* that Switzerland was an example of political wisdom.[40]

The Austrian parliament debated the question of future military neutrality in considerable detail on April 2, 1952. The foreign minister, Karl Gruber, declared that neutrality under international law (meaning that a neutral nation must not grant any military advantage to another state) was for Austria self-evident for various reasons. At the same time Gruber made it very clear that such a neutrality for Austria, like Switzerland's, should be an armed neutrality and would have nothing in common with the neutralist ideas of Austria's Communists who advocated disarmed neutrality. The government's statement on the future status of military neutrality was endorsed by members of not only coalition parties but also of the right-wing opposition.[41]

On June 25, 1953, the Austrian government even undertook unofficial diplomatic steps on this matter, which was kept secret at that time and was little known even after it was first made public in spring 1955.[42] Foreign Minister Gruber went to Lucerne, Switzerland, to pay a visit to Indian Prime Minister Jawaharlal Nehru, who was accompanied by the Indian ambassador to Moscow, K.P.S. Menon. Gruber requested the good offices of the Indian prime minister on behalf of establishing a free and independent Austria. It was reported that Nehru was pleased to accede to the request. Shortly afterward, Ambassador Menon broached the Austrian request to Soviet Foreign Minister V. M. Molotov. Menon said that although he could not speak for Austria, he believed that if Austria declared its readiness not to grant military bases on its territory to foreign powers or to join any military alliance, a way to establish Austria's full, united independence might be found. To this Molotov was said to have replied that a solemn Austrian declaration of neutrality, including the stated obligations, would be useful but not sufficient for the conclusion of the state treaty and the end of occupation.[43]

Subsequently, on June 30, 1953, the Austrian government, without consulting any of the Western powers, sent a memorandum to the Kremlin strongly suggesting that the Austrians would agree to some form of military neutrality if the Soviet Union would sign a treaty. However, Molotov was adamant on German assets and linked the Austrian treaty with a German peace treaty. The issue of German assets dated back to the Potsdam conference (July 1945), where it had been agreed that the Allies would waive reparations from Austria but reserved the right to take over German assets as compensation. The Austrians were disappointed by the Soviet response but persisted on their independence in exchange for their neutrality.[44]

Throughout this period, the West (especially the United States) was reluctant to see a neutral Austria. U.S. defense planners seemed to envision the small country as a nominal member of NATO, unlikely to be a major participant in joint military exercises but vital to the organization simply by virtue of geographic location. Austria was viewed as an important strategic link in the defense of western and southern Europe. Any weakening of Austria by its neutralization would not only create a military vacuum but also have serious impact upon the entire NATO defense concept. Therefore, maintenance of the status quo would be preferable to a neutralized Austria.[45]

On November 26, 1953, the Soviet Union suggested a foreign ministers conference be held in Berlin; the conference began January 25, 1954. On the initiative of U.S. Secretary of State John Foster Dulles, the three Western powers decided to throw the Soviet delegation off balance by agreeing almost immediately to accept the Soviet Union's agenda, which placed a proposal for a five-power conference (including China) on Indochina and consideration of the German situation before discussion of an Austrian treaty (discussion began February 12). Thus, the Berlin conference provided the only occasion on which the future status of neutrality for Austria became the subject of formal and publicized diplomatic exchanges. On the first day of the talks on Austria, Molotov presented a proposal that Austria should not enter any coalitions or military alliances directed against any nation that participated in the war against Nazi Germany and in the liberation of Austria, nor should it permit the establishment of foreign military bases on its territory in order to prevent a new *Anschluss* (annexation). In addition, Molotov demanded that Allied occupation forces remain in Austria until the German peace treaty was signed, even after the conclusion of the Austrian state treaty.[46]

The continuous linkage of the Austrian treaty with the German settlement was rejected by the Western powers as well as by Austria. However, Foreign Minister Leopold Figle, who headed the Austrian delegation, declared on February 16, 1954, that Austria would do everything to keep free from foreign military influences.[47] Moreover, U.S. Secretary of State Dulles also went so far as to commit himself to the principle of neutrality on the Swiss model, as long as the Austrians freely chose that neutrality.

A neutral state is an honorable status if it is voluntarily chosen by a nation. Switzerland has chosen to be neutral, and as a neutral she has achieved an honorable place in the family of nations. Under the Austrian State Treaty as heretofore drafted, Austria would be free to choose for itself to be a neutral state like Switzerland. Certainly the United States would fully respect its choice in this respect, as it fully respected the comparable choice of the Swiss nation.

However, it is one thing for a nation to choose to be neutral. It is another thing to have neutrality forcibly imposed on it by other nations as a perpetual servitude.[48]

The Austrians regarded this statement as significant as a record of support for neutrality as long as that neutrality was freely chosen. The two Austrian officials told Dulles that they had no choice but to make some declaration of military neutrality for Austria in order to avoid partition. Whatevern his personal feeling about neutrality, Dulles publicly insisted in Berlin that the choice belonged to the Austrians alone.[49]

On February 8, 1955, after almost a decade of Allied occupation, the impasse over the reestablishment of Austrian independence by concluding a state treaty was ended by Molotov in his speech to a session of the Supreme Soviet. He dropped the long-maintained obstacle that stood in the way of the Austrian state treaty: Moscow's insistence on a prior or simultaneous peace settlement with Germany. Moscow conceded that as long as the four powers agreed on some guarantees against a union of Germany and Austria, the Allied troops might be withdrawn from Austria without waiting for the conclusion of a German peace treaty. Austria should undertake the obligations pertaining to no military coalitions or alliances or foreign military bases on its territory; the four powers would have to commit themselves to respect these obligations as well.[50]

The three Western powers endorsed the Soviet initiative. After further negotiations, the Austrian government and the Kremlin agreed April 15, 1955, on the so-called Moscow memorandum in which the Austrians gave assurances that the Austrian Republic, in the spirit of the declaration made at the Berlin conference in 1954, would not join any military alliances or permit military bases on its territory and would pursue a policy of independence in regard to all states. In return, the Kremlin agreed that occupation forces of the four great powers would be withdrawn by December 31, 1955.[51]

In consequence of this memorandum, the Austrian state treaty was signed by the four powers on May 15, 1955, and the Austrians regained their unified independence.

Korean Reunification Vis-à-Vis
Yemeni, German, and Austrian Precedents

In the foregoing brief survey of the history of unification of three nations, one can discern some similarities, differences, and uniqueness in the unification process and method. In all three cases, at the time of their unification struggles, there were favorable external changes and impetus that promoted internal unification efforts. In the case of both Yemen and Germany, the weakening of the Soviet empire in its trial period of *perestroika* and *glasnost* prompted their internal desire for unity. Austrian unification was also achieved when Soviet leaders wanted to impress the world with their new policy of "thaw" after the death of Stalin, the architect of the Cold War.

Internally, both divided Germany and divided Yemen had agreed on substantial preparatory arrangements for unification. In Germany, there were the basic treaty of 1972; free legislative elections in the GDR in March 1990; the monetary, economic, and social union in May; and finally the unity treaty in

August. In Yemen both sides agreed on a unity constitution in 1981 and on an accord for a republic and the transitional period in April 1990. However, despite the earlier internal efforts to unify, neither Yemen nor Germany was able to succeed before the Soviet Union changed policy toward its satellites. In other words, the Kremlin withdrew its political and economic support from both East Germany and South Yemen when most needed. Furthermore, because of its internal struggle for democracy, Moscow could not prevent the German or Yemeni merger. In the Austrian case, however, the USSR could have delayed unification much longer. Instead, the Kremlin accepted the Austrian proposal that a reunited, independent Austria would remain permanently neutral like Switzerland. Thus, in permanent neutrality both Austria and the Soviet Union found common ground as a strategic means of promoting their mutual interests or advantages: for Austria, united independence, and for the Soviet Union, a possibility of enticing West Germany to entertain the idea of a neutral, united Germany.

The unique character of Yemen's unification was that the division of Yemen was not a result of World War II. Rather, it resulted earlier from Western colonial policy, and unification was achieved through prolonged, often bitter personal political struggles as well as negotiations between the two ruling groups. In a sense, it might be characterized as a unification "from above" dictated by more populous North Yemen. In contrast, German unification can be said to have taken place "from below" through democratic processes: popular demonstrations followed by general elections. Austrian unification was unique in that one occupying power (the Soviet Union) and Austrian leaders were able to reach a bilateral agreement on the status of postunited Austria— permanent neutrality—and persuade the other three occupying powers, especially the United States, to accept the Austrian-Soviet "memorandum."

Let us now turn to prospects of Korean reunification in light of these three nations' unification achievements. It is clear that none of the three examples would fit to a future Korean reunification scenario, for the Korean experience is different from each of them. However, there are some useful lessons to be learned from the three to help facilitate Korean unity. To begin with, Korea, like Germany and Austria, was divided at the end of World War II as a result of the Cold War between the two victorious superpowers—the Soviet Union and the United States. However, unlike Germany and Austria, the two Koreas went to war in 1950, a conflict initiated by North Korea in its attempt to unify the peninsula by force. Because the war ended in a truce in 1953, not in the imposition of unconditional surrender, the status of war between the two Koreas continued until December 13, 1991, when they signed a nonaggression pact. Nevertheless, their competition for legitimacy still continues. Because of the question of legitimacy and distrust, the North-South joint communiqué of July 4, 1972, could not do much to promote inter-Korean goodwill or the spirit of reconciliation. It is uncertain whether the belated, long-overdue nonaggression pact of 1991 has ended the continuing legitimacy struggle despite limited economic cooperation. Korea has yet to institutionalize the unification process by agreeing on some form of unity constitution similar to what was used in Germany or Yemen.

The two Koreas, however, may never be able to agree on a mechanism that could determine a majority will of the Korean people on the issue of unity through free elections, such as happened in Germany. Nor may it be possible for the Koreans to establish a joint presidential council headed by one of the Korea's leaders as Yemen did, for it is unthinkable and unimaginable to expect an all-Korea ruling council in which Kim Il Sung would not become a hegemon. In Korea, the question of who should rule a united Korea would remain unsettled for a long time to come.

After the Korean War, the two Koreas tried to settle the issue of how and by whom a unified Korea should be governed through a mechanism of general elections, but they were unable to agree on an election format because each side insisted on its own formula that would guarantee it a majority. At present the focus of the method of unification has shifted from elections to a "confederal" or "federal" form of association; thus the electoral process as a means of unification has been abandoned. In light of the current status of the two Koreas, some kind of confederal approach seems reasonable and practical or even inevitable. In this connection, it is interesting to recall that even West German Chancellor Kohl proposed a confederal structure for German unity in late November 1989, soon after the crumbling of the Berlin Wall. However, the dynamic, spontaneous march of events in East Germany forced Kohl to change the course toward general elections in East Germany because it wanted immediate unity.

As to the origins of the German confederal scheme of unification, it was first proposed by East German Prime Minister Otto Grotewohl in 1957 and repeated in 1959, 1961, and 1963 as the official East German unification policy.[52] The main rationale for the confederal scheme was to maintain the two existing different social systems and to establish a future nuclear-free, neutral, unified Germany.[53] This idea of "neutral Germany" was supported by the Kremlin but opposed by the other three occupying powers as well as by West Germany. However, it is interesting to note that in the initial stage of the German unification drama, from the end of 1989 to April 1990, the East Germans as well as the Soviets insisted on a neutral and unified Germany. According to a poll published by the Wickert Institute in February 1990, 92 percent of East Germans and 58 percent of West Germans favored neutrality for a united Germany.[54]

Coincidentally or not, North Korea also adopted a confederal plan for unification in 1960 and repeated it in 1970, 1973, and 1980. The 1980 version, titled "Democratic Confederal Republic of Koryo" (DCRK), became more or less the final North Korean unification formula. Although many of its proposals were repetitions and modifications of the ideas long advanced by Kim Il Sung, it included two new elements: the transformation of the DCRK into a "permanant peace and nuclear-free zone" and its future neutral or nonaligned foreign policy. It is instructive to point out that there was a marked similarity between the East German and the North Korean plans for unification: "confederal and neutral." As pointed out earlier, Chancellor Kohl also entertained the confederal scheme of German unification in its early stage. More interestingly, Kim Il Sung too reiterated the confederal-neutral theme of reunification in 1992. The portion of Kim's statement in this regard in an interview with the *Washington Times* on the occasion of his eightieth birthday (April 15, 1992) is worth quoting in its entirety:

> *Question:* What is your vision for Korea's role in Asia? Are you confident your nation will play a key role in the future?
>
> *Answer:* We don't wish to become a big power. When I advanced the proposal to reunify our country by founding the Democratic Confederal Republic of Korea [sic], I said our country is surrounded by big countries in the world and therefore our country should remain neutral. That is the most favorable status for us— without becoming the satellite of any country. Also, we don't wish to become the agent of any other country.
>
> We should remain an independent, sovereign, non-aligned and neutral state. That is our wish. We should maintain friendly relations with our neighboring countries. And in the meantime we would remain independent and lead a very harmonious life within our nation.[55]

Currently, an interesting and ironic development in the Korean peninsula is that the North Korean proposal of transforming the peninsula into a "permanent peace and nuclear-free zone," as advanced in the 1980 DCRK plan, seems already to have been achieved by the United States and South Korea. On September 30, 1991, President Bush announced that he was withdrawing U.S. tactical nuclear weapons overseas, including South Korea. Two months later, on November 9, President Roh stated that South Korea was free of such weapons and would use nuclear energy only for peaceful purposes, thus paving the way for the historic North-South nonaggression pact in December. After signing this document, the two sides in a joint statement agreed to make the Korean peninsula a nuclear-free zone and pledged to work toward mutual inspection.

Viewed in this light, a confederal or state-to-state linkage for Korea, at least in the initial stage of reunification, might be more appropriate than the German experience. Furthermore, North Korea would resist the West German style of absorptive unification. The Seoul government too seemed to have changed its initial preference for absorptive unity to "community unification" (this may mean a confederal or commonwealth type), which implies a slower, long-term process involving a period of reconciliation, confidence building, and economic development in North Korea especially. The North's 1980 DCRK proposal provided a confederal form of unification but confused confederal and federal structures. In any event, the two Koreas must adjust their unification policies to the changing milieu of internal and international politics of today.

In the Yemeni case, even though it is hard to tell the exact nature of its unification—confederal, federal, or absorptive—the composition of the Presidential Council and the Consultative Assembly is worth noting. The population ratio is five (10 million) to one (2 million) in North Yemen's favor, but three northerners and two southerners made up the council with a northerner as president. The assembly was composed of 159 northerners and 111 southerners with a southerner as prime minister. It is a remarkable feat that the

Yemeni people could agree on power sharing despite the extremely uneven population ratio between the two Yemens. This could be an important lesson for the two Koreas when they confront the issue of power sharing at the time of unification trial. Another unique aspect of Yemeni unification was the constructive role of fellow Arab nations serving as referee and facilitator at critical junctures.

In the Korean experience, there has been no such third-party referee or active facilitator. The two Korean government leaders have always claimed and insisted that they alone are responsible for achieving Korean unity. This attitude, laudable as it may be, will make unification much harder because in the process of the unification game, each Korea inevitably becomes a referee as well as a player. Germany had a referee—the general elections.

One of the outstanding features of German reunification was that it was accomplished with the membership of united Germany in NATO. Some South Korean thinkers have entertained a similar idea—a united Korea within the existing U.S.–South Korean defense alliance. However, such an arrangement would be impossible to achieve because North Korea would certainly reject it. Furthermore, it is contrary not only to the spirit of the joint communiqué of July 4, 1972 (see Appendix A), which emphasized unification through independent Korean efforts, but also to the North Korean ideology of *Juche*.

Let us now turn to the prospect of Korean reunification based on the three examples. No single example is sufficient to be helpful for the Korean situation; the combination of the three is more useful and meaningful. Better yet, Korea must fashion its own unique and separate way of merger in accordance with requirements and conditions of the Korean peninsula, drawing lessons from each of the three. First of all, the key to reducing tensions on the peninsula is active and sincere North-South dialogue and cooperation. Although Koreans themselves must traverse the road to peace and reunification through their own initiatives, it may be necessary to establish a forum for the two Koreas and the four major powers that will guarantee the outcomes negotiated between the two Koreas.

Despite hopeful signs such as the admission of both Koreas to the United Nations and the conclusion of the nonaggression pact, there is potential for a long stalemate in the unification process; resolving the issue of nuclear inspections in North Korea by the International Atomic Energy Agency is a case in point. Today the two Koreas still seem to struggle for advantages in the constant test of wills rather than seek mutual accommodations. Under such circumstances, it is questionable that the status of a denuclearized peninsula as agreed upon can be guaranteed by the two Koreas alone. In this connection, it is worthwhile to recall North Korea's earlier proposal for a nuclear-free peninsula guaranteed by China, the United States, and the Soviet Union. If this idea of a guaranteed denuclearized peninsula were to be accepted by South Korea, it would not be too difficult to envision a guaranteed, neutral reunification of Korea, similar to the Austrian case, that could solve the nuclear issue as well as the problem of other arms control. The processes of reconciliation and reunification need to be based on Korean initiatives, but the final act of unification may require the four major powers' consent and guarantee.

At present, overwhelming majority opinion on Korean unity opposes an absorptive and annexational German-type unification. Analysts of this view cite a host of different facts and reasons existing between the two situations. Whereas German unification was achieved in accordance with the West German basic law (constitution), South Korea does not expect the same with North Korea. Furthermore, West Germany was able to annex the East because of East German emigration to the West. A similar North Korean exodus to the South cannot be expected, for Pyongyang would never allow such emigration to take place. In other words, the opening of North Korean society to the South would mean ipso facto the collapse of its totalitarian political system and its absorption by the South. The all-out effort of North Korea to acquire nuclear weapons could be interpreted in part as its last resort to protect its political system. The North seems to realize that it is engaged in a race that it cannot win, that it is lagging ever further behind South Korea economically and technologically. Seoul is also outstripping Pyongyang diplomatically and gaining new allies, such as Moscow and Beijing, at North Korea's expense. Acquisition of the bomb, however, would turn Pyongyang into an international player that could not be ignored. In any event, Pyongyang seems to be determined not to be absorbed by South Korea.

It would appear, therefore, that the two Koreas are not going the way of the two Germanys. Rather, they will continue to struggle for legitimacy and hegemony despite the weaker status of North Korea. Thus, in order to achieve reunification, Koreans must find a common denominator that benefits the interests of both countries without one side becoming winner or loser. In this context, the Austrian example would help: a neutral Korea, supported by the four major powers, in which the two Koreas could remain politically intact but economically integrated until the process of national reconciliation, confidence building, and cultural exchanges has been completed. Furthermore, because Washington has to phase its forces out of the South, converting its troop withdrawal into a process of neutralizing the Korean peninsula would not be too difficult if the United States so desires.

A number of analysts have argued that unification is not just merging the two Koreas together but creating a new Korea based on new thinking for future generations. A neutral-confederal Korea could be such a new creation, which might prevent the foreign encroachment Korea has experienced throughout its history. It is instructive to recall that prior to the Japanese annexation of Korea in 1910, the pro-Japanese, pro-Russian, pro-Chinese, and pro-U.S. factions contributed to internal political disunity, causing the loss of independence. The murder of Queen Mim by the Japanese in 1895 took place when she courted the Russian influence to counter the Japanese. The 1948 division of Korea, the war, and its current impasse are reflections of such unfavorable historical forces playing upon the Korean peninsula.

There is no guarantee that this tendency toward division will not recur in the postreunification era. Thus, the preservation of independence after unification becomes as important as reunification itself. It is in this context that neutrality serves to foster national independence amid foreign intrigue.

Therefore, the neutrality principle can be used as an ideology of nationalism, a tool to defend national interests, including independence.

Geographical location is a prime factor in a state's survival. States cannot choose their neighbors. Because their location is constant, they must find the best ways and means of coping with their neighbors, especially the stronger ones. Every neighboring state of Korea is stronger than Korea, which necessitates its pursuit of a prudent and balanced foreign policy, and the neutrality principle is a useful guide in such an endeavor.

The important point that emerges from the foregoing analysis is that the neutrality principle can serve as a means of both achieving reunification and maintaining independence after unification. There are those who argue that the end of the Cold War has rendered neutrality useless and irrelevant. But they should be reminded that it was the balance-of-power system or power politics, not the Cold War, that created the doctrine of neutrality. Power politics will continue in the post–Cold War period as well as in the postcommunist era, and so will the doctrine of neutrality. No one can think of creating a new world order free of international conflicts and competition.

In conclusion, the brief survey of Yemeni, German, and Austrian unification might provide some useful lessons for Korea, but Korea has to devise its own formula of unity tailored to its unique history and requirements. However, despite progress toward rapprochement in 1991 and 1992, Korean unification is on hold. German unification seems to have disillusioned Seoul and horrified Pyongyang. It was reported that South Koreans want to put off reunion indefinitely because of the high cost of "absorbing" North Korea—$250 billion over ten years.[56] North Koreans are equally determined not to repeat the fate of East Germany at any cost. In this milieu, the uneasy status quo will continue for some time to come. Meanwhile, even though there is no way of knowing how unification will be achieved in the future, it is prudent for the two Koreas to study a unification policy that would ensure a commitment not only to achieve peaceful unity but also to safeguard the independence of postunited Korea against potential external pressures and intrusions that plagued Korean independence in the past. We have learned some lessons from Germany; much more can be learned from Yemen and Austria—especially from the Austrian example of a neutralized, internationally guaranteed merger, which would help ease the way for Korea's economic union by reducing political risks and by maintaining strategic balance while moving toward gradual integration. Thus, viewed as an alternative to the long-term continuation of U.S. military presence and to the increasing and deepening North Korean fear of being absorbed by the South, the idea of a neutralized confederation merits serious consideration on the part of both Korean governments.

Notes

1. Allen George, "Unified Yemen: New Power in the Arabian Peninsula," *International Defense Review,* November 1990, p. 1227.

2. For general information on Yemen, see Richard F. Nyrop et al., *The Yemens* (Country Studies) (Washington, DC: U.S. Government Printing Office, 1986); and Manfred W.

Wenner, *The Yemen Arab Republic: Development and Change in an Ancient Land* (Boulder, CO: Westview, 1991).

3. Tareq Y. Ismael, *Governments and Politics of the Contemporary Middle East* (Homewood, IL: Dorsey Press, 1970), pp. 387–393.

4. George, "Unified Yemen," p. 1228.

5. *Europa World Year Book 1991*, Vol. 1 (London: Europa Publications, 1991), p. 3055.

6. George, "Unified Yemen," pp. 1228–1229.

7. Ismael, *Governments*, pp. 412–424.

8. *Europa World Year Book 1991*, pp. 3055–3056.

9. Ibid.

10. *Process of Unification* (Washington, DC: Yemen Embassy, 1991), pp. 10–11.

11. Nyrop, *The Yemens*, p. 188.

12. *Europa World Year Book 1991*, p. 3057.

13. Nyrop, *The Yemens*, p. 189.

14. Ibid., pp. 189–190.

15. *Europa World Year Book 1991*, p. 3056.

16. Ibid.

17. *Encyclopedia Britannica* (Book of the Year), 1991, p. 418.

18. *Time*, June 4, 1990, p. 65.

19. For general information on German reunification, see *On the Path to German Unity: Chronology of Events* (Bonn: Inter-Nations Press, 1991); *The Unification of Germany in 1990: A Documentation* (Bonn: Press and Information Office of FRG, 1991).

20. Keesing's Research Report, No. 8, *Germany and Eastern Europe Since 1945* (New York: Charles Scribner's Sons, 1973), p. 1277.

21. Frence A. Vali, *The Quest for a United Germany* (Baltimore, MD: Johns Hopkins University Press, 1967), pp. 181ff; *Europa World Year Book 1991*, p. 1134.

22. Eric G. Frey, *Division and Détente: The Germanies and Their Allies* (New York: Praeger, 1987), pp. 6–7; Vali, *Quest*, pp. 18–20.

23. Frey, *Division*, pp. 9–14; Vali, *Quest*, pp. 62–63.

24. *Europa World Year Book 1991*, pp. 1134–1135.

25. Ibid., p. 1135.

26. Ibid.

27. For the full text of Kohl's ten-point statement, see *German Tribune*, December 10, 1989.

28. *Europa World Year Book 1991*, pp. 1135–1136.

29. Ibid., p. 1136.

30. Stephen F. Szarbo, "Reunited Germany," *Current History*, Vol. 89, No. 550 (November 1990), pp. 357ff. Article 23 (jurisdiction of the basic law) reads: "For the time being, this Basic Law shall apply in the territory of the Laender of Baden, Bavaria, Bremen, Greater Berlin, Hamburg, Hesse, Lower Saxony, North Rhine-Westphalia, Rhineland-Palatinate, Schleswig-Holstein, Wuerttemberg-Baden and Wuesttemberg-Hohenzollern. In other parts of Germany it shall be put into force on their accession." Article 146 (duration of validity of the basic law) reads: "This Basic Law shall cease to be in force on the day on which a constitution adopted by a free decision of the German people comes into force."

31. Thomas L. Friedman, "Moscow Reported to Yield on Neutrality of Germany," *New York Times*, April 7, 1990, p. 1; *Europa World Year Book 1991*, pp. 1136–1137.

32. *Europa World Year Book 1991*, p. 1137.

33. *Facts on File*, September 7, 1990, p. 660.

34. Heinrich Siegler, *Austria: Problems and Achievements Since 1945* (Bonn: Siegler and Co., 1969), p. 277.

35. Ibid.

36. Fritz Bock, "Austrian Neutrality," in Robert A. Bauer, ed., *The Austrian Solution: International Conflict and Cooperation* (Charlottesville: University Press of Virginia, 1982), p. 156.

37. Siegler, *Austria*, p. 10.

38. Quoted in Gerald Stourzh, "Austrian Neutrality: Its Establishment and Its Significance," *International Spectator* 14, March 8, 1960, p. 112.

39. Ibid.

40. Ibid., pp. 112–113.

41. Ibid., p. 113.

42. Ibid., p. 114.

43. Siegler, *Austria*, p. 17.

44. Audrey Kurth Cronin, *Great Power Politics and the Struggle over Austria, 1945–1955* (Ithaca, NY: Cornell University Press, 1986), pp. 126–127.

45. Ibid., pp. 121–122.

46. Ibid., p. 130; Stourzh, "Austrian Neutrality," p. 115.

47. Stourzh, "Austrian Neutrality," pp. 115–116.

48. Quoted in Cronin, *Great Power Politics*, p. 131.

49. Ibid.

50. Siegler, *Austria*, p. 21.

51. Ibid., p. 23.

52. Keesing's Research Report, *Germany and Eastern Europe*, pp. 160–187.

53. Ibid., pp. 177–178.

54. CNN Headline News, "Factoid," March 5, 1990.

55. *Washington Times*, April 15, 1992, p. A11.

56. *U.S. News & World Report*, April 20, 1992, p. 44.

17

The United Nations and Reunification

Tae Hwan Kwak

The United Nations has played a limited but important role in the Korean re-unification process since 1947, when the U.S. government submitted the Korean problem to the UN General Assembly because the U.S.-Soviet joint commission could not solve the problem. The UN's basic goal of achieving a unified Korea has not yet been realized even after forty-five years of Korean debate in the United Nations.

During the Cold War years, the Korean question was viewed as a Cold War issue between the East and the West. The entry of South Korea and North Korea into the UN was impossible because the United States and the Soviet Union were unable to reach an agreement on the admission issue. However, with the end of Cold War politics in the UN and the changing international political-security environment in the 1990s, the two Koreas—the Republic of Korea (ROK) and the Democratic People's Republic of Korea (DPRK)—were finally admitted to the United Nations on September 17, 1991. Their simultaneous but separate admission has had a profound effect on the normalization process in inter-Korean relations and will continue to have positive effects on the peaceful inter-Korean unification process in the years ahead.

In view of an emerging world order in the post–Cold War era, it is meaningful to review the UN's past role and to project its new role in the Korean reunification process. Thus, the purposes of this chapter are (1) to discuss the role of the United Nations in Korean reunification during the Cold War years and (2) to examine the necessary and desirable roles of the UN in bringing about peace and the reunification of Korea in coming decades. What role(s) has the UN played in the Korean reunification process in historical perspective? What could the UN do to solve the Korean question? What could and should the UN do to bring about Korean reunification? What could the UN's new role be now that the two Koreas are members of the UN? These and other related questions are discussed in this chapter.

Historical Perspective of the UN's Role
in Korean Reunification

The Korean peninsula was divided at the thirty-eighth parallel in 1945 after the Japanese military surrender under the U.S. and Soviet military occupation forces. The United States and the Soviet Union attempted to solve the Korean problem through diplomatic bargaining and negotiations from 1945 to 1947, but the joint commission failed to achieve Korean reunification because of conflicting goals of the two superpowers. The United States wanted to establish a unified, independent, and democratic Korea, whereas the Soviet Union wanted a communist Korea.[1] Thus, the U.S. government brought the Korean question to the UN General Assembly in September 1947.[2] On November 14, 1947, it established the nine-member UN Temporary Commission on Korea (UNTCOK) to facilitate establishment of a national government of Korea through general elections.

UNTCOK was not permitted to visit North Korea, but it observed general elections in South Korea in May 1948, which resulted in the formation of the Republic of Korea government on August 15. In September, a separate government—the Democratic People's Republic of Korea—was created in North Korea under Soviet supervision. On December 12, 1948, the third UN General Assembly adopted by a vote of 48 to 6 with one abstention Resolution 195 declaring that "there has been established a lawful government (the Government of the Republic of Korea) having effective control and jurisdiction over that part of Korea where the Temporary Commission could observe and consult and in which the great majority of the people of all Korea reside; that this Government is based on elections which were a valid expression of the free will of the electorate of that part of Korea and which were observed by the Temporary Commission; and that this is the only Government in Korea."[3] The General Assembly established the seven-member UN Commission on Korea (UNCOK) to continue the first commission's work toward achieving unification of Korea. In short, the ROK was established under UN supervision. The United Nations, for almost a half century, has been heavily involved in the Korean question.

When North Korea invaded the South on June 25, 1950, the UN Security Council called for the immediate cessation of hostilities and for North Korea to withdraw its armed forces to the thirty-eighth parallel. On June 27, the council recommended that members furnish such assistance to South Korea as might be necessary to repel the armed attack and restore international peace and security in the area. In response to this resolution, sixteen UN member states sent troops to Korea. This marked the first collective police action against an aggressor. On October 7, 1950, the General Assembly recommended (Resolution 376) that "all appropriate steps be taken to ensure conditions of stability throughout Korea" and established the UN Commission for the Unification and Rehabilitation of Korea (UNCURK)[4] to establish a unified, independent, and democratic government of Korea.

The People's Republic of China (PRC) intervened in the Korean War by sending its troops to North Korea in October 1950. The UN General Assembly adopted a resolution naming the PRC as an aggressor in Korea in February 1951. Meanwhile, the Korean War reached a stalemate. In June 1951, negotiations for a cease-fire began, and after two years of long negotiations an armistice agreement was signed July 27, 1953, by the commanders of the UN forces, the North Korean People's Army, and the Chinese People's Volunteers.

In accordance with article 4 of the armistice and General Assembly Resolution 711 (adopted August 28, 1953), the Geneva political conference on Korea was convened from April 26 to June 15, 1954, to solve the Korean question, but no substantial progress was made.[5] The Geneva conference focused on the unification formula and the withdrawal of foreign troops. The ROK first asserted that an election should be conducted only in North Korea but later accepted the UN view that the UN had the right to supervise an all-Korean election and should not withdraw UN forces until a united government in Korea was established. Because the Geneva conference failed, primary responsibility for the Korean question was returned to the United Nations December 11, 1954 (General Assembly Resolution 811).

In every session from 1947 to 1975, the UN General Assembly reaffirmed that "the objectives of the United Nations in Korea are to bring about, by peaceful means, the establishment of a unified, independent and democratic Korea" and received the annual UNCURK report on Korea. Thus, the Korean question was a perennial issue in the General Assembly. For over two decades, it placed the issue on the agenda of each regular session for "automatic" annual debate, although UN debates on the Korean question did not make tangible progress toward achieving Korean reunification.

The ROK needed to modify its long-standing policy of automatic annual debate in October 1971 when the PRC government assumed China's seat in the Security Council. This replacement was perceived as a grave threat to Seoul's interests by South Korean leaders. The ROK government suspended its policy and decided to raise the Korean issue only when it might be necessary. Thus, the ROK's new policy prevented the Korean question from being discussed at the twenty-sixth General Assembly session in 1971; debate was postponed until the twenty-eighth session in 1973.

In August 1971, for the first time since the division of the Korean peninsula, there had been an inter-Korean dialogue initiated for Koreans themselves to solve the Korean problem. However, in August 1973, talks were unilaterally suspended by North Korea. Meanwhile, North Korea established full diplomatic relations with several European nations in 1973. Also that year, it was admitted to the World Health Organization (WHO) as a member and acquired permanent observer status at the United Nations with the ROK. In the General Assembly's twenty-eighth session that fall, delegates of both South and North participated as observers in the debate on the Korean question; the only substantive decision made was to dissolve UNCURK, which was done in

November.[6] In 1974, the ROK government expressed its readiness to accept a dissolution of the UN Command (UNC) if an alternative arrangement could be made to replace the Korean armistice agreement.

In 1975, North and South expected another diplomatic showdown in the thirtieth session of the General Assembly. North Korea attempted a full-scale diplomatic offensive by demanding the withdrawal of all foreign troops from Korea. On June 17, the United States and South Korea offered to dissolve the UNC in Korea the following January and replace it with U.S. and South Korean officers as parties to the 1953 Korean armistice if the Chinese and North Koreans consented. The offer, made in a letter to the UN Security Council, was aimed at heading off any demand at the General Assembly session that U.S. troops in South Korea under the UN flag be withdrawn. The U.S. and South Korean governments argued that the armistice would be thrown into question if the UNC was dissolved without arrangements for a successor party. The ROK government favored having the Security Council deliberate on an alternative arrangement to the armistice agreement at an appropriate time.

The General Assembly adopted two conflicting resolutions on Korea on November 18, 1975.[7] The Western resolution, sponsored by the United States and twenty-seven other members, was adopted by a vote of 59-51 with 29 abstentions. It called for negotiations to find alternative arrangements for the 1953 armistice agreement by the parties directly concerned (North Korea, South Korea, China, and the United States) and provided for dissolution of the UNC by January 1976. The United States contended that U.S. troops in South Korea were there under the 1954 U.S.-ROK defense treaty.

The pro–North Korean resolution, sponsored by Algeria, the PRC, the Soviet Union, and thirty-nine other nations, was adopted by a vote of 54-43 with 42 abstentions. It called for the immediate dissolution of the UNC, the withdrawal of all foreign troops from South Korea, and the replacement of the armistice agreement with a peace treaty between North Korea and the United States. North Korea contended that South Korea should not be included in the treaty negotiations was not a party to the 1953 agreement.[8] Thus, by adopting these conflicting resolutions, the UN showed its weakness in dealing with the Korean question, and from 1976 to fall 1991, it was not on the agenda. The ROK government did not initiate debates in the UN but instead urged North Korea to solve the Korean problem through inter-Korean dialogue outside of the UN framework.

Admission of the Two Koreas to the UN, 1991

After the ROK government made its first application for admission to the United Nations on January 19, 1949, it applied formally four more times (December 22, 1951; April 21, 1961; July 29, 1975; and September 21, 1975); its bid was supported by nine resolutions by its allies. The North Korean government also applied for membership (February 9, 1949; January 2, 1952); in support were three resolutions by its allies. Whenever South and North applied for membership, both were denied.[9] From 1949 to 1991, neither South Korea nor North Korea could be admitted into the UN primarily because of the use of the veto power by the five permanent members of the Security Council.

South Korea's new policy on UN admission was spelled out in President Park Chung Hee's June 23, 1973, declaration for peace and unification: "South Korea shall not object to its admission to the United Nations together with North Korea, provided that it does not cause hindrance to national unification."[10] President Park also stated that even before its admission to the UN, South Korea would not be opposed to North Korea also being invited at the same time into the UN debate on the Korean question. This declaration indicated clearly that the ROK's policy toward the UN had been revised substantially in response to the changing international environment because it was no longer opposed to simultaneous admission of both Koreas.

North Korea rejected President Park's dual-membership proposal on the grounds that it would perpetuate the division of Korea. President Kim Il Sung made his counterproposal: North Korea would not enter the UN separately, and if the South and the North wanted to enter the UN before unification, they should enter as a single state under the name Confederal Republic of Koryo.[11] North Korea's rationale for rejecting dual membership was that it would be a recognition of the two states internationally and thus the division of Korea would be permanent.

In response, the ROK government argued that dual membership in the UN would not become a hindrance to national reunification—if South and North agreed, there could be a united Korea anytime they wished. Dual membership, South Korea argued, would not freeze the division of the Korean peninsula. The ROK government made its proposal because it believed the entry of North and South into the UN might moderate the North's aggressive behavior and contribute to a peaceful resolution of the Korean reunification issue.

When the Security Council decided not to include the ROK's application for UN membership on the agenda again in September 1975, the ROK government did not have much choice but to take a long break before reapplying. In the late 1980s, the Cold War between the East and the West was on the wane in a rapidly changing international security environment. Revolutionary changes in Eastern Europe and the Soviet Union, the collapse of communism in Eastern Europe, and the end of the Cold War between the United States and the Soviet Union required the ROK to take a fresh look at its foreign policy toward communist states.

There were drastic changes in South Korea's policy toward North Korea and northern neighbors in summer 1988. In his special statement on July 7, President Roh Tae Woo declared that the South would no longer regard North Korea as an adversary but as a member of the Korean National Community; that the South would help North Korea effectively take part in the international community as a responsible member; that the South would continuously carry out its policy of increased cooperation and reconciliation with the North; and that his government would make efforts to put an end to counterproductive diplomatic competition between the South and the North.[12] In the same declaration, President Roh announced his "northern policy" to improve diplomatic relations with the Soviet Union, the PRC, and East European countries. As a result, South Korea established diplomatic relations with Hungary in February 1989 and later with Poland, Yugoslavia, Bulgaria, Czechoslovakia, and Romania. In September 1990, South Korea also established diplomatic ties with the Soviet Union, and the next month South Korea and the PRC agreed to exchange trade offices with de facto consular functions (there had been formal diplomatic relations established with the People's Republic of Mongolia that summer).[13]

South Korea successfully hosted the 1988 summer Olympics in Seoul. The event provided golden opportunities for South Korea to obtain international support for the Korean question in the UN. After the Seoul Olympics, consensus developed in the UN that South Korea should be admitted. By the end of 1990, both the PRC and the Soviet Union—permanent members of the UN Security Council—were inclined not to reject South Korea's application for membership to the UN with North Korea.

In view of favorable international developments, the ROK government made new efforts to enter the UN in 1990, proposing to North Korea in the spring that the two Koreas join the UN simultaneously but separately as a temporary measure pending Korean reunification. If the North refused to join, the South stated that it would apply for membership alone. In response, the North counterproposed May 30 that South Korea and North Korea enter the UN as a single member.[14] The North's proposal was immediately rejected by the South on the grounds that such a plan was utterly unrealistic. North Korea proposed discussion of UN membership as one of three urgent issues at the inter-Korean talks held in Seoul in September 1990, but the two sides did not reach an agreement because of the North's insistence on the joint entry of the two Koreas in a single seat. South Korea, however, decided to postpone the resubmission of its application until 1991. In the meantime, in the 1990 session of the UN General Assembly, over seventy members supported the South's plan for simultaneous but separate admission of the two Koreas; no member favored the North's proposal for joint entry of the two Koreas in a single seat.

In spring 1991, the Soviet Union and the PRC changed their policy on South Korea's application. The Soviet government declared its intention to support South Korea's UN membership at the Soviet-ROK summit meeting held on Cheju Island in April.[15] The PRC had indicated its intention not to veto South Korea's application. Thus, the ROK decided to apply for membership regardless of what action North Korea might take. In view of the unfavorable international developments, North Korea was forced to revise its position on the UN membership issue. On May 27, 1991, the DPRK issued an official statement claiming it had no choice but to enter the United Nations separately, although it had argued for years that dual membership would perpetuate the division of Korea.

As the south Korean authorities insist on their separate UN membership, if we leave this alone, important issues related to the interests of the entire Korean nation would be dealt with in a biased manner on the UN rostrum and this would entail grave consequences. ... The Government of the Democratic People's Republic of Korea has no choice but to enter the United Nations at the present stage as a step to overcome such temporary difficulties created by the south Korean authorities.[16]

It is significant to examine why North Korea decided to seek a separate seat in the UN. What major factors influenced North Korea's change in policy? First, the PRC and the Soviet Union clearly stated that they would not veto South Korea's UN membership application. Second, Japan's demand for simultaneous entry of the two Koreas was an important factor. Third, the DPRK government accepted separate admission to protect the North Korean system from possible "absorption" by the ROK. The survival of the North Korean system was the ulterior motive behind the North's shift in policy. Thus, North Korea wanted to enter the UN as a separate member because it would "enhance the North's legitimacy, bolster its international position, and strengthen its national security."[17]

On August 9, 1991, the UN Security Council unanimously approved the two Koreas' membership applications, and they were finally admitted into the United Nations on September 17. The separate but simultaneous admission of South and North eventually led to a new chapter in inter-Korean relations based on peaceful coexistence and coprosperity between the two Koreas. According to the UN charter (article 4, paragraph 1), "Membership in the United Nations is open to all other peace-loving states which accept the obligations contained in the present Charter and in the judgment of the Organization, are able and willing to carry out these obligations." The admission of the two Korean states to the United Nations requires them to abide by the obligations contained in the UN charter and international law. As members of the UN, the ROK and the DPRK governments should settle their disputes by peaceful means without resort to violent means.

The New Roles of the UN
in the Korean Reunification Process

Since South Korea and North Korea were admitted to the United Nations in September 1991, inter-Korean high-level talks have been productive and thus have paved the road to Korean reunification. South and North in December 1991 signed and in February 1992 effectuated two important agreements: an agreement on reconciliation, nonaggression, and exchanges and cooperation (Appendix B) and a declaration on denuclearization of the Korean peninsula (Appendix C). Nonetheless, the two Koreas need to implement these agreements in good faith to solve the Korean problem themselves.

Although the DPRK entered the UN separately, it still argues that "Korea is one," flatly rejecting the two-Korea policy. North Korea does not politically accept the notion of two Korean states on the Korean peninsula, although its acceptance of separate UN memberships and the South-North agreements have legally nullified the North's one-Korea policy. Under the UN charter, the DPRK must be a "peace-loving" state that is "able and willing to carry out" the obligations in the charter. As a member of the UN, the DPRK is expected to become a more civilized state that will observe in good faith the UN charter and international law. What can and should the UN do to bring about peace and the unification of Korea? As previously discussed, it is argued here that the UN has played a limited but important role in the Korean reunification process. When North Korea crossed the thirty-eighth parallel to unify all Korea by military force, the UN effectively prevented North Korea from achieving its goal. The UN has also provided good offices, mediation, and a forum for solving the Korean problem.

Because both the ROK and the DPRK are now UN members, it should be pointed out that the UN can play new roles, albeit limited, in achieving Korean reunification. One should clearly understand that the UN is not a world government but at best a loose confederation of 183 (as of May 1993) sovereign nation-states. Hence, Koreans should not expect too much regarding what the UN could do to help them bring about the peaceful unification of Korea. Nevertheless, despite its inherent weaknesses and limitations, the UN still can make important contributions to the Korean reunification process.

First, the UN can provide a world forum and a better place for inter-Korean dialogue and international dialogue through which North Korea will learn more about "good behavior" in international relations. Both the ROK and the DPRK will be able to use the UN as a venue for international diplomatic bargaining and negotiations between the two Koreas and the four major powers (the United States, the PRC, Russia, and Japan). Hence, the UN can help achieve cross recognition of the two Koreas by the four powers. The UN also can provide a valuable channel for international economic development cooperation involving the two Koreas and other UN members. The Tumen River economic development project under the auspices of the United Nations Development Program (UNDP) is a case in point.

Second, the UN can still play an important role in converting the 1953 Korean armistice agreement into a peace system on the Korean peninsula because the agreement was signed under UN auspices. The "real" parties to it are undoubtedly South Korea, North Korea, the United States, and the PRC. Hence, the author proposes there be a four-power conference of these parties in New York under the auspices of the UN secretary-general to discuss this critical issue. Other issues for possible discussion include replacing the 1953 armistice with a peace treaty between the PRC and the ROK and a peace treaty between the United States and the DPRK; resolution of these matters would formally end the Korean War.

Henry Kissinger made a similar proposal before the thirty-first session of the UN General Assembly on September 30, 1976. He suggested a conference to discuss ways of adapting the Korean armistice agreement to new conditions and replacing it with a more permanent arrangement. Kissinger proposed a three-phase approach. The first phase would be preliminary talks between North Korea and South Korea to discuss the venue and scope of the conferences. In this phase, the United States and the PRC could participate as "observers or in an advisory role." The second phase would be an international conference with the United States, the PRC, South Korea, and North Korea participating. The third phase would be "a wider conference in which other countries could associate themselves with arrangements that guarantee a durable peace on the peninsula."[18]

Third, the DPRK government will continue demanding U.S. troop withdrawal from South Korea in future UN debates on the Korean question. For their part, the United States and the ROK will equally maintain that the presence of U.S. forces in Korea is based on the 1954 U.S.-ROK mutual defense treaty. Hence, U.S. troops in Korea should stay until a peace system on the Korean peninsula is firmly established.[19] U.S. troop withdrawal from Korea without some UN guarantees would be undesirable. Therefore, an alternative to the presence of U.S. forces in Korea could be a UN peacekeeping force in Korea if the two Koreas will accept this idea. This force should remain under the direction of the UN secretary-general as a symbol of peace on the Korean peninsula.

Conclusion

As discussed in this chapter, the United Nations has played a limited but important role in the Korean reunification process since 1947. During the Cold War years, Korean reunification was one of the issues between the East and the West. The two Koreas' entry into the UN was impossible because the United States and the Soviet Union could not reach an agreement. However, with the end of the Cold War, the two Koreas were finally admitted to the United Nations on September 17, 1991. Their simultaneous but separate admission will have significant effects on the future of inter-Korean relations and the Korean reunification process in coming years.

The UN does not have the power or competence to achieve the goal of Korean reunification but can help both South and North solve their problems pertaining to this goal. In this context, one may define the UN's new roles in the reunification process.

As previously suggested, the ROK and the DPRK governments can effectively use the UN for the purpose of converting the 1953 Korean armistice agreement into a durable peace system in Korea, but they should be willing to compromise and make mutual concessions to solve the Korean problem by themselves. In the final analysis, the new role of the UN in the Korean reunification process needs to be clearly defined, and the UN can and should play a limited but significant role in the effort to achieve Korean reunification in the years ahead.

Finally, the UN can play an active role as communication facilitator between the South and the North, now that the two Koreas are members of the international body. Finally, the UN can provide a forum for inter-Korean bilateral and multilateral negotiations to discuss the Korean question under the auspices of its secretary-general. In this way the issue can be settled through that office providing a mediation role in dispute settlement. As members of the United Nations, both North Korea and South Korea, if they so choose, can solicit the UN to play a constructive third-party role in conflict resolution.

Notes

1. For further details of the joint commission, see Soon Sung Cho, *Korea in World Politics, 1940–1950* (Berkeley: University of California Press, 1967), pp. 114–158.

2. *Yearbook of the UN, 1947–48* (Lake Success, NY: UN Department of Public Information, 1948), p. 81.

3. Cho, *Korea in World*, pp. 220–221.

4. *Yearbook of the UN, 1950* (New York: Columbia University Press in cooperation with the United Nations), pp. 280–283.

5. For further details of the Geneva conference, see Hak-Joon Kim, *The Unification Policy of South and North Korea: A Comparative Study* (Seoul: Seoul National University, 1977), pp. 153–157.

6. For the best analysis of the Korean question at the twenty-eighth General Assembly, see B. C. Koh, "The United Nations and the Politics of Korean Reunification," *Journal of Korean Affairs*, Vol. 3, No. 4 (January 1974), pp. 37–56.

7. For an excellent analysis of UN votes on the two resolutions, see B. C. Koh, "The Battle Without Victors: The Korean Question in the 30th Session of the U.N. General Assembly," *Journal of Korean Affairs*, Vol. 5, No. 4 (January 1976), pp. 43–63.

8. Ibid., pp. 48–55.

9. For South Korea's efforts to enter the UN, see Ministry of Foreign Affairs, ROK, *Han'guk Oegyo 40 nyon, 1948–1988* (ROK's Forty-year diplomacy) (Seoul: Ministry of Foreign Affairs, 1990), pp. 249–253; Warren Whalmin Kim, "On the Admission of Korea to Membership in the United Nations," in *Proceedings of the Fifth Joint Conference of the Korean Political Science Association and the Association of Korean Political Scientists in North America, August 8–10, 1983* (Seoul: Korean Political Science Association, 1983), pp. 247–260; Chong Han Kim, "The Changing Character of South Korea's UN Policy on the Korean Question: A Preliminary Survey," in *Proceedings of the Fourth Joint Conference of the Korean Political Science Association and the Association of Korean Political Scientists in North America, August 10–12, 1981* (Seoul: Korean Political Science Association, 1981), pp. 119–133; Chi Young Park, "Korea and the United Nations," in Youngnok Koo and Sung-joo Han, eds., *The Foreign Policy of the Republic of Korea* (New York: Columbia University Press, 1985), pp. 262–284.

10. President Park Chung Hee, "Special Statement Regarding Foreign Policy for Peace and Unification" (Seoul: Korea Information Service, Inc., 1973), pp. 29–34.

11. *Rodong Sinmun*, June 24, 1973; *New York Times*, June 24, 1973.

12. For further details of the statement and its significance, see National Unification Board, ROK, *A White Paper on South-North Dialogue in Korea* (Seoul: National Unification Board, 1988), pp. 381–403.

13. For an evaluation of the South's northern policy, see Tae Dong Chung, "Korea's Nordpolitik: Achievement and Prospects," *Asian Perspective*, Vol. 15, No. 2 (Fall-Winter 1991), pp. 149–178.

14. *Chosŏn Ilbo*, May 31, 1990.

15. *Korea Newsreview*, April 27, 1991.

16. *Pyongyang Times*, June 1, 1991.

17. For further details, see Hong Nack Kim, "The Two Koreas' Entry into the United Nations and the Implications for Inter-Korean Relations," *Korea and World Affairs*, Vol. 15, No. 3 (Fall 1991), pp. 407–409.

18. For full text, see Henry A. Kissinger, "Toward A New Understanding of Community," secretary of state's speech before the 31st session of the UN General Assembly, Bureau of Public Affairs, Department of State, September 30, 1976.

19. For further discussion on the role of U.S. forces in Korea in the inter-Korean peace process, see Tae Hwan Kwak, "The Reduction of U.S. forces in Korea in the Inter-Korean Peace Process," *Korean Journal of Defense Analysis,* Vol. 2, No. 2 (Winter 1990), pp. 171–194.

18

Ideological Synthesis for Reunified Korea

Han Shik Park

This chapter is written on the premise that any meaningful attempt at reunification of the divided Korean communities must be preceded by concerted efforts at cultivating a system of shared values. This premise is predicated upon the realization that each of the two systems on either side of the DMZ can be expected to accept the existence of each political system along with its bases of legitimacy. The successful inter-Korean talks, held at the prime ministerial level, and all other conciliatory gestures have been carried out in a way that both sides expect to benefit from these maneuvers; but as soon as either side faces unwanted developments tilting against its interests or in the other's favor, conciliatory gestures are disrupted, indicating that the negotiations are guided basically by a zero-sum game. Thus, this mutually exclusive relationship between the two regimes must explore a shared value system designed to facilitate a positive-sum relationship whereby both sides benefit from their interactions.

In light of the preceding factors, this chapter attempts the following: (1) to discern the nature of the political-historical milieu that provides the context in which an ideological synthesis must emerge; (2) to ascertain contrasting patterns of political cultures exhibited by the two Korean regimes; (3) to examine the global environment to which a national identity and a new ideology must adapt and to offer a normative construct that might lay the foundation for a new ideology needed for the reunification of Korea and beyond.

The Erosion of the Cold War World Order System

It is now evident that the era of Cold War politics has ended. But there seems to be little consensus on the causes of this change. The demise of the communist bloc cannot be interpreted simply as the victory of the capitalists in the ideological warfare; a more direct cause might have been its inherent inability to meet the basic needs and rising expectations of the people. Furthermore, the demise of some socialist systems must not lead us to the conclusion that capitalism is an ideal ideology to guide human behavior and the course of social development. Two facts remain indisputable: First, there are oppressing problems in advanced capitalist systems, including human and social degeneration as well as ecological deterioration. Second, the socialist ideal of equality and of every individual being entitled to basic needs is still found in some Third World systems where socialism has been adapted to indigenous conditions, including in the Asiatic systems of China, Vietnam, and North Korea.

These factors notwithstanding, however, the global community has created an ideological vacuum in which human values and belief systems are rapidly becoming irrelevant to contemporary politics. The process of value neutralization in human conduct has been accelerated by the myth of science on the one hand and the universal human desire for material affluence on the other. Indeed, the contemporary human being seems to be guided by material self-interest rather than by any value system. In fact, the concept of "rationality" is perceived as being value neutral because the concept is defined as the pursuit of interest maximization. If we consider that classical philosophers regarded pursuit of self-interested behavior as irrational and of altruistic (benevolent) behavior as rational, the drastic conceptual transformation speaks a great deal about modern civilization. The contemporary syndrome of value neutrality may have been a powerful underlying current behind the erosion of socialism and the age of ideology itself. Under the market culture, we are expected to behave in a highly predictable way in which choice is dictated by the market mechanism of cost/benefit assessment, and there is no overriding value that supersedes material gain. In this sense, human beings may have become little more than physical objects and their behaviors explicable by the law of physics.

In this ideological vacuum, the boat carrying the human species has lost its canvas, and humans themselves are making their journeys without a map. The unguided journey is destined to end in a catastrophe because all the symptoms of illness in the health of the ecology, social systems, and human minds are pushing humankind toward self-inflicted extinction.[1]

An ideology functions as an institutional means of coping with human problems and realizing human aspirations. It induces certain values and conducts and discourages others; it provides legitimacy for certain forms of governance and prohibits others. In other words, an ideology is a codebook that any political system must have, and it should therefore be the crystallization of collective aspirations of a society. Thus, as long as there are human aspirations for development, there should be ideology. Then, what are and what should be today's human aspirations to be incorporated into a new ideology to emerge from the ideological vacuum? This question has to be addressed before we attempt to prescribe an ideology for Korea.

Human aspirations may be perceived in terms of two categories: problem solving and social engineering.[2] Problem solving involves identification, diagnosis, and treatment. Contemporary problems share common characteristics; among them are universality and human degeneration. They are universal in that all peoples in the world share similar problems as evidenced by ecological deterioration, threat to global security by the proliferation of destructive weapons, and degeneration of social structures. These problems pose a certain threat to the very survival of the human species. However, solving these problems is not the ultimate achievement of human aspirations. Society must be engineered in a normatively desirable direction toward the realization of human development, social harmony, and global peace.[3] The two challenges of problem solving and social engineering are not necessarily sequential; that is, one need not wait for problem solving to be completed before venturing into social engineering. Social engineering can in fact be an effective approach to solving certain problems.

To the extent that we have a common fate as fellow travelers on this planet, Korean problems cannot be isolated entirely from the problems of the global community, although they may have their unique additional features. Indeed, the Korean peninsula seems to be the microcosm of the global society as far as the diversity and intensity of problems are concerned. The two Koreas combined might represent a range of diverse life situations that encompass the world itself. Thus, a key to solving the Korean problems might be instrumental in developing ideas and strategies to address world problems.

The Plight and Character of the Korean People

In this century, the Korean people have gone through a great variety of personal and national experiences. In the political realm, they have lived through dynastic rule, thorough exploitation by colonialism, division of the country along with separation of families in the magnitude of 10 million, one of the bloodiest civil wars in human history, and unstable democracies in the South and a centrist xenophobia in the North for nearly half a century resulting in mutually incompatible sets of values, beliefs, and political systems. No other people in the world have experienced such a profound historical diversity. From the economic standpoint, the people have experienced extreme poverty, routine starvation every spring, feudal as well as colonial exploitation, and finally, relative stability and prosperity in recent decades. A variety of economic systems have been experimented with on the Korean peninsula ranging from an intense form of capitalist competition to an extreme kind of planned economy. In the arena of social life, the Korean people have experienced the disruptive process of urbanization, the transition of family as institution, internationalization in the South, and indigenization in the North. The diversity of cultural experience is even more acute. As some say, each of the cultural systems of Confucianism, Buddhism, and Christianity has exhibited more extreme manifestation in Korea than it has in the society of its origin. In this way, Koreans have been deeply influenced by ideas and values that are fundamentally contrasting and divergent. The two ideologies being advocated and practiced today—*Juche* in North Korea and democracy in the

South—might well be as diverse and different as any set of ideologies that have existed in history.

Although diverse experience exists in both the physical and metaphysical arenas, what is truly intriguing is the fact that the heterogeneous attributes in the society and culture have seldom generated serious confrontation or chaotic disunity. With the exception of the untested case of *Juche* versus South Korean democracy, almost all the contrasting forces have coexisted harmoniously: There has been no religious confrontation although the Buddhist, Christian, and Confucian populations are nearly equally matched in numbers. It would not be unusual for a Korean to participate in Confucian rites for ancestor worship, marry in a Christian wedding, and have a burial based on Buddhist rituals.

Paradoxical to the heterogeneous national attributes is the fact that the Korean people share similar national characteristics in such salient areas as language, race, and ethnic identity. Whereas the dividing attributes are of the kind that have been articulated rather than ascribed, the consensual characteristics cannot be altered by will of the people or government policies. It is therefore vital to explore avenues in which these common national characteristics can be exploited selectively to cultivate national consciousness and ideological foundation. The process of identifying and selecting consensual national characteristics should be guided by the ideals and aspirations of the Korean people. Thus we must first address the question of what ideals and aspirations might be established in Korea in this era of globalism.

The first and foremost ideal has to be the restoration and preservation of human dignity. Thus, the aspiration of creating a community in which humankind is dignified is not limited to the Koreans but is common to all peoples. Human dignity requires the material condition of basic needs, the social condition of having a sense of belonging and opportunities, and the political condition of choice making. One aspires to have sufficient food, adequate shelter, and security from political and environmental adversities in order to ensure physical survival. One must also aspire to secure psychological comfort by belonging to other human beings and by gaining access to economic and social opportunities. Finally, human beings must claim masterhood over their natural, social, and political environment through the right to make voluntary choices.

Second, in a world so torn by artificial parameters such as national interest and ethnic and ideological differences, one must reach for peace. Ideally, peace must refer to something more than the absence of conflict. It must mean harmonious coexistence in which relationships are guided by a positive game. Their tormented history makes the Korean people long for meaningful peace. In fact, there might not be another people that has suffered as much from conflict, division, distrust, and the anxieties of a zero-sum game. This experience may richly qualify them to be able to articulate ideas of peace and to construct approaches toward its realization.

Today's global political climate shows a resurgence of ethnic and national consciousness, as evidenced by the former Soviet republics, by Yugoslavia, and by the Kurds of Iraq. Most multiethnic systems are showing signs of rebellious and at least nonconforming behavior toward their traditional political centers. This tendency suggests that ethnic and national groups may have given an appearance of assimilation into the predominant political culture during the Cold Ear era but that the disguised appearance can be unveiled as the externally imposed suppression is lifted.

A nation, unlike a political system, is an "imagined political community" that provides a civil society with cohesion and psychological integration.[4] The sense of belonging can be so emotionally and psychologically strong that personal sacrifice, including life itself, is often absorbed by members of the nation. Members have mysterious and compelling attachment to the nation in such a manner that any behavior or attitude in defiance of group norms is condemned. The degree to which a people has an inward sense of cohesiveness is determined by a number of inherent and situational characteristics of the nation. Among other factors, ethnic homogeneity, longevity of national history, and external hostility might be included as the most crucial determinants of national consciousness.

The Koreans are regarded as one of the most homogeneous peoples in the world. In fact, *The Book of World Rankings* compiled by George T. Kurian ranks Korea as the highest of all nations on the ethnic homogeneity index.[5] It is not only the ethnic makeup of the Korean people that is homogeneous; their norms and behavioral patterns tend to be uniformly exclusive as well. This tendency is richly documented by overseas Koreans who have maintained cultural and ethnic purity while living abroad for generations, often forming "Korea towns" or ethnic regions. They insist on using their own language and preserving cultural values and life-styles.

These ethnic characteristics coupled with the longevity of the nation as a cohesive entity have provided the people with an unwavering sense of belonging. Furthermore, the fact that Korean history is marred by successive domination by superior powers surrounding the peninsula has reinforced the inward sentiment of national consciousness. At the same time, the fact that Korea has had to cope with a hostile environment resulting from its geopolitical characteristics has helped the people learn to be adaptive to changing and different environments. The seemingly contradictory characteristics of salient national consciousness and adaptability may have resulted in generating a form of dualism: unwavering egocentrism and at the same time accommodation (and sometimes submission) to foreign influence. Thus, Korean politics has exhibited inconsistencies between appearances and contents: democracy in institutional appearance and authoritarianism in behavioral content; absolute loyalty in appearance and calculated opportunism in cultural content.

The "imagined" nation of Korea, therefore, can be said to have earned a set of characteristics through its history, and they can provide the underlying foundation upon which a national ideology might be formulated. These characteristics as described here include a series of seemingly contradictory attributes: diversity of experience and homogeneity of ethnicity; metaphysical idealism and practical rationality; collectivism in appearance and individualism in content; exclusiveness toward foreign objects and accommodation of alien influence. Attesting to these diverging attributes are the extremely contrasting patterns of behavioral and institutional manifestations that have indeed been witnessed in recent history culminating in profoundly different life situations in the two Korean communities.

Collectivism Versus Individualism

Korean culture, stemming basically from Confucianism, is inherently collective-oriented. Hedonistic selfishness is condemned and collective interest supersedes personal interest. Although industrial and urban development may have destroyed collectivism in its purest form, values of collectivity—whether it is the family or the state—are still placed above individual interest as a matter of moral imperative. However, the thorough saturation of South Korea with capitalist and market culture has produced what is referred to as the "rational actor" who is essentially an individualist. The rational actor in South Korea has been instrumental to economic expansion through exploring the international market. The law of survival of the fittest has favored the rational actor who is self-centered and aggressive in pursuing individual interest in South Korea. Yet one should note that no matter how "rational" the actor may be, this individual cannot avoid cultural condemnation if the selfish pursuit of interest undermines collective interest of the family, social and cultural organizations, and the state. In other words, the context of South Korean development may have steered the individual to behave for self-interest, but it failed to eradicate the normative ideal of collective good. As a result, a sort of dualism has evolved in the South Korean personality: collective orientation as an ideal value and hedonistic individualism as a practical guide.

North Korea, in contrast, has never departed from Confucian collectivism because it has not been exposed to the capitalist and market culture in which rational-actor behavior is induced. Individual interest should never deviate from state and societal interest. In fact, individual worth is determined by the extent to which the individual makes a contribution to the collective good. According to the *Juche* idea, individuals can overcome limitations and become perfected by attaining the "social-political life" of the state in a similar way that the Christian individual achieves salvation and eternal life through being selfless in God.[6]

Ethnocentrism Versus Internationalism

As discussed earlier, the Korean people by virtue of their ethnic homogeneity tend to be closed-minded and exclusive. Yet the fact that Korea is geopolitically vulnerable to external influence has made the people more adaptive and accommodating. Thus, the two opposing predispositions have been instilled in the political cultures of North Korea and South Korea: The North has formed its orientations centered around ethnocentrism, whereas the South has fostered internationalism. The contrast is extreme and casually felt by visitors to both societies. North Korean *Juche* is based on a de facto recognition of racial superiority, as evidenced by the notion promoted in North Korea that human history originated from the ancient land of Korea and its people are destined to keep human civilization from falling under the "yoke of imperialism." As the emancipator of all the oppressed peoples of the world, the "great leader" Kim Il Sung is claimed to be a global leader, indicating that his immediate people, North Koreans, have the uncommon quality of providing the world with such a leadership. This ethnocentrism has been promoted effectively by the regime through policies of information control and manipulation of political socialization of the masses.[7]

South Korea, by contrast, has been subjected to intensive and extensive foreign influences. In terms of the spiritual life, Western religions of diverse hues have settled in South Korea; on the material level, products from around the world have found their market in Korea; political institutions of all kinds have been transplanted from other countries. Ideas and values have been transferred to South Korea through the proliferation of foreign publications. Tourists from all over the world have come to South Korea and left some wrinkles in the society and culture. Multiple international events have been convened not only in the area of sport such as the Olympics but in the art and commercial arenas as well. All these combined have changed the South Korean society and its people in a profound manner, and they have learned the hard reality that Korea is merely one of many countries and cultures—a humbling experience that induces internationalism.

Spiritual Determinism Versus Material Determinism

It is truly ironic that Marxist materialism has led the North Korean ideology to a sort of spiritual determinism, whereas Western capitalism has become instrumental to the practice of a kind of material determinism in South Korea. One might object to this blunt observation, but the fact remains valid that material power has become almost omnipotent in the South, and the *Juche* idea of the North centers around the notion that human spirit has the power to determine the fate of the human race and history.

Juche claims that the human being is uniquely different from other species in that only humankind has *chajusŏng*, the ability to manage one's life independently of material, social, and political conditions. In fact, there is little resemblance between the Marxist perception of people and society, on the one hand, and the *Juche* conception of human nature and its relationship to the material forces of production and the symbolic environment of the society, on the other.[8]

Because Confucian values tend to favor the spiritual and human dimensions of social life rather than material success, North Korea's *Juche* might be considered relatively more consistent with traditional culture. But whether the desired national consciousness should be traditional or modern is a debatable question.

Traditionalism Versus Modernism

At the risk of oversimplification, one can say that North Korea is past and inwardly oriented, whereas South Korea is more future and outwardly oriented. When North Koreans compare their life condition, they tend to compare themselves with their ancestors rather than with people in other societies. Visitors to North Korea invariably develop the impression that the atmosphere of the society has not changed from the time of national liberation from Japanese colonialism. The prevalence of anti-Japanese sentiment, the exclusive use of Korean characters in all publications, the clothes people wear, and popular literature and the arts are all oriented toward traditionalism and nationalism.

South Korea, on the other hand, is motivated toward modernization, which often translates into Westernization. The streets of Seoul and entertainment establishments in South Korea show remarkable resemblance to the manifestations of Western societies. What is traditional is often regarded as backward and underdeveloped to the extent that modernization tends to be defined in terms of the eradication of traditional values and ways of life.

In the search for a new national consciousness, one must realize that not all traditional elements are underdeveloped. By the same token, one must also realize that not all Western or modern elements are corrupt or inhumane. Here, one must exercise great caution in choosing what is worth preserving and what is worth adopting. This circumspect approach can only be possible with a normative conception of a desirable ideology.

Normative Values and Ideas for a New Ideology

In spite of the fact that national consciousness is surging throughout the world in this post–Cold War era, the global community has clearly become an indivisible and integral single unit. The most dramatic development in this respect is the emergence of a global market in which national boundaries are becoming obsolete. Needless to say, the human species shares one ecosystem on a planet showing signs of deterioration beyond recovery, and we are forced to accept a common fate in matters of security. In short, a global community has emerged, and the extent of its interdependence is growing. No nation can be a viable member of the world system without being assimilated into and becoming an integrated part of the global community.

When a community is formed, cultural norms and values are simultaneously articulated. A culture is the symbolic expression of patterned relationships that emerge in the process of community building. What are the norms and values that emerge from the formation of the global community? In other words, what is the nature of the global culture (globalism) in the context of the contemporary global society?

The primary actor in the global community is the individual rather than the conventional body politic. In fact, the sovereign state will become increasingly obsolete as individual members of the global community find alternative functional entities that maintain cohesiveness and solidarity. One such entity is the ethnic group. Ethnic identity and national consciousness have surged forcefully following the decline of Cold War politics, as seen in the republics of the former Soviet Union and Eastern Europe. The impetus underlying German reunification might also be seen in light of the resurgence of national consciousness. Societies with ethnic diversity are expected to experience turmoil when claims are made for distributive justice; an example is the racial riots in Los Angeles in April and May 1992. Because ethnicity is an ascriptive quality, ethnic animosities and mutual disagreement cannot be settled easily through bargaining or negotiation. Ethnic minority groups demand not only distributive fairness but also a broader claim to human dignity. Human dignity on the part of the individual requires universal and inalienable human rights, including the rights to life and choice. For good reasons, ethnicity has been undermined as being insignificant or even irrelevant for the last few decades. The Cold War order was based on the confrontation between capitalism and socialism, both of which were in defiance of ethnicity. Capitalist classification of people was based on achievement in competition, and it distinguished achievers from nonachievers; whereas Marxist socialism organized population into classes. In either case, ethnicity had no room to stage its legitimate place in the world.[9] But with the changing world order, ethnicity has found a new light in the growing global community. It is in this historical context that the issues of ethnic identity and national consciousness will find a rightful place in the politics of the reunification of Korea.

Given that highly sophisticated weapons are already in the possession of undetermined hands and that weapons proliferation will continue at an explosive pace, the human species is at a crossroads: If we fail to solve ethnic and national problems, humans are indeed doomed. Any effort to resolve ethnic problems requires more than bargaining or negotiation, which is meant for cases of disagreement on the allocation of quantitative values. When the Korean issue is viewed from this perspective, one might note that it will take no less than a miracle to expect a negotiated settlement between the two regimes. What is needed is not negotiation but genuine efforts for peacemaking.

Negotiating may be useful for the postponement of conflict, but it is not a process of peacemaking because peace is more (other) than the absence of conflict. The concept of peace (or any other concept) should be defined in terms of what it is rather than what it is not. Conflict resolution may be necessary, but it is not what peacemaking is about. Peace refers to harmony in which diverse parts find "oneness" through perfection and coordination of the constituent parts. In this case, each of the parts becomes better off through overcoming its individuality and becoming integrated or assimilated into the whole. A perfect analogy may be made in musical harmony. After painstaking trials and learning by musicians during rehearsals, different instruments in a symphonic group will be able to produce a harmony of "oneness." Toward this creation, each part has to perfect its function not in isolation from others but in coordination with them. This coordination must avoid domination by any part but find a rightful place in the totality. The conductor's job is to envision the state of harmony and induce each part toward realization of the vision. The conductor in this case is analogous to political leadership. The leader is one who interprets the music (composition) and helps the community of musicians in pursuing realization of the vision. In this case, the vision is an ideology. The ideology in today's context needs to be globalism.

In short, globalism is an idea in which human development at the individual level and peace at the collective level are promoted. In view of the contrasting national characters as exhibited by the two Korean regimes, what then ought to be the direction in which a new ideology may be formulated— an ideology that not only might facilitate the process of national integration but also could contribute to the goals of a peacemaking global community? In this regard, one might prescribe the nature of national consciousness for the Korean people in terms of what it should not be and what it should be.

1. *From domination to accommodation:* One system should not impose its desires on the other in an attempt to dominate it. As clarified in the discussion about the concept of peace, domination has no place in the pursuit of integration through harmony. There may be values offered by either of the regimes in Korea that might be more conducive to globalism, but they must be legitimized as intrinsic values rather than as means of domination. Despite the appearance of reconciliation between the two regimes, it is undeniable that neither side has ever expressed willingness to compromise on its insistence on being righteous vis-à-vis the other side.

As clearly evidenced in the notion of peace, a harmonious relationship should facilitate mutual adjustment and reinforcement. By interacting with each other and through integration, each of the two sides must expect to be better off than under the status quo. The reality in the history of inter-Korean relations is that each side has sought its basis of legitimacy in repudiating the existence of the other; thus the relationship has been one of mutual exclusiveness or a zero-sum game.[10] Conversely, accepting the other side's proposals has been automatically construed as a defeat, and any proposal originating from the other side has been habitually rejected regardless of the content of the proposal itself. This mentality must be cured if there is to be any progress toward national integration.

2. *Basic needs and the right to life:* Any ideology to be persuasive should be founded on the universal value of human dignity. Human dignity, as alluded to earlier, involves at the very minimum the right to basic needs. No national consciousness or political ideology can be justified if it defies physical existence. One must live first before pursuing any other component of dignified life. For this, one must insist on the production of sufficient food and shelter as well as security. Whether one might pursue self-sufficiency or look to other systems to obtain these basic requirements is an important question. In this regard, there seems to be sharp disagreement between North Korea's *Juche* and South Korea's ideas for modernization. It would seem that self-reliance— to the extent possible without curtailing productivity and resource expansion—might be a meaningful goal for any system.[11] This is because one should be able to make decisions guiding one's own behavior.

3. *Freedom and the right of choice:* Because human beings cannot find dignity without securing certain autonomy from not only the physical world but also social and political capricious manipulations, one might insist on the right of choice. Choice making should be what human behavior itself is all about. If a person behaves only in accordance with someone else's plans, desires, and preferences, such a person is literally a slave. To the extent that the life of a slave is not consistent with human dignity, the right of choice must be regarded as a requisite for a dignified life. Choice making requires among other things the availability of alternatives, information about them, preference or-

dering on the part of the chooser, and the absence of political restrictions on choice-making behavior.

Thus, the range of alternatives in terms of both their quantity and their qualitative diversity must be maximized. This means at least that diverse ideas and ideologies as well as social organizations and cultural associations should be protected and even promoted, including those critical of the political establishment. Furthermore, extensive and unrestricted flow of information concerning the alternatives should be insisted on in the search for a new ideology. Both the North and the South have ample room for improvement in this regard, and the monolithic system of the Pyongyang regime is especially vulnerable to this criticism.

4. *Distributive justice:* The right to choice making can be severely undermined by social and economic inequality and by political power. In fact, a desirable ideology should ensure a broad distribution of resources and values for not only choice making but equality itself. One should not forget that socialism may have faltered seriously in recent years, but the very value of equality advocated by the same ideology should not be discarded, for without economic and social equality, human dignity itself becomes meaningless. Yet one should not be so naive as to expect a perfectly equal society, nor should one consider such a society even desirable. Then, how may the extent of inequality that is allowable be determined? This question is addressed later. For now, a comparison of the two Korean regimes reveals sharp differences in patterns of distribution. North Korea is one of the most egalitarian systems in the world, at least when measured by indices of income distribution by household or occupational categories; South Korea suffers from an increasingly widening gap between the rich and the poor, the result in part of uncontrolled land speculation. Income discrepancies and a certain degree of economic inequality might be conducive to healthy competition, but distributive inequality should be contained within the limit of not provoking social injustice.

5. *The achievement society:* The question of "allowable" degree of inequality was raised in the preceding paragraph. The rationale was that it may facilitate healthy competition and promote a work ethic through positive incentives. Yet no viable definition of the threshold has been persuasively presented. One definition offered here is that inequality should not be inherited; by the same token, the structure of inequality in a society should be changeable by the dynamics of individual achievement. When distributive injustice—thus social and human injustice—is immune to individual achievement, it constitutes a form of "structural violence" threatening the very stability of the regime. Thus, an ideal ideology should incorporate a distributive mechanism whereby economic and social rewards are based on achievement and social contribution rather than ascription and personal connections. In this regard, both Korean regimes seem to be seriously deficient.

6. *The environment:* Human dependence on the natural environment is unavoidable, yet it has always been a human aspiration to alleviate the adversities of nature. In fact, technological development has largely been and should continue to be geared in the direction of controlling the natural environment without destroying it. Unfortunately, today's technologies are seemingly de-

signed to promote human leisure (or perhaps laziness) and conquer (destroy) nature's ecosystem. To this extent, technological evolution has been misguided. Ironically, the technologically and industrially developed societies contribute to greater environmental deterioration. A cursory comparison of the two Korean regimes would lead to the conclusion that the North has been more successful in avoiding environmental decay. However, it is of vital importance for North Korea to make conscientious efforts to avoid ecological deterioration as it pursues economic and industrial development, whereas South Korea might shift its policy from indiscriminate industrial growth to a comprehensive environment policy.

7. *Institutionalization:* The simple fact that a person's longevity has an absolute limit and a society or political community endures beyond the human life span is often forgotten. Laws and principles guiding a society must not be designed to satisfy any particular individual's personal ambition. When principles and legislative ideas are conceived, they need to be centered on the life of the society and be future-oriented. In this sense, laws and guiding principles must be autonomous from any specific individuals. Instead, patterns of government or relationships ought to be institutionalized, personalized.

Koreans are notoriously incapable of distinguishing principles and "ideal types" from concrete cases in which specific persons are involved. For both Koreas and their people in general, laws are made to rationalize and justify individual persons or empirical situations of their choice. In fact, each of the leaders (mostly presidents) of South Korea has changed the state's constitution in order to accommodate his political ambitions or personal desires. Similarly, North Korean politics (and accompanying political ideas) has evolved around Kim Il Sung to the extent that he has become in the political culture an immortal being. This syndrome of personalization of politics is not limited to the level of national government; it is pervasive at all levels of government. Further, this syndrome is not contained within the public sector. Indeed, private organizations including even universities and religious groups, especially in the South, are highly personalized; laws and regulations have merely cosmetic usefulness.

The lack of institutionalization or the practice of personalization of politics leads to factionalism and recurring instability and legitimacy crises. At the same time, this breeds cultism and possible deification of political leaders and promotes nepotism and other forms of corruption, as amply demonstrated in both political systems.

If a new ideology is to avoid the same trap of personal politics and all the accompanying shortcomings, it is imperative for it to cultivate a political culture (and practice) of depersonalization and move toward viable institutionalized politics.

8. *Communicative capability:* The ultimate goals of human dignity and global peace cannot be approached without extensive and intensive communication by individuals and groups with different values and priorities. Communication is necessary when understanding is desirable; it is misunderstanding that is the primary source of conflict at all levels of society. Understanding is not agreement; in fact, agreement does not require understanding. Because dis-

agreement and differences lead to confrontation, the enhancement of under-standing is necessary to avoid conflict. But the real significance of communi-cation is far-reaching and instrumental to peacemaking.

Communication is the exchange of values as opposed to mere facts. Differ-ent values and opinions that might even be mutually incompatible must find a common basis through communication and understanding. For communi-cation to be effective and meaningful, there are a few requisite conditions. First, empathy is required. Without this attitudinal quality, communication can only result in one-sided assertions and misunderstanding. Second, one must also be open-minded—be ready to accommodate other views and opin-ions and willing to adjust one's own perspectives. Third, the absence of con-straint (political or otherwise) on communication must be preserved.

In view of the definition and conditions for communication, one has to con-clude that both Korean regimes are utterly unprepared for meaningful com-munication. The motivations and orientations behind their contacts and nego-tiations seem to suggest that the two sides are not empathetic. Rather, they are self-centered, closed-minded, and unwilling to compromise their positions. In addition, within both societies, especially the North, there appear to be nu-merous constraints upon the expression of ideas and values.

9. *Radical relativism:* The admission of relativism in values and positions on the part of the communicator is a necessary requirement for viable communi-cation. As long as values and opinions are held to be dogmatic, communica-tion cannot work as a vehicle for peacemaking. Unfortunately, the Cold War political culture fed into the hostile relations between the divided regimes of Korea to instill in the political orientations for both sides dogmatic views about each other that left little room for compromise. The long-held impasse in inter-Korean relations has resulted in part from the zero-sum nature of the competition for system legitimacy.

The context of world politics has changed in that relations of political and nonpolitical entities are no longer guided by the ideological nexus. No longer does the legitimacy of a political regime depend on its ability to denounce the ideology of its adversary. It is therefore of vital significance for the two Ko-rean regimes to move their bases of regime legitimacy from mutual rejection to a broader and common basis by incorporating the notion of human dignity. A political system, then, may be regarded legitimate if it can be supportive of and instrumental to enhancing human dignity. Both Korean regimes should realize that each has some areas of strength as well as weakness in their pur-suit of human dignity; better yet, they should realize that they can even com-plement each other because they indeed represent a variety of different at-tributes that must first find their rightful places in order to begin building eventual, lasting harmony.

Conclusion

With the waning of the Cold War world order, the East-West ideological nexus has been dismantled; left in the wake is an ideological vacuum. Con-tending views and claims about a new world order have never produced an authoritative assessment of the current situation. Amid this global transition, inter-Korean relations have evolved to a point that interactions have progressed at a breathtaking pace. Yet the nature of differences and the condition of the impasse between the two Korean regimes are such that the sporadic talks convened at the government level have been dramatized in the media but seldom produced tangible results for peaceful reunification. This chapter was written on the premise that an ideology is a road map designed to guide the course of social change, and that it is imperative for Korea—and for that matter the global community—to advance a new ideology.

Efforts were made here first to discern the contrasting characteristics between the two Korean regimes that would be helpful in diagnosing the sources of problems in interregime dialogue. Second, further efforts were made to identify the kinds of values and ideas that could be used in developing a new ideology that not only might facilitate a meaningful course of Korean reunification but more ambitiously could provide some insights for the emerging global community itself. The view that a desirable ideology should promote dignity for human individuals and peace for the community was put forth. The nine-point proposal led to the conclusion that there is ample room for improvement and change in both systems and that the challenge of generating such an ideology lies ahead for the Korean people.

Notes

1. For further analysis of the process of social change on this premise, see Han S. Park, *Human Needs and Political Development* (Cambridge: Schenkman Publishing, 1984).

2. The term "social engineering" is adopted from Eugene Meehan, *Value Judgement and Social Science* (Homewood, IL: Dorsey Press, 1969).

3. The concept of human development is persuasively espoused by Steve Chilton, who posits culture as the locus of development; see Chilton, *Defining Political Development* (Boulder, CO: Lynne Rienner Publishers, 1988).

4. The concept of "imagined political community" is adopted from Benedict Anderson, *Imagined Communities: Reflections on the Origin and Spread of Nationalism* (New York: Verso, 1983), pp. 15–16.

5. Kurian ranks both North Korea and South Korea as being the only countries with 100 percent ethnic homogeneity. George T. Kurian, comp., *The Book of World Rankings* (New York: Facts on File, 1979).

6. The notion of the "social-political life" has been advanced by *Juche* theorists since the introduction of the concept by Kim Jong Il in his speech entitled "Some Questions on the *Juche* Idea" in 1986. For a concise exposition of the idea of "eternal life," see Koh Rim, *Juche ch'olhak wonron* (Introduction to *Juche* philosophy) (Pyongyang, 1989).

7. The consistent purpose of the massive thirty-three-volume history series *Chosŏn Chŏnsa* (Complete history of Korea (Pyongyang: Science and Encyclopedia Publishing House, 1979–1982) was to convey the idea that Korea is a chosen land and its people are destined to liberate humanity from imperialist oppression.

8. There are numerous publications on the *Juche* interpretation of human nature. In the first volume of the massive book series published in Pyongyang in 1985 by multiple authors entitled *Widaehan Juche Sasang Ch'ongsŏ* (Complete reference of great *Juche* thought), Li Sŏng-jun introduces the philosophical foundation of the ideology.

9. For further exposition of this analysis, see Stephen Ryan, *Ethnic Conflict and International Relations* (Aldershot, Hants, England: Dartmouth, Brookf, 1990), p. xix.

10. For a comparison of the bases of legitimacy of the two regimes, see Han S. Park and Kyung A. Park, "Bases of Regime Legitimacy in North and South Korea," *Korea Observer*, Vol. 18, No. 3 (Autumn 1987), pp. 321–343.

11. For a discussion on the relevance of self-reliance for security, see Han S. Park and Kyung A. Park, "Ideology and Security: Self-Reliance in China and North Korea," in Edward Azar and C. I. Moon, eds., *National Security in the Third World* (Aldershot, Hants, England: Edward Elgar Publishing, 1988), pp. 102–135.

19

Epilogue: Korean Conundrum in the Post–Cold War Era

Young Whan Kihl

The controversy over North Korea's "suspected" nuclear weapons program epitomizes the security dilemma of the Korean peninsula in the post–Cold War era. World attention was focused on Korean security issues once again when North Korea announced its withdrawal from the Nuclear Nonproliferation Treaty (NPT) on March 12, 1993, and then "suspended" the withdrawal on June 11, one day before it was to take effect.

The realization of North Korea's nuclear ambition will usher in new uncertainty and instability in the region. According to the U.S. Central Intelligence Agency's report to the president in December 1993, North Korea probably had already produced one or two nuclear bombs.[1] Media reports indicate that Pyongyang already possessed the capability to add more warheads to its stockpile of nuclear weapons, including 300 missiles with a range of 100 miles or more.[2] In testimony to a House of Representatives foreign affairs subcommittee on July 28, 1993, the CIA's director, James Woolsey, confirmed that North Korea had tested a 620-mile- range missile.[3]

North Korea as a nuclear weapon state naturally poses a threat to the interests of the regional and global powers in Northeast Asia, including Seoul, Tokyo, Beijing, Moscow, and Washington, D.C. South Korea and Japan could be moved to acquire their own nuclear capabilities, thereby unleashing a nuclear arms race in the region. China already has an estimated 9,300 missiles; Russia, 8,100 missiles; and the United States, 9,200 missiles.[4] Given this reality, of the Korean peninsula surrounded by actual and potential nuclear weapon states, a nuclear war scenario involving North and South Korea in the post–Cold War era cannot be ruled out unless the powder keg on the peninsula can be defused in time.

International Responses to the Nuclear Issue

The international community in the post–Cold War era, as during the Cold War itself, naturally hopes to prevent the spread of nuclear weapons. The political communiqué issued on July 8, 1993, by the Group of Seven countries following a three-day economic summit conference of industrial democracies in Tokyo called on North Korea "to retract immediately its decision to withdraw from the NPT, and to fully comply with its nonproliferation obligations, including the implementation of IAEA safeguards agreement and the Joint Declaration on Denuclearization of the Korean Peninsula."[5]

The ASEAN ministerial meeting in Jakarta, July 23–24, 1993, issued a joint communiqué addressing a host of international and regional concerns including the need "to evolve a more predictable and constructive pattern of political and security relationships in the Asia-Pacific."[6] On November 1, the UN General Assembly voted 140 to 1 to urge North Korea to "immediately cooperate" with the IAEA. UN Secretary General Boutros Boutros-Ghali visited Pyongyang and held direct talks with President Kim Il Sung on December 25, but he failed to win North Korea's agreement to allow the resumption of IAEA monitoring of its nuclear installations.[7]

Of the two types of responses open to the international community, negative sanctions (hawkish measures) and positive inducements (dovish measures), neither is completely satisfactory or feasible because of the complexity of the issues. The possible imposition of economic sanctions against North Korea is unlikely to be implemented soon because of China's objection and its possible use of the veto in response to a UN Security Council resolution on the subject. Short of launching a military attack against the North Korean nuclear installations and risking a renewed Korean war, the international community must pursue a policy of positive inducements leading North Korea to terminate its self-imposed isolation. The hawkish proposal to launch a surgical air strike against North Korea is counterproductive and certain to fail because most of Korea's military targets are kept underground and thus are difficult to pinpoint.

U.S.-DPRK Bilateral Talks

The United States has made clear that it wishes to maintain and strengthen the nuclear nonproliferation regime of the IAEA. President Clinton has warned that "North Korea cannot be allowed to develop a nuclear bomb."[8] He also stated that if North Koreans were to use nuclear weapons, it would be the "end of their country as they know it."[9] He repeated this warning at the truce village of Panmunjom during his visit to South Korea in July 1993. This hawkish stance, however, has been circumscribed by a more flexible diplomatic posture of conducting bilateral talks with North Korea on the nuclear issue.

Two rounds of U.S.-DPRK talks were held in 1993, the first in New York from June 9 to 11 and the second in Geneva from July 16 to 19. At the end of the second round of talks, on July 19, 1993, a joint statement was issued on a three-point agreement: (1) North Korea would begin talks with the IAEA to discuss the question of outstanding safeguards, that is, over special inspections; (2) that inter-Korean talks would be reopened to discuss matters of mutual concern, including the nuclear issue; and (3) that a third round of high-level talks would be held within two months to discuss possible U.S. assistance for North Korea to replace existing graphite-moderated reactors with light-water reactors.[10]

As for the conversion of North Korea's nuclear technology from the present system, which uses gas-cooled reactors, to a more advanced system using light-water reactors, not only the United States but other countries including South Korea and Japan could provide such technology if the conditions and terms were right. North Korea seems anxious to expedite the process of acquiring new technology, judging from the report that a disagreement over the pace of the conversions caused a snag in the Geneva talks.[11] The real questions, however, seem to be the cost, the time schedule, and the political will of outsiders to render assistance to North Korea.[12] South Korea, for instance, had already expressed its willingness to help North Korea acquire the new technology providing Pyongyang would give up its current suspected nuclear weapons program. Whether the United States and Japan would do likewise seems not altogether clear.

In any case, it not only would be extremely costly but also would take a long time (probably six to eight years) for North Korea to build a light-water reactor. Construction of new reactors therefore might not offer an immediate solution to the current nuclear impasse.[13] North Korea's successful conversion of its reactor technology, however, will depend upon the help of the international community, including the United States, Japan, and South Korea, in doing away with outdated and dangerous nuclear technology. Nuclear energy programs using light-water reactors are preferred for nuclear power generation in most countries because they are less likely to be used for weapons production.

Exploring Peaceful Avenues for Problem Solving

To dissuade North Korea from actively pursuing its nuclear weapons program, a series of positive incentives have been suggested to the North Korean communist regime by the international community. In the absence of diplomatic ties between the United States and the DPRK, U.S. government financing of joint projects with North Korea, including light-water reactor conversion, is not likely. The initial movement toward expanded activity with North Korea is more likely to come from NGOs through projects funded by private foundations, such as the Rockefeller Foundation's support of the Asia Society initiative toward North Korea.[14] The assumption of this type of NGO activity is that building confidence through the identification of concrete areas of economic, technical, and people-to-people exchange is necessary before official exchange and cooperation with the DPRK.[15]

Private-sector opinions vary greatly, from guarded optimism to pessimism, regarding North Korea as a partner in expanded cooperation. Some suggested measures of cooperation would include lifting restrictions on U.S.-DPRK economic interaction under the existing Trading With the Enemy Act; expanded trade in agriculture and food products; and private-sector participation in energy, infrastructure, mining, the environment, and other areas of economic development. Also included have been U.S. support of the UNDP Tumen River Area Development Program; other UN programs such as the UN Population Fund (UNFPA), the WHO, the Food and Agriculture Organization (FAO), and the UN Industrial Development Organization (UNIDO); and DPRK participation in the Asian Development Bank, IMF, World Bank, and other related activities.[16]

Clearly, the international community will need to convince North Korea to think twice before continuing its suspected nuclear weapons program. The regime's self-imposed isolation is not in tune with global trends, and it will prove to be counterproductive to North Korea in the long run. Renewed tension on the Korean peninsula because of North Korea's hard-line stance on the nuclear issue is not in the best interests of those dedicated to building a foundation for regional peace and stability.

However, the North Korean strategy of nuclear brinkmanship or nuclear blackmail has been very effective from Pyongyang's perspective.[17] Its nuclear weapons program is not irrational or irresponsible in view of the perceived and real security threats from its external environment; it seems sensible because it gives Pyongyang an added valuable strategic asset that it can control now and in the future. Therefore, North Korea will continue to play the nuclear game by pursuing its present course of action, that is, developing nuclear capability and a missile delivery system.

Concrete and specific incentives for North Korea to reverse its present course may be contemplated in three areas: (1) military, diplomatic, and IGO activities; (2) economic, trade, and investment opportunities; and (3) people-to-people and NGO interactions.

On the military and diplomatic fronts, incentives may include the cancellation of the 1994 Team Spirit U.S.-ROK joint military exercise, which North Korea condemns as a nuclear war game directed against it, in exchange for North Korea's withdrawal of forward-deployed troops near the DMZ. The measures may also entail the speedy conclusion of the Japan–North Korea normalization talks, now suspended, with a financial assistance package under Japan's Official Development Assistance (ODA) program, even if North Korea regards the ODA program as "compensation" for Japan's past colonial rule of Korea. Finally, invitations may be extended to North Korea to join the Asian Development Bank and, in due course, the World Bank and the IMF. North Korea may also receive an invitation to send observers to regional economic meetings such as APEC, so as to build bridges with other Asian countries.

On the subject of economic, trade, and investment opportunities, the measures may take the form of a concrete offer to assist North Korea in acquiring the new technology of reactor cooling system conversion. This acquisition would allow North Korea to move from graphite cooling reactors to light-water cooling reactors. This change not only will give North Korea a safer nuclear power system but also will allow outsiders to monitor North Korea more closely. In a more radical vein, an offer may be made for outright purchase of North Korea's nuclear industry and the infrastructure it is now building, such as the plutonium reprocessing plant. If the multiyear Tumen River Basin development project is to materialize, a large-scale economic assistance program through the UNDP or other IGOs may be needed. Other economic and financial measures will entail helping North Korea reduce its debt via debt-equity swaps; promoting and regularizing border trade with China and Russia; and initiating joint venture projects and investments in special economic zones (SEZs), patterned after those in China, which North Korea plans to establish.

Possible avenues of people-to-people and NGO interactions will include a "ping pong diplomacy" of exchanging athletic teams and cultural and artistic troupes and the promotion of academic and scholarly exchanges by sending a U.S. tour group to North Korea (without the United States necessarily receiving a similar group from North Korea at this time). It may also include NGOs' involvement in such areas as relief work, environmental protection, religious mission trips, youth exchanges, and the like. The latter type of NGO activity may take the form of an invitation by Greenpeace to jointly monitor the nuclear waste dumping in the Sea of Japan recently carried out by Russian naval vessels based in Vladivostok.

These measures and others may be suggested to policymakers in many democracies, including policymakers in Washington. Some critics may consider these to be "soft-line" measures appeasing and rewarding an aggressor nation. Yet a second Korean war over any issue, including North Korea's nuclear intransigencies, should be avoided at all costs because it would destroy the economic infrastructure that has been built in South and North Korea.

Pyongyang's Nuclear Brinkmanship: An Analysis

Assuming that North Korea already has nuclear bombs, which is just a worst-case assessment of existing data rather than a fact based on on-site inspections, two questions arise. First, how rational is North Korea's nuclear brinkmanship in a post–Cold War environment? Second, what can the outside world, including the United States, do to deal with the new situation of North Korea as a nuclear weapon state?

As for the first question, it is clear that the Pyongyang regime has employed a high-risk game of nuclear brinkmanship/blackmail.[18] Pyongyang talks tough and keeps options open while it purposely keeps the outside world—including Japan and the United States—guessing at its true intentions. Despite its denial, Pyongyang's official line of "no intention, no capability" regarding nuclear weapons development is not credible. One must therefore assume that Pyongyang is playing for time and seeking to acquire nuclear weapons so as to maintain or enhance its national security.[19] As for the second question, the right package of incentives, including a security guarantee, economic ties, and diplomatic recognition, may be offered to North Korea in exchange for abandonment or trading away of its nuclear program, as happened in South Africa and is contemplated for Belarus and Ukraine.

U.S. intelligence agencies' assessment, based on data collected before the IAEA inspections were suspended by North Korea in 1992, is that North Korea might have extracted as much as 12 kilograms of plutonium from its reactors, enough for two atomic bombs. The accuracy of this assessment can be ascertained only by resumed IAEA on-site inspections, which will reveal how much plutonium North Korea has produced in its two reactors and will also discourage further bomb making. Since North Korea will soon be forced to shut down a reactor at Yongbyon to replace its nuclear fuel rods, the resumption of regular IAEA inspections would establish the amount of spent fuel extracted and diverted for plutonium to manufacture more atomic bombs.[20]

In the fall of 1990, in a rather surprising move, North Korea came close to admitting its intention to manufacture nuclear weapons. When then–Soviet Foreign Minister Eduard Shevardnadze visited Pyongyang in early September, DPRK Foreign Minister Kim Yong-nam reportedly warned that the North would push ahead with nuclear weapons development if the Soviets carried out their plan of recognizing South Korea. Pyongyang's threat did not succeed: Moscow and Seoul established diplomatic relations on September 30, 1990. North Korea then took the rather unusual step of releasing a memorandum a few weeks later that stated that Soviet recognition of the ROK "will leave us no other choice but to take measures to provide ... for ourselves some weapons for which we have so far relied on the alliance." The weapons to which this statement alludes seem likely to be nuclear ones.[21]

So far North Korea has played its nuclear card rather skillfully—a far cry from the Cold War days when North Korea made both strategic and tactical miscalculations regarding U.S. policy. As Ralph N. Clough, writing in 1987, observed, "by relying too much on harsh tactics and leaving the art of diplomacy relatively underdeveloped, North Korea has failed to make significant progress in achieving its objective toward the United States."[22] During the Cold War North Korea's effort to achieve its primary goal, the withdrawal of U.S. forces from South Korea in order to clear the way for reunification of the peninsula on its own terms, was unsuccessful. In the post–Cold War environment, North Korea seems obviously more adept in its diplomatic movement toward the United States, using the nuclear issue as a bargaining chip.

Nuclear diplomacy is a dangerous game. On January 2, 1994, following President Kim Il Sung's New Year's address, the DPRK Foreign Ministry, meeting with the U.S. negotiator in New York, announced that it was now agreeable to international inspection of "the country's seven declared nuclear sites for one-time inspection."[23] When the United States and North Korea reached this agreement "in principle" for one-time inspection, the arrangement was criticized for falling short of the U.S. administration's original goal of getting North Korea to reaffirm its obligations to the NPT, which requires members to submit to periodic inspection of nuclear sites.[24] President Clinton and his administration officials, however, denied a news account that suggested the United States had retreated. A senior administration official even stated that Mr. Clinton "misspoke" earlier when he said that "North Korea cannot be allowed to develop a nuclear bomb." Instead, the official said, the

U.S. position is that North Korea cannot develop its nuclear capability any further and must be open to "full" inspection.[25] This latest gesture by North Korea is another example of North Korea's success at playing the nuclear card.

North Korea's nuclear program could also affect U.S.-Japanese relations. The prevailing view in Japan is that if South Korea responded to Pyongyang's nuclear program by moving its own nuclear program toward weapons capability, or if a reunified Korea were likely to acquire North Korean nuclear weapons, Japan eventually would have to go nuclear. If the security situation on the Korean peninsula deteriorated, the issue of Japanese military involvement likely would arise. However, even if U.S. pressures for Japan to become involved militarily on the Korean peninsula succeeded, a rearmed Japan with possible nuclear weapons would be strongly opposed by all the East Asian governments, including South Korea, which remains suspicious of Japan because of its record before and during World War II.

North Korea's Future: Explosion, Implosion, or Reform?

Pyongyang's nuclear brinkmanship and the peaceful alternatives to North Korea's nuclear program will become immaterial if the North Korean communist regime undergoes radical changes after the passing of its aging leader. The regime of President Kim Il Sung has been intact since 1948, and the nuclear capability gave it a new lease on life in the post–Cold War era. Despite the collapse of communist regimes elsewhere in Europe, North Korea and other Asian communist states have survived.

The present regime of North Korean communism, however, is bound to undergo radical changes in one of three ways: (1) an explosion due to disruptive external impacts (which North Korea has successfully overcome and survived thus far), (2) an "implosion" due to internal pressures generated from within (from a crisis involving the politics of succession, for instance), and (3) orderly reform initiated from within the system. The reality may consist of a mixture of these scenarios.

In view of the learning capacity of the North Korean regime, the last option, orderly and peaceful change, may not be entirely unworkable. President Kim Il Sung has admitted for the first time the failure of economic policy in his country. Kim's New Year's message for 1994 was more conciliatory and less belligerent and self-righteous than in years past. He suggested that North Korea would have to change dramatically in order to develop foreign markets.[26] This realism gives hope for the possibility of orderly change. For these reasons, all the proposed measures for peaceful settlement of North Korea's nuclear problem, as enumerated in the preceding discussion, acquire new relevance and significance.

South Korea's Two-Track Reform Policy: Democratization and Internationalization

In confronting the nuclear issue the South Korean government of President Kim Young Sam has taken the high road of diplomacy rather than military action toward North Korea. South Korea has expressed its concern about pushing North Korea too hard, not wishing to provoke the North to launch a preemptive attack against the South.[27] The joint U.S.-ROK strategy vis-à-vis North Korea was hammered out during President Kim's meeting with U.S. President Clinton in Washington, D.C., on November 23, 1993. The strategy was to make a "thorough and broad" effort to bring about a "final" solution to the North Korean nuclear issue.[28]

A two-track policy of democratic reform at home and international activism abroad seems to have been adopted by the South Korean government in order to solidify its position regarding North Korea. As the first civilian president popularly elected in thirty-two years, President Kim has carried out bold measures of democratic reform aimed at eliminating political corruption, economic irregularities, and social injustices. South Korea has also learned a lesson in confronting North Korea's nuclear program—that it must become a nuclear energy–exporting country in the long term. Without necessarily forsaking plans to maintain a nuclear option to match the North's challenge, the South is determined to advance its research on high technology in the nuclear energy field and to develop nuclear energy sources for peaceful purposes.[29] It is seriously considering the export of peaceful nuclear technology to Southeast Asian countries so as to commercialize the country's advance in the nuclear industry.

President Kim has successfully pushed his ambitious reform agenda at home, including measures to separate "money" and "power" via both asset-disclosure requirements for public officials and the "real name" registry of the financial accounts system. South Korea's ongoing reform, in particular the electoral revolution, was initiated from below and led by indigenous political forces rather than initiated from above and imposed by foreign powers, as in the case of post–World War II Japan. Because of this electoral mandate and popular support, the anticorruption struggle launched by Kim Young Sam seems to have greater promise of success than those initiated by leaders of other Asian countries, such as Japan (under Prime Minister Hosokawa Horihiro) and China (under President Jiang Zemin). South Korea's democracy building is the envy of the leaders of other Asian countries.

The next policy agenda for the Kim government will be to conduct an effective foreign policy characterized by trade expansion and security alliances in the Asia-Pacific region. In the coming years South Korea's existing security ties with its traditional allies, the United States and Japan, will remain important; equally important will be the strengthening of the foundation of an Asia-Pacific economic community. North Korea's suspected nuclear program and its refusal to abide by the IAEA safeguard measures present a special problem to the Seoul government in evolving policy with the United States and Japan as allies.

President Kim's participation in the APEC summit in Seattle from November 19 to 21, 1993, was a reflection of South Korea's "coming of age" in the regional and world arena as a newly industrialized and democratic country. Seoul's diplomacy will need to be strengthened in three areas. First, the existing bilateral security alliance with the United States will need to be preserved.

The new post–Cold War environment has led to the withdrawal of U.S. troops from Europe and the restructuring of the NATO alliance. Second, the possibility of multilateral diplomatic institution building will need to be explored. Regularizing ministerial meetings such as the APEC forum will need to be considered, so as to institutionalize the existing good-neighbor relations that Seoul has maintained with Tokyo, Beijing, Moscow, and other capitals of the Asia-Pacific countries. Third, the regional and global network of cooperation will need to be strengthened. Cross-border activities via private and nongovernmental international agencies will make the ROK truly responsible and active in promoting the noble cause of world peace and friendship into the twenty-first century.

When and if this experimentation in democracy building and diplomatic activisim begins to bear fruit, the positive nationalistic aspiration of the Korean people toward reunification of their divided country will be a natural byproduct. Then Korea in the twenty-first century will regain its lost reputation as "the light in the East."

Korea's Coming Reunification?

Inter-Korean relations in the post–Cold War era have not progressed too far since the signing of the historic agreements on peace and cooperation in 1991, primarily due to North Korean intransigence and failure to resolve the pending nuclear issue. On the Korean peninsula the Cold War glacier has proven difficult to thaw because of the strong and unyielding attitudes of the respective Korean states. The *Juche* idea of the North Korean communist regime, for example, refuses to open the country to IAEA inspections in the name of upholding independence and sovereignty.

Yet the steps toward normalization of the Cold War situation on the Korean peninsula have already been taken, and the institutional framework for peaceful coexistence and cooperation between the two Korean states has been kept intact. What is lacking is the will, not the method, of peace building. Also missing is the determination of the political leadership of North Korea and South Korea to put the terms of agreement into practical action.

In addition to the 1991 inter-Korean agreement on peace and cooperation, advances have also been made in diplomatic relationships between the major powers surrounding the Korean peninsula and the Korean states. With Seoul-Beijing and Seoul-Moscow relations now fully established, the South has been more successful than the North. Talks on Pyongyang-Tokyo and Pyongyang-Washington diplomatic relations will take more time to bear fruit. The unresolved nuclear issue remains an obstacle along the path of institutionalizing peace on the Korean peninsula in the post–Cold War era into the twenty-first century.

Notes

1. This classified assessment was supported by virtually all intelligence agencies but disputed by the State Department's analysts. *New York Times,* December 26, 1993, p. 1.

2. *Time*, June 21, 1993, p. 38.

3. *New York Times*, July 29, 1993.

4. *Time*, June 21, 1993, p. 38.

5. For the text of the communiqué, see *Korea and World Affairs*, Vol. 17, No. 3 (Fall 1993), p. 559.

6. For the text of the communiqué, see ibid., p. 561.

7. *New York Times*, December 28, 1993.

8. This statement was made during NBC's "Meet the Press" program on November 7, 1993.

9. *New York Times*, July 10, 1993. This statement was also made during an interview on July 9, 1993, undertaken while President Clinton was attending the economic summit in Tokyo.

10. The third-round talks did not take place on time because of lack of progress on two items noted in the agreement.

11. *New York Times*, July 20, 1993.

12. For the discussion of North Korea's nuclear program in general, see David Albright and Mark Hibbs, "North Korea's Plutonium Puzzle," *Bulletin of the Atomic Scientists*, November 1992, pp. 36–40; Joseph A. Bermudez, "North Korea's Nuclear Programme," *Jane's Intelligence Review*, September 1991, pp. 404–411; and Leonard S. Spector and Jacqueline R. Smith, "North Korea: The Next Nuclear Nightmare?" *Arms Control Today*, March 1991, pp. 8–13. As for the nuclear reactor conversion issue for North Korea, see Peter Hayes, "What Does North Korea Want?" *Bulletin of the Atomic Scientists*, December 1993.

13. Peter Hayes, "Should the United States Supply Light Water Reactors to Pyongyang?" *Nautilus Working Paper*, 21, November 1993 (Berkeley, CA: Nautilus Institute).

14. Report of an Asia Society research project for the Rockefeller Foundation, "Possible Areas of Cooperation with the Democratic People's Republic of Korea," December 1993.

15. Ibid., p. 7.

16. Ibid.

17. *New York Times*, December 12, 1993 (Week in Review Section); *Washington Post*, April 27, 1993.

18. *New York Times*, December 12, 1993.

19. James Cotton, "North Korea's Nuclear Ambitions," *Adelphi Paper*, 275 (March 1993), pp. 94–106.

20. *New York Times*, "If North Korea Has Bombs" (editorial), December 28, 1993.

21. Andrew Mack, "North Korea and the Bomb," *Foreign Policy*, No. 83 (Summer 1991), p. 89. For the gist of the released memorandum, see Young Whan Kihl, "North Korea's Foreign Relations: Diplomacy of Promotive Adaptation," *Journal of Northeast Asian Studies*, Vol. 10, No. 3 (Fall 1991), pp. 30–45.

22. Ralph N. Clough, "North Korea and the United States," in *The Foreign Relations of North Korea: New Perspective*, Jae Kyu Park ed. (Seoul: Kyungnam University Press, 1987), p. 273.

23. *New York Times*, January 5, 1994.

24. *New York Times*, January 9, 1994.

25. *Wall Street Journal*, January 6, 1994.

26. *New York Times*, January 2, 1994.

27. *New York Times*, November 17, 1993.

28. *Korea Newsreview*, November 27, 1993, p. 6.

29. Young Jeh Kim, "North Korea's Nuclear Program and Its Impact on Neighboring Countries," *Korea and World Affairs*, Vol. 17, No. 3 (Fall 1993), p. 494.

Texts and Documents

Appendix A:
South-North Joint Communiqué
of July 4, 1972

Recently there were talks held both in Pyongyang and Seoul to discuss problems of improving South-North relations and unifying the divided fatherland.

Director Lee Hu Rak of the Central Intelligence Agency of Seoul visited Pyongyang from May 2 to 5, 1972, to hold talks with Director Kim Young Joo of the Organization and Guidance Department of Pyongyang. Second Vice Premier Park Sung-chul, acting on behalf of Director Kim Young Joo, also visited Seoul from May 29 to June 1, 1972, to hold further talks with director Lee Hu Rak.

With the common desire to achieve peaceful unification of the fatherland as early as possible, the two sides in these talks had a frank and openhearted exchange of views and made great progress in promoting mutual understanding.

In the course of the talks, the two sides, in an effort to remove misunderstanding and mistrust, and to mitigate increased tensions that have arisen between the south and the north as a result of the long separation, and further to expedite unification of the fatherland, have reached full agreement on the following points:

1. The two sides have agreed to the following principles for unification of the fatherland:

- First, unification shall be achieved through independent efforts without being subject to external imposition or interference.

Source: A White Paper on South-North Korea Dialogue (Seoul, Korea: Republic of Korea National Unification Board, 1975), pp. 35–37.

- Second, unification shall be achieved through peaceful means, and not through use of force against one another.
- Third, a great national unity, as a homogeneous people, shall be sought first, transcending differences in ideas, ideologies and systems.

2. In order to ease tensions and foster an atmosphere of mutual trust between the south and the north, the two sides have agreed not to defame and slander one another, not to undertake armed provocations against one another whether on a large or a small scale, and to take positive measures to prevent inadvertent military incidents.

3. The two sides, in order to restore severed national ties, promote mutual understanding and to expedite an independent peaceful unification, have agreed to carry out various exchanges in many areas.

4. The two sides have agreed to cooperate positively with one another to seek an early success of the South-North Red Cross Conference, which is currently in progress amidst the fervent expectations of the entire people of Korea.

5. The two sides, in order to prevent unexpected military incidents and to cope with problems arising in the relations between the south and the north directly, promptly and accurately, have agreed to install and operate a direct telephone line between Seoul and Pyongyang.

6. The two sides, in order to implement the aforementioned agreements, settle all the problems that exist in the relations between the South and the North and to solve the question of unifying the country, based on the agreed principles, have agreed to create and operate a South-North Coordinating Committee, jointly chaired by Director Lee Hu Rak and Director Kim Young Joo.

7. The two sides, firmly convinced that the aforementioned agreements correspond with the common aspirations of the entire people eager to see early unification of their fatherland, hereby solemnly pledge before the entire Korean people that they will faithfully carry out the agreements.

July 4, 1972
Upholding the desires of their respective superiors

Lee Hu Rak   *Kim Young Joo*

Appendix B:
Agreement on Reconciliation, Nonaggression, and Exchanges and Cooperation Between the South and the North

(to enter into force as of February 19, 1992)

The South and the North, in keeping with the yearning of the entire Korean people for the peaceful unification of the divided land; reaffirming the principles of unification set forth in the July 4 (1972) South-North Joint Communiqué; determined to remove the state of political and military confrontation and achieve national reconciliation; also determined to avoid armed aggression and hostilities, reduce tension and ensure the peace; expressing the desire to realize multifaceted exchanges and cooperation to advance common national interests and prosperity; recognizing that their relations, not being a relationship between states, constitute a special interim relationship stemming from the process towards unification; pledging to exert joint efforts to achieve peaceful unification; hereby have agreed as follows:

Chapter I   South-North Reconciliation

Article 1: The South and the North shall recognize and respect each other's system.

Source: Agreement on Reconciliation, Nonaggression, and Exchanges and Cooperation Between the South and the North, signed on December 13, 1991 and entered into force as of February 19, 1992, *Korea and World Affairs*, Vol. 16, No. 1 (Spring 1992), pp. 145–148.

Article 2: The two sides shall not interfere in each other's internal affairs.

Article 3: The two sides shall not slander or vilify each other.

Article 4: The two sides shall not attempt any actions of sabotage or subversion against each other.

Article 5: The two sides shall endeavor together to transform the present state of armistice into a solid state of peace between the South and the North and shall abide by the present Military Armistice Agreement (of July 27, 1953) until such a state of peace has been realized.

Article 6: The two sides shall cease to compete with or confront each other in the international arena and shall cooperate and endeavor together to promote national prestige and interests.

Article 7: To ensure close consultations and liaison between the two sides, South-North Liaison Offices shall be established at Panmunjom within three (3) months after the coming into force of this Agreement.

Article 8: A South-North Political Committee shall be established within the framework of the South-North High-Level Talks within one (1) month of the coming into force of this Agreement with a view to discussing concrete measures to ensure the implementation and observance of the accords on South-North reconciliation.

Chapter II   South-North Nonaggression

Article 9: The two sides shall not use force against each other and shall not undertake armed aggression against each other.

Article 10: Differences of views and disputes arising between the two sides shall be resolved peacefully through dialogue and negotiation.

Article 11: The South-North demarcation line and areas for nonaggression shall be identical with the Military Demarcation Line specified in the Military Armistice Agreement of July 27, 1953, and the areas that have been under the jurisdiction of each side until the present time.

Article 12: To implement and guarantee nonaggression, the two sides shall set up a South-North Joint Military Commission within three (3) months of the coming into force of this Agreement. In the said Commission, the two sides shall discuss and carry out steps to build military confidence and realize arms reduction, including the mutual notification and control of major movements of military units and major military exercises, the peaceful utilization of the Demilitarized Zone, exchanges of military personnel and information, phased reductions in armaments including the elimination of weapons of mass destruction and attack capabilities, and verifications thereof.

Article 13: A telephone hotline shall be installed between the military authorities of the two sides to prevent accidental armed clashes and their escalation.

Article 14: A South-North Military Committee shall be established within the framework of the South-North High-Level Talks within one (1) month of the coming into force of this Agreement in order to discuss concrete measures to ensure the implementation and observance of the accords on nonaggression and to remove military confrontation.

Chapter III South-North Exchanges and Cooperation

Article 15: To promote an integrated and balanced development of the national economy and the welfare of the entire people, the two sides shall engage in economic exchanges and cooperation, including the joint development of resources, the trade of goods as domestic commerce and joint ventures.

Article 16: The two sides shall carry out exchanges and cooperation in various fields such as science and technology, education, literature and the arts, health, sports, environment, and publishing and journalism including newspapers, radio and television broadcasts and publications.

Article 17: The two sides shall promote free intra-Korean travel and contacts for the residents of their respective areas.

Article 18: The two sides shall permit free correspondence, reunions and visits between dispersed family members and other relatives and shall promote the voluntary reunion of divided families and shall take measures to resolve other humanitarian issues.

Article 19: The two sides shall reconnect railroads and roads that have been cut off and shall open South-North sea and air transport routes.

Article 20: The two sides shall establish and link facilities needed for South-North postal and telecommunications services and shall guarantee the confidentiality of intra-Korean mail and telecommunications.

Article 21: The two sides shall cooperate in the international arena in the economic, cultural and various other fields and carry out joint undertakings abroad.

Article 22: To implement accords on exchanges and cooperation in the economic, cultural and various other fields, the two sides shall establish joint commissions for specific sectors, including a Joint South-North Economic Exchanges and Cooperation Commission, within three (3) months of the coming into force of this Agreement.

Article 23: A South-North Exchanges and Cooperation Committee shall be established within the framework of the South-North High Level Talks within one (1) month of the coming into force of this Agreement with a view to discussing concrete measures to ensure the implementation and observance of the accords on South-North exchanges and cooperation.

Chapter IV Amendments and Effectuation

Article 24: This Agreement may be amended or supplemented by concurrence between the two sides.

Article 25: This Agreement shall enter into force as of the day the two sides exchange appropriate instruments following the completion of their respective procedures for bringing it into effect.

December 13, 1991

Chung Won-sik
Prime Minister of the Republic of
   Korea

Chief delegate of the South
   delegation to the South-North
   High-Level Talks

Yon Hyong-muk
Premier of the Administration
   Council of the Democratic
   People's Republic of Korea

Head of the North delegation
   to the South-North High-Level
   Talks

Appendix C:
Joint Declaration of the Denuclearization of the Korean Peninsula

(to enter into force as of February 19, 1992)

The South and the North, desiring to eliminate the danger of nuclear war through denuclearization of the Korean Peninsula, and thus to create an environment and conditions favorable for peace and peaceful unification of our country and contribute to peace and security in Asia and the world, declare as follows:

1. The South and the North shall not test, manufacture, produce, receive, possess, store, deploy or use nuclear weapons.

2. The South and the North shall use nuclear energy solely for peaceful purposes.

3. The South and the North shall not possess nuclear reprocessing and uranium enrichment facilities.

4. The South and the North, in order to verify the denuclearization of the Korean Peninsula, shall conduct inspection of the objects selected by the other side and agreed upon between the two sides, in accordance with procedures and methods to be determined by the South-North Joint Nuclear Control Commission.

5. The South and the North, in order to implement this joint declaration, shall establish and operate a South-North Joint Nuclear Control Commission within one month of the effectuation of this joint declaration.

Source: Joint Declaration of the Denuclearization of the Korean Peninsula (initialed on December 31, 1991; signed on January 20, 1992; and entered into force as of February 19, 1992), *Korean and World Affairs* Vol. 16, No. 1 (Spring 1992), pp. 145–148.

6. This joint declaration shall enter into force on the day on which the South and the North exchange notifications of completion of the formalities for the entry into force of the present declaration.

January 20, 1992

Chung Won-sik
Prime Minister of the Republic of
    Korea

Chief Delegate of the South
    Delegation to the South-North
    High-Level Talks

Yon Hyong-muk
Premier of the Administration
    Council of the Democratic People's
    Republic of Korea

Head of the North Delegation
    to the South-North High-Level
    Talks

Appendix D:
Treaty on Basic Relations Between the Republic of Korea and the Russian Federation

(signed November 19, 1992)

The Republic of Korea and the Russian Federation,

Desirous of strengthening the bonds of peace and friendship between the two countries and of promoting closer economic and cultural cooperation between their peoples,

Conscious of the traditional relations between their two peoples and determined to overcome the consequences of the adverse period of their common history,

Convinced that future relations between the two countries should be guided by the common values of freedom, democracy, respect for human rights and market economics,

Affirming their conviction that the development of friendly relations and cooperation between the two countries and their peoples will contribute not only to their mutual benefit but also to the peace, security and prosperity of the Asian and Pacific region and throughout the world,

Reaffirming their commitment to the purposes and principles of the Charter of the United Nations,

Recognizing that the Moscow Declaration of 14 December 1990 shall continue to govern relations between the two countries,

Have agreed as follows:

Article 1

The Republic of Korea and the Russian Federation shall develop friendly relations in accordance with the principles of sovereignty, equality, respect

Source: Treaty on Basic Relations between the Republic of Korea and the Russian Federation, signed on November 19, 1992, *Korea and World Affairs*, Vol. 16, No. 4 (Winter 1992), pp. 744–748.

for territorial integrity and political independence, nonintervention in internal affairs and other generally accepted principles of international law.

Article 2

1. The Contracting Parties shall refrain in their mutual relations from the threat or use of force and shall settle all their disputes by peaceful means in accordance with the Charter of the United Nations.

2. The Contracting Parties shall use, to the maximum extent possible, United Nations mechanisms to settle international conflicts and shall cooperate and endeavour to enhance the role of the United Nations in the maintenance of the international peace and security.

Article 3

1. The Contracting Parties shall develop cooperation for the promotion of stability and prosperity in the Asian and Pacific region.

2. The Contracting Parties shall strengthen their cooperation, including exchanges of information, within the framework of international and regional organizations.

Article 4

1. The Contracting Parties shall hold consultations on a regular basis between their Heads of State, Foreign Ministers and other members of their Governments, or their representatives to discuss matters concerning bilateral relations as well as international and regional issues of mutual interest.

2. The consultations shall normally be held in the Republic of Korea and the Russian Federation alternately.

Article 5

1. The Contracting Parties shall promote the development of broad contacts and ties between their nationals and social organizations.

2. The Contracting Parties shall support contacts and exchanges between the parliaments of the two countries.

3. The Contracting Parties shall encourage direct contacts between their regional and local governments.

Article 6

1. The nationals of either Contracting Party shall, subject to the laws and regulations relating to the entry and sojourn of aliens, be permitted to enter or leave, to travel or stay in the territory of the other Contracting Party.

2. The nationals and juridical persons of either Contracting Party shall, within the territory of the other Contracting Party, enjoy full protection and security in accordance with relevant laws and regulations.

Article 7

1. The Contracting Parties shall promote and develop extensive cooperation between the two countries in the economic, industrial, trade and other fields to their mutual benefit and on the basis of principles generally recognized in international practice.

2. The Contracting Parties shall promote and develop cooperation in the fields of, inter alia, agriculture, forestry, fisheries, energy, mining, communication, transport and construction.

3. The Contracting Parties shall also promote and develop, on the basis of their mutual interest, cooperation in the areas of protecting the environment and the rational use of natural resources.

Article 8

1. The Contracting Parties, recognizing that scientific and technological cooperation will be of great value in advancing the well-being of their peoples, shall develop broad cooperation in the fields of science and technology for peaceful purposes.

2. In the scientific and technological cooperation between the two countries, special attention shall be devoted to promoting exchanges of scientists and the results of scientific and technological research, and encouraging joint research projects.

Article 9

The Contracting Parties shall encourage and facilitate diverse and close contacts and cooperation between the business communities of the two countries.

Article 10

1. In recognition of their respective centuries-old cultural heritages, the Contracting Parties shall promote the development of exchanges and cooperation in the fields of the arts, culture and education.

2. The Contracting Parties shall promote the development of exchanges and cooperation in the fields of the mass media, tourism and sports, and encourage the exchange of young people.

3. The Contracting Parties consider it a matter of special interest to increase the knowledge of each other's languages and cultures in the two countries. Each Contracting Party shall encourage and promote the establishment and activities of cultural and educational institutions for the purpose of providing all persons concerned with broad access to the language and culture of the other Contracting Party.

Article 11

Each Contracting Party shall, within its territory, recognize the rights of its nationals or citizens originating from Korea or Russia to enjoy their own culture, to profess and practice their own religion, and to use their own language.

Article 12

The Contracting Parties, deeply concerned about the growing internationalization of crime, shall promote effective cooperation in their efforts to combat organized crime, international terrorism, illegal traffic in drugs and psychotropic substances, illegal acts aimed against the security of maritime navigation and civil aviation, counterfeiting, smuggling including illicit transboundary traffic in articles of national, artistic, historical or archeological value as well as in animal or plant species under threat of extinction, or parts or derivatives thereof.

Article 13

This Treaty shall not affect the rights and obligations assumed by either Contracting Party under any international treaties and agreements currently in force and shall not be invoked against any third State.

Article 14

The Contracting Parties shall conclude treaties and agreements, wherever necessary, for the implementation of the purposes of this Treaty.

Article 15

1. This Treaty shall be subject to ratification and shall enter into force thirty days after the day of exchange of the instruments of ratification.

2. This Treaty shall remain in force for ten years and shall continue to be in force thereafter until terminated as provided herein.

3. Either Contracting Party may, by giving one year's written notice to the other Contracting Party, terminate this Treaty at the end of the initial ten-year period or at any time thereafter.

DONE at Seoul, this 19th day of November, one thousand nine hundred and ninety-two, in duplicate, each in the Korean, Russian and English languages, all texts being equally authentic.

For the Republic of Korea   For the Russian Federation

Roh Tae Woo   *Boris Yeltsin*
President   President

Selected Bibliography

Only book-length monographs published since 1990 written in English and readily available to the public are included.

Ahn, Byung-joon. *South Korea's International Relations: Quest for Security, Prosperity, and Unification.* Asian Update. New York: The Asia Society, 1991.

Allison, Graham, and Gregory F. Treverton, eds. *Rethinking America's Security: Beyond Cold War to New World Order.* New York: Norton, 1992.

Bandow, Doug, and Ted Galen Carpenter, eds. *The U.S.–South Korean Alliance: Time for a Change.* New Brunswick, NJ: Transaction Publishers, 1992.

Carpenter, Ted Galen. *A Search for Enemies: Alliances After the Cold War.* Washington, DC: Cato Institute, 1992.

Clark, Donald N., ed. *Korea Briefing, 1992.* Published in cooperation with The Asia Society. Boulder, CO: Westview Press, 1992.

———. *Korea Briefing, 1991.* Published in cooperation with The Asia Society. Boulder, CO: Westview Press, 1991.

Cotton, James, ed. *Korea Under Roh Tae-woo: Democratisation, Northern Policy and Inter-Korean Relations.* Canberra: Allen & Unwin, 1993.

Cumings, Bruce. *The Origins of the Korean War Vol. II: The Roaring of the Cataract, 1947–1950.* Princeton, NJ: Princeton University Press, 1990.

Divided Korea. Report of The Asia Society Study Mission. New York: The Asia Society, 1992.

Dupont, Alan. *Australia's Relations with the Republic of Korea: An Emerging Partnership.* Australia-Asia Papers No. 58. Nathan, Australia: Griffith University Centre for the Study of Australia-Asia Relations, 1992.

Foster-Carter, Aidan. *Korea's Coming Reunification: Another East Asian Superpower?* London: The Economist Intelligence Unit, 1992.

Gibney, Frank. *Korea's Quiet Revolution: From Garrison State to Democracy.* New York: Walker and Co., 1992.

Gregor, A. James. *Land of the Morning Calm: Korea and American Security.* New York: Ethics and Public Policy Center, 1990.

Harris, Stuart, and James Cotton, eds. *The End of the Cold War in Northeast Asia.* Melbourne, Australia: Longman Cheshire, 1991.

Hwang, In Kwan. *United States and Neutral Reunified Korea.* Lanham, MD: University Press of America, 1990.

IISS (International Institute for Strategic Studies). *Asia's International Role in the Post–Cold War Era.* Adelphi Papers No. 275. London: Brassey, 1993.

Kihl, Young Whan. *The 1990 Prime Ministers' Meetings Between North and South Korea: An Analysis.* Asian Update. New York: The Asia Society, 1990.

Kihl, Young Whan, Chung In Moon, and David I. Steinberg, eds. *Rethinking the Korean Peninsula: Arms Control, Nuclear Issues and Economic Reformation.* Washington, DC: Georgetown University Asian Studies Center; and Osaka, Japan: International Society for Korean Studies, 1993.

Kim, Byoung-Lo Philo. *Two Koreas in Development: A Comparative Study of Principles and Strategies of Capitalist and Communist Third World Development.* New Brunswick, NJ: Transaction Publishers, 1992.

Kim, Ilpyong J., ed. *Korean Challenges and American Policy.* New York, NY: Paragon House, 1991.

Kim, Young C., and Gaston Sigur, eds. *Asia and the Decline of Communism.* New Brunswick, NJ: Transaction Publishers, 1992.

Korea to the Year 2000: Implications for Australia. Report by the Australian National Korean Studies Centre. Canberra, Australia: East Asia Analytical Unit, Department of Foreign Affairs and Trade, 1992.

Lee, Bum-Joon, and Sung Chul Yang, eds. *The Changing World Order: Prospects for Korea in the Asia Pacific Era.* The KAIS International Conference Series No. 1. Seoul: The Korean Association of International Studies, 1992.

Lee, Chae-Jin, ed. *The Korean War.* Claremont, CA: The Keck Center for International and Strategic Studies, Claremont McKenna College, 1991.

Lee, Chong-Sik, and Se-Hee Yoo, eds. *North Korea in Transition.* Berkeley, CA: Institute of East Asian Studies, University of California, 1991.

Lee, Hong Yung et al., eds. *Korean Options in a Changing International Order.* Berkeley, CA: Institute of East Asian Studies, University of California, 1993.

Lee, Manwoo. *The Odyssey of Korean Democracy: Korean Politics, 1987–1990.* New York: Praeger, 1990.

_____, ed. *Current Issues in Korean-U.S. Relations: Korean-American Dialogue.* A Report of the IFES Korea-U.S. Forum on ROK-U.S. Relations. Seoul: Kyungnam University Institute for Far Eastern Studies, 1993.

Lee, Manwoo, and Richard Mansbach, eds. *The Changing Order in Northeast Asia and the Korean Peninsula.* Seoul: The Institute for Far Eastern Studies, Kyungnam University, 1993.

Levin, Norman D. *Security Trends and U.S.-ROK Military Planning in the 1990s.* Santa Monica, CA: Rand, 1991.

Lim, Gill-Chin, and Jack Williams, eds. *Korea: Its Political and Economic Future.* East Lansing, MI: Asian Studies Center, Michigan State University, 1993.

Macdonald, Donald Stone. *U.S.-Korean Relations from Liberation to Self-Reliance: The Twenty-Year Record.* Boulder, CO: Westview, 1992.

Mazarr, Michael Jr., John Q. Blodgett, Cha Young-Koo, and William J. Taylor, Jr., eds. *Korea 1991: The Road to Peace.* Boulder, CO: Westview, 1991.

Morley, James W., ed. *Driven by Growth: Political Change in the Asia-Pacific Region.* New York: M. E. Sharpe, 1992.

Mosher, Steven W., ed. *Korea in the 1990s: Prospects for Unification.* Brunswick, NJ: Transaction Publishers, 1992.

Niksch, Larry A. *North Korea's Nuclear Weapons Program.* CRS Issue Brief. Washington, DC: Library of Congress, 1993.

Pae, Sung Moon. *Korea Leading Developing Nations: Economy, Democracy, and Welfare.* Lanham, MD: University Press of America, 1992.

Pollack, Jonathan D., and James A. Winnefeld. *U.S. Strategic Alternatives in a Changing Pacific.* Santa Monica, CA: Rand, 1990.

Robinson, Thomas W., ed. *Democracy and Development in East Asia: Taiwan, South Korea and the Philippines.* Washington, DC: AEI Press, 1991.

Sanford, Dan C. *South Korea and the Socialist Countries: The Politics of Trade.* New York: St. Martin's Press, 1990.

Savada, Andrea, and William Shaw, eds. *South Korea: A Country Study.* Washington, DC: U.S. Government Printing Office, 1992.

Scalapino, Robert A. *The Last Leninists: The Uncertain Future of Asia's Communist States.* Creating the Post-Communist Order: Significant Issues Series Vol. 14, No. 3. Washington, DC: The Center for Strategic and International Studies, 1992.

Shapiro, Michael. *The Shadow in the Sun: A Korean Year of Love and Sorrow.* New York: Atlantic Monthly Press, 1990.

Shaw, William, ed. *Human Rights in Korea: Historical and Policy Perspectives.* Cambridge, MA: Harvard University Press, 1991.

Shinn, Rinn-Sup. *North Korea: Policy Determinants, Alternative Outcomes, U.S. Policy Approaches.* CRS Report for Congress. Washington, DC: Library of Congress, 1993.

Speakman, Jay, and Chae-Jin Lee, eds. *The Prospects for Korean Reunification.* Claremont, CA: Claremont McKenna College, 1993.

Storrs, K. Larry. *Communist Holdout States: China, Cuba, Vietnam, and North Korea.* CRS Issue Brief. Washington, DC: Library of Congress, 1993.

Sutter, Robert G. *Korea-U.S. Relations: Issues for Congress.* CRS Issue Brief. Washington, DC: Library of Congress, 1993.

Taylor, Jr., William J., Cha Young-Koo, and John Q. Blodgett, eds. *The Korean Peninsula: Prospects for Arms Reduction Under Global Détente.* Boulder, CO: Westview Press, 1990.

U.S. Department of Defense. *A Strategic Framework for the Asian-Pacific Rim: Looking Toward the 21st Century.* Washington, DC: U.S. Government Printing Office, 1990, 1992.

Winnefeld, James A., et al. *A New Strategy and Fewer Forces: The Pacific Dimensions.* Santa Monica, CA: Rand, 1992.

Yu, Eui-Young, and Terry R. Kandal, eds. *The Korean Peninsula in the Changing World Order.* Los Angeles, CA: California State University, Los Angeles, Center for Korean-American and Korean Studies, 1992.

Acronyms

ANSP	Agency for National Security Planning (South Korea)
APEC	Asia-Pacific Economic Cooperation
ASEAN	Association of Southeast Asian Nations
CBMs	confidence-building measures
CCFMC	County Cooperative Farm Management Committee (North Korea)
CDU	Christian Democratic Union (West Germany)
CIS	Commonwealth of Independent States
CPRF	Committee for the Peaceful Reunification of the Fatherland (North Korea)
CPSU	Communist Party of the Soviet Union
CSCA	Conference on Security and Cooperation in Asia
CSCE	Conference on Security and Cooperation in Europe
CSU	Christian Social Union (West Germany)
DCRK	Democratic Confederal Republic of Korea (North Korea's reunification plan)
DLP	Democratic Liberal Party (South Korea)
DM	deutsche mark
DMZ	demilitarized zone
DP	Democratic Party (South Korea)
DPRK	Democratic People's Republic of Korea (North Korea)
EAEG	East Asia Economic Group
FDP	Free Democratic Party (Germany)
FKTU	Federation of Korean Trade Unions (South Korea)
FLOSY	Front for the Liberation of Occupied South Yemen
FRG	Federal Republic of Germany (West Germany)
GATT	General Agreement on Tariffs and Trade
GDP	gross domestic product
GDR	German Democratic Republic (East Germany)
GNP	gross national product
IAEA	International Atomic Energy Agency
IGOs	intergovernmental organizations
IMEMO	Institute of International Economy and World Politics
INGOs	international nongovernmental organizations
JNCC	Joint Nuclear Control Commission (South-North)

JSP	Japan Socialist Party
KAIS	Korean Association of International Studies
KAL	Korean Air Lines
KDI	Korea Development Institute
KNC	Korean National Community (South Korea's reunification plan)
KW	kilowatt
KWP	Korean Workers' Party
LDP	Liberal Democratic Party (Japan)
MITI	Ministry of International Trade and Industry (Japan)
MW	megawatt
NAFTA	North American Free Trade Agreement
NATO	North Atlantic Treaty Organization
NCND	neither confirm nor deny
NF	National Front (South Yemen)
NGOs	nongovernmental organizations
NICs	newly industrializing (-ed) countries
NIEO	new international economic order
NLF	National Liberation Front (South Yemen)
NPT	nuclear nonproliferation treaty
NSA	nuclear safeguards accord
OMA	orderly marketing agreements
PBEC	Pacific Basin Economic Council
PDRY	People's Democratic Republic of Yemen (South Yemen)
PKO	peacekeeping operations
Pŏmminryon	Pan-National Alliance for Reunification of the Fatherland
PRC	People's Republic of China
ROK	Republic of Korea (South Korea)
SDF	Self-Defense Forces (Japan)
SED	Socialist Unity Party of Germany (East Germany)
SPD	Social Democratic Party (West Germany)
TRADP	Tumen River Area Development Program
UAR	United Arab Republic
UDRK	Unified Democratic Republic of Korea (Chun Doo Hwan's plan for reunification)
UNC	United Nations Command
UNCOK	UN Commission on Korea
UNCURK	UN Commission for the Unification and Rehabilitation of Korea
UNDP	United Nations Development Program
UNP	Unification National Party (South Korea)
UNTCOK	UN Temporary Commission on Korea
UPP	United People's Party (South Korea)
VER	voluntary export restraints
WHO	World Health Organization
WOMP	World Order Models Project
YAR	Yemen Arab Republic (North Yemen)
YSP	Yemen Socialist Party

About the Book and Editor

During the Cold War era, Korea's security agenda was defined largely by superpower rivalry. The goal of U.S. strategy, as reflected in the Truman Doctrine, was to stem the tide of communist expansionism and contain Soviet power within the USSR's existing borders. Korea was cast as a crucial buffer and fulcrum in the balance of power among the major powers surrounding the peninsula, and North Korea's invasion in 1950 of its southern neighbor was seen as a key test of containment policy.

Now that the Cold War is over, it is time to reconsider the Korean peninsula's strategic role in global and regional politics. In this book, leading scholars provide new perspectives on Korea's changing role in the new world order. What are the implications of the dramatic end of the Cold War for East Asia and the Korean peninsula? Will peace and prosperity return to the region, followed by the reunification of divided Korea? Or will history repeat itself in the form of violent conflict and rivalry, as in late nineteenth- and early twentieth-century East Asia? The contributors consider these questions in the context of major powers' policies toward the Korean peninsula, inter-Korean relations, and revived prospects for Korean reunification.

Young Whan Kihl is professor of political science at Iowa State University, Ames. He serves on the editorial board as book editor on Korea of the *Journal of Asian Studies*. His recently published books include *Rethinking the Korean Peninsula: Arms Control, Nuclear Issues, and Economic Reformation* (coeditor, 1993); *Security, Strategy, and Policy Responses in the Pacific Rim* (coeditor, 1989); and *Political Change in South Korea* (coeditor, 1988).

Index